LEGAL
PRACTICE
COMPANION

Sir
faithful

mame
faithful
Sincerely

LEGAL PRACTICE COMPANION

by
Gerald Montagu
BA (Hons), Solicitor

and
Mark Weston
LLB (Hons), Solicitor

Foreword by The Right Honourable Lord Woolf
Master of the Rolls

Foreword to the Second Edition by
The Honourable Mr Justice Lightman

CLT PROFESSIONAL PUBLISHING
A DIVISION OF CENTRAL LAW TRAINING LTD

© G. F. H. Montagu and M. Weston
1997

Published by:
CLT Professional Publishing
A Division of Central Law Training Ltd
Wrens Court
52-54 Victoria Road
Sutton Coldfield
Birmingham
B72 1SX

ISBN 1 85811 152 8

Printed and bound in Great Britain by
Redwood Books, Trowbridge, Wiltshire

'There are three partners in man –
The L'rd (Blessed be He), his [the man's] father
and his mother.'

Babylonian Talmud

Tractate Niddah 31a

I thank them all.

M.W.

'Many rough and cragged by-ways have been ... trodden towards the intricate problems of the Law's mysteries, but no foot-path ... [has been] plainley beaten, so that anyone could ... find the way without being subject to any Aberrations [and which] should safely conduct the Zealous Pilgrim through the sullen deserts, and over the craggy precipicies of this Herculean voyage.'

Compleat Solicitor (London, 1668)

Foreword to the *Companions*

I am wholly in favour of the *Companions*. Legal text books are not often to the fore when it comes to presenting legal information in an attractive, readily understandable and digestible form. However, this is exactly what the *Companions* achieve. The law is becoming ever more complex and there is undoubtedly a need to find new methods of communicating it to those who need to know, whether they be members of the public, law students, practitioners or for that matter judges. They will all find that it is a great advantage to have access to a *Companion*.

This is why the first volume in the series, *The Legal Practice Companion* (LPC) has proved to be a success. It is now in its third edition, having been first published in 1995. *The Intellectual Property and Media Law Companion* and *The Corporate Finance Companion* are worthy successors to the first volume, LPC.

Some of the subjects which are now dealt with by the *Companions* are not ones with which I am particularly familiar and so I was able to find out for myself in practice whether they work. I can assure the potential reader that they do work as far as I am concerned and that they are very user friendly. The very clear method of presentation both provided an overview of the subject and a step by step guide. I am not surprised to learn that it is intended in due course to provide the text of the *Companions* on a CD-ROM. I feel confident that they will translate well to this format since their present style will be very familiar to regular users of information technology.

My enthusiasm for the *Companions* is in part because they complement the reforms I have recommended for civil procedure and which I hope will make our Civil Justice System an appropriate one for the next millennium. I am very conscious that a weakness of the reforms is that in general they were confined to procedural law and left substantive law intact and in a state which means that in the majority of areas it is impenetrable to those to whom it is unfamiliar. This creates a real impediment to access to justice. The virtue of the *Companions* is that they provide a clear path through what is so often a jungle. While the *Companions* will usually provide all that the reader requires, when this is not the case they will be a solid base from which to embark on a more detailed investigation of the tangled undergrowth of the law.

That I find the *Companions* refreshing is no doubt due to the fact that the authors are (by judicial standards) all young and obviously very bright. Because they are either recently qualified or yet to qualify they know the needs of others in their position and how the existing texts do not always meet those needs. They have decided that something can and should be done to provide a solution. LPC was the start and there now follow the *Companions*. They deserve to succeed and I believe that they will succeed in meeting that need. I congratulate the team on their initiative and on what they are achieving and I look forward to the growth of the *Companions* into a complete series.

The Right Honourable, Lord Woolf

Master of the Rolls

Foreword to the *Legal Practice Companion*

The *Legal Practice Companion* is intended as a companion, friend and guide to the student and newly qualified practitioner. Its purpose is achieved with distinction. This work sets out the principles of substantive law in the areas where the reader will need to tread; and civil procedure can no longer be a mystery to those who have this book at hand. The quality of the contents and the clarity of thought and presentation combine to enable the authors, in one volume, to provide a map and a guided tour of legal practice today. Seasoned practitioners will find it valuable to have at their elbows such an up-to-date and reliable summary, and most certainly the *Legal Practice Companion* will occupy a place on my bookshelf.

The Honourable Mr Justice Lightman

Welcome to the *Legal Practice Companion*!

To the Practitioner

This book aims to help provide a guide to law and practice beyond your areas of specialisation. It sets out the context, general 'feel' and basic concepts of an area of law. Its purpose is to serve as a prelude to detailed research. The numerous references aid 'mapping out' research, before clients are given more considered advice based on that research.

The book is intended to provide an *overview* for the practitioner. It is *not* comprehensive - there are numerous specialist works on particular topics that are intended for that purpose. For example, the demands of converting highly complex statutes into digestible points have forced us to focus on those points that seem most relevant. When giving advice, original sources should *always* be checked.

Meeting the needs of practitioners has required an original approach. After discussions with solicitors and trainees, we have evolved a novel format that represents something of a departure for legal publishing. This is reflected in both the choice of material and its presentation.

In this book:

1. procedures are often broken down into steps or flowcharts, so that they can easily be followed.

2. the law is set out schematically and areas are linked together as appropriate. For example, the *Business* section gives an integrated overview of the legal framework within which businesses operate, dealing with corporate governance, employment, and commercial agreements.

3. all this is packaged in one convenient volume. Therefore, for example, the conveyancer will find an outline of the possible tax treatment of the transaction a few pages away - the importance of which has been highlighted recently by Lightman J's judgment in *Hurlingham Estates Ltd v. Wilde & Partners* [1997] STC 627).

4. this book also flags statutes which have received Royal assent, which are not yet in force but are awaiting orders to bring them into force. This ensures that an awareness of how the law *will* work (as well as how it *does* work) is maintained.

We believe that this book will become a valued tool - a trusty companion for the practitioner who will, we hope, keep a copy within reach of his or her desk.

Introduction

Welcome to the *Legal Practice Companion*!

To the Student

With the advent of the **Legal Practice Course,** the worlds of work and law college have moved closer together than ever before. This volume is intended to help in both.

The information required for the compulsory topics and the pervasive topics on the LPC (under the Law Society's *Legal Practice Course Board's Written Standards*) is presented here in one volume. After you complete the course, the source references to lay the basis for your research in practice are included in a format which will quickly become familiar.

Other books and materials usually contain seemingly unwieldy blocks of text, which are often split over numerous pages and volumes. This often hinders grasping masses of information as it often appears unconnected and unclear. The *Legal Practice Companion* breaks new ground by presenting the relevant law and practice in a step by step format - it is all in one volume, and frequently one topic is presented per page. Charts, flow charts and summaries provide an accessible, clear and straightforward overview of modern legal practice. Please note that the book does assume some prior knowledge and comprehension of basic concepts - it is aimed at students undertaking a Legal Practice Course, or equivalent professional examinations. The *Legal Practice Companion,* for example, will not define a shelf company or an either way offence, but it will tell you what to do with them and the procedures that apply to them.

This book is intended:

1. to explain complex parts of the course that you have already covered.

2. to provide a breakdown (aiding comprehension) for parts of the course that you are about to tackle.

3. to present an area of law coherently in one place (for example, taxation and conduct for the whole course are grouped in their own sections).

4. to split topics up so that they appear where they fit best (such as European law in *Business*).

For you, the student, this book is intended to cover all that you need for your courses, and to help you beyond into the world of work. No doubt your annotations will soon cover the pages and this is entirely suitable and to be encouraged. For those of you who can take books into examinations, this presentation of the course, together with your annotations, will be invaluable in helping you pass the LPC exams.

Preface

In the legal profession, like in most careers, there is no substitute for experience. However, the Legal Practice Course helps bridge the gap between the academic study of law and the cut and thrust of practice as a solicitor. The ever-growing number of *Legal Practice Companions* we see on the shelves of junior lawyers reflects the popularity of this work as a useful tool for students and practitioners.

The *Legal Practice Companion* is written by two authors who share their own experience in successfully tackling the demands and pitfalls of the Legal Practice Course. In addition, they are able to apply their experience as trainees and now solicitors in the London offices of the two largest international law firms in the world.

The combination of knowledge of the Legal Practice Course and the demands of actual practice have been distilled into a well-presented, concise, and user friendly work. It should prove an invaluable aid to those on the Legal Practice Course and a useful reference guide when starting at your law firm.

On behalf of the partners of *Baker & McKenzie* and *Clifford Chance,* we wish every success both to Gerald and Mark with the book and to you in your career in the law.

Paul Rawlinson   *Simon Davis*
Graduate Recruitment Partner   *Graduate Recruitment Partner*
Baker & McKenzie   *Clifford Chance*

Acknowledgements

The new Legal Practice Course ...

The first edition of the *Legal Practice Companion* sailed straight into the stormy debate over the Legal Practice Course, bringing as it did into sharper focus the differing emphasis of the proponents of black-letter law and the proponents of skills. The experience of students and practitioners alike in using the *Legal Practice Companion* has demonstrated that access to law and procedure is a prerequisite for developing skills. We have been encouraged by those who realised that the *Companion* was intended to point the way constructively towards higher standards and a more demanding, more practical, introduction to legal practice.

1997 witnessed the first review of the *Legal Practice Course* by the Law Society. We are delighted that, in some areas, the review has led to the inclusion on the course, of material which was covered in earlier editions of *Legal Practice Companion* because we thought it vital for practice, but which at the time that it was included, would have been deemed 'off-syllabus'. Other changes to the course include the emasculation of the previously compulsory 'Wills, Probate and Administration' topic which is now taught as an elective. We question the wisdom of this. This is an area of practice which is still reserved to solicitors by statute and in cutting down on its teaching, the Law Society might well have no reason to complain if the Government gives the green light to 'licensed probate practitioners'.

The new *Companions* ...

The appearance of the *Corporate Finance Companion* and the *Intellectual Property and Media Law Companion* in April 1997 has seen the application of the approach we developed for the *Legal Practice Companion* to new areas. The authors of the new companions have all worked exceedingly hard to run with the torch. It is therefore gratifying that feedback, both from students and practitioners, suggests that the new books in the series meet a very real need which is felt within the profession and further afield. We have all been tremendously heartened by the support of the Master of the Rolls for the series. We are grateful to all who have made this development possible.

Behind the scenes ...

We would like to thank those at Clifford Chance who patiently found time to help, including Frank Jackson and Norman Thomas of the Partnership Finance Department. Also Louise England and Fiona Durrant of the Baker & McKenzie library staff have been invaluable in keeping track of the latest legislation (from March 1997 onwards). Diane Gwynne-Smith runs the excellent library team. Susan Warrington in the tax library at Clifford Chance has cheerfully helped us to efficiently keep track of two Budgets. Inestimable thanks must also go to Elisabeth Tooms and her staff at Allen & Overy (particluarly Jacqui Studd) for helping keep a track of ever-changing law till

Acknowledgements (cont.)

March 1997 and to Clare Maurice, Graduate Recruitment Partner at Allen & Overy for her continued support and encouragement. Thanks also go to Mike Conradi, Jonathan Lipman, Pat Kelleher and Maggie Jarrett (trainees at Baker & McKenzie) for checking certain points and to Aron Youngerwood (summer student) for the same.

We would again like to thank Gill Zeiner of Macfarlanes for her help in developing the typeset for our approach without which the series would not be nearly as attractive as it is. The series would never have taken flight as it has had it not been for Gill's invaluable contribution to the first edition. We have not had the heart to ask David Montagu for the hours which he devoted in previous years to checking the proofs and we hope that he is happy that this edition carries on with his high standards.

Something new ...

Those familiar with the second edition will notice a number of improvements which we have made following suggestions from students, trainees and practitioners and to reflect changes on the Legal Practice Course. Most noticable is the addition of chapters on accounts and the *Solicitors Account Rules*. Both on the old Finals course and more recently on the PSC, this is a topic which has filled people with dread. However, we hope that the innovative presentation of these topics will demystify this area. We have tried to balance the inclusion of new material to reflect changes in the Legal Practice Course with trying to put as little strain as possible both on the binding of the book and on the bank balances of students - both, we are all too well aware, have their limitations!

We would like to again voice the hope that readers will write to us at our firms, as they have done in the past, with suggestions on how the *Legal Practice Companion* can become even more helpful.

Without which ...

And of course, many thanks to our families and friends who put up with us during the writing process. And (just in case!) to anyone else we have missed!

The law ...

Readers will see that we have endeavoured to reflect changes in the law right up until going to press, although the law is generally as stated at 2 July 1997.

Gerald Montagu and Mark Weston,
London, 16 July 1997.

Contents

Conduct

Accounts

Taxation

Wills and probate (outline)

A guide to boxes and conventions

I   Boxes

Legal points and principles
➤ Square boxes contain information relating to a specific area of law or legal principle.

Practice points and principles
➤ Round boxes contain information relating to information that is useful in practice.

II   Legislative citations

➤ At the time of going to press, certain legislation covered in this book has either not yet received the royal assent, or awaits an order from a Minister before it comes into force (this is dependent on the drafting and approval of secondary legislation and/or regulatory codes).

◆ At the time of going to press, the *Finance (No2) Bill (F(No2)B 1997)* has not completed its parliamentary passage.   We understand from the Treasury that the Bill is expected to receive the Royal Assent before Parliament rises for the summer recess. Given the Government's large parliamentry majority and the shortage of parliamentary time, we have assumed that the measures announced by the Chancellor on 2 July 1997 will become law in substantially the form set out in the Bill published on 8 July 1997.   The draft version of the Bill, as published on the Treasury's website, was used in the the preparation of this book. Readers should note that clause numbers may be altered to different section numbers when the Bill is enacted.

Table of abbreviations

Statutes

AA 1870	Apportionment Act 1870.
AA 1996	Arbitration Act 1996.
AEA 1925	Administration of Estates Act 1925.
AEA 1971	Administration of Estates Act 1971.
AE(SP)A 1965	Adminstration of Estates (Small Payments) Act 1965.
AHA 1995	Agricultral Holdings Act 1995.
AIA 1996	Asylum and Imigration Act 1996.
AJA 1920	Administration of Justice Act 1920.
AJA 1952	Administration of Justice Act 1952.
AJA 1982	Administration of Justice Act 1982.
AtEA 1971	Attachment of Earnings Act 1971.
BA 1976	Bail Act 1976.
B(A)A 1993	Bail (Amendment) Act 1993.
BEA 1882	Bills of Exchange Act 1882.
BNA 1985	Business Names Act 1985.
BSA 1986	Building Societies Act 1986.
CA	Companies Act 1985.
CA 1989	Companies Act 1989.
ChA 1989	Children Act 1989.
CA 1992	Charities Act 1992.
CAA 1968	Criminal Appeal Act 1968.
CAA 1990	Capital Allowances Act 1990.
CAA 1995	Criminal Appeal Act 1995.
CCA 1984	County Courts Act 1984.
CDDA 1986	Company Directors Disqualification Act 1986.
CEA 1898	Criminal Evidence Act 1898.
CEA 1968	Civil Evidence Act 1968.
CEA 1972	Civil Evidence Act 1972.
CEA 1995	Civil Evidence Act 1995.
CE(A)A 1997	Criminal Evidence (Amendment) Act 1997.
CICA 1995	Criminal Injuries Compensation Act 1995.
CL(C)A 1978	Civil Liability (Contribution) Act 1978.
CJA 1967	Criminal Justice Act 1967.
CJA 1982	Criminal Justice Act 1982.
CJA 1988	Criminal Justice Act 1988.
CJA 1991	Criminal Justice Act 1991.
CJJA 1982	Civil Jurisdiction and Judgments Act 1982.
CJJA 1991	Civil Jurisdiction and Judgments Act 1991.
CJPO 1994	Criminal Justice Public Order Act 1994.
CLSA 1990	Courts and Legal Services Act 1990.
CPA 1865	Criminal Procedure Act 1865.
CPA 1987	Consumer Protection Act 1987.
CPA 1997	Civil Procedure Act 1997.
CPIA 1996	Criminal Procedure and Investigations Act 1996.
C(S)A 1997	Crime (Sentences) Act 1997.
CYPA 1933	Children and Young Persons Act 1933.
DDA 1995	Disability Discrimination Act 1995.
DTA 1994	Drug Trafficking Act 1994.
EPA 1970	Equal Pay Act 1970.
EPAA 1985	Enduring Powers of Attorney Act 1985.
ERA 1996	Employment Rights Act 1996.
FAA 1976	Fatal Accidents Act 1976.
FA 1930	Finance Act 1930.
FA 1931	Finance Act 1931.
FA 1942	Finance Act 1942.
FA 1958	Finance Act 1958
FA 1963	Finance Act 1963

Table of abbreviations (cont.)

Statutes

FA 1971	Finance Act 1971.
FA 1985	Finance Act 1985.
FA 1986	Finance Act 1986.
FA 1987	Finance Act 1987.
FA 1991	Finance Act 1991.
F(No2) 1992	Finance (No 2) Act 1992.
FA 1993	Finance Act 1993.
FA 1994	Finance Act 1994.
FA 1995	Finance Act 1995.
FA 1996	Finance Act 1996.
FA 1997	Finance Act 1997.
FJ(RE)A 1933	Foreign Judgments (Reciprocal Enforcement) Act 1933.
FLA 1996	Family Law Act 1996.
FLRA 1969	Family Law Reform Act 1969.
FLRA 1987	Family Law Reform Act 1987.
FSA 1986	Financial Services Act 1986.
HA 1957	Homicide Act 1957.
HA 1988	Housing Act 1988.
HA 1996	Housing Act 1996.
HSWA 1974	Health and Safety at Work Act 1974.
IA 1978	Interpretation Act 1978.
IA	Insolvency Act 1986.
IA 1994	Insolvency Act 1994.
I(No2)A 1994	Insolvency (No2)A 1994.
IEA 1952	Intestates' Estates Act 1952.
IHTA 1984	Inheritance Tax Act 1984.
I(PFD)A 1975	Inheritance (Provision for Family and Dependants) Act 1975.
JA 1838	Judgments Act 1838.
JA 1974	Juries Act 1974.
LA 1976	Legitimacy Act 1976.

LA 1980	Limitation Act 1980.
LAA 1988	Legal Aid Act 1988.
LCA 1972	Land Charges Act 1972.
LD(A)A 1888	Law of Distress (Amendment) Act 1888.
LLCA 1975	Local Land Charges Act 1975.
LPA	Law of Property Act 1925.
LP(JT)A 1964	Law of Property (Joint Tenants) Act 1964.
LP(MP)A 1989	Law of Property (Miscellaneous Provisions) Act 1989.
LP(MP)A 1994	Law of Property (Miscellaneous Provisions) Act 1994.
LP(R)A 1938	Leasehold Property (Repairs) Act 1938.
LRA	Land Registration Act 1925.
LRA 1967	Leasehold Reform Act 1967.
LRA 1997	Land Registration Act 1997.
LR(CN)A 1945	Law Reform (Contributory Negligence) Act 1945.
LRHUDA 1993	Leasehold Reform Housing and Urban Development Act 1993.
LR(MP)A 1934	Law Reform (Miscellaneous Provisions) Act 1934.
LR(PI)A 1948	Law Reform (Personal Injuries) Act 1948.
LR(S)A 1995	Law Reform (Succession) Act 1995.
LTA 1927	Landlord and Tenant Act 1927.
LTA 1954	Landlord and Tenant Act 1954.
LTA 1985	Landlord and Tenant Act 1985.
LT(C)A 1995	Landlord and Tenants (Covenants) Act 1995.
MA 1967	Misrepresentation Act 1967.
MCA 1973	Matrimonial Causes Act 1973.
MCA 1980	Magistrates' Courts Act 1980.
MCA 1987	Minors' Contracts Act 1987.
MHA 1983	Matrimonial Homes Act 1983.
MntHA 1983	Mental Health Act 1983.
MWPA 1882	Married Womens' Property Act 1882.

Table of abbreviations (cont.)

Statutes

Table of abbreviations

Statutory Instruments / Law Society regulations

AIEDPO 1986   Administration of Insolvent Estates of Deceased Persons Order 1986.

ATAO(F)R 1988   Assured Tenancies and Agricultural Occupational (Forms) Regulations 1988.

CA(ASMCMAA)R 1997

Companies Act 1985 (Accounts of Small and Medium-Sized Companies and Minor Accounting Amendment) Regulations 1997.

CA(MAA)R 1996   Companies Act (Miscellaneous Accounting Amendments) Regulations 1996.

CA(CD)R 1993   Commercial Agents (Council Directive) Regulations 1993.

CA(DDE)R 1997   Company Accounts (Disclosure of Directors' Emoluments) Regulations 1997.

CA(DR)(SPP)R 1997

Companies Act (Directors' Report) (Statement of Payment Practice) Regulations 1997.

CBNR 1981   Company and Business Names Regulations 1981.

CC(ANEE)R 1987   Crown Court (Advance Notice of Expert Evidence) Rules 1987.

CCF(A)O 1996   County Court Fees (Amendment) Order 1996.

CCR   County Court Rules 1981.

CFAO 1995   Conditional Fee Agreements Order 1995.

CFAR 1995   Conditional Fee Agreements Regulations 1995.

CLA(AR)R 1989   Civil Legal Aid (Assessment of Resources) Regulations 1989.

CLA(G)R 1989   Civil Legal Aid (General) Regulations 1989.

CLA(G)(A)R 1997   Civil Legal Aid (General) (Amendment) Regulations 1997.

CPIA(DDTL)R 1997

Criminal Procedure and Investigations Act (Defence Disclosure Time Limits) Regulations 1997.

D(RPC)O 1996   Deregulation (Resolutions of Private Companies) Order 1996.

HCCCJO 1991   High Court and County Courts Jurisdiction Order 1991.

HCCCJ(A)O 1996   High Court and County Courts Jurisdiction (Amendment) Order 1996.

HMLRFO 1997   HM Land Registry Fees Order 1997.

IPO 1994   Insolvent Partnerships Order 1994.

I(P)R 1971   Indictments (Procedure) Rules 1971.

IR 1971   Indictment Rules 1971.

IS(ICO) 1977   Intestate Succession (Interest and Capitalisation Order) 1977.

IT(E)R 1993   Income Tax (Employments) Regulations 1993.

IT(NP)R 1994   Income Tax (Notional Payments) Regulations 1994.

JD(RI)) 1993   Judgment Debt (Rate of Interest) Order 1993.

LAAPS(R)R 1989   Legal Advice and Assistance at Police Stations (Remuneration) Regulations 1989.

LAAR 1989   Legal Advice and Assistance Regulations 1989.

LAA(S)R 1989   Legal Advice and Assistance (Scope) Regulations 1989.

Table of abbreviations (cont.)
Statutory Instruments / Law Society regulations

LABLAAAAPSRA 1995
    Legal Aid Board Legal Advice and Assistance at Police Stations Register Arrangements 1995.

LACCP(C)R 1989 Legal Aid in Criminal and Care Proceedings (Costs) Regulations 1989.

LACCP(G)R 1989 Legal Aid in Criminal and Care Proceedings (General) Regulations 1989.

LACCP(G)R 1995 Legal Aid in Criminal and Care Proceedings (General) Regulations 1995.

LRR 1925 Land Registration Rules 1925.

LRR 1996 Land Registration Rules 1996.

LT(C)(N)R 199 Landlord and Tenant (Covenants) Act (Notices) Regulations 1995.

MC(AI)R 1985 Magistrates' Courts (Advance Information) Rules 1985.

MC(ANEE)R 1997 Magistrates' Courts (Advance Notice of Expert Evidence) Rules 1997.

MCR 1981 Magistrates' Courts Rules 1981.

MLR 1993 Money Laundering Regulations 1993.

NA(AR)R 1992 National Assistance (Assessment of Resources) Regulations 1992.

NCPR 1987 Non-Contentious Probate Rules 1987.

PO(CTL)R 1987 Prosecution of Offences (Custody Time Limits) Regulations 1987.

RSC Rules of the Supreme Court 1965.

SAR 1991 Solicitors' Accounts Rules 1991.

SCF(A)O 1996 Supreme Court Fees (Amendment) Order 1996.

SDC 1995 Solicitors' Discrimination Code 1995.

SIBR 1995 Solicitors' Investment Business Rules 1995.

SIRC 1990 Solicitors' Introduction and Referral Code 1990.

SPC 1990 Solicitors' Publicity Code 1990.

SPR 1990 Solicitors' Practice Rules 1990.

SD(EI)R 1987 Stamp Duty (Exempt Instruments) Regulations 1987.

SARR 1991 Solicitors' Accountant's Report Rules 1991.

SA(LATP)R 1992 Solicitors' Accounts (Legal Aid Temporary Provision) Rule 1992.

SRO 1994 Solicitors' Remuneration Order 1994.

TCP(GPD)O 1995 Town and County Planning (General Permitted Development) Order 1995.

TCP(UC)O 1987 Town and Country Planning (Use Classes) Order 1987.

TI(DF)O 1996 Trustee Investment (Division of Funds) Order 1996.

TU(PE)R 1981 Transfer of Undertakings (Protection of Employment) Regulations 1981.

UTCCR 1994 Unfair Terms in Consumer Contracts Regulations 1994.

VATR 1995 Value Added Tax Regulations 1995.

VAT(A)(No3)R 1997
    Value Added Tax (Amendment) (No3) Regulations 1997.

Conduct

This chapter examines:

Solicitors' Practice Rules 1990 r.1

➤ This rule is the cornerstone of good conduct.

'A solicitor shall not do anything in the course of practising as a solicitor, or permit another person to do anything on his or her behalf, which compromises or impairs or is likely to compromise or impair any of the following:

a) the solicitor's independence or integrity.

b) a person's freedom to instruct a solicitor of his or her choice.

c) the solicitor's duty to act in the best interests of the client.

d) the good repute of the solicitor or the solicitors' profession.

e) the solicitor's proper standard of work.

f) the solicitor's duty to the court.'

➤ Individual solicitors are liable for any breach of these rules.

➤ All partners of a law firm are jointly and severally liable for any breach of these rules by any fee earner.

A   Taking instructions

I	Advertising
II	Introductions and referrals
III	Accepting instructions
IV	Authority and responsibilities during a retainer
V	Terminating a retainer

I   Advertising

➤ Advertisements must comply with the *SPC 1990,* which forbids:

- ◆ comparisons with other firms, *or*

- ◆ unsolicited intrusion upon members of the public (eg: tele-sales).

➤ Advertisements must comply with *SPR r.2* and:

- ◆ not be in bad taste, *and*

- ◆ contain accurate information and nothing which is misleading, *and*

- ◆ comply with the general law.

II   Introductions and referrals

➤ Introductions by third parties are permitted (*SPR r.3*), provided the *SIRC 1990* and *SPR r.1* are complied with.

- ◆ The solicitor may *not* pay a third party for the introduction.

- ◆ The firm must keep a written record of any agreements for the introduction of clients, showing:

    a) that the clients concerned have been advised impartially, *and*

    b) the income which the firm derives from each agreement with an 'introducer', *and*

    c) that the *SIRC 1990* has been complied with.

➤ A solicitor may refer a client to a third party, provided he:

   a) acts in the client's best interests, *and*

   b) accounts to a client for commissions over £20, or retains the money with the client's prior consent (*SPR r.10*).

➤ A solicitor engaged in investment business must also comply with the *SIBR 1995*, disclosing in writing to the client *before* the client signs any proposal form or application:

   a) the *total* amount of commission due to the solicitor *and* a permitted third party in cash terms, *and*

   b) any subsequent change to the commission reflecting a change in the transaction.

III   Accepting instructions

Money Laundering Regulations

➤ If a solicitor has a new client *and* 'will carry out relevant financial business in the UK', he must ensure compliance with *Money Laundering Regulations* by making enquiries of the new client, to check his identity (eg: by asking to see a passport). There are criminal penalties for non-compliance.

1   A solicitor must always:

➤ take instructions directly from the client (ie: a request for advice on behalf of a potential client should be confirmed personally by the client).

➤ ensure a client is free to instruct whomever he wishes, and is aware of this right (*SPR r. 1*).

➤ accept instructions if the client is eligible for legal aid and the solicitor does legal aid work.

2   A solicitor should *not*:

➤ act in a 'conflict of interest' situation. This arises when any duty a solicitor owes, or might be thought to owe, to a near relative, a third party or to the court, conflicts (or may be likely to conflict) with the client's interests.

➤ act for a buyer and a seller in a 'contract race' (even if *SPR r.6* would otherwise apply - see below), nor may he act for more than one buyer (*SPR r.6A*).   A 'contract race' occurs when a seller of freehold or leasehold land *either* instructs a solicitor to deal with more than one prospective buyer, *or* is known by the solicitor to be dealing with more than one prospective buyer (*SPR r.6A*).

➤ act for both parties in an arm's length conveyancing transaction involving a sale or a grant of a lease (*SPR r.6 as amended from 1 June 1996*) *unless*:

a) no other solicitor or qualified conveyancer is readily available in the area, *or*

b) all parties (or 1 of 2 joint buyers or sellers and the other parties) are established clients, *or*
c) the consideration is £10,000 or less, *or*

d) the seller or lessor is a builder or developer, but is not dealing in that capacity as such, *or*

e) 2 offices of the same firm, or offices of associated firms are instructed,

    and on condition that there is:

a) no conflict of interest, or evidence of undue influence, *and*

b) that the solicitor is not instructed to negotiate the sale of the property, *and*

c) that both parties consent in writing.

Where the parties are associated companies, *or* are related by blood, adoption, or marriage, there is a presumption that the parties are not at arm's length.

♦ Written notification must be given to an institutional lender if a solicitor is *either* acting for the lender, and the borrower is the solicitor himself, or a member of his immediate family, *or* the solicitor is acting for both the buyer and the seller.

♦ A solicitor can act for both borrower and lender on a private (non-institutional) mortgage if there is no conflict of interest and the transaction is not at arm's length.

♦ 'Associated practices' of solicitors may act for both parties provided that separate solicitors acting for the buyer and the seller supervise the transaction for each party, the practices are in different localities and one practice does not refer a client to the other practice.

➤ generally accept instructions on a contingency fee basis (ie: the fee is a percentage of the damages won for the client). However, he may make an approved conditional fee arrangement as specified in *CLSA 1990 s.58* and made in accordance with *SPR rr. 8,18(2)(c)*, the *CFAO 1995* and the *CFAR 1995*. Under such an arrangement, the solicitor will not charge if he loses, but if he wins, there may be an increase in fees. However,

   ◆ the increase in fees must not exceed 100%, *and*

   ◆ the arrangement can only apply to proceedings:
      i)   for personal injury, *or*
      ii) before the European Court of Justice or the European Court of Human Rights, *or*
      iii) concerning insolvency (where proceedings are brought by a company, its liquidator, or administrator when it is in administration, or being wound up), *or*
      iv) when an individual is bankrupt and a trustee in bankruptcy brings proceedings.

➤ accept instructions on a basis which excludes the jurisdiction of the Law Society.

➤ act for a client where the action is malicious.

Fees - quotations and estimates

➤ If a solicitor gives a quotation instead of an estimate of fees, he must do the job for that price.

➤ An estimate of fees should make clear how costs will be calculated; the solicitor must inform the client if it appears likely that costs will exceed the estimate.

➤ If VAT is not mentioned, the client is entitled to assume the price is inclusive of VAT.

---

3   **On accepting instructions, a solicitor should:**

➤ comply with the Law Society's Client Care *SPR r.15*. The solicitor should:

   a) keep the client informed as to the costs which have been, and are likely to be incurred (otherwise he may commit an offence under *CPA 1987 s.20*), *and*

   b) provide details of the firm's complaints procedure, and of appeals to the Law Society, *and*

   c) comply with the Law Society's *Solicitors' Costs Information and Client Care Code* by supplying the necessary and relevant information to the client.

➤ in a 'contract race' for conveyancing clients, immediately inform each buyer's solicitor of the race by telephone or fax, and confirm this in writing (*SPR r.6A*).

Solicitors' Anti-Discrimination Code 1995

➤ A solicitor should not discriminate on grounds of:
   ◆ race,
   ◆ sex,
   ◆ sexual orientation.

➤ A solicitor should not discriminate unreasonably or unfairly on grounds of:
   ◆ disability.

➤ A solicitor may not refuse instructions on the above grounds, or discriminate against his staff on these grounds. If a client asks a solicitor to instruct a barrister of a particular race or sex, the solicitor should try to persuade him otherwise, and if this fails, he should refuse to act.

IV Authority and responsibilities during a retainer

1 Authority

➤ **Non-contentious business:** (ie: before litigation is commenced), a solicitor has 'ostensible authority' to act on the client's behalf (see p.252).

➤ **Contentious business:** a solicitor has 'actual authority' to act on a client's behalf *and to bind a client.*

  ◆ The solicitor should always obtain a client's express authority, preferably in writing, before making any commitment on their behalf, unless the matter is urgent.

  ◆ A solicitor acting without a client's consent may be liable to a third party for breach of warranty of authority.

2 Responsibilities

➤ A solicitor should act in the client's best interests (*SPR r.1*).

➤ A solicitor must not mislead the court (*SPR r.1*).

  ◆ In a criminal case, a solicitor can put the prosecution to proof even if the client admits guilt to the solicitor. However, assisting a client to give perjured evidence would breach the solicitor's duty to the court, and the solicitor should refuse to act if a client attempts this.

  ◆ A solicitor is not obliged to inform the court if it is mistaken about a defendant's criminal record, provided the court does not request any positive representation. If a court requests information, the solicitor must advise the client to tell the truth, and must refuse to act if the client declines.

➤ A solicitor must maintain confidentiality during the retainer *and* after it ceases (*SPR r.1*).

  ◆ The duty is relaxed if:
    a) the client authorises it, *or*
    b) the solicitor believes his advice is being sought in preparation for a non-trivial crime, *or*
    c) a court order requires disclosure, *or*
    d) the police have a search warrant (and documents are not covered by legal privilege), *or*
    e) national security demands it, *or*
    f) the information concerns authorities on which a party intends to rely during a hearing, *or*
    g) the defence calls **expert** evidence (it must be disclosed before a hearing (*PACF s.84(1)*)), or
    h) a legally aided client behaves unreasonably (see p.10).

➤ A solicitor must write regularly to the client keeping him informed of what is (or is not!) happening, the costs incurred, and any action which the client ought to take (*SPR r.15*).

➤ A solicitor must comply with the *Financial Services Act 1986* when advising the client (see p.19).

  ◆ Whether advice is classified as non-discrete investment business, *or* discrete investment business, a firm must abide by various requirements of *SIBR 1995* with regard to record keeping. Eg: *r.16(3)* mandates a solicitor to maintain records of client complaints, and any action taken in response to these over the last 6 years.

➤ A solicitor must comply with the *Solicitors' Accounts Rules* (see p.48).

V   Terminating a retainer

Actions on termination

➤   A solicitor should return the client's papers, unless the solicitor:

   a) holds the papers as the client's agent, *and*

   b) has a lien over them (eg: for unpaid work).

➤   If the client instructs another solicitor, the second solicitor must secure the documents by giving an undertaking as to the costs incurred by the first solicitor.

   ◆ When the client is legally aided, there is no need for such an undertaking.

➤   The retainer may be terminated:

   1 by the client at any time, for any reason.

   2 by the solicitor if there is 'good reason', and reasonable notice is given.

   ◆ When stating the 'good reason', a solicitor must take care not to breach his duty of confidentiality.

   • Eg: if a solicitor acting for an insured person and his insurance company becomes aware that the insured is defrauding the insurers, the solicitor should refuse to act for both parties. The solicitor must maintain confidentiality to both clients, and must therefore not disclose any details to the insurer. A similar situation could occur when a solicitor is acting for both a mortgage company and a house buyer, where the house buyer wishes to obtain a mortgage for more than the property is worth.

   • Circumstances which may entitle, or compel a solicitor to end a retainer include:

   a) a conflict of interest arises, eg: a solicitor for 2 co-accused (with contradictory defences) should decline to act for both, *or*

   Note: where a conflict of interest does not threaten the administration of justice, and both parties consent, then a solicitor may continue acting for one of the parties.

   b) the client instructs a solicitor to break the law, *or*

   c) when confidence between the solicitor and the client breaks down, *or*

   d) when the client does not meet an interim bill during contentious proceedings.

   3 by operation of law.

   ◆ Eg: the solicitor is declared bankrupt or is of unsound mind.

B Costs, legal aid and bills

I Costs - general principles

Solicitors' Practice Rules 1990 r.15 (as amended)

➤ *'Solicitors shall give information about costs and other matters, and operate a complaints handling procedure, in accordance with a Solicitors' Costs Information and Client Care Code...'*

NB: The rule is stated as per a draft amendment that is expected to come into force around October 1997.

➤ Solicitors must keep clients notified of costs from the first meeting until instructions end. In particular:

  a) inform the client of costs at regular intervals (minimum every 6 months) and deliver interim bills where appropriate, *and*

  b) explain to the client (and confirm in writing) any changed circumstances that may affect the amount of costs, the degree of risk or the cost-benefit to the client in continuing with the matter, *and*

  c) tell the client in writing promptly that an estimate or agreed costs cap may be exceeded, *and*

  d) consider the client's eligibility for legal aid if there is a change in his means.

➤ A client will have to bear costs. These costs fall into 2 classes:

  1 **Solicitor-own-client costs:** these are all the expenses which the solicitor incurs on the client's behalf, including fees for expert opinions, applications for police accident reports, counsel's advice, etc, as well as the solicitor's own fees. It is usual to ask for a payment on account to cover expenses which the solicitor expects to incur.

  2 *Inter partes* **costs:** these are expenses which other parties to an action incur and are usually the responsibility of whichever party loses litigation (subject to the court's ruling on costs - pp.317-320).

Contentious matters - solicitors must explain:	
Private clients	**Legally aided clients**
◆ the client's potential liability for his own costs and those of any other party	◆ the client's potential liability for his own costs and those of any other party
◆ the fact that the client will be responsible for paying the firm's bill in full regardless of any order for costs made against the opponent	◆ the effect of the statutory charge and its likely amount
	◆ the client's liability to pay the statutory charge and consequences of failure to do so
◆ the probability that the client will have to pay the opponent's costs as well as the client's own costs if the case is lost	◆ the fact that the cleint may still be oredered by the court to contribute to the opponent's costs if the case is lost even though the client's own costs are covered by legal aid
◆ the fact that even if the client wins, the opponent may not be ordered to pay or be capable of paying the full amount of the client's costs	◆ the fact that even if the client wins, the opponent may not be ordered to pay or be capable of paying the full amount of the client's costs
◆ the fact that if the opponent is legally aided the client may not recover costs even if successful	

II   Legal aid franchising

Legal aid - franchising

➤   Firms may be franchised or non-franchised.

➤   A franchised firm holds a franchise with the Legal Aid Board and is said to be 'quality-checked'.

◆   This allows the firm to claim a higher payment for legal aid work.

◆   This gives the firm an ability to carry out certain decisions without reference to the Legal Aid Board (such as extending Green Form limits).

III   Civil legal aid

➤   There are 2 main forms of civil legal aid:

1   **Green Form scheme**

2   **Legal aid order**

1   **Green Form scheme** (*LAA 1988 Part III, LAAR 1989, LAA(S)R 1989*) (*Form GF1*)

➤ **Purpose:**   advice for up to 2 hours on any matter of English law is paid for by the Legal Aid Board. It does *not* include 'taking a step in proceedings' (ie: representation before a court), making a will if the applicant is under 70, or conveyancing services.

➤ **Merits of claim:** these are irrelevant.

➤ **Means test:** net disposable income that has been received over the previous 7 days including the day of application and disposable capital. The criteria are shown on a 'key card'.

A person on state benefits (a defined list) will qualify automatically on income but may be out of scope on capital

Green Form limits - figures as of 7 April 1997		
Income	Capital	Result
Above £77 **or** Above £1,000		The applicant may be refused aid
£77 or less **and** £1,000 or less		The applicant will get aid

Dependants

The following figures are added to the £77 **income** limits:

a partner	£28.00
dependants under 11	£16.90
dependants 11-16	£24.75
dependants 16-18	£29.60
dependants 18+	£38.90

The following figures replace the £1,000 **capital** limits:

1 dependant	£1,335
2 dependants	£1,535

3+ dependants - add £100 to the £1,535 figure for each additional dependant

➤ **Age:**   for anyone over 16. For minors, a parent's/guardian's capital and income are assessed.

➤ **Procedure:**   the solicitor fills in and returns *Form GF1* to the Legal Aid Board Area Manager, who pays up to a maximum of twice the hourly rate (regardless of number of disbursements).

➤ **Extension:**   authority must be sought from the Legal Aid Board. This is usually granted if a full Legal aid order is being applied for. *Form GF3* must be completed.

Note: franchised firms may be authorised to grant this authority to themselves.

2   Legal aid order (*LAA 1988 Part IV, CLA(G)R 1989, CLA(AR)R 1989*) (*Form CLA1*).

➤ Purpose: for most types of civil claim.

➤ Merits of claim: the test is whether the applicant has:

◆ 'reasonable grounds for taking, defending or being party to the proceedings',

and ◆ particular circumstances that make it reasonable for him to get legal aid.

➤ Means test: an applicant who is employed completes *Form CLA4A*, and his employer completes *Form L17* giving salary details. *Form CLA4B* is used if the applicant is unemployed (*CLA(AR)R 1989*).

◆ The calculation is based upon the applicant's disposable capital and disposable income, together with that of a spouse or unmarried partner over the last year, provided that there is no conflict of interest between them.

◆ An applicant will receive legal aid if his disposable income is £7,595 per annum or below, but may be refused if his disposable capital is above £6,750.

◆ Reassessments of income and capital may take place at any time while the legal aid certificate is in force.

A person on income support will qualify automatically

Legal aid limits - figures as of 7 April 1997		
Income	Capital	Result
Above £2,563 **or** Above £6,750		The applicant may be refused legal aid
£2,563 or less **and** £3,000 or less		The applicant will get legal aid
Above £2,563 **and** Above £3,000 Not above £7,595 Not above £6,750		The applicant will get legal aid, but a contribution is payable

Dependants	Pensioners
The following figures are capital allowances ie: amounts of capital that are ignored for the capital calculation: a partner £1,460	There are also capital allowances for pensioners (not listed here)
dependants under 11 £ 881	**Contribution**
dependants 11-16 £1,291	There is a monthly contribution from income of 1/36th of the excess, over £2,563, over the life of the certificate
dependants 16-18 £1,543	
dependants 18+ £2,028	

Personal injury

NB: There are different limits for personal injury claims:

Replace the £7,595 income figure with £8,370

Replace the £6,750 capital figure with £8,560

➤ Age;   anyone. (Applications for a minor must be made by a 'next friend' or a 'guardian *ad litem*', but are assessed on the basis of a minor's means. If the minor has no income, and £2,500 or less in capital, *Form CLA4F* must be used.)

➤ Procedure: ◆ if a contribution is payable, the Legal Aid Board must make an offer of legal aid to the applicant. If the applicant accepts the offer of legal aid within 28 days, a certificate of legal aid is issued. The contribution may well be refunded if the other side ends up paying *inter partes* costs.

◆ if no contribution is payable, the Legal Aid Board must make an offer of legal aid to the applicant.

➤ Certificate of legal aid:

- ◆ 1 copy is sent to the applicant and 2 to the solicitor (1 of which is to be kept on file and 1 filed at court). Notice of the issue is served on any other parties.

  (NB: No notice of any limitation or restrictions on the legal aid must be given to other parties.)

- ◆ does not entitle a solicitor to reimbursement for expenses which have already been incurred - an important difference between civil and criminal legal aid.

- ◆ may be conditional - the Legal Aid Board may remove restrictions later if asked.

- ◆ should reflect the current state of proceedings and should be amended if necessary (eg: if another party is joined to the proceedings).

- ◆ covers all expenses incurred in the 'reasonable' conduct of a case.

- ◆ places a solicitor under a duty to the Legal Aid Board not to incur unnecessary costs.

  Note: this duty to the Legal Aid Board is in addition to the duty to act in a client's best interests. Where a client is unreasonable compared to the standard of a 'privately paying client of moderate means', the solicitor's duty to the Legal Aid Board takes precedence, and he should make a report to the Board even if this infringes his duty of confidentiality to the client.

➤ **Amendment:**   if the certificate needs to be amended, the Legal Aid Board must issue an amended certificate and notice must be served on all parties to the dispute.

➤ **If the assisted party loses** (*LAA 1988 s.16, CLA(G)R 1989 rr.87-99*):

- ◆ the court may make an order for the loser to pay costs not exceeding a sum that is reasonable in all the circumstances.

- ◆ the Legal Aid Board keeps any contribution paid by the legally assisted loser.

➤ **If the assisted party wins** (*LAA 1988 s.16, CLA(G)R 1989 rr.87-99*):

- ◆ the Legal Aid Board may keep:

  - • any *inter partes* costs awarded in favour of the winner, *and*

  - • any contributions made by the legally aided party, *and*

  - • **the statutory charge** (ie: the Legal Aid Board has the first call on any damages won, to meet its costs in the action).

    - ▪ a person's tools of his trade are exempt from the statutory charge (*CLA(G)(A)R 1997*).

➤ **Costs of an unassisted defendant who wins the action** (*LAA 1988 s.18*):

- ◆ the Legal Aid Board can be ordered to pay the defendant's costs if:

  - a) it is just and equitable to do so, *and*

  - b) the defendant would be exposed to severe financial hardship. (The burden of proof rests on the defendant and this test is strictly applied.)

➤ **Discharge:**   ◆ the certificate:

- • is normally discharged on the conclusion of proceedings, *but*

- • may be discharged earlier, eg: if the client's means change.

➤ **Revocation:**   ◆ this occurs if the client has misled the Legal Aid Board in some way.

- ◆ the solicitor will still be paid by the Legal Aid Board, but the client may be liable for full costs.

IV Criminal legal aid

➤ There are 5 forms of criminal legal aid.

1   **Green Form scheme**
2   **Help from the duty solicitor at a police station**
3   **Court duty solicitor**
4   **ABWOR (Assistance By Way Of Representation)**
5   **Legal aid order**

1   **Green Form scheme** *(LAA 1988 ss.2, 8-13, LAA(S)R 1989)* *(Form GF1)*

➤ As per the civil Green Form scheme (see p.8).

2   **Help from the duty solicitor at a police station** *(LAAR 1989, LAAPS(R)R 1989)*

➤ **Purpose:**   to give advice to a suspect, up to a maximum financial limit (currently around £90). *Not* for representation before a court, unless it is for a guilty plea.

➤ **Extension:**   only in 'urgent necessity' in the interests of justice. It can be extended retrospectively.

➤ **Eligibility:**   anyone who needs advice and assistance at a police station.

➤ **Means test:**   *none.*

3   **Court duty solicitor (limited ABWOR)**

➤ **Purpose:**   representation in court.

➤ **Eligibility:**   representation for anyone in cases of a guilty plea *only*, for a non-imprisonable offence, at a Magistrates' Court.

  ◆ The scheme is for representation for bail, adjournments, *or* pleas in mitigation.
  ◆ The scheme is for up to 1 day, charged at a fixed hourly rate to the Legal Aid Board.
  ◆ The scheme only operates if the defendant would not otherwise be represented, and if he has not received this form of help before. The scheme operates when the solicitor concerned is present in the court precincts, and the court takes the view that the hearing should proceed on that day.

➤ **Means test:**   *none*, the service is free of charge to the defendant.

4   **ABWOR** *(LAAR 1989)*

➤ **Purpose:**   an Assistance By Way Of Representation (**ABWOR**) when there is no court duty solicitor scheme operating.

➤ **Eligibility:**   the scheme operates when the defendant would not otherwise be represented at a hearing for an imprisonable offence, where the hearing concerns bail, *or* an adjournment, *or* mitigation. (The requirement for it to be an imprisonable offence can be overridden if the solicitor considers the circumstances exceptional.) The scheme operates when the solicitor concerned is present in the court precincts, and the court takes the view that the hearing should proceed on that day.

➤ **Means test:**   *none.*

5 **Legal aid order** (*LAA 1988 Part V, LACCP(G)R 1989, LACCP(C)R 1989*)

➤ **Generally:**　　jurisdiction to grant this rests with the courts.

➤ **Purpose:**　　for representation before *either*:

a) Magistrates' Court and Crown Court

- The order covers advice on, and the preparation of, a notice of appeal. (Separate legal aid is necessary for the conduct of the appeal itself.)
- In the Magistrates' Court it covers representation by a solicitor (*LACCP(C)R 1989 r.7(3)*). (**Note:** counsel might act for free or for a reduced fee in return for taking the case when it comes to the Crown Court.)
- In the Magistrates' Court, unless there is a conflict of interest, one solicitor will represent co-defendants (*LACCP(G)R 1989 r.49*). In grave and difficult cases, counsel is allowed.
- In the Crown Court, it covers a solicitor and counsel on standard fees.

or **b) Court of Appeal and House of Lords.**

➤ **Payment:**

Magistrates' Court	Crown Court
- Costs are met on a standard basis - Complex cases are met on an hourly rate scheme covering the work done	- Most cases are met on a standard basis - Certain cases are met on an hourly rate scheme, covering the work done
- Claims are made to the Legal Aid Area Office for payment	- Claims are made to the Crown Court Taxing Office for payment

➤ **Effect:**
- an order is *not* retrospective unless (*LACCP(G)R 1989 r.44(7)*):
  a) the matter is urgent, *and*
  b) an application is made as soon as possible, *and*
  c) a solicitor who performs initial work before an order is granted applies for the order.

➤ **Means test:**
- If a defendant is on income support *or* family credit, there is no means test.
- The means test is otherwise determined by limits on income and capital:
  - free legal aid income limit:　£49.
  - free legal aid capital limit:　£3,000.
    NB:　There are also dependant allowances (not listed here).
- There may be a contribution payable by the defendant to the Legal Aid Board to help meet the cost of his legal aid(*LACCP(G)R 1989*):
  - from capital of the excess over £3,000.
  - (weekly contribution) from income of £1 for every £3 (or part of £3) by which weekly disposable income exceeds the £49 limit.

➤ **Merits:**
- Legal aid *must* be granted in *all* cases (subject to means testing) (*LAA 1988 s.19*), if:
  ✓ the charge is murder, *or*
  ✓ the prosecutor appeals to the House of Lords, *or*
  ✓ (in a Magistrates' Court) a defendant has been remanded in custody, and he may be remanded again, and he wishes for representation (having not been represented when first remanded in custody), *or*
  ✓ a defendant is to be sentenced by the Magistrates' Court or the Crown Court, and is in custody prior to the compilation of reports.

➤ **Merits (cont.):**
◆ legal aid *may* be granted if it is in the 'interests of justice', subject to means. The circumstances (non-exhaustive) when it is appropriate to give legal aid are when (*LAA s.22(2)*):

✓ there is a likelihood of a) a custodial sentence, *or* b) loss of livelihood, *or* c) serious damage to reputation. There is no clear authority as to whether a community sentence under the *CJA 1991* qualifies.

✓ there is a substantial question of law involved (eg: evidential difficulties).

✓ a disability or a linguistic barrier prevents the defendant from understanding the proceedings.

✓ tracing *and* interviewing of witnesses is necessary.

✓ expert cross-examination of a prosecution witness will be required.

✓ it is in the interests of someone other than the accused that the accused is represented.

◆ **Doubts** are resolved in the applicant's favour (*LAA 1988 s.21(7)*).

➤ **Where to apply:**
◆ legal aid for the Magistrates' Court - apply to the Magistrates' Court.
◆ legal aid for the Magistrates' Court on committal or legal aid for appeal to Crown Court - apply to the Crown Court.
◆ legal aid for appeal to the Crown Court against conviction or legal aid for appeal against a sentence in a Magistrates' Court - apply to the Crown Court.

Steps	
1	The applicant should complete an application for legal aid (*Form 1*), and a statement of means (*Form 5*). (No statement of means is necessary if an applicant is on income support, family credit or disability working allowance.)
2	The applicant should apply to the court, so that it can consider the statement of means.
3	The applicant should apply to the Magistrates' clerk, or orally to the court, to consider the application on *Form 1*.

➤ **Procedure:** the court itself grants orders.

➤ **Appeal against a refusal of legal aid:**
◆ the defendant can apply again to the refusing court at trial or other hearing:
  a) if the offence is indictable or triable either way, *and*
  b) if legal aid is refused by a Magistrates' Court (or a Magistrates' Court clerk) in the 'interests of justice test'.
◆ if this is refused, then the defendant may appeal to the Area Committee of the Legal Aid Board, provided that:
  a) the appeal is made within 14 days of receiving notification of the refusal, *and*
  b) the original application was made at least 21 days before any date which had been fixed for transfer or summary trial (*LACCP(G)R 1989 rr.15-17*).
◆ the Area Board may not review a means test; redress is through judicial review.

V   Bills

➤   The calculation of a bill is governed by different rules, depending on whether the business is non-contentious or contentious.

➤   A matter is contentious if proceedings have begun before a court or an arbitrator (*SA 1974 s.87*). (Proceedings before the Probate Court under the *NCPR 1987* are not classed as contentious.)

➤   In both cases various factors are considered:

Contentious business (RSC Ord.62, App. 2)	Non-contentious business (SRO 1994)
The complexity or novelty of the case	
The skill, labour, knowledge, responsibility and time involved	
The number and importance of documents involved (their length is irrelevant!)	
The place and circumstances under which the business is handled	
The value of property involved	
The importance of the matter to the client	
Any other fees and allowances payable to the solicitor or counsel in respect of other items in the same case, but only where the work done has reduced the work which would otherwise be necessary in the case.	Whether registered land is involved
	Approval of the client (express or implied) for what the solicitor has done, and for how much the work costs

➤   A bill must be signed by a partner, and state sufficient information to identify the matter and the period to which it relates.

➤   A bill should state whether VAT is included - if it does not mention VAT, then it is taken to be included.

➤   Disbursements (eg: experts' fees) should be billed separately.

VI Disputed bills

1 Client's remedies

➤ For non-contentious business, a client who is dissatisfied with a bill can ask the Law Society's Remuneration Certificate Department to issue a remuneration certificate *unless*:

a) the bill has already been paid, *or*

b) at least 1 month has passed since the client was told of his right to seek a certificate, *or*

c) the bill is due to be taxed under a High Court order, *or*

d) the bill is over £50,000 (not including VAT and disbursements).

◆ A remuneration certificate costs the client nothing, and if it sets a lower figure, the client need only pay that amount.

➤ Whether the matter is contentious or non-contentious, a client is also entitled to apply to the High Court for taxation (see p.318).

◆ If a client asks for taxation first, he cannot then ask for a remuneration certificate.

◆ The taxation will be on an indemnity basis (see p.317), but 3 presumptions apply (*RSC Ord.62 r.15, CCR Ord.38 r.19A*):

a) it is reasonable to incur expenditure on items that the client has expressly or impliedly approved, *and*

b) the amounts of expenditure are presumed reasonable if the client approved the amounts, *and*

c) it is unreasonable to incur the expenditure on items which are unusual, unless the client was warned in advance that these items might be allowed on a subsequent taxation.

2 Solicitor's remedies

➤ A solicitor can sue on a bill (or threaten to do so), provided that:

a) the bill has been signed by a partner, *and*

b) the client has been notified in writing of the right to request a remuneration certificate, *or* if the bill is for a contentious matter, of his right to taxation at the High Court, *and*

c) 1 month has passed since the bill was delivered to the client (unless the court grants leave to sue earlier than this under *SA 1974 o.69*).

➤ A solicitor can charge interest on an unpaid bill, at the rate due on judgment debts (currently 8%) provided that:

a) 1 month has passed since the bill was delivered to the client, *and*

b) the client has been informed in writing of his right to challenge the bill, *and*

c) for non-contentious business, notice has been given of the right to charge interest, *and*

d) for contentious business, this has been agreed beforehand.

C   Undertakings

> I   Undertakings generally

> II   Enforcement

I   Undertakings generally

Undertakings

➤   An undertaking is '... any unequivocal declaration of intention addressed to somebody who reasonably places reliance on it.'

➤   An undertaking can be given by a solicitor *or* any member of his staff.

➤   An undertaking can be written or oral in form, and it need not use the word 'undertake'.

➤   An undertaking binds the firm, and all the partners are personally liable to ensure its performance.

➤   To avoid incurring liability recklessly, a solicitor should follow these 5 steps before giving an undertaking.

Steps	
1	Ensure that it will be possible to fulfil the undertaking.
2	Obtain a client's authority before giving the undertaking.
3	Put the undertaking in writing.
4	Mark the client's file *on the outside* to warn everyone dealing with it of the undertaking.
5	Ask the recipient for a written discharge, and keep it on the client's file.

➤   It might be a good idea to observe a 'house rule' that only partners can give undertakings.

➤   **Note:**

   a) ambiguities are construed against the person who gives the undertaking.

   b) a solicitor is not released from his obligations if his default is due to circumstances beyond his control.

   c) the Law Society has drafted 'model' undertakings for use in certain situations (eg: conveyancing).

II   Enforcement

➤   The court has jurisdiction over solicitors as they are officers of the court. The court may therefore deal with breaches of undertakings.

➤   Breach of an undertaking is a breach of the professional conduct rules and the Law Society may take disciplinary action. If a client suffers loss as a result, then the solicitor may be liable for damages.

➤   The client also has a right to complain to the Legal Services Ombudsman under the *CLSA 1990*.

D Discipline

I Inadequate professional services/negligence

II Disciplinary bodies

I Inadequate professional services/negligence

➤ There is a distinction between inadequate professional services, negligence and work of low quality.

Inadequate professional services	Negligence	Low quality work

◆ These may include:
  ● breach of the conduct rules
  ● failure to follow instructions
  ● unreasonable delays
◆ There is no need to show damage
◆ The Law Society may take disciplinary action
◆ Complaints are dealt with by:
  ● the Solicitors' Disciplinary Tribunal for misconduct
  ● the Office for the Supervision of Solicitors for other inadequate professional services
	◆ Breach of 'duty of care' to a client or a third party
	◆ Work is performed without 'reasonable skill and care' (*SGSA 1982 s.13*)
	◆ The complainant must show damage
	  ● The test for this depends on whether the action is in contract or tort
	◆ A civil remedy lies in contract for the client, or in tort for a third party
	◆ The Law Society *may* take disciplinary proceedings
		◆ This is to be avoided, but if it falls short of negligence and does not amount to inadequate professional services, it is not actionable

➤ A solicitor should take the following actions on discovering that there are grounds for a claim.

Steps	
1	Inform the firm's insurers, and ask for their advice.
2	Advise the party concerned to seek independent legal advice.
3	Ensure all communications concerning this matter are confirmed in writing.
4	He must not admit liability without the insurer's consent.

II   Disciplinary bodies

1   Office for the Supervision of Solicitors ('OSS') (*CLSA 1990 s.93, SA 1974 s.44A*)

➤ **Structure:** The OSS is split into:

- the Office for Client Relations (dealing with complaints), *and*
- the Office for Professional Regulation (dealing with serious breaches of regulation and professional misconduct).

➤ **Jurisdiction:**

a) professional conduct - *SARs, SPRs* (under the Law Society's jurisdiction, *SA 1974 Sch.1*).

b) negligence, in certain circumstances.

c) breaches of the *SIBR 1995,* as the Law Society is treated as a Recognised Professional Body by the Securities and Investments Board.

➤ **Procedure:** conciliation where possible, else an assistant director at the OSS makes a ruling.

➤ **Appeals:** these are made to the Adjudication and Appeals Committee, which may investigate by:

a) inspecting the solicitor's accounts, *and*

b) demanding the solicitor's file.

➤ **Adjudication and Appeals Committee's powers include:**

- refusing, or imposing conditions on a practising certificate, *or* an investment business certificate.
- reprimanding the solicitor.
- awarding compensation up to £1,000 from the Law Society's Compensation Fund.
- taking the case before the Solicitors' Disciplinary Tribunal.
- ordering the solicitor to pay the client interest on money.
- ordering OSS staff to intervene in the practice where the public is at risk.
- ordering the solicitor to remit fees, or put the matter right at his own expense.
- ordering the solicitor to pay compensation to the client of up to £1,000.
- ordering the solicitor to reduce his bill in whole or in part.

2   Legal Services Ombudsman (*CLSA 1990 ss.21-26*)

➤ **Jurisdiction:** when a client is dissatisfied with the OSS's investigation of a complaint.

➤ **Powers:**   to make a report recommending the Law Society to discipline the offender, *or* to reconsider the complaint, *or* to compensate the injured party or ensure the offender does so.

- The Ombudsman has no powers of enforcement, but the recipient of a report must respond within 3 months.

3   The Solicitor's Disciplinary Tribunal (*CLSA 1990 s.92, SA 1974 s.47*)

➤ **Jurisdiction:**

- criminal conduct, professional misconduct or improper conduct (which may be just dishonourable.)

➤ **Powers:**

- impose a fine of up to £5,000.
- suspend a solicitor.
- strike a solicitor off the roll (ie: prevent him from practising).
- restore a solicitor to the roll.
- order payment of costs incurred during the investigation and the hearing.

➤ **Appeal:** to the Divisional Court of the Queen's Bench; thereafter to the House of Lords.

E *Financial Services Act 1986*

Steps

1 **Is an 'investment' involved?** (If so, go to **Step 2**)

'Investments' Part I Schedule 1	NOT 'Investments'
◆ Insurance policies with an investment element ◆ Unit trusts ◆ Company shares ◆ Debentures ◆ Government and public securities	◆ Insurance policies against risk (ie: no investment element) ◆ Building society shares ◆ Building society deposit and share accounts ◆ Bank deposits ◆ National savings (NS certificates, premium bonds) ◆ Mortgages over land

2 **Is the activity listed?** (If so, go to **Step 3**)

Activity	Description
◆ Dealing	Buying or selling
◆ Arranging	Fixing through a third party (but not referral)
◆ Managing	Control rather than just safekeeping
◆ Advising	About a specific investment (includes advising on others' advice)
◆ Establishing or operating collective investment schemes	

3 **Is it an excluded activity?** (If not, go to **Step 4**)

Excluded activity	Description
◆ Dealing as a principal	Acting privately on one's own behalf
◆ Sale of a company	Sale of 75% or more of the voting shares
◆ Necessary advice or arranging	Essential to the legal advice *and* no element of 'separate remuneration'
◆ Acting as (*not* for) a personal representative (PR) or trustee	No element of separate remuneration

4 **The solicitor must be authorised to conduct investment business by the Law Society, else he is in breach of the *FSA 1986*.** (Go to **Step 5**)

5 **Is the activity 'discrete investment business'?**

If so, the *SIBR 1995* apply in full. If not, the *SIBR 1995* apply in part.

Avoiding 'discrete'	Activity description
◆ Incidental business ◆ Permitted third parties ('PTPs')	The investment is subordinate to legal advice. (NB: However, unit trusts and life policies *are* discrete)
	A solicitor with an investment business certificate who acts as a disclosed agent for a named client is a PTP
	A person may also be authorised *in his own* right to conduct investment business, eg: a stockbroker. If a member of IMRO is involved as a PTP for the client, the solicitor should set up a procedure for 'full disclosure', to ensure transparency

➤ Even for non-discrete activity, some *SIBR* requirements governing record-keeping must be followed.

➤ A non-exempt person who carries out investment business without authorisation commits an indictable criminal offence which carries a prison sentence of up to 2 years (*FSA 1986 s.4(1)*).

➤ An agreement made by, or through, an unauthorised person is unenforceable unless a court consents (*FSA 1986 s.4(2)*).

➤ Breaches of the *SIBRs* carry liability to compensate for resultant losses, and invite disciplinary action.

F   Professional ethics

I   Conveyancing with non-solicitors

II   Criminal law - the prosecution's duties

III Criminal law - the defence's duties

IV   Civil litigation - disclosure

I   Conveyancing with non-solicitors

➤   When dealing with a buyer or seller who is not represented by a solicitor or a licensed conveyancer, a solicitor should:

  ◆ ensure he does not inadvertently commit an offence under *SA 1974 s.22* (eg: transferring title to land, or contracting to do so for profit without authorisation from the Law Society).

  ◆ tell his client he is dealing with an unrepresented party.

  ◆ consult the Law Society's published guidelines and write to the other party warning them (tactfully!) of the law, and asking them to confirm that they are not in danger of breaching it.

  ◆ not accept undertakings as these will not be enforceable. (He may be negligent in his duty to his client if he does so.)

  ◆ advise the other party to seek proper legal advice. (The solicitor does not owe a duty to the other side to explain anything to them himself.)

II   Criminal law - the prosecution's duties

The prosecution's duties

The duty of the prosecution is to ensure all material evidence is put before the court in a

dispassionate and fair manner. *All* relevant facts should be put before the court,

including, after conviction, facts relevant to mitigation.

➤   There is a duty to give evidence to the defence that the prosecution does not intend to use, eg: if the prosecution has in its possession the statement of a material witness showing the innocence of the defendant, it is its duty to disclose it to the defence. (See the 'Disclosure' provisions p.377).

➤   There is a duty to tell the defence if a prosecution witness gives evidence which is inconsistent with an earlier statement.

III   Criminal law - the defence's duties

> ### The defence's duties
> The defence has a duty to the court and a duty to the client.

➤ **When the client admits his guilt to the solicitor**, the solicitor is unable to act. However, on a plea of 'not guilty', he can still put the prosecution to proof.

➤ **When the client pleads 'guilty', but has a defence**, the solicitor can act. He can put the client's defence, but must advise the client that in mitigation it may not be possible to rely on the facts constituting the defence.

➤ **When the client gives inconsistent instructions**, the solicitor can act (if there is no false evidence).

➤ **The solicitor must never disclose the defence case without the client's consent.**

➤ **The solicitor has a positive duty to assist the court on points of law.**

➤ **The solicitor has a negative duty not to mislead the court on points of fact.**

➤ **If the client wishes to give a false name or address to the court,** the solicitor must try to persuade the client to be truthful. If he does not succeed, the solicitor cannot act.

➤ **If the court has an incorrect list of the client's previous convictions,** the solicitor may not correct the list without the consent of the client. If there is no such consent, the solicitor must refuse to act.

➤ **If for *any* reason, the solicitor is unable to act, he may not be able to say why without breaching a client confidence.** He should just say that it is impossible for him to act, without saying why.

➤ **If the prosecution does not realise that its detention limits are about to run out,** the defence owes a duty to the client not to remind the prosecution of this (see p.346).

IV   Civil litigation - disclosure

➤ The solicitor should make his client aware that it is important to:
   ◆ preserve carefully all documents for disclosure whether they:
      • help the client's case, *or*
      • harm the client's case.
   ◆ be truthful when dealing with such documents because:
      • the solicitor has a duty not to mislead the court, *and*
      • from the client's point of view, if it later arises at trial that documents have been withheld, lost, or 'destroyed', it may critically prejudice the client's case.

Accounts

This chapter examines:

Conventions in the presentation of accounts

➤   If a figure is underlined, this means it is being added or subtracted along with those *above* it.

➤   The answer may be placed in the column to the right of the underlined figure if there is one, or if there is no such column, directly below.

➤   The purpose of this is to help in the addition or subtraction of totals and subtotals.

➤   Final answers are usually double-underlined.

A Basic bookkeeping

Step 1	Produce 'T' accounts

➤ In a double entry accounting system, every transaction is recorded twice in order to produce an ongoing error check in the figures.

◆ 'T' accounts are used, named after the shape of the lines drawn.

● These are 'fictional' devices which set out what is happening to particular items in a business.

■ Items can be assets, liabilities, receipts in or payments out eg: cash, a vehicle, debtors, etc.

NB: 'T' accounts are *not* real accounts in the sense of a bank account.

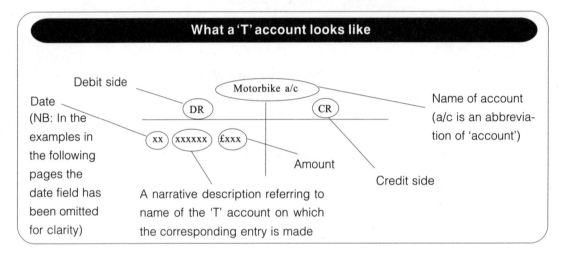

➤ A debit on 1 side of a 'T' account = a credit on 1 side of another 'T' account.

◆ Total debits *must* equal total credits.

➤ As many 'T' accounts as necessary are used. **It is easiest to start with the cash account entry.**

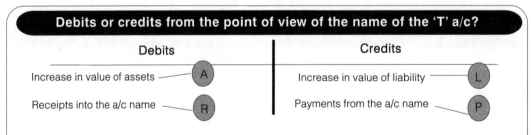

Hint: For the cash account, think of DR as all moneys coming into the cash a/c and CR as all monies paid out. Then work the double entry from there for the corresponding accounts.

Hint: After the cash account the rest of the 'T' accounts may be done in any order.

➤ The collection of 'T' accounts taken together' is known as:

◆ the general ledger, *or*

◆ the nominal ledger.

Step 1	Example

Facts: Alpha and Beta start together as solicitors on 1 January, 1997. Each puts £15,000 into the new partnership. In the first year the following events occur:

	DR	CR
Staff salaries	27,000	
Rent	10,000	
Company motorbike	4,000	
Office equipment bought on credit	6,500	
Misc. and general expenses	1,500	
Bills delivered		90,000

> They have only collected £62,000 of bills delivered and you will see that they still owe £6,500 for the office equipment.

Hint: Start with the cash account and work through the other accounts.

The 'T' accounts

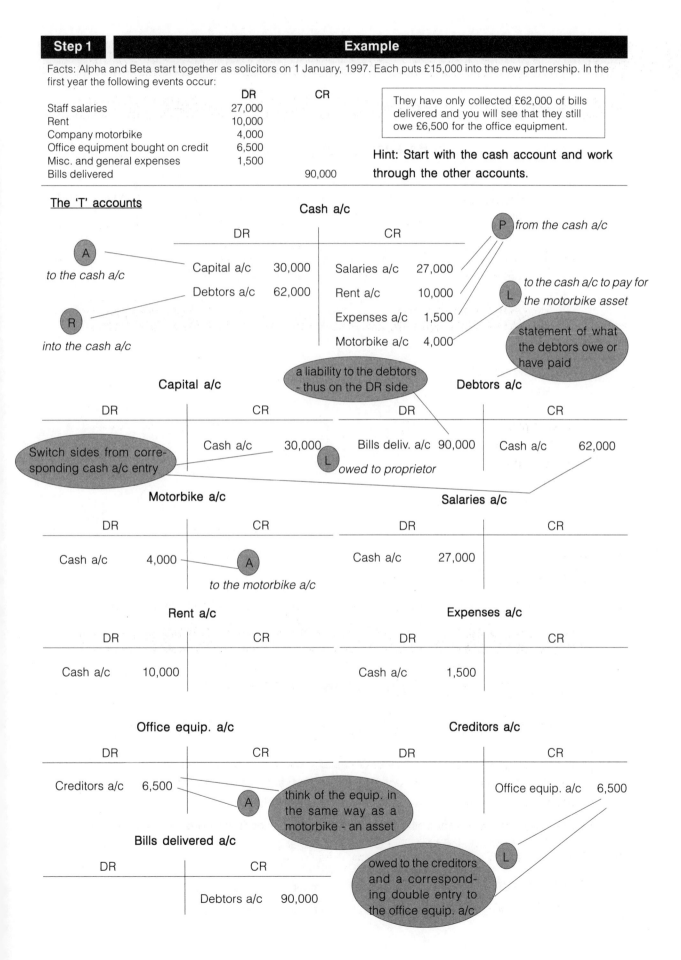

Cash a/c

DR			CR		
Capital a/c	30,000		Salaries a/c	27,000	
Debtors a/c	62,000		Rent a/c	10,000	
			Expenses a/c	1,500	
			Motorbike a/c	4,000	

A — to the cash a/c

R — into the cash a/c

P — from the cash a/c

L — to the cash a/c to pay for the motorbike asset

statement of what the debtors owe or have paid

a liability to the debtors - thus on the DR side

Capital a/c

DR		CR	
		Cash a/c	30,000

L — *owed to proprietor*

Switch sides from corresponding cash a/c entry

Debtors a/c

DR		CR	
Bills deliv. a/c	90,000	Cash a/c	62,000

Motorbike a/c

DR		CR	
Cash a/c	4,000		

A — *to the motorbike a/c*

Salaries a/c

DR		CR	
Cash a/c	27,000		

Rent a/c

DR		CR	
Cash a/c	10,000		

Expenses a/c

DR		CR	
Cash a/c	1,500		

Office equip. a/c

DR		CR	
Creditors a/c	6,500		

A — *think of the equip. in the same way as a motorbike - an asset*

Creditors a/c

DR		CR	
		Office equip. a/c	6,500

L — *owed to the creditors and a corresponding double entry to the office equip. a/c*

Bills delivered a/c

DR		CR	
		Debtors a/c	90,000

Step 2	Balance the 'T' accounts and produce a trial balance

A. Balancing the 'T' accounts

➤ The aim of balancing accounts is to draw the line under everything that has occured so far in each 'T' account and carry on into the next period with just one figure - so starting the process for each 'T' account all over again.

➤ Balancing off the 'T' accounts is the process of adding all the entries on each side of a 'T' account and working out what the difference is and on which side that difference falls.

➤ The balance is carried forward to the next period.

➤ There are 5 steps in this procedure which are set out (❶ to ❺) in the example opposite.

B. Producing the trial balance

➤ The purpose of producing a trial balance is to check the arithmetic in all of the 'T' accounts.

➤ A trial balance is produced as follows:

 ◆ take each of the DR 'balance brought forward' entries (from the 'T' accounts with a balance brought forward on the DR side) and add them together to reach a total, *and*

 ◆ take each of the CR 'balance brought forward' entries (from the 'T' accounts with a balance forward on the CR side) and add them together to reach a total, *and*

 ◆ if the arithmetic is correct, the totals should be the same because of the double entry system whereby every time a CR is made, a corresponding DR is made, so total CR = total DR.

➤ The method of setting this out is illustrated in the example opposite.

Step 2	Example

Facts: Continued from step 1.

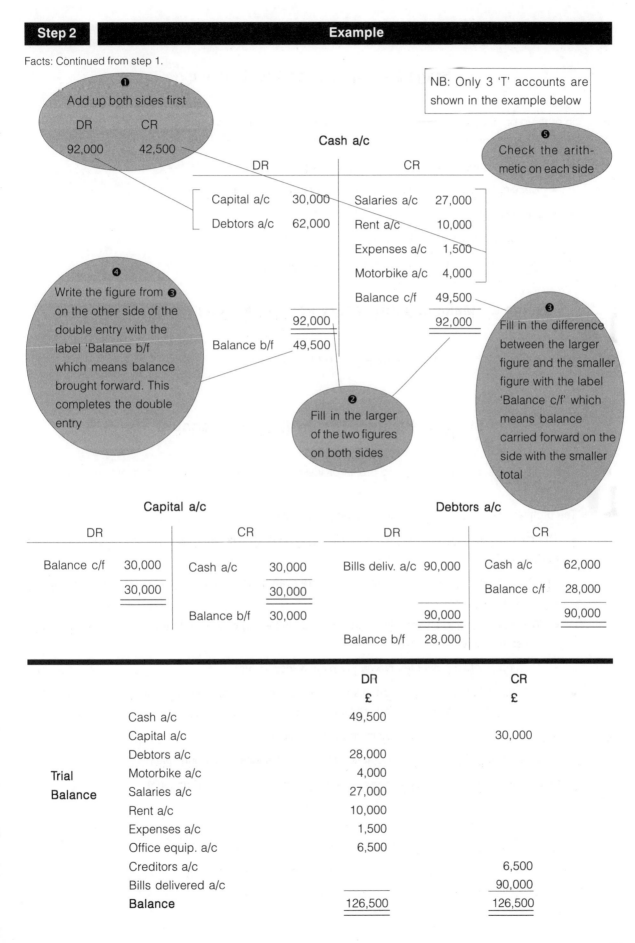

❶
Add up both sides first

DR	CR
92,000	42,500

NB: Only 3 'T' accounts are shown in the example below

❺
Check the arithmetic on each side

Cash a/c

DR			CR	
Capital a/c	30,000	Salaries a/c	27,000
Debtors a/c	62,000	Rent a/c	10,000
		Expenses a/c	1,500
		Motorbike a/c	4,000
		Balance c/f	49,500
	92,000		92,000
Balance b/f	49,500		

❹
Write the figure from ❸ on the other side of the double entry with the label 'Balance b/f which means balance brought forward. This completes the double entry

❷
Fill in the larger of the two figures on both sides

❸
Fill in the difference between the larger figure and the smaller figure with the label 'Balance c/f' which means balance carried forward on the side with the smaller total

Capital a/c

DR		CR	
Balance c/f	30,000	Cash a/c	30,000
	30,000		30,000
		Balance b/f	30,000

Debtors a/c

DR		CR	
Bills deliv. a/c	90,000	Cash a/c	62,000
		Balance c/f	28,000
	90,000		90,000
Balance b/f	28,000		

		DR £	CR £
	Cash a/c	49,500	
	Capital a/c		30,000
	Debtors a/c	28,000	
Trial	Motorbike a/c	4,000	
Balance	Salaries a/c	27,000	
	Rent a/c	10,000	
	Expenses a/c	1,500	
	Office equip. a/c	6,500	
	Creditors a/c		6,500
	Bills delivered a/c		90,000
	Balance	126,500	126,500

Step 3	Produce final accounts (Profit & loss account and balance sheet)

Stage 1 - Mark up the trial balance

➤ In order to produce the 2 final accounts, it is necessary to mark every item on the trial balance as being destined for the profit & loss account or the balance sheet.

 ◆ Receipts and payments will go on the profit and loss account.

  ● Receipts and payments have the nature of being ephemeral - coming and going.

 ◆ Assets and liabilities will go on the balance sheet.

  ● Assets and liabilties have a more permanent nature.

➤ An example of this marking is shown in the example opposite.

Stage 2 - Make any necessary adjustments as per pp.32-35.

➤ The example on the right has no necessary adjustments to make.

Stage 3 - Produce the profit & loss account

➤ The profit & loss account shows the profits or losses that the business has made during a particluar period.

➤ The profit & loss account is part of the double entry system.

 ◆ This means that to put entries into the profit & loss account, it is necessary to close off the relevant 'T' account.

 NB: Relevant 'T' accounts are those which are relevant to the profit & loss account from the marking up of the trial balance.

  ● This means writing an entry labelled 'P&L a/c' on the opposite side to the 'balance b/f' entry with the same figure.

  ● Then complete the double entry in the profit & loss 'T' a/c.

 ◆ The relevant 'T' accounts for which this has been done are at zero and are said to be closed for the period in question. The new period will start from a zero balance again.

➤ There are 2 'styles' of presenting a profit and loss account.

 ◆ Style 'A' is technical and is a presentation of the profit & loss 'T' account itself.

 ◆ Style 'B' is more user-friendly and is a re-writing of the profit & loss 'T' account.

Step 3	Example

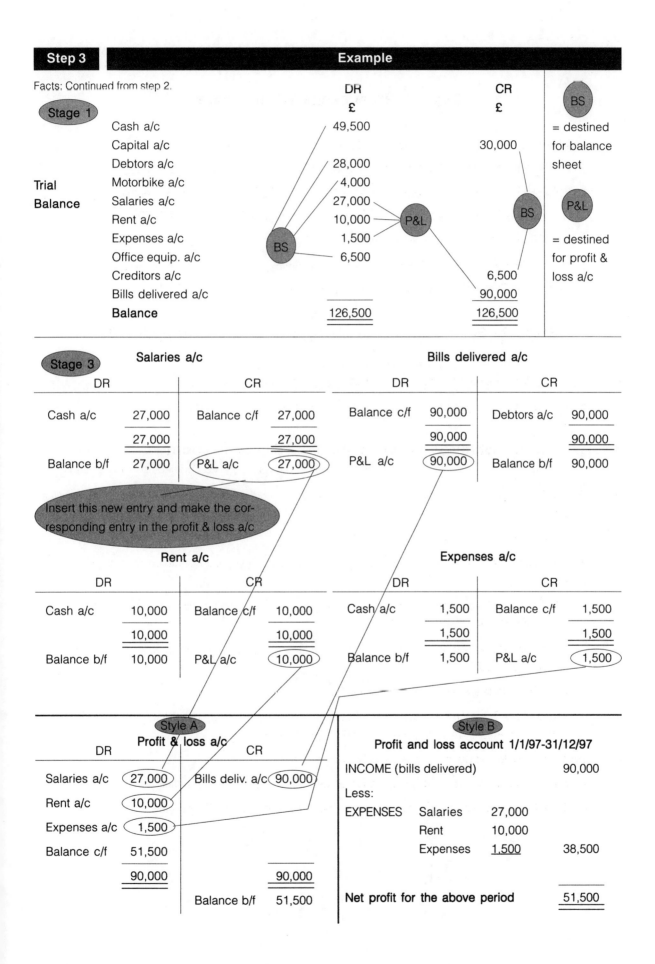

Facts: Continued from step 2.

Stage 1

Trial Balance

	DR £	CR £	
Cash a/c	49,500		BS
Capital a/c		30,000	= destined for balance sheet
Debtors a/c	28,000		
Motorbike a/c	4,000		
Salaries a/c	27,000		P&L
Rent a/c	10,000		= destined for profit & loss a/c
Expenses a/c	1,500		
Office equip. a/c	6,500		
Creditors a/c		6,500	
Bills delivered a/c		90,000	
Balance	126,500	126,500	

Stage 3

Salaries a/c

DR		CR	
Cash a/c	27,000	Balance c/f	27,000
	27,000		27,000
Balance b/f	27,000	P&L a/c	27,000

Insert this new entry and make the corresponding entry in the profit & loss a/c

Bills delivered a/c

DR		CR	
Balance c/f	90,000	Debtors a/c	90,000
	90,000		90,000
P&L a/c	90,000	Balance b/f	90,000

Rent a/c

DR		CR	
Cash a/c	10,000	Balance c/f	10,000
	10,000		10,000
Balance b/f	10,000	P&L a/c	10,000

Expenses a/c

DR		CR	
Cash a/c	1,500	Balance c/f	1,500
	1,500		1,500
Balance b/f	1,500	P&L a/c	1,500

Style A

Profit & loss a/c

DR		CR	
Salaries a/c	27,000	Bills deliv. a/c	90,000
Rent a/c	10,000		
Expenses a/c	1,500		
Balance c/f	51,500		
	90,000		90,000
		Balance b/f	51,500

Style B

Profit and loss account 1/1/97-31/12/97

INCOME (bills delivered)			90,000
Less:			
EXPENSES	Salaries	27,000	
	Rent	10,000	
	Expenses	1,500	38,500
Net profit for the above period			51,500

29

Step 3...   **Produce final accounts (Profit & loss account and balance sheet)**

Stage 4 - Produce the balance sheet

➤   The balance sheet performs 2 functions:

a) it is a snapshot of the business's assets and liability's at a particular date, *and*

b) it is a check that 'Assets of the business = Liabilities of the business (ie: capital employed)'.

◆   The form of the balance sheet is derived from the equation as follows:

Assets = Liabilities

Assets = Inside liabilities (owed to the proprietor ie: capital and profit) + Outside Liabilities

Assets = (Opening capital and profit) + Outside liabilities

Assets - Outside liabilities = Opening capital and profit

➤   The balance sheet is *not* part of the double entry system.

◆   This means there is no adjustment to the 'T' accounts.

➤   The balance sheet is made up by taking the items from the marked up trial balance *and* taking the final figure from the profit and loss account and putting them into the balance sheet form. There is a pro forma balance sheet set out on p.38.

➤   The net assets [ie: (fixed + current assets) less (fixed + current liabilities)] should match the opening capital and profit. This is because it shows how the company capital is employed and tied up in assets and liabilities.

Step 3...   **Example (cont.)**

Stage 4

A 'snapshot' as of this date

Balance sheet as at 31st December, 1997

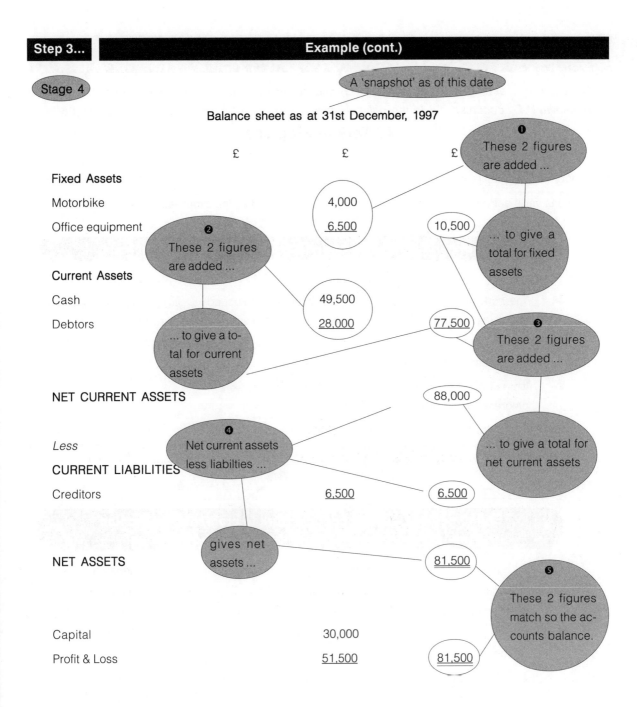

	£	£	£
Fixed Assets			
Motorbike		4,000	
Office equipment		6,500	10,500
Current Assets			
Cash		49,500	
Debtors		28,000	77,500
NET CURRENT ASSETS			88,000
Less			
CURRENT LIABILITIES			
Creditors		6,500	6,500
NET ASSETS			81,500
Capital		30,000	
Profit & Loss		51,500	81,500

❶ These 2 figures are added ...

... to give a total for fixed assets

❷ These 2 figures are added ...

... to give a total for current assets

❸ These 2 figures are added ...

... to give a total for net current assets

❹ Net current assets less liabilties ...

gives net assets ...

❺ These 2 figures match so the accounts balance.

All figures used on this balance sheet are from the marked up trial balance

31

B   Advanced bookkeeping

All advanced bookeeping in this section (A - G) necessitates changes to the profit & loss account (and other relevant 'T' accounts) and to the balance sheet. There is a fully worked example on pp.36-37.

A. Work in progress

➤ Work in progress is work that is being undertaken by the firm but which has not yet been been billed.

➤ It has value and this value must be shown in the same period as the expenses spent to produce it.

End of period 1 - taking period 1 work in progress into account

Profit & loss account	Balance sheet
◆ The work in progress 'T' a/c should be debited with the period 1 work in progress figure (see p.24 because it is an asset).	◆ Add work in progress under CURRENT ASSETS as per the pro forma on p.38.
◆ The profit & loss a/c should be credited with the period 1 work in progress figure (completing the double entry).	
◆ If presenting the account in style B (see p.28), add the work in progress for period 1 to bills delivered.	

Bills delivered · Start · Period 1 · End · Work in progress

End of period 2 - taking period 2 work in progress into account and taking out period 1 work in progress from account

Profit & loss account	Balance sheet
◆ The work in progress 'T' a/c should be debited with the period 2 work in progress figure (see p.24 because it is an asset).	◆ Add work in progress under CURRENT ASSETS as per the pro forma on p.38.
◆ The profit & loss a/c should be credited with the period 2 work in progress figure (completing the double entry).	

- The 'T' a/cs will now be accurate as the period 1 work in progress was billed and gradually paid, the necessary entries will have been made in the work in progress a/c to bring the period 1 work in progress a/c to zero.

◆ If presenting the account in style B (see p.28), add the work in progress from period 2 to bills delivered and subtract the work in progress from period 1 from bills delivered.

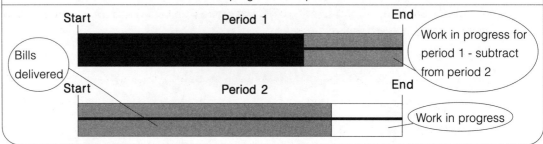

Start · Period 1 · End · Work in progress for period 1 - subtract from period 2

Bills delivered · Start · Period 2 · End · Work in progress

B. Bad debts

➤ Sometimes it is obvious that specific debts will not be paid by specific debtors and it is necessary to write off those debts.

➤ Adjustments:

◆ the balance sheet, by amending the profit & loss figure (see below) and the current assets, *and*

◆ the profit & loss account and other 'T' accounts:

● The debtors a/c is credited with an entry labelled 'bad debts a/c' and the amount.

● The bad debts a/c is debited with an entry labelled 'debtors a/c' and the amount. This is then closed off to the profit & loss account.

▪ In Style 'B' presentations, bad debts is an expense of the business.

Eg: (showing the amendments to 'T' accounts only).

The facts are as on pp.25, 27 and 29 but it becomes obvious that £1,500 will never be paid:

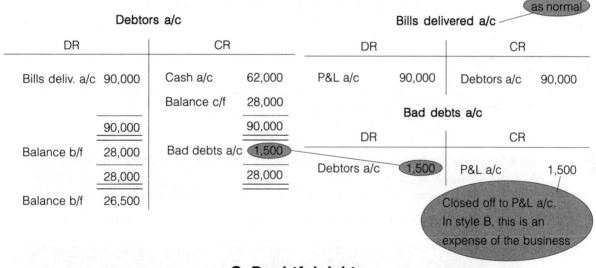

C. Doubtful debts

➤ It is careful accounting to make a provision for doubtful debts (unlike bad debts which is knowledge that a *specific* debtor will not pay).

◆ The figure chosen is based on experience of debts that as a fact have not been paid in the past and is usually a percentage of total debtors.

➤ Adjustments:

◆ the balance sheet, by amending the profit & loss figure (see below) and the current assets (by subtracting the figure from debtors), *and*

◆ the profit & loss account and other 'T' accounts:

● The doubtful debts a/c is credited with an entry labelled 'profit & loss a/c' and the amount.

● The profit & loss a/c is debited with an entry labelled 'doubtful debts a/c' and the amount.

▪ In Style 'B' presentations, the doubtful debts are an expense of the business.

D. Payments in advance (prepayments)

➤ These are payments made in the current accounting period for goods/services in the following period.

➤ Adjustments:

◆ the balance sheet, by adding the prepayment as a current asset and amending the profit & loss figure (see below), *and*

◆ the profit & loss account and other 'T' accounts:

• if the account with the prepayment is for example, rent, close off from the rent a/c to the profit & loss account the amount **actually paid out** for the period less the prepayment. The prepayment goes in in the CR column (of the rent a/c) (under the profit and loss a/c entry) as the "balance c/f" figure with the corresponding double entry figure being in the DR column as the balance b/f. This is the amount brought forward into the next accounting period.

NB: the cash a/c should always reflect the sums **actually paid** during the account period.

■ In Style B presentations, subtract the prepayment from the rent figure.

E. Payments in arrears (accruals)

➤ These are payments that will be made in the next accounting period for goods/services used in the current accounting period.

➤ Adjustments:

◆ the balance sheet, by subtracting the accrual by putting it in as a current liability and amending the profit & loss figure (see below), *and*

◆ the profit & loss account and other 'T' accounts:

• if the account with the accrual is for example, water, only close off from the water account to the profit & loss a/c an amount equal to the cash paid out less the prepayment. Carry forward the prepayment into the next account period.

■ In Style B presentations, add the accrual to the water figure for the period.

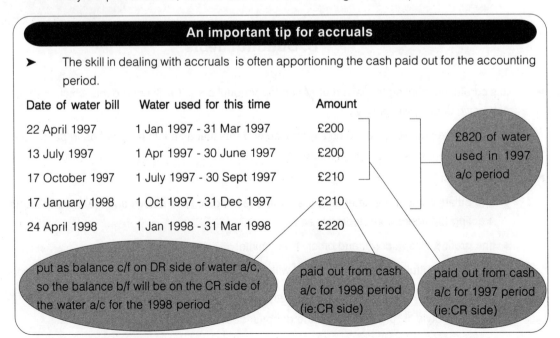

An important tip for accruals

➤ The skill in dealing with accruals is often apportioning the cash paid out for the accounting period.

Date of water bill	Water used for this time	Amount
22 April 1997	1 Jan 1997 - 31 Mar 1997	£200
13 July 1997	1 Apr 1997 - 30 June 1997	£200
17 October 1997	1 July 1997 - 30 Sept 1997	£210
17 January 1998	1 Oct 1997 - 31 Dec 1997	£210
24 April 1998	1 Jan 1998 - 31 Mar 1998	£220

£820 of water used in 1997 a/c period

put as balance c/f on DR side of water a/c, so the balance b/f will be on the CR side of the water a/c for the 1998 period

paid out from cash a/c for 1998 period (ie:CR side)

paid out from cash a/c for 1997 period (ie:CR side)

F. Depreciation

➤ Depreciation is a charge made to the business each year to reflect the loss in value of an asset, eg: if a £5,000 motorbike is expected to last the business for 5 years, we will charge a cost of £1,000 per year to the business.

◆ The actual figure charged per year, although a 'guesstimate' is usually based on the experience of accountants.

➤ Adjustments:

◆ using the motorbike example above, each year on the balance sheet under the fixed asset 'motorbike' there should be an entry labelled 'accumulated depreciation'. This will be listed as £1,000 in the first year, £2,000 in the next year until it reads £5,000 in the fifth year giving an asset value of nil.

◆ 'T' accounts:

● the motorbike a/c will have already have £5,000 listed on the DR side (as it is an asset - see p.24).

● the accumulated depreciation a/c will already have the accumulated depreciation (for previous accounting years) listed on the CR side. Add to the CR side the depreciation for this year's accounting period and perform the 'balance c/f' and 'balance b/f' procedure to give a total figure for accumulated depreciation (for previous accounting periods and this accounting period) on the CR side.

● the depreciation a/c should have this year's (and only this year's) motorbike depreciation put on the DR side and the account should be closed off to the profit & loss account.

■ In Style B presentations, this year's depreciation is an expense of the business.

G. Disposal of fixed assets

➤ When a business sells assets, it will make a profit or loss on the sale.

➤ This profit is reported at the end of the profit & loss account as seperate figure from the main profit figure of the business. (Since the mainstream income of the business is not derived from the buying and selling of assets, the figure from this is listed as seperate, otherwise this would confuse the true proifit and loss figures.)

➤ When asset A is sold:

◆ put in the CR column of the asset A a/c, the label 'transfer to disposal a/c' and the cost price - this clears the asset A 'T' account, *and*

◆ put in the DR column of the accumulation depreciation a/c the accumulated depreciation for asset A and update the accumulation a/c by doing the balance c/f - balance b/f procedure, *and*

◆ put in the DR column of the fixed asset disposal a/cthe label 'Asset A a/c' and the cost figure (thus completing the double entry for (a) above), *and*

◆ put in the CR column of the fixed asset a/c the label 'accumulated depreciation a/c' and the final accumulated depreciation figure for asset A (thus completing the double entry for (b) above), *and*

So far this has cleared off asset A from the main accounts into a special asset disposal account.

◆ put in the DR column of the cash account the sale price, *and*

◆ put in the CR column of the fixed asset disposal a/c, the sale price. Balance off the fixed asset disposal a/c and take the profit to the profit & loss a/c.

■ Style B presentations and adjustments to the balance sheet are self-explanatory.

Fully worked example

Sue, Grabbit & Run, a firm of successful solicitors in Erehwon, set up business on 1 January 1990. The accountants draw up a trial balance as at 31 January 1997 for the 1997 year of business. Produce a balance sheet and profit & loss account based on the following trial balance and extra facts:

Trial balance:	£	£
Opening capital in the business		50,000
Bank loan		80,000
Loan interest	9,000	
Balance in office account - cash	110,000	
Office equipment and computers - cost	20,000	
Office equipment and computers - accumulated depreciation		10,000
Messengers motorbikes - cost	14,000	
Messengers motorbikes - accumulated depreciation		4,000
Bills delivered		170,000
Work in progress as at 31 December 1996	80,000	
Debtors	13,500	
Creditors		8,500
Salaries	60,000	
Office rent	13,500	
Electricity	2,000	
Water	500	
	322,500	322,500

❶

Mark all items on the trial balance as destined for the BS or the P&L a/c

☐ **BS**

▨ **P&L**

Unmarked BS and P&L

- The office owes party contractors (ie: creditors) £1,000 (not yet in the account) for the 1996 office Xmas party.
- The office rent paid in advance at 31 Dec. 1997 is £2,000.
- The electricity accrued as at 31 Dec. 1997 is £400.
- The water accrued as at 31 Dec. 1997 is £100.
- It has been decided that a provision for doubtful debts of £8,500 should be made.
- Depreciation for the year is 20% of cost on office computers and equipment.
- Depreciation for the year is 15% of cost on messengers motorbikes.
- Work in progress at 31 December 1997 is £40,000.

❷

BS and P&L

Profit & Loss account for Sue Grabbit & Run for 1997 a/c period

INCOME

Bills delivered			170,000
Less: last year's work in progress			80,000
			90,000
Add: this year's work in progress			40,000
			130,000

Total income for this year

LESS:
EXPENSES

Salaries		60,000	
Loan interest		9,000	
Xmas party expense		1,000	
Office rent	13,500		
Less: rent advance	2,000	11,500	
Electricity	2,000		
Add: electricity accrual	400	2,400	
Water	500		
Add: water accrual	100	600	
Provision for doubtful debts		8,500	
Depreciation			
1997 office/computers (20% of £20,000)	4,000		
1997 motorbikes (15% of £14,000)	2,100	6,100	99,100

See the box on 'conventions in the presentation of accounts' on p.23 to understand how the underlining of numbers works

Total expenses for this year

NET 1997 PROFIT	**30,900**

Fully worked example (continued)

Balance sheet of Sue, Grabbit & Run as of 31st December, 1997

FIXED ASSETS

Office equipment and computers - cost		20,000	
Less accumulated depreciation (10,000+4,000)		14,000	6,000
Messengers motorbikes - cost		14,000	
Less accumulated depreciation (4,000+2,100)		6,100	7,900	13,900

[pre 1997 office equip. depreciation]   [1997 office equip. depreciation]

[pre 1997 motorbike depreciation]   [1997 motorbike depreciation]

ADD: CURRENT ASSETS

Work in progress 1997			40,000	
Debtors	13,500		
Less provision for doubtful debts	8,500	5,000	
Prepayments		2,000	
Cash		110,000	157,000

LESS: CURRENT LIABILITIES

Creditors	8,500		
Add creditors not yet in accounts	1,000	9,500	
Accruals			
Electricity	400		
Water	100	500	10,000

NET CURRENT ASSETS	**160,900**

LESS: LONG TERM LIABILITIES

Bank loan	80,000
NET ASSETS	**80,900**

Capital and profit

Capital	50,000	
Net 1997 profit	30,900	**80,900**

Pro-forma balance sheet

Balance sheet of [   ] as of [   ]

		V-W should equal AA+BB

FIXED ASSETS

Asset 1 - cost	A		
Less accumulated depreciation for asset 1	B	C (A+B)	
Asset 2 - cost	D		
Less accumulated depreciation for asset 2	E	F (D+E)	G (C+F)

ADD: CURRENT ASSETS

Work in progress current period		H
Debtors	I	
Less provision for doubtful debts	J	
Less provision for bad debts	K	L(I+J+K)
Prepayments (X+X+X+X+X+X+X etc.)		M
Cash at bank		N
Petty cash		O	P(H+L+M+N+P)

LESS: CURRENT LIABILITIES

Creditors	Q	
Add creditors not yet in accounts	R	S(Q+R)
Accruals (X+X+X+X+X+X+X+X etc.)		T	U(S+T)

CLIENT BALANCES

Client bank account	Y	
Less client ledgers (owed to clients)	Y	NIL(Y-Y)	NIL

NET CURRENT ASSETS — V(G+P-U)

LESS: LONG TERM LIABILITIES

Bank loan	W

NET ASSETS — V-W

Capital employed

Capital	if partnership accounts, this is the partners'	AA
Net 1997 profit	capital and current accounts (see p.40)	BB	AA+BB

C   Bank reconciliations

➤   It is often necessary to 'reconcile' the bank statements of the business with the cash ledger (ie: the cash 'T' account) as a cheque on the double entry accounting. They may not match up because of:
  ◆   bank charges/bank interest on the statement but not in the cash book, *and/or*
  ◆   cheques received by the business but not yet paid into/credited onto the bank account, *and/or*
  ◆   cheques paid out by the business but not yet cashed by those to whom they have been given, *and/or*
  ◆   error on the bank statement (quite common!) or in the cash book.

❶   Make sure the starting balances on the cash ledger and the bank statement are the same by bringing the previous month's transactions up to date. Then, cross off all similar items that appear in both the bank statement and the cash ledger and circle those that are different.

❷   write into the cash ledger all outstanding items (see grey boxes below)

❸   draw up a reconciliation statement to match the bank statement to the cash ledger - the end figures should be the same!

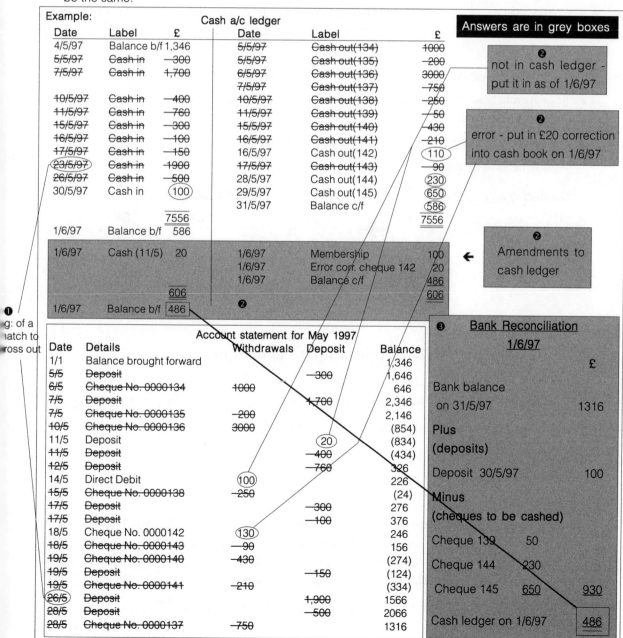

D   Partnership accounts

➤   With partnership accounts, certain changes are made to the different areas of the accounts.

➤   The differences when dealing with partnerships are 4:

a) partners may take interest on their capital contributions to the partnership, *or/and*

b) partners may draw a salary for themselves, *or/and*

c) partners will share profits according to a set formula (usually based on an agreed percentage), *or/and*

d) partners may take drawings from the business for themselves.

A. The trial balance

➤   Remember - a trial balance is a listing of all the balances of the 'T' accounts. Although the changes below are listed from the trial balance stage, they in fact occur much earlier when the individual 'T' accounts are worked on.

➤   In addition to the usual trial balance (p.26), the following changes should be made:

◆   any net profit listed on the trial balance is usually, by convention, a figure taken before any of (a)-(d) above have been out.

◆   the capital account entry is split into an entry per partner:

eg: trial balance excerpt:

Non-partnership accounts		
	DR	CR
capital		X

→

Partnership accounts		
	DR	CR
Partner's 1 capital		A
Partner's 2 capital		B
Partner's 3 capital		C

B. The appropriation accounts

➤   An appropriation account is a breakdown of how profit is distributed to each partner. It is not a 'T' account.

➤   The appropriation account lists the profit for the relevant period broken down into 3 elements:

a) interest on capital, *and*

b) salary, *and*

c) profit division.

➤   The appropriation account is usually broken down into as many time segments as is necessary for the accounting period. Each segment represents a fixed group of partners *and* fixed levels of the list of (a)-(c) at the top of this page. If any of these change (eg: new partners are taken on, partners retire, profit share ratio changes etc.) it is necessary to start a new appropriation account for the new segment of time.

➤   The worked example opposite sets out how to set out the appropriation account.

Fully worked example

Alpha runs his garage business but due to pressure of work he decides to take on a new partner. On 1 August 1997 he takes on Beta who in exchange for a 35%partnership and a yearly salary of £2,000, agrees to put £10,000 in to the partnership. Alpha decides to take £1,000 p.a. salary from the time Beta joins. Both partners agree to take 5% p.a. interest on capital from the time Beta joins. Below is a trial balance for the 1997 period. Draw up the appropriation account and the partners current accounts (for current a/cs, see section C overleaf).

Trial Balance for period ending 31 December 1997

	DR £	CR £
Cash a/c	49,500	
Recovery van a/c	4,000	
Mechanical equip. a/c	6,500	
Staff salaries a/c	17,000	
Expenses a/c	12,500	
Rent a/c	10,000	
Debtors a/c	28,000	
Creditors a/c		7,500
Bills paid		139,500
Partners' capital accounts:		
Alpha		20,000
Beta		10,000
Partners' drawings:		
Alpha	45,500	
Beta	4,000	
Balance	177,000	177,000

NB: Profit for the period is bills paid (£139,500) less staff salaries (£17,000), expenses (£12,500) and rent (£10,000)

= £100,000

Alpha & Beta
Appropriation account
1 January 1997 - 31 July 1997

	£	£	£
Net profit (7 out of 12 months = 7/12 of total profit) ie 100,000 x (7/12)			58333.33
Alpha (the owner)			58333.33

Alpha & Beta
Appropriation account
1 August 1997 - 31 December 1997

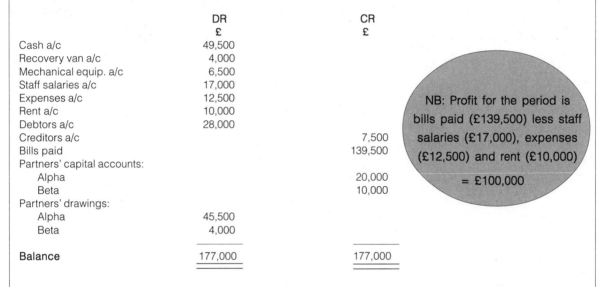

	£	£	£
Net profit (5 out of 12 months = 5/12 of total profit) ie 100,000 x (5/12)			41666.67 ❶
Interest on capital			
Alpha (5/12 x £20,000 x 5%)		416.67	
Beta (5/12 x £10,000 x 5%)		208.33	625.00 ❷
Partners' salaries			
Alpha (5/12 x £1000)		416.67	
Beta (5/12 x£2000)		833.33	1,250.00 ❸
Profit division			
Alpha (65%)		25864.59 ❺	
Beta (35%)		13927.08	39791.67 ❹
			41666.67 ❶

First - write these

Fifth - split ❹ into individual partners

Second - calculate interest on capital and total

Third - calculate partners' salaries and total

Fourth - write inprofit division [❶ - (❷ + ❸)]

C. The current accounts

➤ Each partner will have a current account, showing how much the business owes him (or how much he owes the business!).

➤ Each current account will be in a 'T' a/c format.

   ◆ The example below is based on the facts on the previous page:

Current a/c - Alpha

DR		CR	
		31.12.97	
		profit div no.1	58,333.33
		31.12.97	
		int. on capital	416.67
31.7.97		31.12.97	
Drawings	45,500.00	partner salary	416.67
31.7.97		31.12.97	
balance c/f	39,531.26	profit div no.2	25,864.59
	85,031.26		85,031.26
		31.7.97	
		balance b/f	39,531.26

Current a/c - Beta

DR		CR	
		31.12.97	
		int. on capital	208.33
31.7.97		31.12.97	
Drawings	4,000.00	partner salary	833.33
31.7.97		31.12.97	
balance c/f	10,968.74	profit div	13,927.08
	14,968.74		14,968.74
		31.7.97	
		balance b/f	10968.74

➤ The current accounts are also presented in a certain format as notes to the balance sheet (see D below).

D. The balance sheet

➤ The 'capital employed' section of the pro forma balance sheet (p.38) is made up of:

   ◆ the partners' capital accounts, *and*

   ◆ the partners' current accounts.

➤ A note to the balance sheet lists the make-up of the current accounts.

➤ ALWAYS do the capital account first, followed by the balance sheet, even though they are displayed the other way round.

➤ An example based on the facts from the previous example is on the facing page.

E. Revaluations of assets

➤ A revaluation of each asset is usually carried out on a change in the partnership or a change in the profit-sharing ratio between them.

➤ A revaluation 'T' a/c is opened and the following ajustments are made:

	Revaluation a/c	Asset a/c	Partner capital a/c	any credits/ debits are in the agreed partner ratio of sharing profits and losses
Increase in asset value	CREDIT	DEBIT		
Decrease in asset value	DEBIT	CREDIT		
Profit on revaluation (close revaluation a/c)	DEBIT		CREDIT	
Loss on revaluation (close revaluation a/c)	CREDIT		DEBIT	

Fully worked example (continued)

Balance sheet of Alpha and Beta as of 31st December 1997

	£	£	£
FIXED ASSETS			
Recovery van - cost		4,000	
Mechanical equipment - cost		6,500	10,500
ADD: CURRENT ASSETS			
Debtors		28,000	
Cash at bank		49,500	77,500
LESS: CURRENT LIABILITIES			
Creditors		7,500	7,500
NET CURRENT ASSETS			80,500
NET ASSETS			80,500
Capital employed			
Capital accounts			
Alpha	20,000		
Beta	10,000	30,000	
Current accounts (see note 1)			
Alpha	39,531.26		
Beta	10968.74	50,500	80,500

Do the balance sheet after the current accounts

Notes to the balance sheet
Note (1)

Do this first

Current accounts	Alpha	Beta
Interest on capital	416.67	208.33
Partners' salaries	416.67	803.33
Profit division no. 1	58,333.33	0.00
Profit division no.2	25,864.59	13,927.08
	85,031.26	14,938.74
Less drawings	45,500.00	4000.00
Balance	39,531.26	10,938.74

Put these figures into the balance sheet

E   Interpreting accounts

I	Generally
II	Ratios

I   Generally

➤   When compiling accounts, accountants make use of guidance which the accountancy profession produces (under the auspices of the Accounting Standards Board).

➤   This guidance is published in 'Statements of Standard Accounting Practice' (SSAP) and 'Financial Reporting Standards' (FRS); gradually the FRSs are replacing SSAPs.

➤   Where a feature of the accounts is unusual, or requires explanation, it should be explained in the 'Notes' found at the back of the accounts.   These 'Notes' are an important aid to understanding accounts.

➤   In addition to information to be found in the 'Notes' the use of ratios provides a rough and ready way to:

   ◆   identify trends in a business (by comparing ratios in successive sets of accounts), *and / or*

   ◆   compare a business with other businesses in the same sector, or of a similar size.

➤   Some frequently used ratios, which are examined below, are designed to measure:

   a) profitability.

   b) financial risk.

   c) cashflow.

   ●   Ratios should be used with extreme caution - like all statistics they are misleading if looked at in isolation.   Ratios are best used as a stimulus to ask questions about an enterprise (eg: why is 'dividend cover' so low?) rather than as a source of objective information.

II   Ratios

A. Profitability

➤   The ratios which are used to assess a business' profitability, including the following:

1   Return on capital employed ('ROCE')

   ➤ This ratio relates 'profit before tax' ('PBIT') to the working capital invested in a business.

   ➤ ROCE can be expressed as:

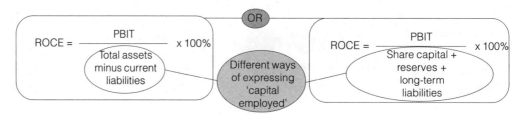

2 Asset turnover

➤ This ratio indicates the volume of sales the enterprise is generating using its assets/capital.

➤ The formula is:

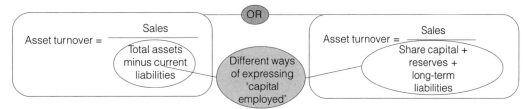

$$\text{Asset turnover} = \frac{\text{Sales}}{\text{Total assets minus current liabilities}}$$

OR — Different ways of expressing 'capital employed'

$$\text{Asset turnover} = \frac{\text{Sales}}{\text{Share capital + reserves + long-term liabilities}}$$

3 Profit margin

➤ This ratio can be used to measure an enterprise's gross profit margin (before general expenses are deducted) or net profit margin (after general expenses are deducted).

$$\text{Gross margin} = \frac{\text{Gross profit (sales less cost of sales)}}{\text{Sales turnover}} \times 100\%$$

$$\text{Net margin} = \frac{\text{Net profit (sales less all costs)}}{\text{Sales turnover}} \times 100\%$$

4 Ratios for companies with share capital

➤ **Earnings per share ('EPS'):** this shows how much profit is earned on each share.

$$\text{Earnings per share} = \frac{\text{Profit}}{\text{Number of issued shares}}$$

◆ EPS has in the past frequently been used (indeed over used) as an indicator of whether shares are under or over priced. It is open to abuse, as the calculation of 'profit' or the use of complex capital structures mean that it can be manipulated. Note also the importance of cultural / economic influences when interpreting EPS as, for instance, the EPS is traditionally lower in the UK and the USA (eg: 10x-15x) than stock markets than on the Japanese market (eg: 20x-25x).

➤ **Dividend cover:** this relates the dividends a company pays to the profits the company earns.

$$\text{Dividend cover} = \frac{\text{Earnings per share}}{\text{Dividend per share}}$$

◆ Note that a dividend cover of less than 1 means that the company is paying dividends out of retained profits earned in previous years, a cover of 1 or more indicates dividends are being paid out of current earnings. Public companies often maintain a dividend cover of 1.5 to 3 (eg: in the latter case £1 paid out for every £3 of profits).

B. Financial risk

➤ The following ratios are used to assess whether a company is likely to be unable to meet its obligations to its creditors.

1 Gearing

➤ Gearing relates debt finance to equity finance.

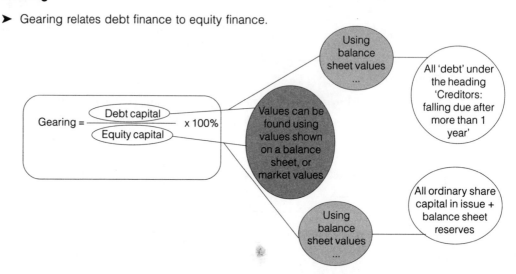

- ◆ Gearing can be measured in a number of different ways. For example, 'Total capital' can be used instead of equity capital.

➤ Whether 'gearing' (also known as 'leverage') is too high, or too low, depends on market conditions and the business sector in which the enterprise is operating. The higher the gearing, the more the equity capital may be perceived to be at risk.

2 Interest cover

➤ This ratio is a measure of credit risk - it shows how comfortably an enterprise can meet its interest obligations to creditors.

$$\text{Interest cover} = \frac{\text{PBIT}}{\text{Interest charges}}$$

3 Working capital

➤ This ratio reflects the amount of capital which is used to finance the enterprise from day-to-day.

$$\text{Working capital} = \text{'Current Assets'} - \text{'Current Liabilities'}$$

- ◆ Put another way, 'working capital' equals 'net current assets'.

C. Cashflow

➤ Cashflow is essential to any enterprise. Without sufficient liquidity to pay its liabilities as they fall due even an enterprise which on paper is extremely profitable will go bust.

➤ The following ratios offer a measure of how liquid an enterprise is:

1 Stock turnover ratio

➤ This ratio shows the average number of days it takes an enterprise to turn its stock over.

$$\frac{\text{Stock in hand}}{\text{Costs of goods sold}} \times 365$$

2 Debtor days

➤ This ratio reveals the average number of days' credit which the enterprise's customers are allowed.

$$\frac{\text{Trade debtors}}{\text{Sales}} \times 365$$

3 'Acid test' ratio

➤ This ratio can be useful if an enterprise necessarily has a slow stock turnover and it should normally exceed 1:1.

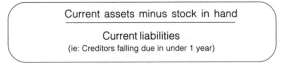

$$\frac{\text{Current assets minus stock in hand}}{\text{Current liabilities}}$$
(ie: Creditors falling due in under 1 year)

4 Current ratio

➤ This ratio demonstrates whether an enterprise can meet its current liabilities.

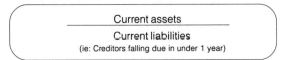

$$\frac{\text{Current assets}}{\text{Current liabilities}}$$
(ie: Creditors falling due in under 1 year)

F   Solicitors' Accounts Rules 1991

I	Overview
II	*SAR Part I* - General
III	*SAR Part II* - Controlled Trusts
IV	*SAR Part III* - Interest
V	The Future ...

I   Overview

➤   The *SARs* apply to all firms of solicitors (sole practitioners, partnerships or incorporated). A firm must submit to the Law Society an annual report compiled by an accountant stating that the *SARs* have been complied with (*SARR 1991*).

➤   A breach of the *SARs* is professional misconduct.

➤   The overriding purpose of the *SARs* is to ensure that client money, in 'client account', is kept separate from the solicitor's money, in 'office account'.

➤   Client account may be a bank current or a deposit account (the bank must be in England or Wales), or a deposit account at a building society.

II   SAR Part I - General

'Client money'

➤   'Client money' is (*SAR r.2*):

... money held or received by a solicitor on account of a person for whom he or she is acting in relation to the holding or receipt of such money ...

... either as solicitor or, in connection with his or her practice as solicitor, as agent, bailee, stakeholder or in any other capacity ... **except for**:

a) money held or received on account of a trust of which the solicitor is a controlled trustee, *or*

b) money to which the only person beneficially entitled is the solicitor ... or in the case of a firm of solicitors, one or more of the partners in the firm.

◆ Money can, therefore, be 'client money' even if the solicitor does not have a retainer with the beneficial owner of the money.

◆ For money to be 'client money' it must be 'received' by and controlled by the solicitor.

◆ Money held by a firm as 'stakeholder' is 'client money'. If, however, it is held on behalf of more than one firm it is not client money; the Law Society recommend that it should be recorded in the ledgers of all the firms operating the account.

➤   'Client money' does **not** include:

◆ where a firm is acting for a partner (or a sole practitioner for himself), a partner's money.

● If a partner and their spouse are clients, money is held for both parties (as trustees) so the money is 'client money'.

◆ a cheque held to a third party's order (until released) as there is no delivery until release (*BEA 1882*).

A. Payments into client account

➤ Only money which the *SARs* 'require or permit' a solicitor to pay into client account, may be a paid into client account (*SAR r.6*).

➤ Client money **must be paid into client account** 'without delay' (*SAR r.3*).

◆ The Law Society has glossed this to mean the day of receipt or, if that is not possible, the following day.

➤ The following **may be paid into client account**:

a) trust money (*SAR r.4*) (see p.52), *and*

b) the solicitor's own money to open the account, *and*

c) money paid in to replace money that has been withdrawn in contravention of the *SARs, and*

d) a cheque or banker's draft which is not 'split' (*SAR r.5*), *and*

e) a payment in settlement or part settlement of a bill of costs, to which the solicitor alone is beneficially entitled (provided that the money does not remain on the client ledger longer than 7 days from receipt) (*SAR r.5A*).

➤ A solicitor **may withhold client money from client account** if (*SAR r.9(1)*):

a) the money is received as cash and is without delay paid in the ordinary course of business to the client or on the client's behalf to a third party, *or*

b) the money is received as a cheque or draft endorsed in the ordinary course of business to the client, or a third party on the client's behalf, and the solicitor does not pass the sum through a bank or building society account, *or*

c) the solicitor pays the money into a separate bank or building society account in the name of the client, or of some person designated by the client in writing or acknowledged by the solicitor to the client in writing.

➤ A solicitor **must withhold client money from client account** if:

a) the client requests the solicitor to withhold money from client account, 'such request either [being] in writing from the client or acknowledged by the solicitor to the client in writing' (*SAR r.9(2)(a)*), *or*

b) the money is received by the solicitor from the client in full or partial reimbursement of money 'expended' by the solicitor on behalf of the client (*SAR r.9(2)(b)*), *or*

◆ 'Expended' means more than just noted on a bill of costs. According to Law Society guidance, it involves drawing and dispatching a cheque in respect of an item of costs (other than a cheque to be held to the solicitor's order),

c) the money is expressly paid to the solicitor *either:*

i) for or towards payment of the solicitors' costs in respect of a bill of costs or other written intimation of the amount of costs incurred has been delivered for payment; *or*

◆ 'Costs' includes fees, charges, disbursements expenses and remuneration and costs (including VAT) in respect of which a solicitor has incurred a liability but excludes fees of counsel or other lawyer, or of a professional or other agent, or of an expert instructed by a solicitor' (*SAR r.2*).

- Payments received from the Legal Aid Board are an exception to general rule relating to money received from a client in respect of which a solicitor has incurred a liability to another lawyer, agent or expert. A payment from the Legal Aid Board may be paid without delay into office account provided that within 14 days of receipt any part of the payment which relates to unpaid fees still remaining unpaid is transferred to client account (*SA(LATP)R 1992*).

ii) as an agreed fee for business undertaken or to be undertaken (*SAR r.9(2)(c)*).

- ◆ Where fees are agreed, no bill or other written intimation of costs needs to be delivered. However, any money received on account of general fees (outside a fee agreement) is client money and must be paid into client account.

B. Withdrawals from client account to meet costs and disbursements

➤ Money may be withdrawn from client account if that money is:

a) properly required in full or partial reimbursement of money expended by the solicitor on behalf of the client, *or*

b) for or towards payment of the solicitors' costs (as defined in *SAR r.2*, see p.48) where ...

... a bill of costs (or other written intimation of the amount of costs incurred) has been delivered to the client *and* ...

... it has been made clear in writing to the client that money held for him is being or will be applied towards or in satisfaction of such costs (*SAR r.7*)

C. Transfers between client ledgers

➤ An amount cannot be transferred from one client ledger to that of another client unless the solicitor would be otherwise permitted to withdraw that amount from client account on behalf of the first client and pay it into client account on behalf of the second client (*SAR r.10(1)*).

➤ No amount in respect of a 'private loan' may be paid directly, or by means of a transfer between client ledgers, out of funds held on account of the lender without the lender's prior written authority (*SAR r.10(2)*).

- ◆ A 'private loan' is a loan which is not 'provided by an institution which provides loans in the course of its activities'. Consequently, this rule does not apply where a solicitor acts for a building societies or bank which is lending money, but it would apply where a trustee makes a loan to a beneficiary using trust funds held in client account.

Record keeping

➤ A solicitor must keep properly written up record of all dealings with client money (ie: client money received, held or paid by the solicitor), irrespective of whether that money is paid into client account under *SAR r.3* or is withheld from client account under *SAR r.9* (*SAR r.11(1)*).

♦ The record (ie: a client ledger) must also distinguish a particular client's money from other money held in client account.

♦ Each client ledger must show a current balance (but there is no requirement to keep a historic record of previous balances) (*SAR r.11(1)(c)*).

♦ Transfers between client ledgers must be recorded through the cash account, or a separate record (often known as a transfer journal, or 'TJ') (*SAR r.11(2)(a)*).

♦ A solicitor must keep a record of all bills of costs (distinguishing between profit costs and disbursements), and must record all bills and intimations of costs delivered to clients (*SAR r.11(4)*).

➤ There is no obligation to keep a separate client ledger for a borrower and lender in a conveyancing transaction provided that (*SAR r.11(3)*):

a) the funds belonging to each client are 'clearly identifiable' (eg: the fact that an amount represents a mortgage advance from a particular lender must be clearly stated in the borrower's ledger), *and*

b) the lender is an institutional lender providing mortgages in the normal course of its activities. (Consequently, this relaxation of the general rule does not apply if the lender is a private individual).

➤ At least once every 5 weeks, a solicitor must compare the balances in client ledgers with the cash account balance, prepare a reconciliation showing the cause of any difference between the two balances and reconcile the cash account with balances shown on client account pass books or statements and money held elsewhere (*SAR r.11(5)*).

➤ A withdrawal from client account must not be made unless there is specific authority signed by (*SAR r.11(6)*):

a) a solicitor with a current practising certificate, *or*

b) a person employed by the solicitor, being ...

  i) a solicitor,

  ii) a fellow of the Institute of Legal Executives (of not less than 3 years standing), *or*

  iii) a registered foreign lawyer who is a partner or director of the practice, or

  iv) a licensed conveyancer if an office deals solely with conveyancing.

♦ A solicitor must keep all cheques and copies of authorities (other than cheques) signed under *SAR r.11(6)* for at least 2 years, or must seek confirmation from a bank or building society that it will retain them for at least 2 years (*SAR r.11(9)*).

➤ A solicitor must keep all accounts, books, ledgers, records, and bank statements as printed and issued by a bank or building society, for at least 6 years from the date of last entry in each document (*SAR r.11(9)*).

III   SAR *Part II* - Controlled trusts

➤   'Trust money' is money held or received by a solicitor which is ...

... not 'client money', *and*

... which is subject to a trust of which the solicitor is a trustee whether or not the solicitor is a 'controlled trustee' of such a trust (*SAR r.2*).

◆   A 'controlled trustee' is a solicitor who is a sole trustee or co-trustee only with one or more of his partners or employees.

◆   Note that the terms 'client money' and 'trust money' are mutually exclusive.

➤   'Trust money' may be held in client account, notwithstanding that it is not 'client money' (*SAR r.4*).

➤   If the solicitor is a 'controlled trustee' then trust money which is not paid into client account must be paid into a 'controlled trust account' for that particular trust.

◆   A 'controlled trust account' is a current account or a deposit account with a bank, or a deposit account with a building society in the title of which the word 'trustee' or 'executor' appears, or which is otherwise clearly designated as a 'controlled trust account' and kept solely for money subject to a particular trust of which the solicitor is a controlled trustee.

◆   Bar certain minor exceptions, only trust money may be paid into a 'controlled trust account'.

◆   A solicitor may split a cheque or banker's draft in which trust money is comprised (if this is practicable), but if a payment is not split the money must be paid into client account (not the 'controlled trust account').

◆   A solicitor who receives controlled trust money as cash, or in the form of a cheque or banker's draft, may pay cash to a third party, or endorse a cheque / banker's draft to a third party without passing the money through the 'controlled trust account'.

◆   Withdrawals from a 'controlled trust account' are only permitted if an amount is:

a)   properly required for payment in execution of the trust, *or*

b)   transferred to client account, *or*

c)   paid in by the solicitor to open or maintain the account, *or*

d)   paid into the account in contravention of the *SARs*.

◆   The record-keeping requirements in relation to controlled trusts are set out in *SAR r.19*.

IV   SAR Part III - Interest

➤   If the solicitor and the client have not made a written agreement to the contrary, the solicitor must usually account to the client for interest on money held on account as follows (*SAR r.21*):

Amount on deposit	Time before interest is due to the client
Minimum £1,000	For up to 8 weeks
Minimum £2,000	For up to 4 weeks
Minimum £10,000	For up to 2 weeks
Sum over £20,000	For up to 1 week For under 1 week if this is 'fair and reasonable'

➤   If money is not held in a designated deposit account, a rate of interest must be paid which is equivalent to the interest which would have accrued on deposit (or the gross equivalent if the interest had been net of tax) (*SAR r.20*).

 ◆   This means that the client should not be at a disadvantage if a designated deposit account is not used. It also leaves scope for the solicitor to make money. As the client account aggregates different clients' money into a large pool a better rate of interest should be derived than on smaller deposits representing each client's individual money - the solicitor may retain the margin between the two rates.

➤   These rules do not apply to money in respect of which the solicitor is a controlled trustee, or if the solicitor holds non-controlled trust money as a trustee (not in his capacity as a solicitor) (*SAR r.26(b)*). Note, however that trust law applies and that this requires the solicitor to account to the trust for all interest.

➤   These rules do apply to money held as 'stakeholder' - interest is paid to whoever the stake is finally paid to (*SAR r.24*) (unless agreed otherwise in writing (*SAR r.26(c)*).

V   The Future ...

➤   The core of the *SARs* has remained unchanged since 1935 and the rules are meant to be safe rather than innovative.

➤   Change may, however, be on the way.

◆   The Law Society has published a consultation paper recommending a radical overhauls of the *SARs* in the hope of removing unnecessary red-tape, increasing the protection afforded to client funds, and (we are promised) rewriting the rules 'in plain English' (*Law Society Gazette*, 29 May 1997).

➤   The new rules will not come into force until after a consultation exercise has been completed and the new rules have been approved by the Law Society's Council and the Master of the Rolls.   Until this process is considerably more advanced no date will be fixed for the commencement of the new rules.

◆   In practice the new rules are not expected to be in force until (at the earliest) well into 1998.

➤   The proposed changes include:

a) Client money (*SARs Part I*)

●   *Simplification*: by allowing (in limited circumstances, and under strict conditions such as the requirement that a transfer be made within 2 working days) an office account to be used for unpaid professional disbursements.

●   *Tightening*:   the rules governing the transfer:

i) of billed costs out of client account after a bill of costs has been sent out, *and*

ii) of money to or from client account, ...

... by providing that the transfer must take place within 14 days, unless unpaid professional disbursements are temporarily held in office account.

b) Controlled trust provisions (*SARs Part II*)

Tightening by means of *Simplification*.

c) Deposit interest provisions (*SARs Part III*)

●   *Simplification*: by replacing the table showing the period of time after how long interest should be paid to a client on particular amounts with a *de minimis* of £20, above which interest must be accounted for to the client.

●   *Tightening*: forbidding 'contracting out' of the provisions by using standard terms (currently permitted under *SAR r.26*).

G Keeping accounts as a solicitor

I	Generally
II	Particular entries

I Generally

➤ In order to comply with *SAR rr.3, 6* (see p.49), a solicitor must use separate bank accounts for client money and office money. Separate cash account ledgers must be kept for each bank (or building society) account (these show amounts paid into / withdrawn from each account).

➤ A solicitor must keep a separate ledger for each client (*SAR r.11*) (these show amount received from / paid out for each client).

♦ Since there are two separate cash accounts (one for office money and the other for client money), each client effectively has two ledgers - one dealing with that client's 'client money' and the other with that client's 'office money'.

➤ The diagram below shows how the two sets of ledgers relate to each other.

♦ The Cash Account shows two separate accounts kept with a bank or building society (client account and office account). The Client Ledger shows the money which the firm is liable to the client for (client money) and which the client owes the firm (office money).

♦ Note that double entries are **never** made between the 'office' and 'client' ledgers, but between the those ledgers and the related ledgers in the Cash Account (for instance, when money is paid out of one account and into the other, eg: when a bill of costs is settled).

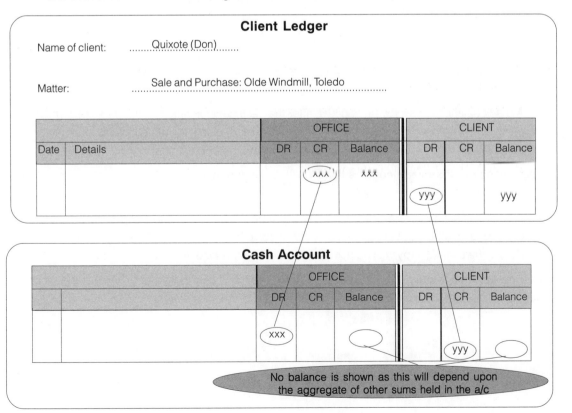

➤ Various formats can be used for ledgers, but the example below illustrates some important features of a Client Ledger comprising two separate sets of 'T' accounts (known as 'ledgers'), one showing office money and the the client money:

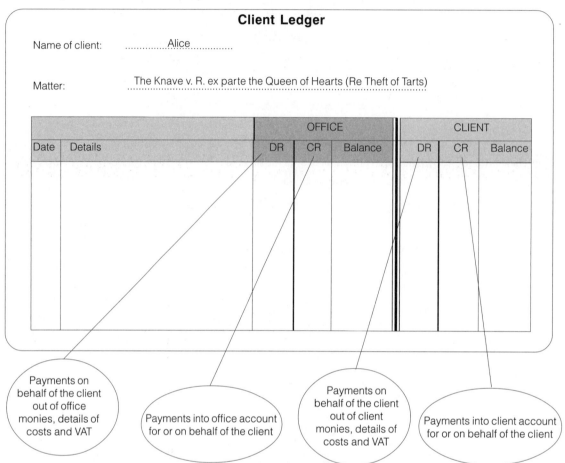

Client Ledger

Name of client: ....Alice...............

Matter: The Knave v. R. ex parte the Queen of Hearts (Re Theft of Tarts)

Date	Details	OFFICE			CLIENT		
		DR	CR	Balance	DR	CR	Balance

Payments on behalf of the client out of office monies, details of costs and VAT

Payments into office account for or on behalf of the client

Payments on behalf of the client out of client monies, details of costs and VAT

Payments into client account for or on behalf of the client

➤ **The balance in the office ledger should be a debit balance** - it indicates how much the client owes the firm for costs, disbursement etc.

◆ A credit balance (shown by putting 'CR' after the balance) indicates that more has been paid into the office account than is owed by the client to the solicitor - it usually (but not always, see below for the treatment of 'agreed fees') shows that the *SARs* have been breached.

➤ **The balance in the client ledger should be a credit balance** - it indicates how much money the solicitor holds on the client's behalf.

◆ A debit balance (shown by putting 'DR' after the balance) indicates that money has been withdrawn which does not belong to the client - the *SARs* have been breached and remedial action should be taken immediately (ie: by making good the deficiency with office money).

➤ **Description** - always 'describe' the corresponding account entry (so that you can match the entries to each other) then add any further information, see p.57 for an example.

A note on terminology

In the following pages the word 'Ledger' is used to refer to the Client Ledger recording office and client money associated with a particular client. It is also used to refer to Cash Account and other ledgers recording client or office monies (eg: Profit Costs a/c).

A 'ledger' dealing with 'client money' or 'office money' is called a 'column'. This is purely to avoid the confusion often occasioned by using the term 'ledger' is more than one sense. According to accountancy terminology, the 'columns' are themselves 'ledgers' (ie: separate 'T' accounts) relating respectively to 'office money' and 'client money' which are written up, for the sake of convenience, in the same 'Ledger'.

Terminology - an illustration

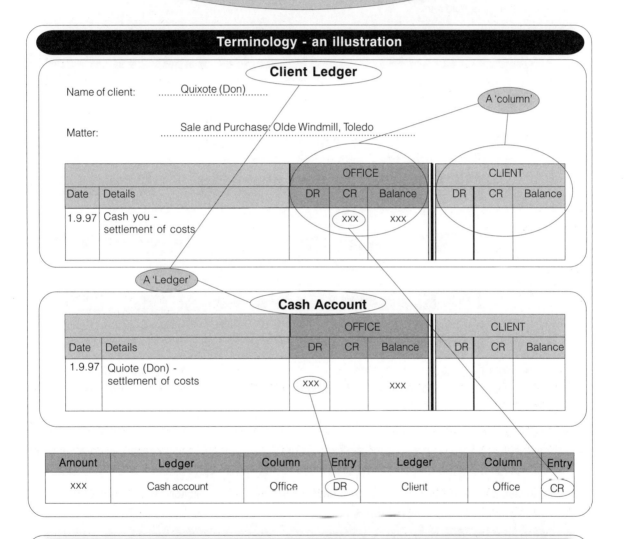

Problem solving hints

➤ Get into the habit of thinking of entries in a particular order with its own logic, eg: (following the cash)

    a) is it client money or office money? (This dictates which 'column' is correct)

    b) is it a receipt into Cash account (always DR) or a payment out of Cash account (always a CR)?

    c) which Ledger should the corresponding CR entry (or DR entry) go in?

      ... does the column 'balance' as it should, or would the proposed entries breach the *SARs*?

II Particular cases

1 Costs and disbursements

➤ When a bill of costs is delivered to a client the following entries are made (see p.100 for VAT):

Amount	Ledger	Column	Entry	Ledger	Column	Entry
Costs	Client	Office	DR	Profit costs account	Office	CR

➤ When the bill is paid *either*:

a) the payment should be paid into office account as office money (*SAR r.9(2)(c)*), *or*

Amount	Ledger	Column	Entry	Ledger	Column	Entry
Costs	Cash account	Office	DR	Client	Office	CR

b) if the payment is mixed with other monies which are client money, and the solicitor does not split the cheque, the cheque should be paid into client account and the relevant amount subsequently transferred to office account.

	Amount	Ledger	Column	Entry	Ledger	Column	Entry
Into client a/c	Payment	Cash account	Client	DR	Client	Client	CR

	Amount	Ledger	Column	Entry	Ledger	Column	Entry
Out of client a/c	Costs	Cash account	Client	CR	Client	Client	DR

	Amount	Ledger	Column	Entry	Ledger	Column	Entry
Into office a/c	Costs	Cash account	Office	DR	Client	Office	CR

- Note that it is very unusual to 'split' a cheque as cheques are nowadays often crossed 'a/c payee' and so cannot be split. If a cheque is 'split', both portions are accounted for as separate payments into office and client account.

➤ Disbursements and sums paid on the client's behalf may be paid from client account if there is a sufficient balance and the solicitor has express or implied authority to make the payment. If there is not enough money in client account, then office money must be used.

➤ If a client pays a solicitor as reimbursement for sums which the solicitor has expended for the client, such a sum is office money (*SAR r.9(2)(b)*).

2 Agreed fees

➤ A payment from a client in respect of agreed fees is office money and should not be paid into client account (*SAR r.9(2)(c)(ii)*). (This may create a credit ('CR') balance in the office account - but this will be cancelled by a corresponding debit ('DR') in the office account when the solicitor issues his bill).

Amount	Ledger	Column	Entry	Ledger	Column	Entry
Costs	Cash account	Office	DR	Client	Office	CR

3 Sums received on account of costs

➤ These are client money and should be entered on the client account.

Amount	Ledger	Column	Entry	Ledger	Column	Entry
Costs	Cash account	Client	DR	Client	Client	CR

4 VAT

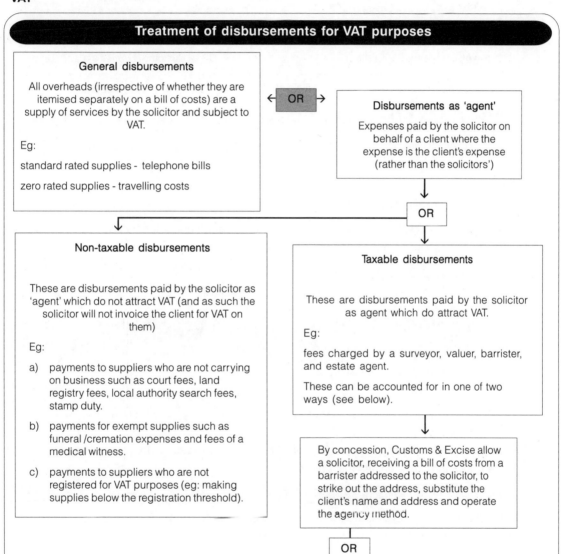

Treatment of disbursements for VAT purposes

General disbursements

All overheads (irrespective of whether they are itemised separately on a bill of costs) are a supply of services by the solicitor and subject to VAT.

Eg:

standard rated supplies - telephone bills

zero rated supplies - travelling costs

OR

Disbursements as 'agent'

Expenses paid by the solicitor on behalf of a client where the expense is the client's expense (rather than the solicitors')

OR

Non-taxable disbursements

These are disbursements paid by the solicitor as 'agent' which do not attract VAT (and as such the solicitor will not invoice the client for VAT on them)

Eg:

a) payments to suppliers who are not carrying on business such as court fees, land registry fees, local authority search fees, stamp duty.

b) payments for exempt supplies such as funeral /cremation expenses and fees of a medical witness.

c) payments to suppliers who are not registered for VAT purposes (eg: making supplies below the registration threshold).

Taxable disbursements

These are disbursements paid by the solicitor as agent which do attract VAT.

Eg:

fees charged by a surveyor, valuer, barrister, and estate agent.

These can be accounted for in one of two ways (see below).

By concession, Customs & Excise allow a solicitor, receiving a bill of costs from a barrister addressed to the solicitor, to strike out the address, substitute the client's name and address and operate the agency method.

OR

As principal

(when the supplier's invoice is made out in the solicitor's name).

VAT charged is the solicitor's input tax: the solicitor recovers it from Customs & Excise and charges the VAT to client as output tax.

As Agent

(when the supplier's invoice is made out in the client's name)

The solicitor pays the VAT inclusive amount. He ignores VAT for his bookkeeping purposes and seeks reimbursement from the client for the VAT.

➤ A solicitor, like any taxable person, is obliged to charge VAT ('output tax') on supplies of services and may recover VAT ('input tax') on supplies attributable to taxable supplies which he or she makes. For a fuller explanation of how VAT works see p.100.

➤ A taxable person's liability to HM Customs & Excise is recorded in a Customs & Excise account.

➤ When a bill of costs is delivered to a client the following double entries must be made:

Amount	Ledger	Column	Entry	Ledger	Column	Entry
Costs (ex VAT)	Client	Office	DR	Profit costs account	Office	CR

Amount	Ledger	Column	Entry	Ledger	Column	Entry
VAT	Client	Office	DR	Customs & Excise a/c	Office	CR

➤ When an expense is paid (including VAT) the following double entries must be made:

Ledger	Column	Entry	Amount	Ledger	Column	Entry
Cash account	Office	CR	← Expense → including VAT →	Nominal expenses / Customs & Excise	Office	DR

● In order to ease a subsequent bank reconciliation the apportionment between the expense and the VAT is recorded as in the following example:

Cash Account

Date	Details		OFFICE			CLIENT		
		DR	CR	Balance		DR	CR	Balance
1.1.1998	Mousetraps 240							
	VAT 42		282	282				

➤ When net VAT is paid to Customs & Excise (ie: output tax exceeds input tax for the accounting period) the following double entries must be made:

Amount	Ledger	Column	Entry	Ledger	Column	Entry
Net VAT	Cash account	Office	CR	Customs & Excise a/c	Office	DR

5   Deposits (Conveyancing transactions)

➤ A deposit can be held as agent for the for the seller, or as stakeholder. In both cases a deposit is 'client money' (*SAR r.2*, see p.48).

➤ The accounting treatment differs depending on how deposit monies are held.

◆ **As agent:** the solicitor may account immediately to the client for the deposit.

Amount	Ledger	Column	Entry	Ledger	Column	Entry
Deposit	Cash account	Client	DR	Client	Client	CR

◆ **As stakeholder:**

a) The solicitor should not account immediately to the client for the deposit - the deposit is recorded in a separate ledger, the 'stakeholder account'.

Amount	Ledger	Column	Entry	Ledger	Column	Entry
Deposit	Cash account	Client	DR	Stakeholder a/c	Client	CR

b) On completion, a transfer is made from the 'stakeholder account' to the client's ledger account. This transfer between the 'stakeholder account' and the client's ledger is a transfer between client ledgers and although there is therefore no need to record the transfer in the cash account (as no money is being withdrawn from client account), the transfer must be noted in both client accounts (*SAR r.11(2)(a)(i)*), stating in both cases 'transfer of deposit TJ' (for 'transfer journal').

Amount	Ledger	Column	Entry	Ledger	Column	Entry
Deposit	Stakeholder a/c	Client	DR	Client	Client	CR

● One 'stakeholder account' ledger will suffice for all stakeholder monies held by a solicitor (as it is all 'client money'), there is no need to have a separate ledger for each client in relation to whom the solicitor is a stakeholder.

6   Mortgages

➤ A solicitor may either treat an institutional lender as a separate client, or may take advantage of *SAR r.11(3)* and simply record a mortgage advance in the buyer's ledger noting the lender's interest, see p.51.

7 Insurance premiums

➤ When a solicitor receives an insurance premium from a client, prior to accounting to an insurance company for the net premium (ie: the gross premium less the solicitors' commission), the insurance company is treated as the solicitors' client for the purposes of the *SARs*.

➤ A commission of less than £20 may be paid into office account if the solicitor has the client's permission to retain it (*SPR r. 10*) (see p.2), otherwise it is 'client money'.

➤ If the solicitor receives commission **without accounting to policyholder** for it the double entries are:

a) On payment by the policyholder:

Amount	Ledger	Column	Entry	Ledger	Column	Entry
Commission	Client (Insurance Co)	Office	DR	Commission account	Office	CR

Amount	Ledger	Column	Entry	Ledger	Column	Entry
Gross premium	Cash account	Client	DR	Client (Insurance Co)	Client	CR

- Note that there is no entry in the ledger account of the policyholder (assuming the policyholder is a client of the solicitor) as the payment is received as 'client money' held on behalf of the insurance company.

b) On payment by the solicitor to the insurance company.

	Amount	Ledger	Column	Entry	Ledger	Column	Entry
Out of client a/c	Net	Cash account	Client	CR	Client (Insurance Co)	Client	DR

	Amount	Ledger	Column	Entry	Ledger	Column	Entry
Out of client a/c	Commission	Cash account	Client	CR	Client (Insurance Co)	Client	DR

	Amount	Ledger	Column	Entry	Ledger	Column	Entry
Into office a/c	Commission	Cash a/c	Office	DR	Client (Insurance Co)	Office	CR

- The commission account is an office ledger - at the end of the year the balance will be closed off to the solicitor's profit and loss account as income.

➤ If the solicitor receives commission **which he is obliged to account to policyholder for**.

Amount	Ledger	Column	Entry	Ledger	Column	Entry
Gross premium	Cash account	Client	DR	Client (Insurance Co)	Client	CR

- There is an entry in the ledger account of the policyholder as the payment is received as 'client money' for which the solicitor must account to the policyholder.

Amount	Ledger	Column	Entry	Ledger	Column	Entry
Commission	Client ledger (Insurance	Client	DR	Client (Policyholder)	Client	CR

- Mark the entry as being 'a transfer of commission TJ' as a transfer between client ledgers (*SAR r. 11(2)(a)(i)*).

- No entries are made in the Commission account as the commission is accounted for to the policyholder as 'client money'. An internal transfer between client ledgers is made (which does not therefore go through the cash account as no money is drawn out of client account).

Amount	Ledger	Column	Entry	Ledger	Column	Entry
Net premium	Cash account	Client	CR	Client (Insurance Co)	Client	DR

8   Returned cheques

➤ A solicitor must record a cheque received from a client in that client's ledger without delay (*SAR r.3*). Consequently, a client ledger may show uncleared funds as well as cleared funds.

Amount	Ledger	Column	Entry	Ledger	Column	Entry
Cheque	Cash account	Client	DR	Client	Client	CR

➤ If a client's cheque bounces the solicitor must make entries in the client's ledger and cash account showing that the cheque has been returned (ie: these reverse the entries made when the money was received).

Amount	Ledger	Column	Entry	Ledger	Column	Entry
Returned cheque	Cash account	Client	CR	Client	Office	DR

➤ If the solicitor has drawn on uncleared funds there will have been a breach of the *SARs* as the money drawn from client account will effectively belong to other clients of the solicitor. The solicitor must immediately make good this breach by making a compensating transfer from office account into client account.

- Note that drawing on uncleared funds is not itself a breach of the *SARs*.

9   Deposit interest

➤ The accounting treatment depends upon whether interest is held on a separate designated deposit account (ie: an account in the client's name, solely for holding money belonging to the named client), or the solicitor accounts to the client for interest.

➤ **If a designated deposit account is used:**

a) the solicitor must record the transfer of money to the designated deposit cash account.

Amount	Ledger	Column	Entry	Ledger	Column	Entry
Payment in	Cash account	Client	DR	Design. deposit a/c	Client	CR

b) on an interest payment by the bank:

Amount	Ledger	Column	Entry	Ledger	Column	Entry
Interest	Desig. deposit a/c	Client	DR	Client	Client	CR

c) in order to draw money from the designated deposit account the solicitor will have to transfer monies from the designated deposit account to general client account (ie: an account containing mixed client monies) as there will not generally be a cheque book facility on a designated deposit account. This involves reversing the entries in a) above.

Amount	Ledger	Column	Entry	Ledger	Column	Entry
Payment out	Cash account	Client	CR	Design. deposit a/c	Client	DR

- If money is transferred to a designated deposit account no entry need be actually made in the client ledger (as the credit balance indicating the funds owed to the client does not change), but it is good practice to record on the ledger that money has been placed in a designated deposit account.

➤ **If a solicitor pays money in lieu of interest:**

a) the solicitor must make a payment out of his own funds in lieu of interest. This can be done *either*:

- by a transfer from office account to client account, *or*

Amount	Ledger	Column	Entry	Ledger	Column	Entry
Interest	Cash account	Office	CR	Interest paid a/c	Office	DR

Amount	Ledger	Column	Entry	Ledger	Column	Entry
Interest	Cash account	Client	DR	Client	Client	CR

- by an office account cheque paid to the client.

Amount	Ledger	Column	Entry	Ledger	Column	Entry
Interest	Cash account	Office	CR	Interest paid a/c	Office	DR

10   Abatements and bad debts

➤ When a solicitor reduces a bill (known as 'abatement'), the client ledger must record the abatement and corresponding entries must be made in respect of VAT relating to the amount written off. The double entries are as follows:

Amount	Ledger	Column	Entry	Ledger	Column	Entry
Write-off	Client	Office	CR	Costs abatement a/c	Office	DR

Amount	Ledger	Column	Entry	Ledger	Column	Entry
VAT on write-off	Client	Office	CR	Customs & Excise a/c	Office	DR

➤ If client debt which has been outstanding for more than 6 months is written-off, a solicitor may generally claim VAT relief in respect of the 'output tax' that the solicitor will have paid to Customs & Excise one month after the end of the accounting period during which the supply to which the debt relates was made (VATA *1994 s.36*, see also *VATR 1995 rr.165-172* and *FA 1997 s.39*). A successful claim will be recorded by the following double entries:

Amount	Ledger	Column	Entry	Ledger	Column	Entry
VAT relief	Client	Office	CR	Customs & Excise a/c	Office	DR

➤ Any bad debt is treated on the same principles as an abatement.

Taxation

This chapter examines:

Income or capital?

Income is usually a receipt or expense which recurs, eg: rent money or buying paperclips.

Capital is usually a once-off payment for an asset, eg: paying for office furniture.

Individuals are presumed to be domiciled, resident and ordinarily resident in the UK.

Companies are presumed to be resident in the UK

A Income tax

References in this section are to the TA 1988, unless otherwise stated.

I Payment

➤ Two major reforms affecting the assessment and collection of income tax were introduced for the tax year 1996/97:

- ◆ self assessment, *and*
- ◆ payment on account (See further p.84).

II Calculation

A. Individuals as private persons

Steps	
1	**Calculate the individual's total 'statutory income' under Schedules A-F**
2	**Calculate the 'total income' (ie: subtract 'charges on income')**
3	**Calculate the 'taxable income' (ie: subtract 'personal reliefs')**
4	**Calculate the tax payable on the 'taxable income'**

Step 1 | **Calculate an individual's 'statutory income'**

➤ Income is taxed under Schedules in the *Taxes Act 1988*. Different rules govern assessment under each Schedule. A loss under a Schedule gives a nil assessment for that Schedule.

Schedule	Type of income
A	Rents and receipts from land in the UK (*s.15(1)*)
D Case I Case II	Profits of trade in the UK (*s.18(3)*) Profits of a profession or vocation (*s.18(3)*)
D Case III	Interest, annuities, trust income and other annual payments (*s.18(3)*)
D Case IV Case V	Income from foreign securities (*s.18(3)*) Income from foreign possessions (ie: other than securities) (*s.18(3)*)
D Case VI	Income not caught elsewhere (*s.18(3)*)
E Case I, II and III	Income deriving from an office, employment, and pensions (*s.19(1)*)
F	Dividends and other company distributions (*s.20*)

Schedules B and C have been repealed

Exemptions
- ◆ Interest on National Savings certificates (*s.46*) and TESSA accounts (*s.326A*)
- ◆ The first £70 of interest earned on National Savings Bank deposits (*s.325*)
- ◆ Interest on personal injury damages or death damages (*s.329*)
- ◆ Personal Equity Plan dividends (*s.333*)
- ◆ Certain social security benefits (eg: child benefit) (*s.617(2)*)
- ◆ Scholarship income (*s.331*), provided it is not chargeable under *s.165(1)*
- ◆ Gross income up to £4,250 from letting a furnished room in a 'main residence' (*FA(No2)1992 Sch 10*)
- ◆ Maintenance from a former spouse under a court order or written agreement in the hands of the recipient (*s.347A(1)*)

➤ Where tax is deducted at source, 'gross up' the income to its value *before* tax was deducted to arrive at the 'statutory income' (eg: multiply by 100/80 for a 20% deduction).

Schedule A

➤ Rents and income from UK property - this is known as a income from a 'Schedule A business'.

➤ Part of a premium received on the grant of a lease with a term not exceeding 50 years, or on the surrender or variation / waiver of a lease (even if the original term exceeded 50 years), may be treated as an income receipt and as a part disposal for CGT purposes - for the apportionment see *s.34* (see also *TCGA 1992 Sch. 8* for CGT treatment).

➤ **Deductible expenditure and capital allowances:** calculated on Schedule D Case I principles.

➤ **Capital allowances:** see p.78.

Schedule D Case I and II, 'income profit' = 'chargeable receipts less deductible expenditure'

➤ A chargeable receipt a) derives from income not capital, *and* b) derives from the taxpayer's trade.

➤ **Deductible expenditure:** expenses of an income nature that are 'wholly and exclusively' incurred for the purposes of a trade, profession, or vocation are deductible (*s.74(1)*, *Mallalieu v. Drummond* [1983] 2 AC 861).

➤ **Capital allowances:** see p.78.

Schedule D Case III, interest, annuities, trust income and other annual payments

➤ From 6 April 1996 an individual pays tax at the lower rate only, currently 20%, on most payments of gross interest (ie: before lower rate tax is deducted at source) other than certain annuities and foreign income which are still taxed at the basic rate of 23%. Whether an individual claims a rebate, need pay nothing more, or owes tax, depends on the rate at which he pays tax (*s.1A*).

Non-taxpayer ↓ Full rebate (20%)	20% and 23% taxpayer ↓ No more tax to pay	40% taxpayer ↓ 20% more tax to pay

➤ Before the introduction of self assessment, the year of assessment could be either the current year or the preceding year, depending on whether income was received net of tax or gross. Under the new rules all 'new sources' of income arising on or after 6 April 1994 are assessed on the current year basis (ie: the year in which it accrues), although for a partnership with Case III income, its basis period (see p.72) serves as the period of assessment if this differs from its accounting period (*s.111(4)*).

Bank*, Building society* interest and trust income	Unaffected by the move to self assessment
Debenture interest, National Savings interest[†], annuities	Transitional rules for 1996/97 (*FA 1994 Sch.20*)

*	Non-taxpayers and lower rate taxpayers can receive the gross amount without a deduction at source, if they send the correct form to the institution which holds their money
†	Tax on National Savings certificates and accounts is not deducted at source, but is paid gross and assessed from the tax return

➤ **Deductible expenditure:** none. However, if a debenture holder is borrowing money to lend it to a company, then the interest may be a 'charge on income'.

Schedule D Case IV, income from foreign securities

Schedule D Case V, income from foreign possessions (other than securities)

➤ **Deductible expenditure:** none (unless income is from a trade, profession or vocation which is computed on Schedule D Case I and II principles). Consider whether relief is availiable (eg: under a double tax treaty) for tax paid, or deducted, abroad.

Schedule D Case VI, other income

➤ 'Full amount' of any income not caught by another Schedule. This is assessed in a similar fashion to Schedule D Case III, so income arising during a current tax year is assessed, although a partnership's basis period serves as the period of assessment if this differs from its accounting period (*s.111(4)*).

➤ **Deductible expenditure:** on Case I principles (*s.69*).

Schedule E, 'emoluments of office or employment' , Case I

(Cases II & III which may apply if the taxpayer is not both resident and ordinarily resident in the UK during the tax year are not coverd here)

➤ These are benefits which derive from an office or employment. They can come *either* from an employer *or* from a third party. In addition to cash sums (eg: a monthly salary), Schedule E catches payments in the form of goods or services (known as 'benefits in kind').

*Assessment of benefits in kind depends upon the amount of remuneration the individual receives for the purpose of this Schedule. Apply category 'A' then **either** option 'B' or option 'C'.*

Category 'A'

➤ For all employees, benefits in kind include:

a) a gain on the exercise of share options (*s.135*) (options granted under approved schemes involving shares with a value of £30,000 or less are exempt (*s.185*)).

b) non-cash vouchers (*s.141*) and credit tokens (*s.142*), which are taxed on the cost to the voucher provider of providing the goods or services which the employee enjoys via the voucher or token.

c) low rent and rent-free accommodation which bear tax on the value of the benefit to the employee (*s.145*) unless the accommodation falls within limited exceptions in *s.145(4)* (eg: necessary for the 'proper performance of his duties'). If the cost of providing the accommodation exceeds £75,000, there is an additional charge assessed on the cost to the employer of providing this benefit (*s.146*).

d) training on a 'qualifying course' (*s.588-589*) and certain other training (*s.200C*), but not in relation to work related training (*TA s.200B, 200D*).

e) counselling on the termination of an employment (*ss.589A-589B*).

f) relocation expenses unless these qualify for exemption under *Schedule 11A* and do not exceed £8,000.

g) sport and recreation facilities (*s.197G*).

h) sick pay (*s.149*), maternity pay (*s.150*) and income support (*s.151*).

i) pensions (*s.133*).

j) a lump sum at the start *or* end of employment (*s.148*). Any sum paid on injury or death is exempt from tax, as is a sum not exceeding £30,000 if not paid under an employment contract (*s.188*).

NB: relief from tax under Schedule E for profit related pay, which has previously been available on remuneration up to £4,000 a year, is being phased out and will cease altogether in respect of periods beginning on or after 1 January 2000 (*FA 1997 s.61*).

Option 'B'

Employees earning less than £8,500 a year

Non-taxable items	Taxable items
◆ Private use of a car. ◆ Interest free loan. ◆ Medical insurance.	Any goods or services (other than those subject to the specific statutory provisions outlined above) which are convertible into cash (*Tennant v. Smith [1892] AC 150*). Tax is calculated on the cash equivalent value of the benefit in the employee's hands.

Option 'C' (ss.153-168)

i) Directors (unless working part-time *and* owning under 5% of the company's shares).

ii) Employees with emoluments £8,500 or more a year.

Benefit	Taxable value	Exemptions or exceptions
Loan (*s.160*)	Interest saved by comparison with an official rate which is set periodically	Loan under £5,000 (*s.161*) Interest under MIRAS (*s.353*)
Company car (*s.157*)	Tables in Schedule 6 (*TA 1988*) relate to a car's original value, its cubic capacity and age. The resulting figure is then modified to reflect the proportion of business use	
Pension scheme (*s.597*)	Cost to the employer in providing the benefit	Contributions which the employer and the employee make to approved pension schemes are not chargeable (*ss.639, 643*)
Child care facilities		When the care is provided on premises made available by the employer, and the employer wholly or partly finances the care (*s.155*)
Mobile phone (*s.159A*)		The phone has no private use, or the employee makes good the cost
Other benefits (*s.154*)		Expense 'made good' by the employee (*s.156*)

Deductible expenditure (this is very restrictively defined)

The burden of proof rests upon the employee to show that expenditure is:

a) 'wholly, exclusively and necessarily' on behalf of the business, *and*

b) 'incurred in performance of his duties' (*s.198(1)(c)*).

There are different rules for:

◆ **Pension contributions:** contributions to a personal (*s.639*) or occupational pension scheme (*s.592(7)*) are deductible up to certain limits. An employee's national insurance contributions are not deductible (*s.617(3)*).

◆ **Travelling expenses:** the expense has to be 'necessarily expended' in the performance of duties (*ss.193-195, s.198(a)-(b), 198A*), unless it is an 'incidental overnight' expense (*FA 1995 s.93*).

◆ **Capital expenditure on machinery and plant:** if it is 'necessary' for the performance of duties, this is treated as an 'allowance' and set off in the same manner as a 'capital allowance' under Schedule D Case I (*s.198(2)*).

Tax due under Schedule E (together with national insurance contributions) is collected under the PAYE scheme (*ss.143-144A, ss.203-211, IT(E)R 1993, IT(NP)R 1994*) which generally obliges employers to pay tax directly to the Inland Revenue within 14 days of the fifth of the month following the month in which either the payment takes place or the benefit in kind is conferred.

Schedule F

➤ **Distributions** (*s.231*): for a fuller explanation of the imputation system see p.95. The receipt of a tax credit by an individual currently has the following consequences (*s.1A*):

Non-taxpayer ↓ Full rebate (20%) (for distributions before 6 April 1999, but no rebate thereafter)	20% and 23% taxpayer (10% on or after 6 April 1999) ↓ No more tax to pay	40% taxpayer ↓ 20% more tax to pay (32.5% on distributions on or after 6 April 1999 (*F(No2)B 1997 c.31*)

➤ **A close company writes off a loan to a participator** (*ss.419-421*): the amount written off is 'grossed up', so the sum which the company laid out to finance the loan (including tax corresponding to the rate of advance corporation tax (see p96)) is assessed as the shareholder's income. Since the company has already, with the payment to the Revenue, satisfied the shareholder's liability for basic rate tax, the shareholder has effectively postponed liability for higher rate tax (see p.76).

Non-taxpayer, 20% and 23% taxpayer ↓ No more tax to pay	40% taxpayer ↓ 20% more tax to pay (32.5% on release or write off on or after 6 April 1999 (*TA s.421* as amended by *F(No2)B 1997 Sch. 4 para 11*))

➤ **A company repurchases its own shares** (*s.20*): the difference between the original issue price of the shares and their value on sale may be taxed as if it were a dividend. Alternatively, the gain may be subject to CGT if conditions discussed on p.224 are fulfilled.

➤ **Deductible expenditure:** none (*s.20(1)*).

Step 2 — 'Total income' = 'statutory income' - 'charges on income'

➤ **Charges on income**

a) Payment to a former spouse under a court order, *or* agreement after 14 March 1988, *or* through the Child Support Agency (*s.347B*). From 1995/96 relief is only 15% (*s.347B(5A)*).

b) Interest on qualifying loans which the taxpayer takes out (*s.353*):

- as a PR to pay inheritance tax (*s.364*).

- to buy, improve or develop a 'main residence' (*s.354*). The borrower must own legal title to the property and occupy it. Relief is 15% (10% from 6 April 1998) up to £30,000, and it can be deducted at source under MIRAS (*TA s.369*) (*TA* as amended *FB(No2) 1997 cc.15-16*).

- to invest in a partnership (*s.362*): buy a share in, lend or contribute capital to a partnership (subject to restrictions in *s.363*).

- to invest in a close company (not a close investment holding company) (*ss.360-360A*) (subject to restrictions in *s.363*) (see p.77)

- to invest in an employee controlled company (ie: 50%+ of the voting rights or ordinary shares are held by employees) which is not quoted on the Stock Exchange's Official list within 12 months of the company becoming an employee controlled company (*s.361*) (subject to restrictions in *s.363*). The taxpayer works full time for the company (or a 51% subsidiary) and *either*:

  i) lends money to a trading company or the holding company of a trading group, *or*

  ii) acquires ordinary shares in such a company or pays off a loan financing such an acquisition.

c) Payments to fund a qualifying vocational training course where the individual rather than an employer pays for the course. Tax is deducted at source and reflected in a lower charge for fees. A higher rate taxpayer can claim an additional 16% rebate from the Inland Revenue (*FA 1991 s.32*).

d) A gift to charity which is a 'qualifying donation', ie: not relieved as a covenant or under a payroll-giving scheme, and is not less than £250 (*FA 1990 s.25*).

e) A loss on the sale of shares in a qualifying unquoted trading company for which the individual was the original subscriber (*s.574*).

Step 3	'Taxable income' = 'total income' - 'personal reliefs'

➤   These reliefs depend on the individual's personal circumstances.

Personal relief (*s.257*): dependent on age		
Under 65	£4,045	
Over 65, but under 75*	£5,220	
Over 75*	£5,400	
***Additional* relief for married couples (*s.257A*): dependent on age**		
Under 65†	£1,830	The couple live together for part of the year
Either spouse over 65 and under 75*†	£3,185	By default this relief goes to the husband, unless the couple elect before the beginning of the tax year to share it differently
Either spouse over 75*†	£3,225	The spouse can claim any allowance unused by the other spouse at the end of the year
* Relief is *only* available on income up to £15,600 (*s.257A(5)*)		
Other *additional* reliefs		
Single parent's allowance (*s.259*)	£1,830	The taxpayer is unmarried, divorced, separated, widowed and has a child who is under 16, or under 18 in full-time education. The number of children is irrelevant to the level of relief
Widow's bereavement allowance † (*s.262*)	£1,830	A widow is entitled to this relief in the year her husband dies, and if she has not remarried before the start of the next year, she may also claim it for that year
Blind person (*s.265*)	£1,280	If the taxpayer is registered blind Husbands and wives can both claim this relief
† Relief is restricted to 15% (*s.256*)		

Step 4	Calculate the tax payable on the 'taxable income'

➤   Income £0 - £4,100:   taxed at the 'lower rate' of 20% (*s.1(2)(aa)*).

➤   Income £4,101 - £26,100 :   taxed at the 'basic rate' of 23% (*s.1(2)(a)*).

➤   Income over £26,100:   taxed at the 'higher rate' of 40% (*s.1(2)(b)*).

Trustees

➤   UK resident trustees of discretionary trusts and accumulation and maintenance trusts (see p.112 for definition), pay income tax at 34% (*ss.686-687*) (Distributions made on or after 6 April 1999 will be taxable at 25% to compensate for the reduction in the tax credit (*TA s.686(1AA)* as inserted by *F(No2)B 1997 c.32*)).

➤   Trustees of fixed interest trusts have tax at 20% deducted at source on investments and savings, and are subject to basic rate tax at 23% on other income.

➤   Trustees have no personal allowances, but may claim capital allowances and loss relief in respect of any trade they carry out as trustees.

B. Individuals as sole traders/partners

Follow the 4 steps in '*A. Individuals as private persons*',

BUT use these additional rules.

Step 1	Set the 'accounting date'

➤ Profits are taxed by reference to an 'accounting date' (*s.60(3)(b)*), unless special circumstances give rise to a 'basis period'. A 'basis period' arises when *either*:

- ◆ the business ceases for good (*s.63*), *or*
- ◆ an accounting date is other than 5 April (*s.62(2)(1)*), or is changed for certain reasons (*s.62A(1)*).

➤ There is some flexibility in the Inland Revenue's approach to 'accounting dates'.

- ◆ An accounting date fixed for a particular day which falls on different dates (eg: the Last Night of the Proms), will be treated as the same accounting date provided the date does not alter by more than 4 mean days in any year (*Inland Revenue Publication, SAT1*).
- ◆ An accounting date on 31 March will be treated as if it were 5 April (*SAT1*).

➤ Special rules set the basis period during the first 3 years of a business. During the first year, the basis period runs from commencement to the following 5 April (*s.61(1)*). Thereafter, the rules align the basis period with the accounting period as quickly as possible.

- ◆ Alignment happens in year 2 if *either*:
  a) there are 12 months or more between commencement and the accounting date (*s.60(3)(a)*), *or*
  b) there is a change of accounting date between years 1 and 2 (*s.62(2)(a)*), ...
  ... in which case the basis period is the 12 months to the new accounting date.
- ◆ Alignment happens in year 3 if *either*:
  a) there are 12 months or less between commencement and the accounting date (*s.61(2)(a)*), *or*
  b) the accounting date is changed in years 1 or 2 so that the new date is less than 12 months after the business began (*s.61(2)(b)*), *or*
  c) the basis period for year 2 actually ends in year 3 (*s.60(1)*, *s.60(4)(b)*), ...
  ... in the case of a) and b) the basis period in year 2 is the first 12 months, but for c) the basis period is the tax year itself.

Step 2	Claim any 'overlap relief'

➤ When basis periods overlap, 'overlap relief' is available. The profit from the preceding year attributable to the overlapping days is apportioned, and used as a relief to prevent a double liability (*s.63A*).

➤ A loss cannot be used more than once, so overlap relief cannot be used to recycle any other form of loss relief such as relief under *s.380* (*s.382(4)*).

Step 3	Claim any loss relief

	Period	Loss can be claimed ...	Use on ...
Start-up relief s.381	First 4 tax years	... over the 3 tax years before the year in which the loss incurred	... any income
Terminal loss relief s.388	Final year	... the final tax year and the 3 years preceding it	... trading income
Schedule A relief s.379A	Any accounting year	... the next tax year of taxable income; any excess in future years	... any income
Carry across relief s.380, subject to restrictions, s.384		... the tax year in which the accounting year of the loss ends, and the preceding year	
Carry forward relief s.385		... the next tax year with taxable profit, and any excess in future years	... trading income

➤ Using s.380 wastes personal reliefs as this relief must be used on the whole of income

➤ Using s.385 allows personal reliefs to be set off against other income

➤ s.385 can be claimed whether s.380 is used or not

➤ If s.385 is used with a s.380 loss, then s.385 can only be claimed to the extent that a loss remains unused after s.380 has been claimed

Relief under s.379A for Schedule A income is not available to companies (FA 1995 s.39(1))

Relief on incorporation of a business s.386

If a trading loss is unrelieved when the business is transferred to a company 'wholly or mainly in return for the issue of shares' (ie: shares form at least 80% of the consideration), this loss can be carried forward and provide relief against dividends *or* salary which the former trader or partner gains from the company in future years

Tax efficient investments such as venture capital trusts (*TA s.842AA, TCGA 1992 s.100*)) and Enterprise Investment Schemes (*TA ss.289-312, TCGA 1992 ss.150-150C*) and PEPs, are really beyond the scope of this book, however, for an outline see pp.112-113

C. Partnerships

Steps

1 **Send in the partnership return**

2 **Split the profit or loss amongst the individual partners**

Step 1   Send in the partnership return

➤ The partnership must send in a return giving details of the firm's business for an accounting period (eg: partnership income, profit allocation and any capital allowances claimed) (*TMA 1970 s.9*).   Claims for expenditure and capital allowances etc which affect profits and losses of the partnership are made when the partnership return is completed (*TMA 1970 s.42*).

  ◆ Expenditure incurred by a partner must be included on the partnership return; a claim as an individual will be disallowed.

  ◆ Claims for allowances for plant and machinery owned by a partner, but used by the partnership, must generally be made on the partnership return (*CAA 1990 s.65(1)*).

Step 2   Split the profit or loss amongst the individual partners

➤ Profit and loss are calculated for the partnership as a whole (*s.111(2)*).

➤ Partners complete individual self assessments, each being liable for their own share of the profits under the profit sharing ratio during the period of assessment concerned (net of any deductions successfully claimed by the partnership).

  ◆ Partners are generally not jointly and severally liable for taxation arising on the profit earned by each other (*ss.111(3)-111(4)*). (Note that they could be so liable prior to the introduction of self assessment.)

Continuance of partnerships
➤ Under the old rules, before the introduction of self assessment, a partnership was deemed to discontinue if its membership changed, unless the partners elected for it to continue.
➤ If the membership of a partnership changes after 6 April 1994, then it will be deemed to continue unless none of the partners continues in the business (*s.113*).

B Close companies

I	Generally
II	Taxation of a 'close companies' and its 'participators'

I Generally

➤ For corporation tax purposes, a 'close company' is a company that is *either*:

a) 'controlled' by 5 or fewer 'participators', *or*

b) 'controlled' by its directors, *or*

c) has amongst its shareholders 5 or fewer 'participators', or directors who are 'participators' *and* on a winding-up of the company these 'participators' would be entitled to receive the greater part of the company's assets.

- 'Control' means control as defined in *TA s.416*

  - For the definition of 'control' in *TA s.416,* and the also for the (different) definition of 'control' in *TA s.840,* see p.77. (Both definitions are used in the *Taxes Act* and it is important to make sure that the correct definition is used in the right place).

- A 'participator' is a person who has a share or interest in the capital or the income of a company and specifically someone entitled to acquire capital or voting rights, or to ensure income or assets will be deployed for his benefit, or entitled to distributions or the proceeds of a premium or redemption paid by the company, or certain loan creditors (*TA s.417(1)*).

  - The definition of 'director' is a wide one, and focuses on substance rather than the title (*TA s.417(5)*).

➤ Companies which may not be close companies for corporation tax purposes include:

- companies not resident in the UK (*TA s.414*).

- quoted companies, if shares bearing not less than 35% of the votes at a general meeting have been unconditionally allotted or acquired so that members of the public enjoy them beneficially (*TA s.415*).

- companies controlled by one or more non-close companies and which could only be treated as a close company by including a non-close company as one of the 5 participators, or by including non-close loan creditors on an liquidation (*TA s.414(5)*).

➤ The definition of a 'close company' is different in repect of the taxation of individuals who hold shares in such companies.

- For IHT purposes, the definition of a 'close company' is the same as for corporation tax purposes except that:

  a) it includes non-resident companies, *and*

  b) the test for a 'participator' disregards the interests of loan creditors (*IHTA 1984 s.94*).

- For capital gains tax purposes, the definition includes non-resident companies (*TCGA 1992 s.13*).

II Taxation of a 'close company' and its participators

➤ The taxation treatment of a 'close company' depends on whether it is also a 'close investment holding company'.

➤ The rules in **A. 'Close companies'** apply to all 'close companies', the additional rules in **B. 'Close investment holding companies'** apply only to 'close investment holding companies'.

Definition of a 'close investment holding company'

➤ A close company is a 'close investment holding company' unless it exists during an accounting period 'wholly or mainly' for one of 6 purposes.

♦ These purposes include carrying on a trade on a commercial basis, and investing in land provided the land is not intended to be let to connected persons (*TA s.13A(2)*).

A. 'Close companies'

1 Loans to 'participators' (*TA ss.419-421*) (See p.70 for the participator's position if the loan is written off)

➤ A company pays notional ACT, at the same rate as the rate of ACT (20%), to the Inland Revenue on a loan to a participator (eg: if the company wishes to lend £100 gross it pays £20 notional ACT to the Revenue and the participator receives £80).

♦ Notional ACT, it is not ACT so it may not be set off against mainstream corporation tax (see p.97).

➤ This does not apply if *either*:

a) the loan is in the usual course of business for a company whose business is moneylending, *or*

b) the following conditions are fulfilled:

   i) the company's total loans to the 'participator' stand at less than £15,000, *and*

   ii) the 'participator' owns 5% or less of the shares in the company, *and*

   iii) the 'participator' works full time for the company (*s.420(2)*).

➤ If a claim for repayment is made within 6 years of the end of the accounting period in which the repayment is made, the Inland Revenue refund the tax to the company.

2 Expenses of 'participators', and their 'associates', taxed as distributions (*TA s.418*)

➤ An expense to benefit a 'participator' or a participator's 'associate', is a 'qualifying distribution' on which the company must pay ACT; the participator is taxed under Schedule F(*TA s.418(2)*).

➤ A charge to tax under this section is excluded if the 'participator' is taxed on the benefit under *TA s.154* (*TA s.154* is the general charging provision for benefits in kind received by directors and employees earning £8,500 or more a year, see p.69) (*TA s.418(3)*).

3 Attribution of capital gains to a 'participator' (*TCGA 1992 s.13*)

➤ Capital gains made by a non-resident company (which would be close if UK resident) are apportioned to 'participators' in that company in proportion to their beneficial interest in the company.

4 Liability to IHT on a transfer of value by a 'close company' (*IHTA 1984 s.94(1)*)

➤ A transfer at an undervalue by a close company is treated as a transfer out of a 'participator's' estate and is chargeable to IHT. Liability rests primarily on the company, although limited recovery is possible from each 'participator' or the transferee (*IHTA 1984 s.202(1)*).

♦ Altering the rights of unquoted share or loan capital is treated as a transfer (*IHTA 1984 s.98(1)*.

5   Relief on interest on loan to, or to buy ordinary shares in, a close company (*ss.360-360A, 363*)

➤ The individual:

a) has a 'material interest' (he or an associate control more than 5% of the ordinary shares or would be entitled to more than 5% of the assets of the company distributable amongst 'participators' in the company), *or* he (or his associate) already own shares in the close company, *and*

b) the taxpayer spends the majority of time working for the company when the interest is paid, *and*

♦ he lends money to a close company, *or*

♦ borrows money for the close company to use in the course of its business, *or*

♦ to purchase ordinary shares in a close company.

B. 'Close investment holding companies'

1   Rate of corporation tax

➤ Tax is paid at the full corporation tax rate of 31% (ie: not the smaller company's rate of 21%).

2   Restricted right to a tax credit

➤ If the main purpose of a distribution is to allow the company to pay the tax credit to someone who is entitled to reclaim the credit, and the distribution is waived by any of the shareholders, the right to a tax credit may be restricted to what is 'just and reasonable' (*TA s.231(3A)-(3D)*).

♦ This is intended to prevent distributions being rigged to enable shareholders (such as those with losses, or unused personal allowances) to receive a disproportionate share of the company's profits (NB: from 6 April 1999 these rules will be repealed and replaced by *s.231(3AA)* by new rules (*FB(No2)B 1997 c.30*)).

Definitions of 'control' in the *Taxes Act*

➤ The test for 'control' set out in *s.416*, is complex, but involves establishing that a person exercises, is able to exercise or entitled to acquire, direct or indirect control over a company's affairs. Examples of such control include the possession of, or entitlement to acquire:

a) the greater part of a company's issued share capital or of the voting power in a company.

b) enough of the company's issued share capital as would entitle that person to receive the greater part of the income of the company if that income were to be distributed amongst the 'participators' in the company.

c) on a winding-up of the company, to receive the greater part of the assets of the company which would be available for distribution amongst the 'participators' in the company (*s.416(2)*).

● For a definition of 'participators' see p.75.

➤ In addition to the definition of 'control' in *s.416*, there is another definition of 'control' in *s.840* used in certain other contexts. For the purposes of *s.840*, a person has 'control' over a company (the 'relevant company') if that person has power to secure ...

a) by means of the holding of shares or the possession of voting power in or in relation to the relevant company or any other company, *or*

b) by virtue of any powers conferred by the articles of association or other document regulating the relevant company or any other company, ...

... that the affairs of the relevant company are conducted in accordance with the wishes of that person.

C Capital allowances

I   What allowances are and how they may be used

II   Who can claim allowances

III   What allowances can be claimed

I   What allowances are and how they may be used

A. What allowances are

➤   Capital allowances allow the depreciation of capital assets to be brought into account for taxation purposes and offset against income profit (earned by traders, partners and companies).

➤   Different methods of depreciation are used for different types of asset:

4% straight line		25% reducing balance		
Period	Straight line depreciation	Period	Reducing balance	Depreciation
1	£4	1	£100	£25 (25% of £100)
2	£4	2	£56.25	£18.75 (25% of £75)
3	£4	3	£42.19	£14.06 (25% of £56.25)

and so on ... until allowances reach £100 (NB: the majority of the value of a 25% allowance is extracted over 7 years, thereafter the allowance becomes less significant

B. How allowances may be used

➤   A capital allowance may be set against 'income profits' and used to create a loss for Schedules A or D.

◆   If there is more than one item of plant and machinery, an allowance is granted on a 'pool' (separate pools exist for some cars, 'short life' assets (eg: computers), Schedule A assets and 'long life' assets).

➤   When a 'capital' asset is sold, the sum written down against the 'capital allowance' is compared with the proceeds of sale to determine whether a balancing charge or allowance arises.

◆   If the sale proceeds (or original cost if less) exceed the sum written down (in respect of the asset, or the pool if there is a pool), a balancing charge arises on the excess taxed as a chargeable receipt of the trade.   If the proceeds are less than the sum written down, the shortfall is deductible from chargeable receipts of the trade.

II   Who can claim allowances

➤   For plant and machinery, the general rule is that a person may claim a capital allowance if:

a)   while carrying on a trade that person has incurred capital expenditure on the provision of machinery or plant wholly and exclusively for the purposes of the trade, *and*

b)   in consequence of incurring that expenditure, the machinery or plant belongs or has belonged to that person (*CAA 1990 s.24(1)*).

➤   For industrial buildings, the general rule is that a person can claim a writing down allowance if:

a)   at the end of a chargeable period that person is entitled to an interest in a building or structure, *and*

b)   at the end of that chargeable period the building or structure is an industrial building or structure, *and*

c)   that interest is the relevant interest in relation to the capital expenditure incurred on the construction of that building or structure (*CAA 1990 s.3*).

III   What capital allowances can be claimed

➤   A capital allowance can be claimed:

a) **25% on a reducing balance basis** for plant and machinery (*CAA 1990 ss.22, 24*).

b) **6% on a reducing balance basis** for certain plant and machinery which constitute 'long life assets' that are expected to have a useful economic life of at least 25 years (*CAA 1990 ss.38A-38H* inserted by *FA 1997 Schedule 14*).   This treatment does **not** apply to:

i)   a person (other than a lessor) who incurs expenditure during a chargeable period of 12 months not exceeding £100,000.

ii)   expenditure on any of the following (*CAA 1990 s.38B*):

- machinery or plant which is a fixture in, or provided for use in, any building which is wholly or mainly for use as a dwelling house, retail shop, showroom, hotel or office.

- a car.

- prior to 1 January 2011 certain types of ship (basically seagoing vessels).

- prior to 1 January 2011 the provision of a railway asset wholly and exclusively for the purposes of a railway business.

c) **4% on a straight line basis** for industrial buildings (*CAA 1990 ss.3-4*).

d) in certain cases allowances are accelerated and / or offered on special terms, eg: investment in enterprise zones (known as 'enterprise zone allowances or 'EZAs') (*CAA 1990 ss.1, 6, 10A-10D,17A*), mineral extraction (*CAA 1990 ss.98-121*), agriculture and forestry (*CAA 1990 ss.122-133*), dredging (*CAA 1990 ss.132-134*) and scientific research (*CAA 1990 ss.136-139*).

➤   For expenditure incurred on plant or machinery (subject to certain exclusions) from 2 July 1997 to 1 July 1998 a first year allowance may be claimed, provided that the expenditure is incurred by a 'small company' or a 'small business' (*CAA 1990 ss.22-22A* as inserted by *F(No2)B 1997 cc.42-43*).

◆   The normal rate of allowances is doubled (ie: the rate of first year allowances is 50%, unless the plant or machinery is a 'long life' asset' in which case the rate is 12%) (*CAA 1990 s.22* as amended by *F(No2)B 1997 c.42*). This accelerates the allowances so that, where expenditure is incurred between 2 July 1997 and 1 July 1998, twice as much of the expenditure can be set-off against the enterprise's income profit for the chargeable period.

Definition of a 'small business' and a 'small company	
'Small company'	'Small business'
➤ A 'small company' is a company which is: a) 'small or medium sized' for the purposes of *CA s.247* during the financial year of the company in which the expenditure is incurred, *and* b) is not a member of a large group when the expenditure is incurred (*CAA 1990 s.22A* as inserted by *F(No2)B 1997 c.43*)	➤ A 'small business' is, basically, a business which were one to take all its trades together and prepare its accounts as if it were a hypothetical company would qualify as a 'small or medium sized' for the purposes of *CA s.247* (*CAA 1990 s.22A* as inserted by *F(No2)B 1997 c.43*)
'Small or medium sized' for the purposes of *CA s.247*	
➤ A company is 'small or medium' sized for the purposes of *CA s.247* if, broadly speaking, it satisfies 2 of the following conditions: a) turnover of not more than £11.2 million, *or* b) assets of not more than £5.6 million, *or* c) not more than 250 employees	

D Capital gains tax

References in this section are to the Taxation of Chargeable Gains Act 1992, unless stated otherwise.

I Payment

➤ CGT payable by individuals is, for 1996/97 and subsequent years, assessed and paid under the new regime of self assessment, see p.84.

II Calculation

Steps	
1	**Identify the disposal**
2	**Calculate the 'chargeable gain' or 'allowable loss' on *a* disposal**
3	**Calculate the 'taxable gain' for the tax year on *all* disposals of chargeable assets, taking due account of exemptions and reliefs**
4	**Calculate the tax due**

Step 1	**Identify the disposal (*ss.22-28*)**

➤ A sale *or* gift of a 'chargeable asset' (*s.15(2)*). Note that a disposal to a spouse (*s.58*), or charity (*s.257*), does not give rise to a chargeable gain or an 'allowable loss' for CGT.

Step 2	**Calculate the 'chargeable gain' or 'allowable loss' on *a* disposal**

➤ Take *either* the market value of the asset on its 'disposal' (*s.17*) *or* the consideration on its sale, and subtract the 'allowable expenditure'. The allowable expenditure is calculated by adding up the following:

   ◆ the initial cost of the asset. If the asset was acquired before 31 March 1982, then use *either*:
   a) its value on that date, *or*
   b) the cost of acquisition, whichever produces a smaller loss or gain (*s.35*).

   ◆ any expense 'wholly and exclusively' incurred in enhancing the asset's value (not routine maintenance) (*s.38*).

   ◆ the cost of establishing title to the asset, and any costs incurred in disposing of it (*s.38*).

➤ Then subtract the 'indexation allowance', which accounts for the impact of inflation on the gain.

   ◆ Where an asset was owned on 31 March 1982, the indexation allowance can be taken *either*
   a) from the asset's value on 31 March 1982, *or*
   b) from the 'actual expenditure' on the asset (ie: acquisition, maintenance, etc), whichever carries a higher indexation (*s.54*).

   Note: since 30 November 1993, this allowance only serves to reduce or extinguish a gain, it cannot be used to increase the size of a loss, nor to convert a gain into a loss.

| **Step 3** | **Calculate the 'taxable gain' for the tax year** |

➤ Add up the total 'chargeable gains' for the tax year and deduct:

◆ any 'allowable losses' from that tax year (*s.2(2)(a)*), *and*

◆ any 'allowable losses' from previous tax years not previously brought into account for CGT (*s.2(2)(b)*),

➤ Ensure that relevant exemptions and reliefs are left out of account:

Exemptions for ... individuals ... and ... companies	
Annual exemption of £6,500 for the tax year being assessed (*s.3(2)*) (£3,250 for trustees)	✘
'Wasting assets' which have a life of under 50 years (*ss.44-45*)	✓
Tangible moveables if the consideration is less than £6,000 (*s.262*)	✓

A private dwelling house which is used as a 'main residence' (or which has been used as such during the period of ownership) and land up to half a hectare (*s.222*). The following periods of absence are permitted:
 	
➤ the first year of ownership (*Extra Statutory Concession D49*)
 	
➤ up to 3 years' absence for any reason, split over as many periods as the owner's absence (*s.223(3)(a)*)
 	
➤ for as long as the owner is employed outside the UK (not self-employed) (*s.223(3)(b)*)
 	
➤ up to 4 years of absence within the UK at the reasonable behest of an employer (*s.223(3)(c)*)
 	
➤ the last 3 years of ownership (*s.223(1)*)
 	
Note
 	
➤ Married couples can only use this exemption for one house - if they own more than one, they must choose which qualifies for the exemption (*s.222(5)*)
➤ The exemption will be reduced proportionately to the extent the property is used for business purposes (*s.223(2)*)
➤ Trustees can claim exemption from CGT so long as the occupier was entitled to occupy the house *either*
  a) as tenant for life, *or*
  b) under the terms of the trust (*s.225*)
➤ Land over half a hectare will not come within the exemption unless the owner can show it is for the 'reasonable enjoyment' of the house (*ss.222(2)-222(3)*)
➤ If land of up to half a hectare is sold off, but the house is retained, the exemption will apply to the land sold (*s.222(4)*)
	✘

An indication of whether a relief or exemption is available for companies has been included as a quick aide-mémoire - to avoid confusion please note that (apart from this instance) these pages relate to the application of capital gains tax to individuals (not companies). For companies, which do not pay capital gains tax, but corporation tax calculated according to the CGT principles, see p.91.

Reliefs for ...	individuals ...	and ... companies
Retirement relief (*ss. 163-164, Schedule 6*) **Person** a) 50 or over *or* ill *and* b) disposes of a 'business interest' *and* c) owned the 'interest' for at least 1 year i)　**An individual** carrying on a business may claim relief when: 　a) the asset is used for the business *and* b) an 'interest' in business as well as the asset itself is disposed of ii)　**A shareholder** may claim relief when: 　a) the asset is in a personal trading company *and* b) he is a full-time officer/employee of the company 　　　NB: Relief is reduced if rent is charged by an amount which the Inland Revenue deem 'just and equitable' 　**Relief:** the rate of relief depends on the size of the gain: 　➤　100% relief: gains of up to £250,000 　➤　50% relief: gains of between £250,000 and £1,000,000 　**Amount of relief:** this depends on how long the 'interest' being disposed of has been owned: 　➤　10 years or more: full relief 　➤　1-10 years: the years of ownership divided by 10		✗
Roll-over relief on the replacement of 'qualifying assets' (*ss. 152-157*) 　Qualifying assets: a) goodwill *and* b) land *and* c) fixed plant and machinery 　➤　A replacement is acquired *either* within 1 year prior to the disposal *or* within 3 years after the disposal 　➤　The replacement asset does not have to be of the same kind as the asset disposed of 　　NB: For a shareholder the assets must be used by a personal trading company 　　NB: Relief is restricted if the asset is not used in the seller's trade throughout the period of ownership *or* if 　　　the whole proceeds are not reinvested in a new qualifying asset		✓
Roll-over relief on investments in unquoted shares and shares quoted on AIM (*ss. 164A-164M*) 　➤　Any gain on the disposal of assets sold after 16 March 1993 to purchase shares in an unquoted company 　　◆　The replacement is acquired within 1 year prior to the disposal *or* within 3 years after it		✗
Roll-over relief on the incorporation of a business (*s. 162*) 　➤　The business is transferred to a corporate body as a going concern 　　◆　The business is transferred with all its assets (ignore cash) 　　◆　The relief only applies to the proportion of the gain for which the consideration is in shares		✗
Hold-over relief on gifts of business assets (*s. 165, Schedule 7*) 　Qualifying assets: a) used by the business, *or* b) shares in a personal trading company, *or* c) unquoted shares 　➤　The disposal was a gift, *or* at below market value 　➤　There must be a joint election for relief by the donor and the donee 　　NB: any IHT due is deductible from CGT as an 'expense' (*s.260(7), s.165(11)*)		✗

Note
i)　If **hold-over** relief or **roll-over** relief is used, the annual exemption may not be used with respect to the asset concerned. **Retirement relief**, however, can be used with any other exemption
ii)　**Roll-over** relief treats the disposal as representing neither a gain nor a loss; it reduces the value of the consideration for the new asset by the amount of the gain realised on the disposal of the old asset
iii)　**Hold-over** relief holds any gain over so as to reduce the consideration which the transferor would have received on a sale at market value, and reduces the consideration for which the transferee acquires the asset by the same amount

Step 4	Calculate the tax due

Individuals: tax is paid on the 'chargeable gains' for the year of assessment at the same rate as the top slice of income tax (see p.29) (*s.4*).

Trustees: trustees of discretionary trusts, and trustees of accumulation and maintenance trusts pay tax at 34% (*s.5*).

Partnerships: calculate the 'chargeable gain' by subtracting a partner's share of an asset's acquisition cost from that partner's share of the asset's disposal value. It is the individual responsibility of each partner to ensure that his CGT is paid (*s.59*).

Instalment option

➤ The instalment option enables tax to be paid in 10 annual instalments, where:

a) the disposal was a gift (*s.281(1)(a)*), *and*

b) hold-over relief is not available, as opposed to not claimed (*s.281(1)(b)*), *and*

  • Normally, the 'instalment option' is not available for sole traders/partners as there is 'hold over' relief.

c) the property disposed of was (*s.281(3)*):

  • land, *or*

  • a controlling shareholding in a quoted or unquoted company, *or*

  • a minority holding in an unquoted company.

Tax efficient investments such as venture capital trusts (*TA s.842AA, TCGA 1992 s.100*)) and Enterprise Investment Schemes (*TA ss.289-312, TCGA 1992 ss.150-150C*) and PEPs, are really beyond the scope of this book, however, for an outline see pp.112-113

E Self assessment for individuals

I Assessment of income tax and capital gains tax by individuals

➤ An individual must submit a tax return, usually in response to a notice issued to him by the Inland Revenue, stating his liability to income tax and capital gains tax (*TMA 1970 s.8(1)(a)*).

➤ The tax return creates a legal charge to tax which is due from the individual. The date by which the return must be submitted (the 'filing date') depends on whether the individual does a self assessment.

  ◆ If he only wishes to supply information, without doing a self assessment, he must submit the return on or before 30 September following the end of the tax year or if a notice is issued after 31 July following the end of the tax year (*TMA 1970 s.9(2)*) within 2 months of the notice being issued.

  ◆ If he is prepared to assess his own tax, then he must submit the return on or before 31 January following the end of the tax year, unless the return is issued to him late (after 31 October), in which case, he has 3 months from when the return is issued (*TMA 1970 ss.8(1)(a), 8(1A)*).

➤ If the Inland Revenue do not issue a notice, the individual is under a duty to notify them of any chargeable income or capital gain within 6 months of the taxable event in respect of which tax falls due, unless the individual is exempt as:

  ◆ no chargeable income and gains arise in the year of assessment (above the exempt amount), *and*

  ◆ his net income tax liability is nil *or* tax deducted at source covers any liability (*TMA 1970 ss.7(3)-7(7)*).

➤ If a return is submitted, but the self assessment is not completed, the Inland Revenue are under a duty to complete it (*TMA 1970 s.9(3)*).

➤ Records relevant to calculating tax liability must be kept: there is fine of up to £3,000 for non-compliance (*TMA 1970 ss.12B(1)-12B(6)*).

	Individual	Sole trader/partner
Time the return is issued	Within 1 year of the **filing date**	Within 5 years of the **filing date**
Obligation expires	1 year after the **filing date**	5 years after the **filing date**, or when a formal Inland Revenue enquiry is finished or becomes impossible

➤ Penalties for failing to submit a return are hefty: £100 automatically if a return is not submitted on time, a further £100 if it is still outstanding 6 months later, and then up to £60 a day (*TMA 1970 ss.93(2)-93(4)*). If no return is sent in at all, the Inland Revenue may, within 5 years of the end of the year of assessment, estimate the tax and make a determination stating the tax due (*TMA 1970 s.28C*).

II Payment of income tax and capital gains tax by individuals

➤ Tax is payable 'on account' on 31 January during the year of assessment, and on 31 July following the end of the year. Any corrective 'balancing' payment is due on the next 31 January (*TMA 1970 s.59A(2)*).

➤ Interest runs on tax due 'on account', or as a balancing payment (*TMA 1970 ss.59A-59B*) from the date the payment is due (*TMA 1970 s.86*). Interest on overpaid tax is paid to the taxpayer (*s.824, TCGA s.283*).

➤ A surcharge of 5% is levied on tax outstanding 28 days after it falls due, and there is a further 5% surcharge if the tax is still unpaid 6 months after it is due (*TMA 1970 s.59C*).

F Inheritance tax

References in this section are to the Inheritance Tax Act 1984, unless otherwise stated.

I Payment

Payment
a) 6 months from the end of the month of the chargeable transfer, *or*

b) for lifetime transfers made between 5 April and 1 October, 30 April in the next following year (*s.226*).
   IHT on 'instalment property' is payable in 10 equal annual instalments, with the first due 6 months from the end of the month of death, rather than on delivery of the Inland Revenue account (*s.227*). It is available for:
   i) land, *and*
   ii) an interest in a business, *and*
   iii) shares (quoted and unquoted) which entailed control of a company immediately prior to death, *and*
   iv) unquoted shares if *either*:
   - they form a large holding (10% of the nominal capital of a company worth £20,000 or more),
   or - the Inland Revenue accepts 'undue hardship' would follow if payment was due immediately,
   or - IHT on the instalment option exceeds 20% of the total IHT due on the estate as a whole.

If the instalment property is sold, tax and interest are both payable immediately (*s.227(4)*).

Interest runs ...

... 6 months after a chargeable transfer: on non-instalment property vesting in PRs, land that is 'instalment property', GBRs, LCTs, PETs (on death) and life interests in possession (*s.233*).
... from the instalment date: sums unpaid on the date they are due under the instalment option (*s.234*).

Property	Liability for IHT		Burden (if a will is silent)
Vesting in the PRs	PRs: are liable to the extent that resources fall into their hands or would do so but for their default (*ss.200, 204*)		Residuary beneficiary
Jointly and nominated			Beneficiary
LCTs, PETs	Donor and donee (*s.199*)	PRs for IHT is unpaid after 12 year after the end of the month of death (*s.204(8)*)	Donee
GBRs			
Life interest in possession	Donee and trustees (*s.199*)		Donee and trust fund

II Calculation

During life (L)

Steps

L1 Identify a 'transfer of value' which reduces the estate's value

L2 Value the transfer

L3 Deduct any exemptions or reliefs

L4 Cumulate transfers over 7 years and calculate the tax due

'PET' - Potentially Exempt Transfer
'LCT' - Lifetime Chargeable Transfer
'GBR' - a Gift in respect of a which a donor Reserves a Benefit under *FA 1986 s.102*.

On death (D)

Steps

D1 Identify property deemed to pass on death: 'the free estate'

D2 Value the 'free estate'

D3 Deduct any exemptions, reliefs or deductible property

D4 Calculate IHT on death, on pre-death chargeable transfers (LCTs, PETs, GBRs) and on the 'free estate'

Steps L1 and L4	Identify the lifetime transfer and calculate the tax due

Lifetime transfers which are potentially chargeable

Transfer	Definition	Tax on transfer	Cumulation on death	Tax on death
Lifetime chargeable (s.2)	a) To a discretionary trust (Gross up transfer) b) To a company	Up to £215,000 at 0% Over £215,000 at 20% Cumulate LCTs over 7 years prior to the LCT	LCTs and chargeable PETs over 7 years prior to death	Tapering relief: year 6-7: 8% year 5-6: 16% year 4-5: 24% year 3-4: 32% Otherwise death rate at 40% Credit is given for tax already paid
Potentially exempt (s.3A)	a) To an individual b) To an accumulation and maintenance trust c) To a disabled trust	Nil, unless the donor dies within 7 years, then cumulate LCTs over 7 years prior to the PET	If a PET becomes chargeable, add it to the cumulative total	Tapering relief applies (as above)

Steps L2 and D2	Value the transfer and/or the 'free estate'

➤ The value of a lifetime transfer is the value of the asset transferred at the time of the transfer (s.160).

➤ The probate value is the value of the death estate minus any lifetime transfers of value.

Valuation

Bank, building society a/c	The balance of the account and interest which has accrued to the date of death
Debts	Sums owed to the deceased. Overpaid income tax is reclaimed and accounted for on CAP D3 (s.174)
Life interest in trust	The capital value of the beneficial interest which the deceased enjoyed *and* income accrued but unpaid at death (s.49)
Insurance	If it matures on the deceased's death and the estate is beneficially entitled, the sum it produces on maturing. If it matures on another event, the value of premiums paid less any sum paid to surrender rights under the policy before death (s.167)
Quoted shares	In accordance with the Stock Exchange *Daily Official List* on the day of death. The value for IHT is the 'sell' price plus one quarter of the difference between the 'sell' and the 'buy' price Prices are usually quoted 'cum div.' (ie: with the right to the next dividend). If the dividend has been declared but not paid, the price is quoted 'ex div.' as only those registered on the company's Register of Members when the dividend is declared are entitled to receive the dividend. If the testator dies before payment of the dividend, his estate is entitled to any declared dividend. The dividend is treated as a separate asset in the estate, and the estate's gross value is calculated by adding the dividend to the 'ex div.' price of the shares
Unquoted shares	The open market value. The firm's accountants and the firm itself will advise on a valuation. The latest annual accounts should be consulted as a guide (s.168)
Land	The open market value. Estate agents will advise on this. The figure must be agreed with the local district valuer before the estate is wound up (s.160)

Loss relief on death

For some assets, the sale price may replace the probate value *if* it is lower than their aggregate probate value.

➤ Sale within 1 year of shares and securities quoted on a Stock Exchange at death (ss.178-189).

> Note: if qualifying investments are cancelled (and not replaced by the institution which issued them), they are treated as having been sold.

➤ Sale within 4 years of land (ss.190-198).

Steps L3 and D3	Deduct any exemptions, reliefs and (on death) deductible property

Exemptions, reliefs and deductible items *available on life only* per tax year

➤ £3,000 per annum, which can be carried forward for 1 year so that £6,000 becomes available in a given year.

➤ Normal expenditure (*s.21*).

   ◆ Regular payments + the transfer is from income + the transferror retains sufficient income to maintain his standard of living.

➤ PETs which are not yet chargeable *or* have become extinct as they occurred more than 7 years before death.

➤ £250 small gift exemption for gifts up to this sum to any particular individual (*s.20*).

➤ Marriage: a) up to £5,000 from a parent, b) up to £2,500 from a remoter relation, c) up to £1,000 from a non-relation (*s.22*).

Exemptions, reliefs and deductible items *on life and death*

Exemptions	➤ Gift to spouse (*s.18*) ◆ The transfer of a lifetime interest in possession is treated as capital within this exemption ◆ On death, a gift qualifies for exemption if it is immediate *or* conditional on survivorship for up to 1 year ➤ Gift to charity (*ss.23-26*) ➤ Gift for the public benefit (*ss.30-35*). Providing that: a) the Treasury classes the asset as being as of national, artistic, historic or scientific interest, *and* b) an undertaking is given that the asset will i) remain in the UK, *and* ii) be preserved, *and* iii) be open to public access	
Business property relief (*s.105*)	Relief is at 100%	➤ A business *or* an interest in a business property ➤ Any shares in an unquoted company
	Relief is at 50%	➤ Quoted shares if the transferror had control of the company immediately before the transfer ➤ The transferror is a partner *or* controls a company *and* transfers land, buildings, machinery or plant which were wholly or mainly used for the business
	Property must be owned for 2 or more years before the transfer takes place (*s.106*)	
Agricultural property relief (*ss.115-24*)	Relief is at 100%	➤ The transferor used the property for agriculture for 2 years prior to the transfer, *or* ➤ The transferor owned land used for agricultural purposes during the last 7 years and is entitled to occupy it within 1 year (or the land is let under an agricultural tenancy granted on or after 1 September 1995)
	Relief is at 50%	➤ The transferor owned land used for agricultural purposes during the last 7 years and the land is subject to a tenancy granted before 1 September 1995

Exemptions, reliefs and deductible items *available on death only*

Quick succession (*s.141*)	Relief is a fraction of the tax already paid on a previous transfer: 1-2 years before death: 80% 2-3 years before death: 60% 3-4 years before death: 40% 4-5 years before death: 20%	➤ Tax was paid on a chargeable transfer to the deceased within the last 5 years ➤ Tax is payable on the deceased's estate
Woodlands (*ss.125-130*)	Timber is exempt	➤ Timbered land not qualifying for agricultural property relief ➤ Timber itself (not the land) is exempt provided the land was bought at least 5 years before death
Funerals (*s.162*)	Fully deductible	➤ Reasonable burial expenses are deductible
Debts (*s.505*)		➤ Debts incurred for money or money's worth are deductible

Liabilities are deductible (*s.5(3)*) unless the deduction is excluded (*s.162*) (More complex liabilities are not dealt with here)

Step D1	Identify property deemed to pass on death

Identifying the 'free estate' on death (*IHTA 1984 ss.5, 200*)

➤ Assets to which the testator is beneficially entitled and which pass under the will or on intestacy, eg: a life assurance policy in the deceased's name and in his favour.

➤ Assets passing outside the will or intestacy:

   ◆ to which the deceased is beneficially entitled under property law: joint tenancies, nominated property (Friendly societies, Industrial and Provident societies, some TSB accounts, with deposits up to £5,000)

   ◆ to which the deceased is deemed to be beneficially entitled to for IHT purposes: GBRs, life interest under a trust

Step D4	Calculate IHT on death, on pre-death chargeable transfers

Calculation of IHT on the death estate

LCTs and PETs	Any of these occurring within 7 years prior to the death represent additional liability	(See *Step L1*, p.86)
Tax rate on 'free estate'	Not exceeding £215,000 at 0% Exceeding £215,000 at 40%	

Note
In calculating these bands, cumulate LCTs and PETs which occurred in the 7 years prior to death

Apportionment of IHT over the estate

Subject to instructions to the contrary in the will, the IHT burden is 'apportioned' over the whole estate by the formula:

$$\text{Estate rate} = \frac{\text{Tax payable}}{\text{Taxable estate}}$$

The tax due on each asset is calculated by multiplying the value of the asset by the 'estate rate'.

G Calculation of corporation tax

References in this section are to the Income and Corporation Taxes Act 1988, unless otherwise stated.

I	Calculation
II	Loss relief

I Calculation

Steps	
1	**Calculate 'income profit'**
2	**Calculate 'capital profit'**
3	**Calculate 'total profit'**
4	**Deduct 'charges on income'**
5	**Calculate the corporation tax due**

Step 1	**Calculate the 'income profit'**

(Profit under Schedules A, D and F) plus (Profit on 'loan relationships', foreign echange and financial instruments) less (any available losses (see p.94)).

Schedule A income

➤ Income under Schedule A is calculated differently from Schedule A income enjoyed by an individual, sole trader or partner (*FA 1995 s.39(1)*).

   ◆ Deductible expenditure is subject to special rules set out in the *Taxes Act* (*s.25(2), ss.26-43*) For coporation tax, unlike income tax, the general rules is that Schedule A expenses can only be deducted when they have been paid (rather than when they accrue, ie: fall due).

➤ Part of a premium received on the grant of a lease with a term not exceeding 50 years, or on the surrender or variation / waiver of a lease (even if the original term exceeded 50 years), may be treated as an income receipt and as a part disposal for CGT purposes - for the apportionment see *s.34* (see also *TCGA 1992 Sch. 8* for CGT treatment).

➤ Subtract any **capital allowances**, or add any **balancing charges** see p.78.

Schedule D Case I and Case II trading income ('chargeable receipts' minus 'deductible expenditure')

➤ **Chargeable receipts** a) derive from income not capital, *and* b) derive from the company's trade.

➤ **Deductible expenditure:** expenses of an income nature that are 'wholly and exclusively' incurred for the purposes of a trade, profession, or vocation are deductible (*s.74(1)*). Case law governs whether expenses are deductible (see eg: *Mallalieu v. Drummond* [1983] 2 AC 861).

➤ Subtract any **capital allowances**, or add any **balancing charges** see p.78.

Schedule D Cases IV, V and VI income

➤ See p.67.

Schedule F income

➤ Qualifying distributions received from UK companies are FII which is not taxable, see p.95 (provided the company is not a dealer in securities in which case the net distribution is taxable (*TA s.95* as amended by *F(No2)B 1997*).

Profits on 'loan relationships' (and FX and FI in outline)

➤ A company has a 'loan relationship' when:

a) it stands in the position of a creditor or a debtor as respects a money debt, *and*

b) the debt arises from a transaction for the lending of money (*FA 1996 s.81*) (eg: not a trade debt).

- A 'money debt' is a debt in any currency which is to be settled by the payment of money, *or* the transfer of a right to settlement of a debt which is a money debt) (*FA 1996 s.81*).

➤ Profits and losses are calculated using one of the 'authorised accounting methods' (*FA 1996 s.85*):

◆ **the accruals basis:** allocates income and expenditure to the period to which it relates, irrespective of when payment is made or received.

◆ **the mark-to-market basis:** the fair market value at the accounts date.

- Broadly speaking, the accounting method used is that followed in a company's statutory accounts (*FA 1996 s.86*). There are rules in the legislation governing how accounting methods may be used and what happens when different methods are used with respect of a particular loan relationship (*FA 1996 ss.89-90*).

- In certain situations, an accruals basis must be used (eg: *FA 1996 s.87* (parties to a relationship are 'connected'), *s.92* (the 'creditor' relationship in respect of a convertible security), *s.93* (asset-linked debt)).

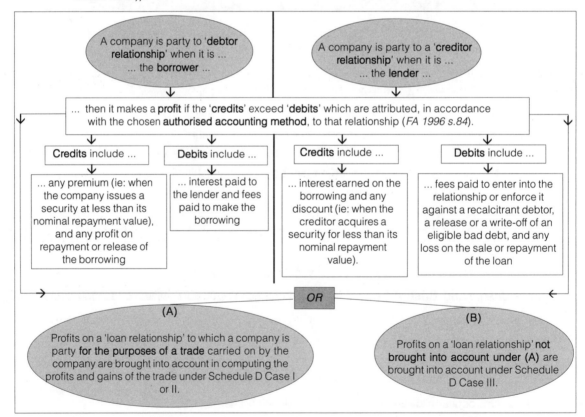

➤ Various anti-avoidance provisions may prevent a company gaining deductions in respect of interest or other 'debits'. The details of this legislation are beyond the scope of this book.

◆ Provisions of general application include *TA ss.209(2)(d)-(e), TA s.787* and *FA 1996 Schedule 9 para 13*.

◆ There are also rules which apply in particular circumstances, eg: *FA 1996 Schedule 9 para 6(1)* which restricts the availability of 'debits' for a creditor when a debt between connected parties becomes a bad debt.

➤ The general intention of this regime is that 'capital' gains and losses (as well as 'income' profits and losses) on money debts should be taxed and relieved as income (*FA 1996 s.80(1), 84(1)(a)*). There are however exceptions when only 'income' is in the regime, eg:

- ◆ a creditor relationship, if a 'loan relationship' is a convertible security (*FA 1996 s.92*).

- ◆ a relationship linked to the value of chargeable assets (unless the disposal of the asset would take place as an integral part of a trade carried on by the company) (*FA 1996 s.93*).

➤ Foreign exchange (Forex) gains and losses, and gains and losses on financial instruments (FI) (eg: options, swaps and derivatives) are brought into account under complex legislation which in principle aims, like the 'loan relationship' rules, to follow accountancy treatment.

- ◆ The primary legislation relating to Forex is in the *FA 1993 (ss.92-95, 125-170)* and that relating to FI in *FA 1994 (ss.147-177)*.

➤ For the treatment of losses on 'loan relationships', Forex and FI, see p.56.

Transfer Pricing

Transfer Pricing
➤ If property is sold and the buyer 'controls' (as defined in *s.840*, see p.77) the seller, or visa versa, or both are 'controlled' by the same person or persons, and the price is not an 'arms' length price' the Revenue may in certain circumstances substitute an 'arm's length price' for tax purposes (known as 'transfer pricing') (*ss.770-773*) (see *Ametalco UK v. IRC* [1996] STC (SCD) 399).

Step 2	Calculate 'capital profit'

Steps	
I	**Identify the disposal**
II	**Calculate the 'taxable gain' or loss on _a_ disposal**
III	**Calculate the 'taxable gain' on all disposals for the accounting period, taking account of exemptions and reliefs**

Step I	Identify the disposal (*TCGA 1992 ss.22-28*)

➤ A sale *or* gift of a 'chargeable asset' (*TCGA 1992 s.15(2)*).

Step II	Calculate the 'taxable gain' or 'allowable loss' on _a_ disposal

➤ Take *either* the market value of the asset on its 'disposal' (*s.17*) *or* the consideration on its sale, and subtract the 'allowable expenditure'. The allowable expenditure is calculated by adding up the following:

- ◆ the initial cost of the asset. If the asset was acquired before 31 March 1982, then use *either*:

    a) its value on that date, *or*

    b) the cost of acquisition, whichever produces a smaller loss or gain (*s.35*).

- ◆ any expense 'wholly and exclusively' incurred in enhancing the asset's value (not routine maintenance) (*s.38*).

- ◆ the cost of establishing title to the asset, and any costs incurred in disposing of it (*s.38*).

> Then subtract the 'indexation allowance', which accounts for the impact of inflation on the gain.

- ◆ Where an asset was owned on 31 March 1982, the allowance can be taken *either*

    a) from the asset's value on 31 March 1982, *or*

    b) from the 'actual expenditure' on the asset (ie: acquisition, maintenance, etc), whichever carries a higher indexation (*s.54*).

    Note: since 30 November 1993, this allowance only serves to reduce or extinguish a gain, it cannot be used to increase the size of a loss, nor to convert a gain into a loss.

Step III	Calculate the 'taxable gain' for the accounting period

> Add up the total 'chargeable gains' for the accounting period.

> Then deduct:

- ◆ any 'allowable losses' from that accounting period (*TCGA 1992 s.2(2)(a)*), *and*

- ◆ any 'allowable losses' from previous accounting periods not brought into account to corporation tax (*TCGA 1992 s.2(2)(b)*), *and*

> Ensure relevant exemptions and reliefs are left out of account:

Exemptions
'Wasting assets' which have a life of under 50 years (*TCGA 1992 ss.44-45*)
Tangible moveables if the consideration is less than £6,000 (*TCGA 1992 s.262*)

Reliefs
Roll-over relief on the replacement of 'qualifying assets' (*TCGA 1992 ss.152-157*)
Qualifying assets: a) goodwill *and* b) land *and* c) fixed plant and machinery (*ss.155-156*) ➤ A replacement is acquired *either* within 1 year prior to the disposal *or* within 3 years after the disposal ➤ The replacement asset does not have to be of the same kind as the asset disposed of **NB:**Relief is restricted if the asset is not used in the seller's trade throughout the period of ownership *or* if the whole proceeds are not reinvested in a new qualifying asset
Roll-over relief on paper for paper transactions (*TCGA 1992 ss.127-137*)
➤ See *Corporate Finance Companion, 1ˢᵗ Edition,* p.54

Step 3	'Total profit' = 'income profit' + 'capital profit'

Step 4	Deduct any 'charges on income'

> Since the introduction of 'loan relationships' in *FA 1996* the 'charges on income' in respect of which deductions can be claimed against a company's 'total profits' have been reduced to (*s.338*):

a) certain annuities and annual payments (not being payments in respect of loan relationships), *and*

b) certain charitable donations (ie: those falling within *s.339*), *and*

c) patent royalties, mining rents / royalties and payments for easements.

- ◆ Note that certain detailed conditions (which are beyond the scope of this book) must be satisfied for charges on income to be deducted.

| Step 5 | Calculate the corporation tax due |

➤ The rates are fixed for a financial year: if the rate changes during the accounting period, the taxable profit is apportioned across the applicable tax rates.

Full rate of 'mainstream corporation tax':   31% on profits over £1,500,000.

Tax rate on profits between £300,000 and £1,500,000:   33.5% ⟩— relief is effectively given at this marginal rate

Tax rate on profits under £300,000:   21% ⟩— the 'small companies rate' of corporation tax

● Note that these rates are as amended by (F(No2)B 1997 c.18).

➤ Franked investment income (ie: dividends and tax credits accruing on shares owned by the company) is ignored when paying tax, but it is included when calculating the rate of tax applicable (see p.97).

II   Loss relief

➤   Companies may use their losses in a number of ways.

	Loss can be claimed ...	Use on ...

Carry-across and carry-back relief *s.393A*	a) ... for the accounting period, *and*
	b) ... any unrelieved loss may be carried back against any profits from an accounting period in the previous 1 year[†] , *provided*:
	  i) the company is carrying on the same trade as it had been in the earlier year, *and*
	  ii) the loss is set against later years first
	
	[†] This was 3 years for periods starting before 2 July 1997. There are transitional rules for periods straddling 2 July 1997 (*F(No2)B 1997 c.40*)
		... total profits

Losses (trading) other than terminal losses *s.393*	... following accounting periods, against losses of the trade, for as long as the company carries on the trade	... trading income

NB: special rules apply for losses on a Schedule D Case V trade (*s.393(5)*) and Schedule D Case VI losses (*s.396*)

NB: a company which is a member of a group of companies can claim group relief (see the *Corporate Finance Companion*, 1st edition p.67)

Loan relationships, Forex and FI

➤   Special rules govern the use of losses on 'loan relationships'.

♦   'Debits' on 'loan relationships' to which a company is a party **for the purposes of a trade carried on by it** are deductible in computing the profits of that trade (*FA 1996 s.82(2)*) and losses may be relieved under the normal rules for the set-off of losses on income (ie: *TA ss.393-396*).

♦   All the 'debits' and 'credits' on 'loan relationships' to which a company is party **otherwise than for the purposes of trade carried on by it** are aggregated respectively together.   If the 'non-trading debits' exceed the 'non-trading credits', a company has a 'non-trading deficit' on its 'loan relationships'. A 'non-trading deficit' may be dealt with in one of 4 ways (*FA 1996 s.83(2)*):

a)   set-off against profits from the same accounting period (in the priority required by *FA 1996 Schedule 8 para 1*).

b)   relieved through group relief (see the *Corporate Finance Companion*, 1st edition p.67).

c)   carried back against profits which were attributable to loan relationships taxed under Schedule D Case III and earned over the previous 1 year (*FA 1996 Schedule 8 para 3* as amended by *F(No2)B 1997 c.40*. (For accounting periods beginning before 2 July 1997, the period was 3 years - there are transitional provisions for accounting periods straddling the 2 July 1997)).

d)   carried forward against profits for the next accounting period (providing the profits are not classed as trading income within *s.393A*) - this option is used to the extent that the others are not claimed (*FA 1996 s.83(3)*).

➤   These rules also apply to Forex (*FA 1993 ss.128-130*) and FI (*FA 1994 ss.159-160*) losses.

H The imputation system

References in this section are to the Income and Corporation Taxes Act 1988, unless otherwise stated.

I	Generally
II	Payment of ACT and MCT
III	FII and Surplus FII
IV	Foreign income dividends (FID)s and 'special dividends'

I Generally

➤ When the imputation system was introduced in 1972, the aim was to restrict the extent to which profits made by companies and distributed to their shareholders were subject to double taxation: first as the company's profits and secondly as income in the hands of its shareholders.

◆ Although this logic has gradually been eroded and has been virtually abandoned in the Chancellor's Budget statement on 2 July 1997, this background still helps to understand the rules set out in this section. The changes contained in *F(No2)B 1997* provide for the two stage withdrawal of the 'tax credit' which has been the mechanism through which tax paid by a company has been 'imputed' to its shareholders:

Stage 1 for distributions made on or after 2 July 1997:

a) pension funds ceased to be entitled to repayment of a 'tax credit'. Pension funds will suffer a reduction in their income and pension fund trustees will need to consider whether the funds they are responsible for administering meet the solvency requirements under *PA 1995*. Corporate schemes may need topping up by employers if the scheme is to pay out a pension tied to the employee's final salary (ie: a 'defined benefit scheme'), holders of personal pensions may need to increase contributions to their pensions to make good the shortfall.

b) companies lost the entitlement to reclaim the tax credit element associated with FII (see p.97).

Stage 2 for distributions made on or after 6 April 1999:

a) individuals will only be entitled to a tax credit equal to 1/9th of the distribution received by the shareholder (ie: 10% of the gross distribution including the tax credit).

b) charities will cease to be entitled to repayment of the tax credit. However, charities will benefit from transitional rules which apply to distributions made on or after 6 April 1999 and before 6 April 2004 and which are intended to cushion charities from the resulting drop in their income.

◆ The term 'tax credit' suggests a 'credit' for which a taxpayer could claim a cash repayment from the Inland Revenue.

● This will, on 6 April 1999, become something of a misnomer as no UK resident shareholders will be entitled to a cash repayment. The only shareholders who may be entitled to claim a (much reduced) repayment in respect of a 'tax credit' will be shareholders resident in foreign jurisdictions who are entitled to claim repayment under a 'double tax treaty' with the UK.

➤ In outline, the system now works as follows:

◆ When a company makes a 'qualifying distribution' it pays advance corporation tax (ACT) at the same rate as the lower rate of income tax (currently 20/80ths) of the gross distribution (*s.14*).

- A 'qualifying distribution' (eg: a dividend) paid by a company to its shareholders. Exceptions, which are not 'qualifying distributions', include certain bonus shares and securities.

- Subject to certain limits (see p.97), the company can set the ACT it has paid in an accounting period against its mainstream corporation tax (MCT) liability for that period (*s.14(3)*).

◆ Shareholders currently receive a tax credit or are treated as having paid tax at the lower rate on account of the ACT which the company has paid. Quite how this works depends on the tax status of the shareholder and the type of the distribution. Although FIDs are treated differently (see p.98), the basic principle for distributions which are not treated as FIDs is that:

a) **an individual** receives a tax credit (*TA s.231(1),(3)* as amended by *F(No2)B 1997 c.30*):

The tax credit	
Before 6 April 1999	On or after 6 April 1999
20% of the distribution (ie if the company distributes £100, then £20)	1/9th[†] (£8.89) of the net distribution (£80) received by the shareholder
[†] This is equivalent to 10% of the gross distribution (£88.89) the shareholder receives	

- **non-taxpayers** can currently claim a repayment of the credit at the end of the tax year, but will not be able to do so in respect of distributions made on or after 6 April 1999.

- **lower (20%)** and **basic rate (23%) taxpayers** have no further income tax liability in relation to the distribution (*s.231*). For distributions made on or after 6 April 1999, their liability will be at the 'Schedule F ordinary rate' - 10% of the gross distribution (*s.1A(1A)* as inserted by *F(No2)B 1997 c.31(3)*). The tax credit will satisfy this liability.

- **higher-rate (40%) taxpayers** currently owe an extra 20% more tax (*s.1A*). For distributions made on or after 6 April 1999, their liability will be at the 'Schedule F upper rate' - 32.5% (*s.1B* as inserted by *F(No2)B 1997 c.31(5)*).

b) **a company** receives 'franked investment income' (FII).

- The term FII refers to both the distribution *and* the tax credit.

- A company can use the tax credit element of the FII to prevent itself having to pay ACT on the onward distribution of FII to its shareholders. This is known as 'franking' a distribution. A company used to be able to use FII for other purposes (eg: it could set FII off against losses) but this has been stopped for accounting periods beginning on or after 2 July 1997, see p.98.

c) **a pension** fund used to be able to reclaim a tax credit, but cannot do so in respect of distributions made on or after 2 July 1997 (*s.231A* as inserted by *F(No2)B 1997 c.19(2)*).

d) **a charity** may reclaim a tax credit on distributions made before 6 April 1999, thereafter it may claim transitional relief for distributions made before 6 April 2004 (*F(No2)B 1997 c.35, Sch. 5*).

➤ Note that the Inland Revenue may restrict or deny a tax credit in certain circumstances, for instance if a distribution is abnormally large and not commercially justified (*ss.703-709*). A further anti-avoidance provision, *s.231B*, has been introduced by *F(No2)B 1997 c.28* to counteract arrangements designed to pass on the value of a tax credit to a person who would not (without such arrangements) be entitled to it.

Higher rate taxpayer's liability

	Distributions before 6 April 1999		Distributions on or after 6 April 1999	
		£		£
Distribution (net of ACT)		80		80
Tax credit	(20% of income)	20	(10% of 88.89, or 1/9th of 80)	8.89
Gross income		100		88.89
Higher rate tax	(40%)	40	(32.5% of 88.89)	28.89
After tax income		60		60

➤ Note that individuals who hold shares through a PEP will not be able to reclaim the tax credit in respect of distributions made on or after 6 April 1999. PEPs (and TESSAs) will be replaced by the Individual Savings Accounts (ISA). Little is known about precisely how the ISA will work, except that it will be intended to encourage savings amongst those who are less well off.

II   Payment of ACT and MCT

➤ ACT is paid to the Revenue 14 days after the end of the quarter in which the distribution is made (*Schedule 13 paras 1, 3*).

➤ MCT falls due 9 months after the end of each accounting period, which runs from 1 April to 31 March (*s.10(1)*). Under the 'pay and file' system companies must pay the Inland Revenue a sum equal to what they anticipate their corporation tax liability will be (*s.10(2)*). The Inland Revenue then assesses the company's tax liability to reach a final figure - any excess tax which the company has paid is refunded to it, and the company will have to meet any further liability - in both cases, with interest.

➤ If the ACT which the company pays on distributing profits to shareholders exceeds the amount it can set off against MCT, it will have 'surplus ACT', see *Corporate Finance Companion,* 1st edition p.58.

III   FII and Surplus FII

➤ Companies do not pay corporation tax on dividends or distributions they receive from companies resident in the UK (*s.208*). This prevents a company's profits being subject to double taxation in the corporate sector - first in the hands of the company which makes the distribution and secondly as income profit for the company that receives the distribution.

◆ FII is the gross amount of the distribution a company receives, together with the tax credit.

◆ FII is taken into account in working out the rate of corporation tax applicable to a company for an accounting period, but is ignored when calculating the tax actually due

➤ A company may use FII it receives to frank qualifying distributions it makes (ie: it need not pay ACT on a distribution of franked income).

➤ Where FII exceeds the franked payments which a company makes to shareholders, it has surplus FII.

◆ Surplus FII can be rolled forward to frank qualifying dividends in future accounting periods.

● The ability which existed for accounting periods beginning before 2 July 1997 to offset FII or surplus FII against certain losses and to recover payment of the tax credit has been abolished (*s.242*) (*F(No2)B 1997 c.20*).

IV   Foreign income dividends (FIDs) and 'special dividends'

A. FIDs

➤   FIDs were introduced in *FA 1994* to help companies which had amassed surplus ACT and to make the UK a more attractive jurisdiction for international headquarters companies (an 'IHC') with sources of substantial foreign income.

◆   It will not be possible to pay a FID on or after 6 April 1999 (*F(No2)B 1997 c.36(1)*) and the FID rules are being repealed (*F(No2)B 1997 Schedule 6*).

➤   The basic principle of a FID is that a company pays ACT on a dividend as usual, but to the extent that the dividend can be matched to foreign profit and that the company has 'surplus ACT' available, it can subsequently recover the ACT.

➤   An IHC which pays a FID does not need to pay ACT at all when the FID is paid to shareholders (*s.246T*), but will have to pay ACT if it subsequently emerges that it did not merit an IHC treatment.

◆   The complicated three tiered test which needs to be satisfied to be an IHC is beyond the range of this book.

◆   The test, set out in *TA s.246S,* shall cease to apply for accounting periods beginning on or after 6 April 1999 (*F(No2)B 1997 Schedule 6 para 3(3)*).   The Chancellor has announced that 'similar' rules will be introduced with effect from 6 April 1999, but at the time of going to press these rules have not been published.

B. '*Schedule 7* distributions'

➤   The *FA 1997* includes legislation to discourage the use of 'special dividends' in takeover bids and as a means of returning capital to shareholders.   This appears to have been a response to the perceived cost to the Exchequer associated with 'special dividends' that were being targeted during the early 1990s with increasing sophistication at exempt funds, such as pension funds.   Exempt funds were (prior to 2 July 1997) entitled to reclaim the 'tax credit' from the Inland Revenue and therefore effectively turn the tax credit into cash.

◆   *Schedule 7* will cease to apply in respect of distributions made on or after 6 April 1999 (*F(No2)B 1997 c.36(3)*).

➤   A '*Schedule 7* distribution' is a 'qualifying distribution' made by a company:

either   a) i)   on the redemption, repurchase or purchase of its own shares, *or*

    ii)   on the purchase of rights to acquire its own shares (*FA 1997 Schedule 7 para 1(2)*),

and/or   b)   when arrangements are or have been made by virtue of which:

▪   the fact that the distribution is made, *and/or*

▪   the time when the distribution is made, *and/or*

▪   the form of the distribution, *and/or*

▪   the amount of the distribution, ...

    ... is or was made referable to a 'transaction in securities' (*FA 1997 Schedule 7 para.1(3)*).

➤ Certain dividends are exempted from treatment as a '*Schedule 7* distribution'.

◆ There is a specific exemption for pre-sale distributions if there is a 'major change' in the ownership of the company in a period beginning on the day the distribution is made and ending on the 14th day after the day on which the distribution was made (*FA 1997 Schedule 7 para 6*).

● A 'major change' involves the acquisition by 1 person, or by 2 or more persons, of a holding of 75% or more of a company's ordinary share capital.

➤ The drafting of Schedule 7 has attracted considerable criticism. For the Inland Revenue's view on this, see *Tax Bulletin, June 1997*.

C. FIDs and '*Schedule 7* distributions' under the imputation system

➤ A FID is treated differently in the hands of different types of shareholder.

◆ An individual does *not* receive a tax credit, but is treated as having met his liability to basic and lower rate tax (*TA s.246D*). Since there is *no* tax credit, a basic rate taxpayer is *not* entitled to a refund of basic rate tax (20%).

◆ A company is *not* treated as receiving FII (*TA s.246E*).

◆ An exempt institution such as a pension fund or a charity is *not* entitled to claim a repayment in respect of the ACT.

➤ A '*Schedule 7* distribution' is deemed to be a FID, so a shareholder receiving a '*Schedule 7* distribution' receives similar treatment in respect of a '*Schedule 7* distribution' as for a FID (*FA 1997 Schedule 7 para 2*).

➤ Distributions will cease to be treated as FIDs from 6 April 1999 (*F(No2)B 1997 c.36*).

I   Value added tax (VAT)

I   Generally
II   VAT and land - the election to tax
III   Capital goods scheme
IV   Penalties

I   Generally

➤ A registered person accounts periodically to HM Customs and Excise for VAT on 'output' (sales) of goods and services in the course of business, and any VAT on 'inputs' (*VATA s.1*).

➤ VAT is designed, in theory, to pass a tax charge on the value added by manufacturers and suppliers to the final customer (a non-taxable person, or one who makes exempt supplies).

➤ A taxable person who can attribute all his inputs to taxable supplies (ie: all supplies other than exempt supplies) pays no tax insofar as he reclaims 'input' tax he has paid to his suppliers against 'output' tax which he receives from his customers.   The attribution of 'inputs' to 'outputs' is governed by *VATR 1995 rr.99-116*.

➤ A taxable person pays HM Customs and Excise the amount by which a business' 'output' exceeds its 'input', unless 'input' exceeds 'output' in which case he claims a rebate of the excess 'input' tax.

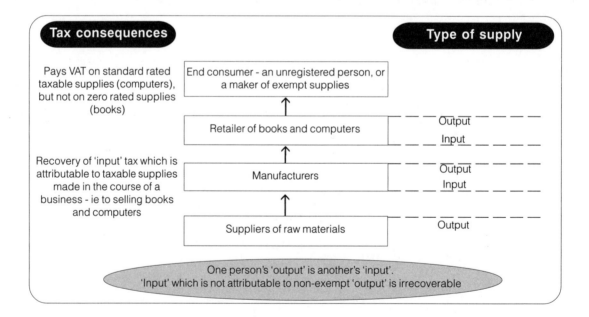

➤ A sole trader, partnership, or company which makes 'taxable supplies' of 'goods or services' in the course of a business exceeding £48,000 (£49,000 from 1 December 1997) a year must register for VAT with HM Customs and Excise as a 'taxable person' (*VATA 1994 s.2*). Partners and trustees must register jointly. For lower turnovers registration is optional; it is only advisable if reclaimable 'input' tax outweighs the extra cost to customers of the VAT which must be charged to them, and the administrative burden is not judged too inconvenient.

➤ Supplies of goods and services are standard rated at 17.5% unless they fall within the categories set out in the boxes below.

Exempt supplies (*VATA 1994 s.31(1), Schedule 9*)

➤ Some grants (including assignments and surrenders) of interests in or over land (*Group 1*).
  ◆ Supplies which do not fall within this exemption are listed in *Items1(a)-(n)* in *Group 1*. They include supplies which are zero rated and some which are standard rated.
  ◆ If the option to tax is exercised, the exemption does not apply (see p.78).
➤ Insurance and reinsurance services (*Group 2*).
➤ Postal services (*Group 3*).
➤ Betting, gaming and lotteries (*Group 4*).
➤ Finance (*Group 5*).
  ◆ Supplies within this group include transactions in money, transactions in securities, underwriting security transactions, running current, deposit or savings accounts, and managing unit trust schemes.
➤ Education (*Group 6*).
  ◆ This exemption embraces education services by 'eligible bodies', examination services, certain private tuition, services provided by youth clubs, research and vocational training.
➤ Health and welfare services (*Group 7*).
➤ Burial services (*Group 8*).
➤ Trade union subscriptions (*Group 9*).
➤ Sporting services (*Group 10*).
➤ Works of art (*Group 11*).
➤ Fund-raisng events (*Group 12*).

Zero rated (*VATA 1994 s.30(2), Schedule 8*)

➤ Food (*Group 1*).
  ◆ Certain foods are, however, standard rated, eg: supplied in the course of a catering business, hot take-aways, or food sold for consumption on the premises where the supply is made, pet food, luxury and 'frivolous' foods.
➤ Sewage and water services (*Group 2*).
➤ Books and newspapers (*Group 3*).
➤ Talking books and wireless sets (*Group 4*).
➤ Certain buildings and civil engineering works (*Group 5*).
  ◆ This includes the first grant of a 'major interest' in land (ie: of a freehold or a lease with a term exceeding 21 years) by a person who:
    i) constructs a building designed as a dwelling, or converts a building or part of a building into one or more dwellings.
    ii) constructs a building, or converts a non-residential building or part of a building, for a 'relevant residential purpose'.
    ii) constructs a building for a 'relevant charitable purpose'.
➤ Supplies of and in relation to certain protected buildings that are listed buildings or scheduled monuments (*Group 6*).
➤ Certain international services (*Group 7*).
  ◆ Services on goods obtained in, or imported into, EEC States and for export from the EEC:
    a) i) by or on behalf of the supplier, or ii) where the recipient of the services belongs in a place outside the EEC.
  ◆ Making arrangements for i) the export of goods from the EEC, ii) a supply of services of the description in item a), or iii) any supply of services which is made outside the EEC.
➤ Transport (*Group 8*).
  ◆ This includes supplies of ships and aircraft, passenger transport services and some freight transport.
➤ Caravans and houseboats (*Group 9*).
➤ Gold (*Group 10*).
➤ Bank notes (*Group 11*).
➤ Drugs medicine and aids for the disabled (*Group 12*).
➤ Certain imports/exports (*Group 13*).
➤ Tax free shops (*Group 14*).
➤ Supplies to or by charties (*Group 15*).
➤ Clothing and footware (*Group 16*).
➤ Commodities traded on terminal markets such as futures transactions (*SI 1973/173*).
➤ Goods exported to third countries (*VATA 1994 s.30(6)*).

Supplies rated at 8% (5% from 1.09.97) (*VATA 1994 s.2(1A), Schedule A1*)

➤ Fuel and power (for domestic use, or use by a charity other than in the course of a business).

II   VAT and land - the option to tax

➤   A taxable person may waive the exemption from VAT in respect of a supply of land which he would otherwise make as an exempt supply under *VATA 1994 Schedule 9, Group 1*.

➤   This is known as the 'option to tax' and is governed by *VATA 1994 Schedule 10 paras 2-6*.   It is subject to some restrictions in that it:

  ◆   does not apply in relation to zero rated supplies within *VATA 1994 Schedule 8, and*

  ◆   if made in respect of part of a building, it covers the whole building.

  ◆   does not apply if at the time of the grant there is an intention or expectation that the land will become 'exempt land' and it is bought by a developer, financier or a connected person (broadly, land other than land used by a taxable person wholly or mainly for making supplies which are not exempt) (*VATA Schedule 10 para 3(AA)* inserted by *FA 1997 s.37*).

➤   An election must fulfil the following conditions (with effect from 1 March 1995):

  ◆   it may be in any form, *but*

  ◆   it must be notified in writing to HM Customs and Excise within 30 days of its being made (there is discretion to extend this period).

➤   If a taxable person wants to elect and he has already made exempt supplies in relation to the land, he should seek clearance by writing to their VAT office, unless the circumstances fall within *Customs & Excise's Notice 742 December 1995 para 8.6* which lists when permission will be granted automatically.

➤   From 1 March 1995, an election can be revoked, with the written permission of the Commissioners, if it is done *either*:

  ◆   within 3 months of the election becoming effective provided that no input tax has been recovered and the land has not been sold as part of a TOGC (Transfer Of a business as a Going Concern), *or*

  ◆   20 years or more after the election took effect.

Some advantages and disadvantages of opting to tax	

✔ VAT on developing or purchasing the land or building will be recoverable
✔ Input tax will be recoverable on the landlord's overheads attributable to the taxable supply
✔ A landlord will be able to recover VAT on continuing maintenance costs such as expenditure on service charges
✔ If a tenant is fully taxable, it will be able to recover VAT on service charges (this is impossible if the service charge is an exempt supply)
	✘ Compliance costs associated with issuing VAT invoices etc
	✘ A future disposal of the building may be adversely affected as:
	  a) the disposal may be standard rated, so stamp duty will be paid on a greater amount
	  b) even if the disposal is part of a TOGC (so that VAT will not fall due) the buyer will also have to opt to tax
	✘ Some tenants, whose business activities are not fully taxable, will have to bear the cost of VAT which they will be unable to recover (eg: insurers or underwriters who carry out exempt business)
	✘ The capital value of the property may be affected if local market conditions discriminate for or against buildings which are taxable

III Capital goods scheme

➤   Under this scheme 'input tax' recovered in respect of a capital item is adjusted over a period of 5 (a) below) or 10 (b) below) years   (Further adjustments are made if, during the period over which the adjustment is made, the item is sold, lost or stolen, the taxable person de-registers, or a lease in respect of the item expires) (*VATR 1995 rr.114-115*).

➤   A capital item qualifies for the scheme (as amended on 3 July 1997 by *VAT(A(No3)R 1997 r.10*) if it is:

a) of a value not less than £50,000 and is computer equipment (*VATR 1995 r.113(a)*), or

b) of a value not less than £250,000 and is:

   i)   an interest in land, a building (or part of a building), a civil engineering work (or part of civil engineering work) acquired as a standard rate supply (*VATR 1995 r.113(b)*), or

   ii) an interest when the taxable person changes the use of a building (or part of a building) which was previously used for a residential or charitable purpose (*VATR 1995 r.113(c)*), or

   iii) an interest in a building (or part of a building) when the taxable person either makes an exempt supply or ceases to be completely taxable (*VATR 1995 r.113(d)*), or

   iv) a building (or part of a building) which the owner constructed and used for the first time on or after 1 April 1990 (*VATR 1995 r.113(e)*), or

   v)   a building which has had its floor area increased by not less than 10% (*VATR 1995 rr.113(f)*).

c) a building refurbished or fitted out by the owner if the expenditure on taxable supplies (other than zero rated supplies) of services and of goods fixed to the building is not less than £250,000 (*VATR 1995 r.113(h)*).

IV Penalties

Penalties for evading VAT			
Offence	Statute	Penalty	Punishment
Default surcharge	*VATA s.59*	Civil	Failure to send in the 3 monthly return within 1 month of the end of each quarter: the surcharge rises to as much as 20% of the tax due over this period
Dishonest conduct	*VATA s.60*	Civil	Fine equal to the tax evaded by dishonestly acting *or* omitting to act, so as to avoid paying tax
Misdeclaration or neglect	*VATA s.63*	Civil	Fine equal to 15% of the tax the offender attempts to avoid by *either* understating his liability, *or* overstating the rebate due to him, *or* not taking reasonable steps to draw an error to HM Customs and Excise's attention (subject to *de minimis* limits)
Failure to register	*VATA s.67*	Civil	Fine equal to 10%-30% of the tax due, on a rising scale relative to the length of time during which the offender was unregistered (for up to 18 months)
Breach of regulations	*VATA s.69*	Civil	Failure to keep certain records is punishable by a fine of up to £500 Other infringements carry a daily penalty
Fraudulent evasion	*VATA s.72*	Criminal	It is an indictable offence to knowingly or deceitfully avoid VAT. The penalty may be an unlimited fine and imprisonment for up to 7 years

J   Stamp duty

I   Calculation

II   Collection and penalties

I   Calculation

Steps	
1	**Is there a dutiable instrument?**
2	**What is the head of charge and what is the rate of charge?**
3	**Is there an exemption or relief?**
4	**Does duty have to be paid, or can it be deferred?**

(This section focuses on stamp duty on sales, other heads of duty (eg: fixed duties) are not considered)

Step 1   **Is there a dutiable instrument?**

A. Is there an 'instrument'?

➤   Stamp duty is a charge upon 'instruments' (*SA 1891 s.1*).

   ◆   Note therefore that because stamp duty arises upon 'instruments', stamp duty can be avoided altogether if an agreement is oral and transfer is by delivery.   If however the agreement relates to shares or securities consider whether there is a SDRT charge (see p.110).

      ●   However, in such cases care must be taken that the terms of the agreement are not subsequently recorded in a memorandum of agreement as such a memorandum will be stampable (this is known as the 'memorandum rule').

B. Does the 'instrument' relate to stampable property?

➤   A stamp duty charge only arises when an instrument relates to 'property' for which stampable consideration is given.

   ◆   Certain things, such as know-how, are not 'property' for stamp duty purposes.

➤   Agreements for the transfer of goods (other than those annexed to land as a 'fixture') (*SA 1891 s.59(2)(c)*).

C. Is there stampable consideration?

➤   Stampable consideration comprises money, stock/marketable securities (*SA 1891 s.55*) and debts (*SA 1891 s.57*), or if land is sold any consideration (*FA 1994 s.241*).

| Step 2 | What is the head of charge and what is the rate of charge? |

A. Generally

➤ Depending on which head of charge applies, duty is either:

a) 'fixed' (50p), *or*

b) calculated by reference to the value of the stampable consideration passing under the instrument (known as 'ad valorem' duty).

B. Heads of charge

➤ An instrument liable to stamp duty under 2 heads of charge may be charged the higher (*Speyer Brothers* v. *IRC* [1908] AC 92). But an instrument chargeable under a specific head of charge is not usually charged with greater duty under a more general head (*North of Scotland Bank* v. *IRC* 1 SC 149).

Heads of charge		
Head of charge	Property	Rate of charge
Conveyance or transfer on sale (*SA 1891 Schedule 1*)	Stock or marketable securities	50p for every £100 or part of £100
	Property other than marketable securities	a) consideration does not exceed £60,000 • with *FA 1958 s.34(4)* certificate: nil • otherwise: ▪ if the consideration does not exceed £500 -50p for every £50 or part of £50, *or* ▪ if the consideration exceeds £500 but does not exceed £60,000 - £1 for every £100 or part of £100 b) consideration exceeding £60,000 but not exceeding £250,000: • with *FA 1958 s.34(4)* certificate - £1 for every £100 or part of £100 • otherwise £2 for every £100 or part of £100 c) consideration exceeding £250,000 but not exceeding £500,000: • with *FA 1958 s.34(4)* certificate - £1.50 for every £100 or part of £100 • otherwise £2 for every £100 or part of £100 d) consideration over £500,000: £2 for every £100 or part of £100 *FA 1958 s.34(4)* requires certification that the transaction effected by the instrument does not form part of a larger transaction or series of transactions in respect of which the amount or value, or aggregate amount or value, of the consideration exceeds that amount (*FA 1963 s.55* as amended by *F(No2)B 1997 c.49*) b)-d) apply to an instrument executed on or after 8 July 1997, but not to an instrument executed pursuant to a contract made on or before 2 July 1997 (*F(No2)B 1997 c.49(6)-(7)*)
Conveyance or transfer other than on sale (*SA 1891 Schedule 1*)		Fixed duty of 50p

Main heads of charge

Head of charge	Charge		Rate of charge

Contracts or agreements for sale
(*SA 1891 s.59*)
	➤ Agreements relating to *either*:
	a) an **equitable interest** in any property, *or*
	b) **any interest** (ie: including a legal interest) an any property **except**
	  i) land, *or*
	  ii) goods, wares and merchandise, *or*
	  iii) stock or marketable securities (Note that agreements for the sale of securities fall outside the stamp duty, but such agreements may be liable to SDRT), *or*
	  iv) ships or vessels or any part of them, *or*
	  v) property outside the UK.
			As a 'conveyance or transfer on sale (see p.10)
			
			If such an agreement is stamped, and an instrument of transfer is subsequently executed in accordance with the agreement, there is no double charge to duty (*SA 1891 ss.59(5)-(6)*).

Repurchase of own shares by a company	When a company files a return at Companies House within 28 days of receiving the shares (*CA 1985 s.169*), the return is treated as an 'instrument'.		Duty is payable at the rate of 50p per £100 or part of £100 (*FA 1986 s.66*).
Lease or tack	Leases of land (ie: not licences) (also, not leases or licences of personal property)	Duty is charged on rent and any premium. **Rent** Furnished lettings: there is no duty on a term certain of under 1 year if the rent is under £500, if rent is over £500 duty is £1 Other leases bear duty depending on the rent in accordance with tables in *FA 1982 s.128(3)-(4)*. Note that the nil rate under a) does not apply if the rent exceeds £600 a year (*FA 1963 s.55(2)*). **Premiums** Duty is charged as for a conveyance or transfer on sale (p.106) on the premium **Surrenders and variations** These may also bear duty, but this is beyond the scope of this book	
Bearer instruments (On issue or first transfer)	The details are beyond the range of this book - note that the head of charge exists and check in a specialist work (see also *FA 1963 ss.59-61, FA 1967 s.30, FA 1997 s.105*)		

When any property is conveyed:
a) in consideration of a debt due to that person, *or*
b) subject to the payment of money (whether secured or unsecured) (eg: a mortgage) ...
... the debt is treated as the consideration for the conveyance and is chargeable with ad valorem duty at the rate of 50p per £100 or part of £100 (*SA 1891 s.57*).

Step 3   Is there an exemption or relief?

1   **Exemptions under *SI(EI)R 1987* from the head 'conveyance or transfer on sale'**

➤ An instrument falling under one of the following categories is exempt if it provides for:

a) the vesting of property subject to a trust in the trustees of the trust on the appointment of a new trustee, or in the continuing trustees on the retirement of a trustee.

b) the conveyance or transfer of property the subject of a specific devise or legacy to the beneficiary named in the will (or his nominee).

c) the conveyance or transfer of property which forms part of an intestate's estate to the person entitled on intestacy (or his nominee).

d) the appropriation of property in satisfaction of a general legacy of money, or in satisfaction of any interest of surviving spouse and in Scotland also of any interest of issue within *FA 1985 s.85(4), (6), (7)*.

e) the conveyance or transfer of property which forms part of the residuary estate of a testator to a beneficiary (or his nominee) entitled solely by virtue of his entitlement under the will.

f) the conveyance or transfer of property out of a settlement in or towards satisfaction of a beneficiary's interest, not being an interest acquired for money or money's worth, being a conveyance or transfer constituting a distribution of property in accordance with the provisions of the settlement.

g) the conveyance or transfer of property on and in consideration only of marriage.

h) the conveyance or transfer of property in connection with divorce (within *FA 1985 s.83 (1)*).

i) the conveyance or transfer by the liquidator of property which formed part of the assets of the company in liquidation to a shareholder of that company (or his nominee) in or towards satisfaction of the shareholder's rights on a winding-up.

j) the grant in fee simple of an easement in or over land for no consideration in money or money's worth.

k) the grant of a servitude for no consideration in money or money's worth.

l) the conveyance or transfer of property operating as a voluntary disposition inter vivos for no consideration in money or money's worth nor any consideration referred to in *SA 1891 s.57*.

m) the conveyance or transfer of property by an instrument varying a disposition on death within *FA 1985 s.84(1)*

- Note that these regulations only apply to instruments executed on or after 1 May 1987 and the nature of the instrument must be certified in accordance with *SD(EI)R 1987 r.3. r.3* requires a certificate stating that the donor / transferror or his solicitor, or someone authorised to do so (using their own knowledge), certifies that the instrument falls within category [A-M] in the Schedule to the *SD(EI)R 1987*.

- If there is no certificate of exemption, duty of 50p is due.

2   **Mortgages granted after 1 August 1971**

➤ Mortgages granted after 1 August 1971 are also exempt from duty (*FA 1971 s.64*).

3   **Corporate reorganisations - under thehead 'conveyance or transfer on sale'** *(FA 1986 ss.75-77)*

➤ See the *Corporate Finance Companion, 1ˢᵗ edition,* pp.85-86

4 **Associated companies (*FA 1930 s.42* as amended)**

➤ See the *Corporate Finance Companion, 1ˢᵗ edition* p.84.

5 **Loan capital (*FA 1986 s.79*)**

➤ 'Loan capital' includes any debenture stock, corporation stock or funded debt, by whatever name known, issued by a body corporate or other body of persons (*FA 1986 s.78*).

➤ *FA s.1986 s.79* provides an exemption for an instrument on transfer of 'loan capital' from all stamp duties (*FA 1986 s.79(4)*) unless:

a) at the time the instrument is executed, the instrument carries a right (exercisable then or later) of conversion into shares or other securities, or to the acquisition of shares or other securities, including loan capital of the same description (*FA 1986 s.79(5)*), or

b) at the time the instrument is executed or any earlier time, it carries or has carried a right:

- to interest the amount of which exceeds a reasonable commercial return on the nominal amount of the capital, *or*

- to interest the amount of which falls or has fallen to be determined to any extent by reference to the results of, or of any part of, a business or to the value of any property, *or*

- on repayment to an amount which exceeds the nominal amount of the capital and is not reasonably comparable with what is generally repayable under the terms of issue of loan capital listed in the Official List of The Stock Exchange (*FA 1986 s.79(5)*).

Step 4	Does duty have to be paid, or can it be deferred?

➤ An instrument must be correctly stamped if it relates to any property situated or any matter or thing done or to be done in the UK, otherwise it will be inadmissible in evidence before a civil court in the UK (*SA 1891 s.14(4)*) and may not be registered (*SA 1891 s.17*).

➤ If an instrument is executed outside the UK, the 30 day period (after which penalties become due) only begins to run when the instrument is first received into the UK (*SA 1891 s.15(2)(a)*).

➤ Consequently, if an instrument does not need to be received into the UK (eg: for production in evidence before a civil court, or enrolment in the UK (eg: on a share register)), the payment of duty can be deferred indefinitely or at least until it becomes necessary to bring the instrument into the UK. To this extent, stamp duty is sometimes referred to as a voluntary imposition.

- Executing (and retaining) an instrument outside the UK is, therefore, sometimes an element in stamp duty planning, although care must be taken that execution does not take place in a jurisdiction with higher stamp duty than the UK (and that there is no memorandum of the agreement which is subsequently made in or brought into the UK).

II   Collection and penalties

➤   When stamp duty was introduced in 1691, it was intended that instruments should be written on pre-stamped paper; however if ordinary paper is used (invariably the case) duty may be paid *either* within 30 days of the instrument being executed *or* within 14 days of the Stamp Office issuing an assessment where adjudication is requested during the 30 day period.

➤   Late stamping invites the following penalties (in addition to the stamp duty due):

◆   a fixed penalty of £10, *and*

◆   interest at 5% per annum on duty of over £10 which is outstanding, *and*

◆   a sum equal to the amount of duty outstanding (*SA 1891 s.15*).

➤   The *Stamp Acts* do not provide any general statements of who is liable to pay duty.   However, an unstamped document may not generally be produced in evidence before a court (*SA 1891 s.14(4)*), or enrolled on a register (*SA 1891 s.17*) (eg: a share register) so the onus is usually on whoever wishes to prove title (usually the transferee / buyer) to pay duty.

◆   Any arrangement or undertaking for assuming liability on account of the absence or insufficiency of stamp, or any indemnity against such liability, absence or insufficiently is void (*SA 1891 s.117*).

●   Attempts are sometimes made to circumvent this prohibition by covenanting to pay duty if and when an instrument executed outside the UK is received into the UK.   Opinion is divided as to whether such a covenant is enforceable.

➤   The following rules govern, in some instances, who is liable to pay penalties for late stamping:

◆   a tenant under a lease, or a person contracting for a lease to be granted (to himself or another)   (*SA 1891 s.15(2)*).

◆   a buyer or transferee under the head 'conveyance or transfer for sale' (*SA 1891 s.15(2)(d)*).

◆   the transferee on receipt of a depository receipt   (*FA 1986 s.72(6)*).

➤   Different heads of charge have various fines and penalties.   In most cases, the Commissioners can recover a penalty, but a fine requires High Court proceedings.

K Stamp duty reserve tax ('SDRT')

I   Generally

II   The principal charge

Generally

➤ Stamp duty reserve tax ('SDRT') is *not* a stamp duty.   It is a separate tax.

➤ SDRT is a tax on agreements relating to 'chargeable securities'.
- ◆ A 'chargeable security' includes:
  - stocks, shares or loan capital, *and*
  - interests in, or dividends, arising from stocks, shares or loan capital, *and*
  - rights to allotments of, or to subscribe for, or options to acquire, stocks shares or loan capital, *and*
  - units under a unit trust scheme (*FA 1986 ss.93(3)-93(6)(a)*), ...
    - ... *unless* the securities are issued by a body corporate not incorporated in the UK *and* the securities are:
      - not registered in a register kept in the United Kingdom by or on behalf of the body corporate by which the securities are issued, *or*
      - in the case of shares they are not paired with shares issued by a body corporate incorporated in the United Kingdom (*FA 1986 s.93(4)*).
  - ◆ Loan capital which is exempt from all stamp duties by under the loan capital exemption in *FA 1986 s.79(4)* (see p.108) is not a 'chargeable security' (*FA 1986 s.99(5)*).

➤ SDRT falls on an agreement, not the instrument of transfer. Where there is a SDRT charge and within 6 years of the SDRT charge arising:

a) a transfer is executed in relation to the securities to which the agreement related, *and*

b) stamp duty paid on the transfer ...

... the SDRT charge is cancelled (*FA 1986 s.92*).

➤ On an agreement to transfer 'chargeable securities' a SDRT charge arises irrespective of whether:

a) the agreement, transfer, issue or appropriation in question is made or effected in the UK or elsewhere, *and*

b) any party to the agreement is resident or situate in any part of the UK (*FA 1986 s.86(4)*).

- Note that an oral agreement can be within the charge to SDRT.

II   The principal charge

➤ The 'principal charge' to SDRT is imposed when one person (A) agrees with another (B) to transfer (whether or not to B) 'chargeable securities' for money or money's worth (*s.87(1)*).

- ◆ There is an SDRT charge:

    a) if the agreement is conditional, on the day on which the condition is satisfied, *and*

    b) if the agreement is unconditional on the day on which the agreement is made (*s.87(3)*).

- ◆ Duty is charged at 0.5% (*s.87(6)*).   Liability to the SDRT charge falls upon (B) (*s.91(1)*).

➤ The precise requirements for the various exemptions are beyond the scope of this book, but note that the following 2 exemptions in particular exist:

1   Intermediaries (*FA 1986 ss.88A-88B as inserted by FA 1997 s.97*)

➤ Agreements entered into by 'intermediaries' effected on an EEA exchange or a recognised foreign exchange are exempted from a *s.87* charge.

- ◆ An 'intermediary' is, broadly speaking, a member of an EEA exchange or a recognised foreign exchange who is recognised as an intermediary by the exchange and who carries out a bona fide business of dealing in chargeable securities but does not carry on an 'excluded business'.

    - ● An 'excluded business' includes any business which consists wholly or mainly in the making or managing of investments or any business which consists of the insurance business or acting as trustee / managing investments on behalf of a pension fund.

2   Public issues of securities (*FA 1986 s.89A*)

➤ This exemption applies to various categories of issuing houses and intermediaries who enter into agreements, conditonal on the admission of the securities concerned to the Stock Exchange's Official List, for the transfer of chargeable securities in order to facilitate the offer of the securities to the public.

➤ There are other SDRT charges, in addition to the 'principal charge', but these are beyond the scope of the book, as are the precise requirements for the various exemptions to the 'principal charge'.

L   Problem solving hints

➤ Often a transaction incurs liability for more than one tax - the transfer of an asset may incur CGT and IHT, and have income tax implications. Set out below are some approaches to tax-planning.

I   During a client's lifetime

➤ Submit self assessment returns and make payments on account on time to avoid large penalties.

➤ If a taxpayer is not resident in the UK (See *IR 20*), or may be able to establish a non-UK domicile (eg: he was born outside the UK, or regards another country as his real long-term home to which he intends to return), take specialist advice about possible tax savings.

➤ Make full use of income tax loss reliefs.

➤ Make full use of a married couple's personal allowances and their individual basic rate bands. If the marriage is stable, consider transferring assets from one spouse to the other so that they receive income more tax efficiently. (There will be no CGT to pay as transfers between spouses do not give rise to a 'chargeble gain' or an 'allowable loss'.)

➤ Make full use of CGT 'allowable losses' and use exemptions or reliefs (roll-over or hold-over).

➤ Consider investing in an Enterprise Investment Scheme ('EIS'), a Venture Capital Trust (VCT), a Personal Equity Plan ('PEP') and Tax Efficient Savings Scheme Account (TESSA) which have various advantages with regard to both income tax and CGT.

The EIS (outline) (*TA ss.289-312, TCGA 1992 ss.150-150C*)

➤ If a company raises money for a qualifying business activity, and both the individual and the issuing company meet certain conditions for different relevant periods, then:

   a) any gain realised on a disposal of the eligible shares after five years is tax free, *and*

   b) income tax relief (at 20%) at the time of the share issue, *and*

   c) if there is a loss on the disposal of EIS shares further income tax relief is available.

➤ An individual cannot invest more than £100,000 in a tax year in EIS.

The VCT (outline) (*TA s.842AA, TCGA 1992 s.100*)

➤ Investment in a VCT may entitle the investor to:

   a) income tax relief (at 20%) on the amount subscribed for *new* shares in a VCT (for subscriptions of up to £100,000 in any tax year) and CGT exemption on the disposal of such shares (a loss on such a disposal will not be an allowable loss), *and*

   b) exemption from income tax on dividends in respect of ordinary shares (either purchased or subscribed for, at up to £100,00 in a tax year), *and*

   c) deferral of a CGT charge on a disposal of any asset if the disposal can be matched against an investment in a VCT under a) and the investment is made within 12 months before or 12 months after the disposal concerned.

➤ A VCT does not pay tax on chargeable gains which it makes.

The PEP (outline) *(FA 1989 s.39, Sch.8, SI 1989/469)*

➤ An individual can invest up to £6,000 a tax year in a general PEP and up to £3,000 a year in a single company PEP. A PEP manager invests the money in qualifying investments (certain shares and corporate bonds)

    a) any gain is exempt from CGT (but a loss is not an allowable loss), *and*

    b) distributions are exempt from income tax (taxpayers can currently recover the tax credit, but this will cease to be the case in respect of distributions on or after 6 April 1999)

The TESSA (outline) *(TA s.326A-326C)*

➤ An individual can deposit £3,000 in the 12-month period from the date on which the TESSA is opened and £1,800 each year, subject to an overall limit of £9,000.

➤ Interest and bonuses on a TESSA are exempt from income tax an CGT.

➤ Where 'related property' (property which is jointly owned) is valued for IHT, ensure it is discounted to reflect the unsaleability of the share concerned by itself - discounts of , eg: 10%-30% can be allowed.

➤ When making lifetime gifts, make full use of exemptions and reliefs.

    ◆ Time gifts to gain the benefit of tapering relief for IHT (eg: plan gifts while still in good health, and do not wait until approaching 100). On death, the value of the transfer is frozen at the value at the time of the *inter vivos* transfer.

    ◆ PETs: if the donor survives 7 years they are exempt.

    ◆ If the donor has plenty of disposable income, make regular gifts using the exemption under *IHTA 1984 s.21* - unlike a PET these gifts are completely exempt irrespective of whether or not the donor survives for 7 years.

➤ A LCT to a discretionary trust will invite a 10 year charge on the settlor or the trust fund on the tenth anniversary of the gift. The rate of tax does not exceed 6%. Tax is calculated on a notional transfer, which the settlor is treated as having made on the anniversary, assessed under a special formula set out in *IHTA 1984.*

➤ Unlike a discretionary trust, an accumulation and maintenance trust is not an LCT and is not subject to a 10 year charge. A trust must last for under 25 years or be for beneficiaries descended from a common grandparent, vest in possession by a specified age (not over 25), and until the interest vests income must be accumulated or used on a discretionary basis for the beneficiaries (*IHTA 1984 s.71*).

➤ Use the nil rate band fully.

    ◆ One way of achieving this is through a flexible nil rate band gift in a will. An amount equal to the unused nil rate band available on death is either left on discretionary trust to the executors to distribute within 2 years in accordance with a letter of wishes, or is left absolutely to named beneficiaries (ideally these should not be exempt beneficiaries such as a spouse or charity).

➤ Assign the benefit of a life assurance policy and any life interest in possession.

➤ Avoid making gifts and reserving the benefit (GBRs).

> ➤ Retain property necessary to maintain the donor's standard of living and security. If advising a client who is elderly, read the Law Society's guidelines 'Legal services for elderly people - gifts of property: implications for future liability to pay for long-term care' (*Professional Standards Bulletin No. 15, March 1996*).

> ➤ Advise elderly clients considering disposing of their home of the consequences if they subsequently need residential care.

> ◆ The local authority determines the level of fees which the resident must contribute by reference to means testing under *NA(AR)R 1992 (as amended)*.

> • Means testing does not cover a minimum charge which is payable by the resident, and leaves the resident a personal allowance. The test relates to income and capital. Broadly, a resident is only entitled to have fees subsidised if their capital does not exceed £16,000, and they qualify for a tapering subsidy below that figure. A home is taken into account unless:

> a) the property is occupied by a spouse, partner or relative who is *either*:

> i) incapacitated, *or*

> ii) aged 60 or over, *or*

> iii) a child under 16 who the resident is obliged to maintain.

> b) someone else occupies the property *and* the local authority uses its discretion.

> c) the person's stay in care in only a temporary one.

> ◆ If the gift prevents the donor from funding care, the local authority may only fund a basic level of care. This may leave the donor dependent on others to supplement fees for better care.

> ◆ The anti-avoidance provisions are formidable:

> • if a 'significant' motivation for the gift is to prevent a local authority imposing a charge on the client's home to pay for care, the authority can:

> a) place a charge on property transferred to a third party while the donor is in care, or within 6 months of going into care (*HSSAA 1983 s.21*), *or*

> b) place a charge on property owned by a resident in a care home (interest runs from the date of death) (*HSSAA 1983 ss.22, 24*), *or*

> c) recover fees as a civil debt in the Magistrates' Court (*NAA 1948 s.56*).

> • When outstanding fees reach £750, a local authority can take insolvency proceedings and have the transaction set aside as a transaction at an undervalue, or as a transaction intended to defraud creditors (*IA 1986 ss.339-341, 423-425*) (see pp.128, 135).

> ➤ Do not resort to 'associated operations' (ie: a series of operations concerning a particular asset or a series of operations carried out by reference to each other which are designed to escape IHT). They will be ineffective as IHT is due under the anti-avoidance provisions (*IHTA 1984 s.268*).

II   On a client's death

> ➤ Alter gifts in a will by a variation or disclaimer.

> ➤ Make efficient use of IHT and CGT loss reliefs.

> ➤ Dispose of property so as to make full use of the three CGT annual exemptions which are available.

Wills and Probate (outline)

This chapter examines:

A Valid wills

A. Generally

There are three requirements for a valid will.

1   The testator has testamentary '**Capacity**'.

2   The testator has general *and* specific '**Intention**' to make the will.

3   The testator's signature and the form of the will must comply with the required '**Formalities**'.

	Requirements	Presumed to be satisfied ...	Safeguards
1 **Capacity** (must have both a) and b))	a) 'Soundness of mind, memory and understanding' (*Marquess of Winchester's Case* (1598) 6 Co Rep 32a)	... if the testator comprehends: the nature of the act, *and* the general extent of his property, *and* the moral claims on the estate. ... the will appears to be rational *and* the testator generally has capacity. A mental state is presumed to persist, so if the testator generally lacks capacity, it must be shown that he possessed it when making the will	➤ Obtain a written medical opinion on the testator's capacity, and ask the person giving this opinion to witness the will ➤ Make a detailed file note of the circumstances
	b) over 18 years of age*		
2 **Intention**	a) General: intention to make *a* will *and* b) Specific: intention to make *this particular* will The testator must intend the will to be valid unconditionally on execution (*Corbett v. Newey* [1996] 2 All ER 914, CA)	... if the testator has capacity when he executes the will. However, this presumption does not arise if: ➤ the testator is blind or illiterate, *or* ➤ 'suspicious circumstances' exist: the testator did not give free approval due to force, fear, undue influence, or because he mistook the will's contents	➤ Explain the meaning of all the clauses ➤ Ensure the client reads the will, and that it is as he wishes. If necessary, read it aloud in the presence of the witnesses, and alter the attestation clause to record this act ➤ If a gift to the solicitor is 'significant' (over £2,000 *or* 10% of the estate), recommend the client takes independent legal advice
	Intention and **Capacity** must be present *either*: a) when the will is executed (*Banks v. Goodfellow* [1870] LR 5 QB 549), *or* b) when the solicitor is instructed to prepare a will if a) these instructions are followed in the will, *and* b) when the testator executes the will, he comprehends that he previously gave instructions to draw it up (*Parker v. Felgate* [1883] 8 PD 171)		

3
 	
Formalities*
	➤ A will may be handwritten, typed or printed
	➤ The will is properly executed if:
	  ◆ a testator, or another at his direction, signs anywhere on the will, *and*
	  ◆ the signature is intended to validate the will, *and*
	  ◆ 2 people witness the signature by signing the will *or* acknowledging the testator's mark in his presence *(WA 1837 s.9)*
	Note:
	a) a witness must be physically and mentally present at execution, and able to give evidence of this, eg: a child must understand the significance of acting as a witness
	b) a witness does not have to see the testator sign, or know the document is a will
	c) both witnesses must be present at the same time
	d) the testator need not see the witnesses sign
			➤ An attestation clause is evidence that these requirements have been met
			
			➤ A witness who is blind, drunk, or mentally unsound is not suitable
			
			➤ A witness should not be a beneficiary *or* married to a beneficiary at the time, as a gift to them lapses. A partner must not witness a will with a charging clause for his firm (*WA 1837 s.15*).
			
			But if 2 capable witnesses sign, a signature by a beneficiary or their spouse will not cause a gift to lapse (*WA 1837 s.1*)

	Burden of proof: rests on the person relying on the will - the 'propounder' of the will (*Griffin & Amos v. Ferard* (1835) 1 Curt 97)		

* Not applicable to 'privileged' wills made by members of the armed forces on active service, or sailors at sea.

B. Alterations

Wills Act 1837 s.21	Presumptions

➤ Before execution alterations are valid
➤ After execution alterations are void unless *either:*
  a) the testator and the witnesses initial the alteration in the margin, *or*
  b) a subsequent codicil republishes the will and confirms the alteration
	➤ Completed blanks predate execution (eg: date)
	➤ Other alterations postdate execution

Problems

If the alteration is void and the original wording is:

a) **legible**: the alteration is disregarded and the original is admitted to probate

b) **illegible**: probate is granted as if there is a blank, unless *either*:

  i) there is evidence that the testator intended to revoke the wording if the substitution was valid ('conditional revocation'), *or*

  ii) the testator had no intention to revoke the original wording, in which case the original wording is effective if extrinsic evidence reveals it, or if the original script can be successfully revealed

C. Revocation

There are 6 ways to revoke the whole *or* part of a will.

1   **Express revocation** (*WA 1837 s.20*)

    ➤ The insertion of suitable words in a subsequent will or a codicil executed as a will.

2   **Implied revocation**

    ➤ When a disposition is inconsistent with an earlier will, the original disposition is revoked and superseded insofar as it is incompatible with the subsequent disposition.

3   **Dependant relative revocation** (*Re Irvine* [1929] 2 IR 485)

    ➤ When the replacement of a disposition is conditional on a specified event: if the event does not occur, the earlier disposition remains valid, otherwise the conditional disposition is substituted for it.

4   **Marriage** (*WA 1837 s.18* as amended *AJA 1982*)

    ➤ Marriage revokes a will, unless the will shows contrary intention.

    ➤ A will made on or after 1 January 1983 in anticipation of marriage, with a clause displaying the testator's intent that the will (or part of it) should remain valid after marriage, will be valid, *provided that*:

      a) the will names a particular person as the intended spouse, and this person is married, *and*

      b) the testator's intention 'appears from the will . . . at the time it was made'; extrinsic evidence is inadmissible.

    ➤ Marriage does not revoke a mutual will as a trust arises on the death of the first to die, and this trust is not revoked by a subsequent marriage (*Re Goodchild (deceased)* [1996] 1 All ER 670, Ch D).

5   **Divorce** (*WA 1837 s.18A as amended by LR(S)A 1995 s.3* for deaths on or after 1 January 1996)

    ➤ If a marriage ends in divorce or annulment, the appointment of an ex-spouse as executor *or* trustee, or a gift to the spouse, take effect as if the former spouse died on the day of the dissolution or annulment.

6   **Destruction** (*WA 1837 s.20*)

    a) Burning, tearing *or* otherwise destroying the will, *and*

    b) destruction by the testator *or* by some person in his presence and by his direction, *and*

    c) destruction with the intention of revoking the will.

       ◆ Destruction must be physical - crossing a will out, or writing 'revoked' across it is insufficient.

       ◆ Symbolic destruction is not sufficient. Destruction of part may only revoke the part destroyed; this depends on the condition of any remains and quite which part of the will is destroyed.

         ● Destruction of a signature revokes the whole will (*Hobbs v. Knight* (1838) 1 Curt 768).

         ● If parts are cut out, only those parts are revoked (*Re Everest* [1975] Fam 44).

        ◆ The presumption is that a missing will is intentionally destroyed.

B Contents of a will

I　　Common clauses

II　　Hints on drafting and interpretation

I　Common clauses

1　Commencement

➤ States the testator's name and address.

➤ The words 'last will and testament' are evidence of an intention to make a will.

2　Revocation of previous wills

➤ Quite what is revoked depends on the wording of the clause.

- ◆ 'Wills' refers to wills and codicils.
- ◆ 'Testamentary dispositions' covers wills, codicils and privileged wills.

3　Disposal of remains

➤ This is a request, it does not bind the executors.

➤ If organ donation or medical research are envisaged, the testator should carry a donor card and inform his family. Details should be kept with the will of how to contact HM Inspector of Anatomy (organ donation) and/or the Department of Health (research).

4　Appointment of executors

➤ Individuals

These should be suitable, willing and capable of taking a grant of representation (not a minor, a convicted criminal, or a bankrupt). Private individuals will not charge, but they may need to engage professionals who will bill the estate. It is advisable to appoint a minimum of 2 people.

➤ Trustees

A maximum of 4 may apply for a grant of probate, so avoid appointing more than this.

➤ Banks and trust corporations

For large complex estates, where the extra expense involved is justified, and the slightly more impersonal approach which may be taken is not a concern.

➤ Solicitors

An individual partner may retire or cease to practice, so appoint the firm in the alternative.

a)　Ensure the will appoints partners acting at death, rather than those at the time of the will, *and*

b)　provide for the firm's amalgamation, change of name, or future incorporation, *and*

c)　include a charging clause which authorises the firm to charge, defines the work for which it can charge, and lets it charge a commercial rate.

➤ Public trustee

This is expensive and inconvenient, but available if there is no alternative.

5 **Appointment of guardians** (*ChA 1989*)

➤ A parent with 'parental responsibility' may appoint a guardian for a minor under the age of 18.

◆ An unmarried father does not have 'parental responsibility' unless he is granted it by a court order.

◆ If both parents have 'parental responsibility', then an appointment is effective on the death of both parents; where both appoint different guardians, the responsibilities are shared between them.

➤ An appointment must be written, dated and signed; it can be revoked in the same fashion *even* if the original appointment was by will *s.5(3)*. No codicil is needed to revoke an appointment, but divorce and annulment revoke the appointment unless the appointment shows a contrary intention (*ChA 1989 s.6(3A)* as amended by *LR(S)A 1995 s.4*).

◆ Ensure both parents appoint the same guardian and that the person consents.

◆ Financial provision for the care of the children should be made by appointing the guardian trustee of a fund, with power to spend income and capital for the children's benefit.

6 **Legacies**

➤ These are classified as 'General', 'Demonstrative', 'Specific', 'Pecuniary' or 'Residuary' (see p.121).

7 **Administrative powers**

➤ PRs and trustees have restricted powers under the general law to administer trust funds.

➤ The will may extend powers granted under the general law (see p.121).

8 **Attestation clause**

➤ This is not compulsory, but it is evidence that the will has been properly executed.

Note: a space for the date is left either in the 'Commencement', or in the 'Attestation' clause.

II   Hints on drafting and interpretation

Class closing rules

Unless the will excludes the class closing rules, these will determine how a class gift is construed.

Vested gifts

a) 'To the children of X' - if there are members of the class alive at the time of the testator's death, the class closes then, otherwise it remains open until X dies.

b) 'To S for life, remainder to the children of X' - as in **a**), but the class *may* close from S's death.

Contingent gifts

c) 'To the children of X who attain the age of 21' - if the contingency has been fulfilled, the class closes at X's death, and it includes any children alive at the testator's death who have reached, or who may in the future reach 21. Otherwise the class closes as soon as one of X's children fulfils the contingency.

d) 'To S for life, remainder to the children of X who attain the age of 21' - as in c), but the class *may* close from S's death.

Gifts to individuals within a class: 'to *each* of the children of X' - the class closes on the testator's death.

Early closing: the class in b) and d) may close immediately the prior interest fails, then the gift operates like a) or c) respectively.

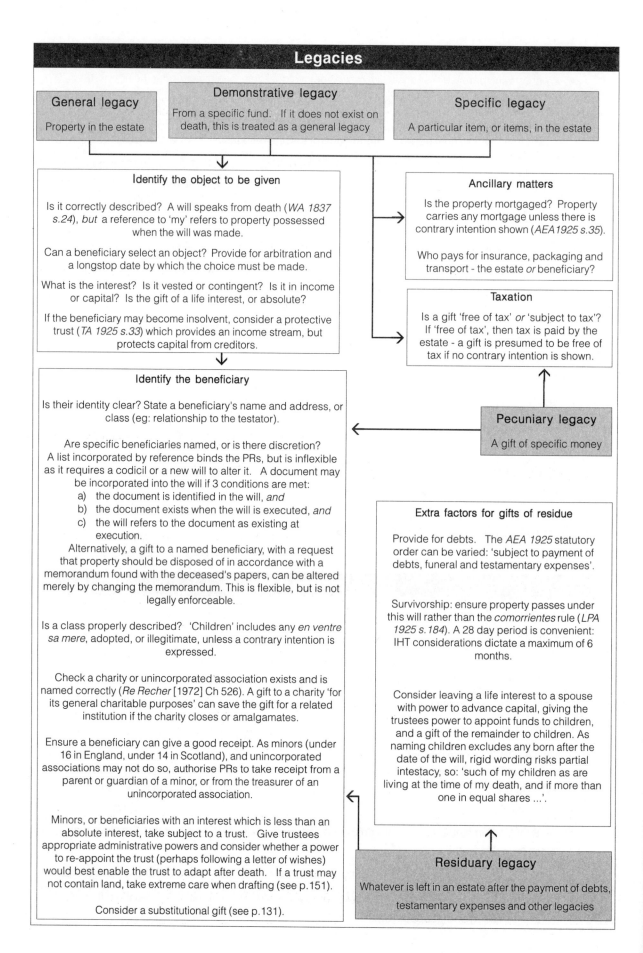

Legacies

General legacy
Property in the estate

Demonstrative legacy
From a specific fund. If it does not exist on death, this is treated as a general legacy

Specific legacy
A particular item, or items, in the estate

Identify the object to be given

Is it correctly described? A will speaks from death (*WA 1837 s.24*), *but* a reference to 'my' refers to property possessed when the will was made.

Can a beneficiary select an object? Provide for arbitration and a longstop date by which the choice must be made.

What is the interest? Is it vested or contingent? Is it in income or capital? Is the gift of a life interest, or absolute?

If the beneficiary may become insolvent, consider a protective trust (*TA 1925 s.33*) which provides an income stream, but protects capital from creditors.

Ancillary matters

Is the property mortgaged? Property carries any mortgage unless there is contrary intention shown (*AEA 1925 s.35*).

Who pays for insurance, packaging and transport - the estate *or* beneficiary?

Taxation

Is a gift 'free of tax' *or* 'subject to tax'? If 'free of tax', then tax is paid by the estate - a gift is presumed to be free of tax if no contrary intention is shown.

Identify the beneficiary

Is their identity clear? State a beneficiary's name and address, or class (eg: relationship to the testator).

Are specific beneficiaries named, or is there discretion? A list incorporated by reference binds the PRs, but is inflexible as it requires a codicil or a new will to alter it. A document may be incorporated into the will if 3 conditions are met:
a) the document is identified in the will, *and*
b) the document exists when the will is executed, *and*
c) the will refers to the document as existing at execution.
Alternatively, a gift to a named beneficiary, with a request that property should be disposed of in accordance with a memorandum found with the deceased's papers, can be altered merely by changing the memorandum. This is flexible, but is not legally enforceable.

Is a class properly described? 'Children' includes any *en ventre sa mere*, adopted, or illegitimate, unless a contrary intention is expressed.

Check a charity or unincorporated association exists and is named correctly (*Re Recher* [1972] Ch 526). A gift to a charity 'for its general charitable purposes' can save the gift for a related institution if the charity closes or amalgamates.

Ensure a beneficiary can give a good receipt. As minors (under 16 in England, under 14 in Scotland), and unincorporated associations may not do so, authorise PRs to take receipt from a parent or guardian of a minor, or from the treasurer of an unincorporated association.

Minors, or beneficiaries with an interest which is less than an absolute interest, take subject to a trust. Give trustees appropriate administrative powers and consider whether a power to re-appoint the trust (perhaps following a letter of wishes) would best enable the trust to adapt after death. If a trust may not contain land, take extreme care when drafting (see p.151).

Consider a substitutional gift (see p.131).

Pecuniary legacy
A gift of specific money

Extra factors for gifts of residue

Provide for debts. The *AEA 1925* statutory order can be varied: 'subject to payment of debts, funeral and testamentary expenses'.

Survivorship: ensure property passes under this will rather than the *comorrientes* rule (*LPA 1925 s.184*). A 28 day period is convenient: IHT considerations dictate a maximum of 6 months.

Consider leaving a life interest to a spouse with power to advance capital, giving the trustees power to appoint funds to children, and a gift of the remainder to children. As naming children excludes any born after the date of the will, rigid wording risks partial intestacy, so: 'such of my children as are living at the time of my death, and if more than one in equal shares ...'.

Residuary legacy
Whatever is left in an estate after the payment of debts, testamentary expenses and other legacies

Powers under the general law	Drafting considerations
Appropriate property to pay a pecuniary legacy ➤ *AEA 1925 s.41*: PRs can appropriate property provided a beneficiary does not suffer, *and* that beneficiary consents	Relieve PRs of the duty to obtain a beneficiary's formal consent
Insurance ➤ *TA 1925 s.19*: power to insure against fire damage for 75% of the value of property. The premium is paid from income alone	Power to insure against all risks, to the full market value on sale Permit PRs to pay a premium from income *or* capital
Receipt ➤ *LPA 1925 s.21*: a married minor can only give receipt for income ➤ *AEA 1925 s.42*: PRs can accept receipt on behalf of minors with an absolute interest from trustees who may be appointed for this purpose	Authorise PRs to accept receipt from a parent, guardian of a minor under 16, to avoid appointing trustees Cater for receipt if a minor's interest is contingent, *or* if a married minor receives capital
Investment ➤ *TIA 1961*: investment powers are very limited, this Act is due to be repealed	Remove the statutory restrictions. Enable trustees to invest as absolute owners (and to buy land)
Land ➤ Until *TLATA 1996* came into force, land was held on a strict settlement under *SLA 1925* unless it is given to a trustee on an 'immediate binding trust for sale'	*TLATA 1996* prevents new strict settlements arising and creates a system of 'trusts of land'. Check pp.150-151 and consider how to achieve the testator's wishes in the light of the changes which the Act makes
Income *TA 1925 s.31*: power to use income for the 'maintenance, education or benefit' of a beneficiary. Trustees must act 'reasonably' and with regard to other sources of maintenance for the beneficiary ➤ At the age of 18, a beneficiary of an absolute or contingent interest is entitled to income ➤ Accumulated income is released if the beneficiary has a life interest in capital, otherwise accumulations and capital are retained until the gift vests absolutely	Give the trustees discretion to make payments as they think fit Postpone a beneficiary's right to receive income, and/or capital, until after the statutory age of 18 Note: the rule against cumulation imposes a long-stop of 21 years after the testator's death, after which the beneficiary must be allowed access to the capital
Capital *TA 1925 s.32*: trustees may use money for a beneficiary's 'advancement or benefit' whether the beneficiary's interest is absolute or contingent ➤ Any payments are subtracted when capital vests absolutely ➤ The holder of a prior life interest must consent in writing ➤ Only half a beneficiary's presumptive or vested interest may be advanced	Increase the capital which trustees can advance Give the trustees discretion to distribute capital without making deductions in respect of prior advancements
Apportionment: complex bureaucratic formulae ➤ *Howe v. Dartmouth* (1802) 7 Ves 137: 'wasting, hazardous and unauthorised' assets, and those which produce no income are sold, so that a life tenant benefits from capital ➤ *Allhusen v. Whittell* (1867) LR 4 Eq 295: debts, administration and tax are apportioned between capital and income ➤ *AA 1870 s.2*: rent and dividends are income arising daily: they are treated as capital before death, and income thereafter	These rules can be expressly excluded to assist the administration of the trust If the will creates a trust of land under *TLATA 1996*, then the rule in *Howe v. Dartmouth* may be automatically excluded (*Re Pitcairn* [1896] 2 Ch 199). However, this will occur if a will trust does not contain land so exclude the rules expressly
Charging ➤ Equity bars PRs and trustees from profiting from their duties	Allow professional PRs to charge a commercial rate for their time
Power to operate business (run by sole trader) ➤ PRs can only run a business to preserve its sale value. They are restricted to using assets the business relied on at the testator's death (*Re Hodson, ex parte Richardson* (1818) 3 Madd 138)	PRs can be permitted to use assets from the general estate to run the business, or it may be left as a specific legacy

C Intestacy

Steps	
1	**Discover the extent of the estate passing on intestacy**
2	**Property passes to the PRs on statutory trusts (*AEA 1925 s.33*)**
3	**Deduct funeral, testamentary and administrative expenses *and* debts**
4	**Set aside a pecuniary legacy fund**
5	**Work out who is entitled to the property (apply the statutory order of entitlement)**
6	**Consider whether the spouse wishes to exercise his/her rights**

Step 1   Discover the extent of the estate passing on intestacy

➤ Only property capable of passing by will can pass on intestacy.

Step 2   Property passes to the PRs on the statutory trusts

➤ Property passes to PRs on the statutory trusts (*AEA 1925 s.47*).

➤ The terms of the trust dictate that the gift is construed as being:

   ◆ to those entitled within a class, in equal shares, *and*

   ◆ to all 'living' persons within the class, including any children *en ventre sa mere, and*

   ◆ on the death of a member of a class who was entitled on the intestate's death, to that beneficiary's issue in equal shares, *and*

   ◆ contingent on the beneficiary marrying *or* reaching the age of 18.

   Note: if a contingency is not met, the failed interest is disregarded, and the distribution of the estate is reassessed as if the failed interest had never existed.

➤ The trustees have:

   ◆ powers of maintenance and advancement given by the *TA 1925 ss.31-32, and*

   ◆ (from 1 January 1997), power to sell. Previously, trustees were under a duty to sell with a power to postpone sale and a direction that the deceased's 'personal chattels' should not be sold without a 'special reason' such as the payment of debts and administration expenses (*AEA 1925 s.33*). When *TLATA* came into force the duty to sell and convert ceased to apply (*TLATA 1996 Schedule 2 para 5*).

Step 3   Deduct funeral, testamentary and administrative expenses

Step 4   Set aside a fund from which to pay pecuniary legacies

Step 5 | **Work out who is entitled to property**

A. The statutory order of entitlement

➤ A surviving spouse takes priority over anyone else. Depending on the size of the estate, the spouse may share an interest with one class of kinsmen (see the chart below); if one class exists those classes further down the line are excluded (*AEA 1925 s.46*).

➤ If there is no spouse, blood kin take in the statutory order:

a) issue, *then*

b) parents, *then*

c) brothers and sisters of whole blood, *then*

d) brothers and sisters of half-blood, *then*

e) grandparents, *then*

f) uncles and aunts of whole blood, *then*

g) uncles and aunts of half-blood, *then*

h) *bona vacantia* goes to the Crown, the Duchy of Lancaster, or the Duke of Cornwall; there is discretion to provide for those an intestate 'might reasonably have been expected to make provision' for,

➤ For deaths on or after 1 January 1996, the spouse is treated as not having survived the intestate if he or she dies within a period of 28 days beginning on the day of the intestate's death (*AEA 1925 s.46(2A)* as inserted by the *LR(S)A 1995 s.1*).

➤ When *FLA 1996 s.21* comes into force (on a day to be appointed by the Lord Chancellor, expected to be on or after 1 January 1999), if a person dies intestate while a separation order is in force and the parties are still actually separated, any property subject to the intestacy rules passes as if the survivor had predeceased the intestate.

	Size of estate	Spouse's entitlement	Others' entitlement
Spouse alone		Everything passing on intestacy	Nothing
Spouse and issue	Estate under £125,000	Everything (including personal chattels)	
	Estate over £125,000	Personal chattels absolutely £125,000 statutory legacy* Life interest in half the residue	On the statutory trusts: ➤ half the residue, *and* ➤ interest in remainder of residue
Spouse, no issue[†] but other kin	Estate under £200,000	Everything (including chattels)	Nothing
	Estate over £200,000	Personal chattels absolutely £200,000 statutory legacy* Half the residue absolutely	On the statutory trusts: ➤ half the residue
No spouse			Everything on statutory trusts

[†] Issue: children and other descendants including adopted, legitimated and legitimised children

* Statutory legacy:
 a) this is paid free of tax and costs. It also includes interest from the date of death until the legacy is paid to the spouse
 b) the value of any personal chattels is not taken into account in establishing whether the estate is worth £125,000 or £200,000

Step 6   Consider whether the spouse wishes to exercise his/her rights

1   **A spouse's right to redeem a life interest**

➤ The spouse may choose to convert the life interest into a lump sum.

➤ The spouse must notify the PRs within 1 year of the date when the grant of representation is issued.

    a) All those entitled to the remainder may, if they are *sui juris*, agree the value of the life interest in writing with the spouse. Otherwise the sum is calculated according to *IS(ICO) 1977*.

    b) The entitlement of other beneficiaries is recalculated.

    c) IHT is recalculated and the spouse bears any resulting charge.

2   **A spouse's right to appropriate the matrimonial home (*IEA 1952 s.5* and *Schedule II*)**

➤ The spouse can demand that PRs transfer the house to him/her as part of the inheritance to which he/she is absolutely entitled.

Steps

 The spouse must notify the PRs within 1 year of the date when the grant of representation is issued.

 The house is valued at the time of appropriation, not death. If its value exceeds the spouse's entitlement, he or she can pay the difference to the estate as 'equality money'.

NB: if the spouse is the sole surviving PR, then the President of the Family Division must be notified of an intention to invoke either of these statutory rights. This is done by lodging the notification together with the original grant at the Probate Registry so that this intention can be recorded on the grant.

D   Probate and administration

I   Overview of solicitor's role

II   Applying for a grant of representation (outline)

I   Overview of a solicitor's role

A solicitor's duty to PRs

1   Advise on succession and revenue law.

2   Prove the testator's will.

3   Administer the estate.

4   Prepare estate accounts.

How to carry out this duty

1   Take instructions directly from the PR.

2   Obtain the deceased's will.

3   Attend to the deceased's wishes as regards cremation, organ donation, etc, in consultation with the PRs.

4   Secure property (ie: check an empty house is locked and insured, locate and safeguard documents of title to assets).

5   Attend to financial arrangements (ie: loans to support a family pending grant of probate or during the administration of the estate).

6   Obtain the death certificate.

7   Compile a list of the deceased's assets and liabilities. This list should be continuously updated during the administration of the estate, to show their state at any given time and what steps have been or are being taken with regard to them.

8   Discover details of all the beneficiaries (ie: ages and addresses).

9   Protect PRs from personal liability against unknown or missing creditors or beneficiaries.

10   Prepare the oath and the Inland Revenue account.

11   Obtain a grant and make office copies of the grant.

12   Collect and realise assets.

13   Pay debts.

14   Pay legacies.

15   Ascertain and distribute residue.

II   Applying for a grant of representation (outline)

➤   A PR's duty is (*AEA 1925 s.25* as amended *AEA 1971 s.9)*: 'to collect and get in the real and personal estate of the deceased and administer it according to law'.

➤   A grant of representation is necessary to administer the rest of the deceased's estate as the executor(s) will need to be able to prove that he/they are entitled to sell or dispose of assets.

➤   The procedure for '**Swearing the oath**' and '**Applying for the grant**' is as follows:

Steps	
1	**Decide what sort of grant is appropriate.**
2	**Ascertain who is entitled to take a grant.**
3	**Choose and complete the correct form of Inland Revenue account.**
4	**Fill in the oath.**

Swearing the oath

➤   Executors complete the jurat before an independent solicitor or commissioner for oaths (*not* an executor).

➤   Executors and a solicitor, or a commissioner for oaths, initial the will and any codicils.

Applying for the grant

➤   Send to the Probate Registry (using a District Registry may minimise publicity):

◆   the oath (*NCPR r.8), and*

◆   the will, *and*

◆   the court fee, *and*

●   The basic fee is calculated by reference to the value of the net estate. Add to this 25p for each office copy of the grant of representation requested. Work out how many copies to ask for by reference to the number of assets for which the grant will need to be produced).

◆   a fee sheet showing how the fee was calculated *and*

◆   the Inland Revenue account (unless the estate is 'excepted').

➤   The Probate Registry usually issues the grant in 5 to 15 days.

➤   Where an estate is 'excepted', the Inland Revenue has 35 days after the grant is issued in which to demand the production of an account.

◆   If the PRs discover other assets, making it necessary to submit an account, then they must tender an account to the Inland Revenue within 6 months of making this discovery.

E Problems which can arise

There are five areas in which difficulties are likely to arise (this list is not exhaustive!).

- I Obtaining a grant and interpreting the will
- II A claim under the *I(PFD)A 1975*
- III Breach of duty by a PR
- IV A PR's death
- V Failure of a gift

I Obtaining a grant and interpreting the will

---

1 Someone objects to the issue of a grant (*NCPR r.44*)

➤ A caveat is lodged with the Probate Registry to prevent the issue of a grant.

2 A person entitled to take an oath fails to do so *or* fails to renounce.

Citation to take or refuse a grant (*NCPR r.47*)

➤ When an executor has intermeddled, but not taken steps to acquire a grant within 6 months of the testator's death, then unless the executor can show good reason for his inaction, the citator can apply to court for an order allowing letters of administration to be issued under *NCPR r.20*.

➤ An applicant wishes to 'clear off' those with prior entitlement to a grant who have not applied for a grant.

3 A person entitled to a grant wishes to prove his right when another contests it.

Citation to propound a will (*NCPR r.48*)

➤ To compel a named person with an interest in the estate (beneficiary or executor) to prove a will if they can.

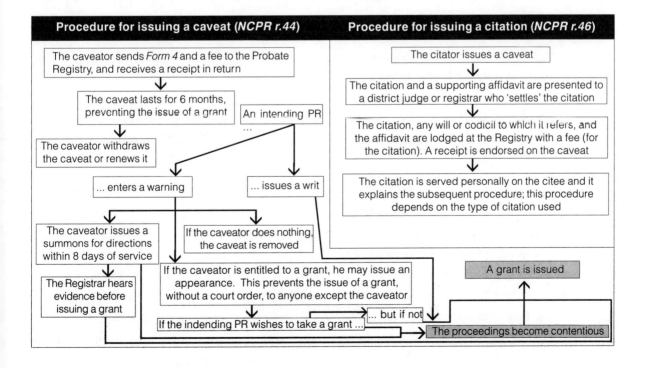

4   The Registrar requires additional evidence before issuing the grant

Affidavit of due execution (*NCPR r.16*)

➤ This is necessary if *either* an attestation clause is not present *or* is corrupt, *or* there is some doubt about the execution due to uncertainty about the testator's capacity or intention.

➤ The affidavit is sworn by witnesses to the execution of the will.

Affidavit as to knowledge and approval (*NCPR rr.13,16*)

➤ This is necessary if the testator was blind, *or* illiterate, *or* frail, *or* there were suspicious circumstances.

➤ The affidavit is sworn by a witness, *or* anyone who went through the will with the testator and can give first-hand factual evidence.

Affidavit of plight and condition (*NCPR rr.14,16*)

➤ This is necessary if there are *either* alterations to the will after its execution, *or* a mark suggesting that other documents were originally attached to the will, *or* signs of an attempt to revoke the will.

➤ An affidavit is sworn by anyone with relevant first-hand factual knowledge.

Lost will (*NCPR rr.15,16*)

➤ Such a will is presumed to be destroyed with the intention to revoke it.

➤ If this presumption can be rebutted, or evidence can be produced to show *either* that the will existed after the testator's death *or* that a copy (or reconstruction) of it is accurate, then the Registrar may grant probate on the production of an affidavit testifying to these facts.

5   The validity of a codicil is doubted

➤ The executor(s) should commence a probate action under *NCPR r.45*.

6   The interpretation of the will is uncertain

➤ PRs may seek clarification from the court by issuing a 'construction summons' - usually this is done through an application to the Chancery Division of the High Court, but the County Court has jurisdiction for actions with a value up to £30,000.

◆ The admission of extrinsic evidence is permitted if the will is a) meaningless, *or* b) *prima facie* ambiguous, *or* c) ambiguous in the light of evidence (other than evidence of the testator's intention) (*AJA 1982 s.21*).

◆ The court can rectify the will so as to carry out the testator's intentions, if the will's failure to do this is due to a clerical error *or* the draftsman's failure to understand the testator's instructions (*AJA 1982 s.20, NCPR r.55, Re Segelman (deceased)* [1995] 3 All ER 676, ChD).

◆ The court can make an order authorising PRs to act as instructed by a barrister who has been practicing for at least 10 years. The barrister can resolve matters of construction which are *not* disputed. This absolves the PRs of liability and, since the court does not hear any argument, saves the estate expense (*AJA 1985 s.48*).

II   A claim under the *I(PFD)A 1975*

➤ The *I(PFD)A 1975* allows close family, dependants and co-habitees to seek provision from an estate when none is made under a will or the intestacy rules.

➤ Unless the value of the claim is clearly within the County Court's jurisdiction (ie: under £30,000), an application is made to either the Chancery Division, or the Family Division of the High Court.

➤ The High Court procedure is governed by *RSC Ord.99* and in the County Court by *CCR Ord r.48*.

➤ The costs of pursuing litigation are considerable, and the defence will often send a 'Calderbank' letter to the plaintiff so that the plaintiff is liable for costs incurred after the letter (see p.247).

III   Breach of duty by a PR

➤   The standard of duty is that of 'utmost good faith', except for professional trustees when it is higher.

   ◆   Liability is personal and unlimited (*Kennewell v. Dye* [1949] Ch 517).

   ◆   A breach of duty occurs if a PR fails to preserve the value of the estate's assets, *or* to distribute the estate as required by the will and statute, *or* uses the estate's assets for the wrong purposes (eg: self-enrichment).

➤   Likely claimants include the following.

   ◆   **Missing beneficiaries**

      ●   The PRs should advertise to locate them, but if this fails they should seek a 'Benjamin' order from the court (*Re Benjamin* [1902] 1 Ch 723). This shields the PRs from liability, but it does not prejudice the claimant's (or his PRs') right to pursue assets from other beneficiaries of the estate.

   ◆   **Creditors who are unknown to the PRs**

      ●   The PRs should protect themselves by:

         a)   advertising in the *London Gazette,* and in a local newspaper in the vicinity of land the deceased owned, as well as anywhere else which seems appropriate (*TA 1925 s.27*). Claimants have 2 months to answer advertisments; distribution should not begin until this period ends.

         b)   searching HM Land Registry, the Central Land Charges Department and conducting local land searches to reveal any charges subsisting over land in the estate.

      ●   Creditors may be able to pursue assets into the hands of the beneficiaries with a tracing action in equity.

   ◆   **Claimants under the *I(PFD)A 1975***

      ●   A PR should not distribute the estate until 6 months after the grant of representation has been issued, thereafter there will be no personal liability under the *I(PFD)A 1975*, although the estate will be subject to any order which the court makes under its discretion to waive the limitation period.

   ◆   **Creditors who are unpaid after an 'unreasonable' delay**

      ●   PRs should pay debts from before the deceased's death with 'due diligence' (*Re Tankard* [1942] Ch. 69).

      ●   PRs owe this duty to beneficiaries *and* creditors alike; any attempt to alter this duty by will is void.

   ◆   **Beneficiaries when debts are paid from the wrong property**

      ●   Where the interests of some beneficiaries are prejudiced, the doctrine of marshalling applies, so that their loss is made good from the rest of the estate.

   ◆   **Landlords**

      ●   Leaseholds (except statutory tenancies under the *Rent Acts*) vest in a PR in his 'representative' capacity, and *may* do so in a 'personal capacity' as a result of actual or constructive entry into possession (see table overleaf).

Liability	Release for PRs
In 'representative' capacity (*Re Bowes* (1887) 37 Ch D128)	
Under privity of estate: rent and breaches of covenant prior to death (to the extent that property is in their hands)	On the assignment, expiry or surrender of the lease
Under privity of contract: where the deceased was the original lessee Note: abolished for new leases granted on or after 1 January 1996 (*LT(C)A 1995 ss.1-5*)	a) PRs satisfy existing claims arising under the lease, *and* b) set aside money against any fixed or ascertained sums which the deceased had agreed in respect of the property, *and* c) assign it to a beneficiary or a purchaser (*TA 1925 s.26*)
In 'personal capacity' (*Re Owers, Public Trustee v. Death* [1941] Ch 389)	
Liable as assignees of the deceased's interest for: ➤ covenants: liability is unlimited for any breach ➤ rent: liability is limited to rent which the PRs actually receive, or would have done so if they had acted with diligence	On the assignment, expiry or surrender of the lease, PRs can seek to protect themselves in one of 3 ways: a) taking out insurance, *or* b) seeking an indemnity from the beneficiaries, *or* c) creating an indemnity fund which is distributed to the beneficiaries once the liability has ended
Note: a landlord's remedies against beneficiaries are unaffected by any of this	

Relieving PRs of liability
Either a) by the court if the PR 'acted honestly and reasonably and ought fairly to be excused' (*TA 1925 s.61*),
or b) in the form of an indemnity from a beneficiary's interest in the estate when the court is shown the written consent of a beneficiary who has been fully informed of the breach (*TA 1925 ss.62,68(1)*),
or c) where the beneficiary (being *sui juris*) who has been fully informed of the breach of trust (known as '*devestavit*') consents to it (*Walker v. Symonds* (1818) 3 Swan 1 at 64).

IV   A PR's death

➤ If a PR dies before a grant is issued, then his rights to the grant die with him.

➤ After a grant has been issued, one PR can administer the estate if the other PRs die: this is known as the chain of administration (*Flanders v. Clarke* (1747) 3 Atk 509).

➤ On the death of a sole surviving PR, the PR's executor steps into the deceased PR's shoes and shoulders all burdens and powers to administer the first testator's estate as well as the PR's estate (*AEA 1925 s.7*).

➤ Where a grant of probate or letters of administration are made to a deceased PR, and the chain of representation is broken, a grant *de bonis non administratis* is sought from the court in favour of whomever is entitled under *NCPR r.20* or *NCPR r.22* (Blackstone, *Commentaries,* (14th ed) *506*).

V   Failure of a gift

A gift can fail through **Ademption, Lapse,** or **Abatement**.

1   Ademption

➤ As a will 'speaks from death', property given in the will may not still form part of the estate on death. If the substance of the gift, rather than its form has altered, then the gift fails.

2   Lapse

a) joint tenants: if a tenant predeceases the testator, the remaining tenant(s) take the gift in full - the gift does not lapse unless they all predecease the testator.

b) tenants in common: if one tenant predeceases the testator, the gift as a whole lapses.

c) class: remains valid *unless* all members of a class have predeceased the testator.

d) witness: this lapses *unless* the witness's signature merely supplemented those of 2 other valid witnesses.

e) divorced spouse: this lapses unless the will shows contrary intention (*WA 1837 s.18A*).

3   Abatement

➤ Where the estate is not able to meet all the legacies, and there is no contrary intention in the will, general legacies abate in equal proportions (*Re Whitehead* [1913] 2 Ch 56).

➤ Demonstrative legacies do not abate with general legacies, unless the fund out of which the demonstrative legacies are to be paid is insufficient to pay them all (*Roberts v. Pocock* (1748) 4 Ves 150).

➤ If the estate is unable to meet all its debts, specific legacies abate amongst themselves, otherwise they do not abate with general legacies.

Substitutional gifts

➤ A gift which adeems *or* lapses falls into residue, unless the will contains a valid gift over in favour of another beneficiary. The *WA 1837 s.33* implies a substitutional gift to the testator's lineal descendants where the original gift was to the testator's children or remoter issue, and the intended donee predeceases the testator.

◆ There is no clear authority whether *WA 1837 s.33*:

a) saves a contingent gift if the original donee has not satisfied the contingency before dying, *or*

b) allows issue to take on satisfying the contingency specified for the original donee, *or*

c) applies to class gifts 'to children living at my death'.

◆ A will should therefore always provide an express substitutional provision in case the named beneficiary predeceases the testator - this avoids uncertainty and ensures that the testator's wishes are followed.

Conveyancing

This chapter examines:

HM Land Registry plan colouring

➤ Red edging round a title.

➤ Green edging round land removed from the title.

➤ Blue shading over land subject to rights of way.

➤ Brown shading over land over which the registered title enjoys right of way.

➤ Green shading over areas of land within the title which do not form part of it.

It is not compulsory to adopt this scheme, but it is good practice to do so.

A   A chronological conveyance

The conveyance is divided into nine separate steps, outlined below.

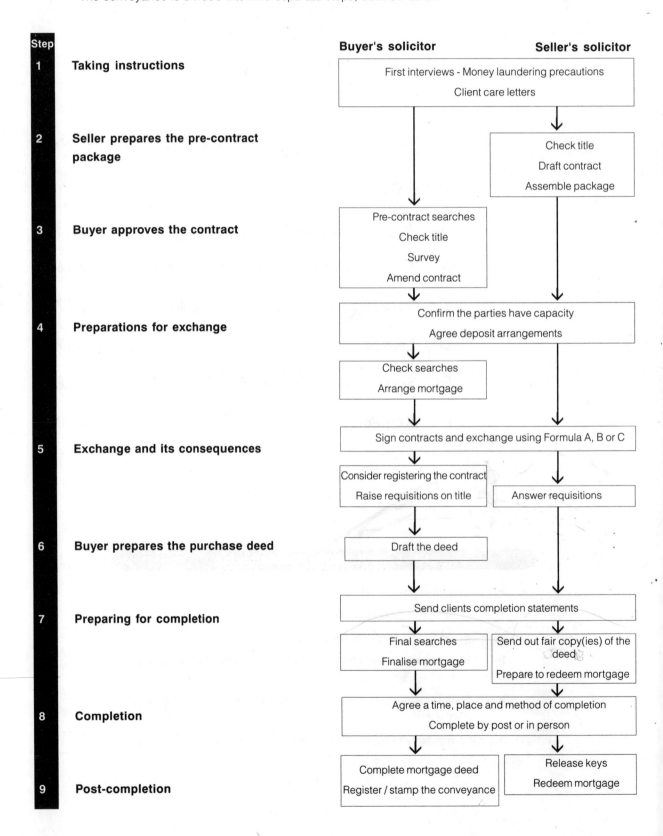

Step		Buyer's solicitor	Seller's solicitor
1	**Taking instructions**	First interviews - Money laundering precautions Client care letters	
2	**Seller prepares the pre-contract package**		Check title Draft contract Assemble package
3	**Buyer approves the contract**	Pre-contract searches Check title Survey Amend contract	
4	**Preparations for exchange**	Confirm the parties have capacity Agree deposit arrangements	
		Check searches Arrange mortgage	
5	**Exchange and its consequences**	Sign contracts and exchange using Formula A, B or C	
		Consider registering the contract Raise requisitions on title	Answer requisitions
6	**Buyer prepares the purchase deed**	Draft the deed	
7	**Preparing for completion**	Send clients completion statements	
		Final searches Finalise mortgage	Send out fair copy(ies) of the deed Prepare to redeem mortgage
8	**Completion**	Agree a time, place and method of completion Complete by post or in person	
9	**Post-completion**	Complete mortgage deed Register / stamp the conveyance	Release keys Redeem mortgage

Step 1	**Taking instructions**

I   First interviews

II   Post-interview formalities

I   First interviews

With the seller

Is there a conflict of interest? There are special provisions regarding this in *SPR r.6* (see p.3).

[handwritten: r.392 Professional Conduct]

> Seller's name and address: . . . .
> Seller's home and business telephone: . . . .
> Buyer's name and address: . . . .
> Estate agent's name and address: . . . .
> Buyer's solicitor's name, address, telephone, fax, DX: . . . .
> Property address: . . . .

Finance

➤ *Proceeds*:

   ◆ will these cover the costs of sale, pay off a mortgage and/or fund another purchase?

   ◆ where should money be paid (bank details, account number)?   If the solicitor is to hold any client money comply with the *Money Laundering Regulations 1993*.

➤ *Deposit*:

   ◆ has a preliminary deposit been paid? (Take a copy of the receipt for the file.)

   ◆ has a deposit been agreed?

➤ *Taxation*: will CGT be payable?

➤ *Mortgage*: will this need to be redeemed? (Note the name(s) and address(es) of lender(s).)

➤ *Solicitor's fees*: explain what these will be (see p.4).

Property

➤ *Tenure*: freehold or leasehold? Will there be a full or limited title guarantee?

➤ *Deeds*: if a client does not hold them, obtain the address of whoever does (eg: building society).

➤ *Contents*: ask the client to fill out a fixtures and fittings form listing the property's contents.

➤ *Property*: are restrictive covenants breached? Have planning and use regulations been obeyed?

➤ *Residents:* are there any third parties with rights to occupy the property?

Transaction

➤ *Completion*: when convenient, synchronisation? (ie: Is the seller co-ordinating a purchase?)

➤ *Terms*: have any particular terms been agreed?

With the buyer

As for the seller plus -

Finance

➤ *Money*: can the client afford the acquisition, including the associated costs (eg: legal fees - estimate the cost of the searches, etc)?

➤ *Deposit*: will bridging finance be needed while an existing property is sold?

➤ *Mortgage*: is this already arranged, or is advice needed?

◆ Do not unwittingly give advice qualifying as DIB without authorisation (see p.19).

◆ Comply with *SIRC 1990* if your firm has a relationship with a mortgage provider (see p.2).

Property

➤ *Intended use of the property*?

➤ *Survey*: the *caveat emptor* principle applies; the buyer chooses what sort of survey to have.

➤ *Location*: are plans, or special searches necessary?

➤ *Insurance:* how will the buyer protect himself from exchange to completion (see p.140)?

Transaction

➤ *Who is buying the property*: is advice about co-ownership needed?

◆ For a joint tenancy the 'four unities' must be present - of 'interest', 'title', 'time' and 'possession'. If a joint tenant dies, the property passes to the survivor(s).

◆ A tenancy in common arises if the 'four unities' are not present, if severance is implied or stated in a conveyance or transfer *or* under an equitable presumption. Tenants' share(s) pass by will or under the intestacy rules.

➤ *Client's present property*: will it be sold, or will notice have to be given to a landlord?

II   Post-interview formalities

➤ Write the client a *r.15* letter (see p.4) summarising what was agreed at the meeting, what will happen next, what if anything the client needs to do, and your likely fees.

◆ Ask the seller to fill in a Property Information Form which should ideally have been supplied at the interview, but may otherwise be enclosed with this letter.

➤ Fill out an attendance note.

➤ Write to the other party, explaining who you are acting for, and how you can be contacted.

◆ Explain whether you intend to use the *Law Society's Standard Terms and Conditions* and whether you wish to follow the *Law Society's Protocol*.

◆ The *Protocol* should only be used if the other party is represented by a solicitor or a licenced conveyancer (see p.20).

➤ Write to the estate agents to inform them you have been instructed and to ask for a copy of their particulars. (These provide information about the property which it is useful to have on file.)

Step 2   **Seller prepares the pre-contract package**

> I   Check details of the seller's title
>
> II   Draft the contract
>
> III   Assemble the pre-contract package

I   Check details of the seller's title

➤ Find and trace the root of title (see pp.142 -144).

Unregistered land	Registered land
Obtain title deeds ◆ If a mortgagee holds the deeds as security, he will usually release them in return for an undertaking from the solicitor that he will be paid first out of any proceeds of sale	Obtain office copy entries of the Register

II   Draft the contract

➤ All contracts take a similar form, and will generally include three sections:

a) parties to the sale.

b) conditions of the sale.

c) memorandum of agreement.

➤ For the sake of convenience, the *Law Society* has produced *Standard Terms and Conditions*. These provide the model around which the following guide is based.

➤ When drafting a contract there are three layers of terms.

◆ The first layer is the open contract rules: these are terms which common law implies into contracts in the absence of any contrary intention between the parties.

◆ The second layer is the 'Standard Terms and Conditions' (*StC*): these form the backbone of the *Law Society's Standard Terms and Conditions,* and are found in small print on the inside pages of the Law Society's contract.

◆ The third layer is the 'Special Conditions' (*SpC*): these override the *Standard Terms and Conditions,* and are found on the back of the Law Society's contract.

➤   The solicitor should:

   a) be aware of the open contract rules, *and*

   b) understand the effect of each *Standard Term and Condition, and*

   c) if a client's needs have not been catered for, he should draft a *Special Condition.*

Complete the *Standard Terms and Conditions*

Agreement date	Leave this blank on the draft; fill it in on the engrossed contract on exchange

Seller	Seller's full name and address

Buyer	Buyer's full name and address

Property
 	
Freehold /
Leasehold
	Delete 'Freehold' or 'Leasehold' as applicable
	
	Plan
	
	The contract should state whether a plan is:
	
	   a) 'for identification purposes only' - the verbal description of the property prevails, *or*
	
	   b) 'as more particularly delineated on the plan'. The plan prevails if doubt arises
	
	A scale of 1:1250 is sufficient, except for flats and units which need a smaller scale
	
	Do not rely on the Land Registry plan - it is only for 'general purposes of identification' (*LRR r.278*)
	
	The seller is not usually obliged to make a statutory declaration (*StC 4.3.1*), but where the physical extent of the property is uncertain the buyer should insist that he does so
	
	The plan is usually paid for by:
	
	   a) the seller if it is reasonable of the buyer to require one (*StC 4.3.2*), *or*
	
	   b) the buyer in other circumstances

Root of title/ **Title number**	*Unregistered land*: describe the root of title eg: 'the conveyance dated . . . between . . . (1) and . . . (2)' *Registered land*: the title number on the Property Register

Incumbrances
on the property
	The seller should disclose:
	
	   a) latent defects affecting the title to the property, *and*
	
	   b) anything the seller does, or should, know about (*StC 3.2.2.1(c)*), *and*
	
	   c) overriding interests in the property held by a third party, *and*
	
	   d) the existence of any occupiers
	
	The seller should disclose fully, as *SpC 2* prevents the buyer raising questions about incumbrances at a later date, provided they have been disclosed in the contract
	
	The seller need *not* disclose:
	
	   a) his mortgage (*StC 3.1.2(d)* obliges the seller to remove this before the sale), *or*
	
	   b) physical defects apparent on inspection (*StC 3.1.2(b)* puts the buyer on notice of these)
	
	Note that the buyer accepts the property in the physical state it is in on exchange (*StC 3.2.1*)

Title guarantee
 	
(full / limited)
	Delete as appropriate and/or qualify by a *SpC* if appropriate. If this is left blank, the seller gives full title guarantee (*StC 4.5.2*)
	
	The *LP(MP)A 1994* implies covenants into a contract governing the disposition of land (whether or not for valuable consideration). The covenants affirm that in the purchase deed the disposer:
	
	    1 has the right to dispose of the property (*s.2(1)*), *and*
	
	    2 will at his own cost give the title he purports to give (ie: title which is sufficient to satisfy the Chief Land Registrar) (*s.2(2)*), *and*
	
	  a) a beneficial freeholder may give a **full title guarantee**
	
	    3 that the title is free of all charges and incumbrances and third party rights (*s.3(1)*)
	
	  b) a trustee, fiduciary, PR or mortgagee (*s.12*) will give a **limited title guarantee**
	
	    4 that no right or charge over the property has been granted to a third party since the last disposition for value (*s.3(3)*)
	
	  c) a leaseholder (*s.4*) (in addition to 1-3, or 1,2 & 4) covenants that at the time of the disposition:
	
	    5 there is no breach of the tenant's obligations and nothing to render the lease liable to forfeiture, *and*
	
	    6 the lease is valid and subsisting
	
	  d) a mortgagor covenants to perform all enforceable obligations under a rentcharge or lease (*s.5*)
	
	Note that these covenants may be modified by deleting *SpC 3* and drafting an appropriate *SpC*

Completion date	Under the open contract rules, this is in a 'reasonable time' *StC 6.1.1* specifies that completion will occur 20 working days after the contract date and that time is not of the essence unless a notice to complete is served If another date is envisaged fill it in here
Contract rate	This is the rate of interest at which compensation is paid for delayed completion (*StC 7.3.2*) The rate is 'The Law Society's interest rate from time to time in force' (*StC 1.1.(g)*); this rate is currently 4% above Barclays base rate
Purchase price	Fill this in as agreed
Deposit	This is 10% of the purchase price (*StC 2.2.1*) If the sum agreed differs, then fill in the agreed value here If the deposit is held as 'agent' for the seller (rather than stakeholder), then draft a *Special Condition* to this effect; this may, for example, happen where the seller is buying another property and wishes to use the deposit monies for the purchase
Amount for chattels	Fill this in as agreed (details are found on the *Fixtures, Fittings and Contents Form*), or delete *SpC 4*
Balance	Add together the 'Purchase price' and the 'Amount of chattels', then subtract the 'Deposit' Stamp duty may be payable on the sale if the consideration exceeds £60,000; the value of chattels is disregarded in working out how much (if any) stamp duty is payable

Consider drafting *Special Conditions*:

Vacant possession	Delete one of the alternative versions of *SpC 5* If the property is subject to leases or tenancies, then insert the details here
Liability on covenants	*StC 4.5.4* makes the buyer indemnify the seller against all future breaches of covenants. The buyer may seek a *SpC* that '*StC 4.5.4* shall not apply' The buyer's solicitor may try to include a *SpC* under which the seller indemnifies the buyer for any past breaches, *or* any which are current on the day of completion

Insurance	Common law passes risk to the buyer on exchange unless loss is due to the seller's lack of care
	
	StC 5.1.1 places risk with the seller until completion. Unfortunately, under this *StC*:
	
	  a) the seller is under no obligation to insure the property during this time (*StC 5.1.3*), *and*
	
	  b) the buyer may rescind if damage prevents the seller completing with the property in substantially the same state as on exchange (*StC 5.1.2(a)*)
	
	There are various possible solutions via *Special Conditions* to the lack of certainty this creates:
	
	  a) oblige the seller to insure to completion, ensure that the terms of the policy protect the buyer's interest in the property (and that the buyer receives written notice that his interest is noted on the policy)
	
	  b) cover the property under a block policy maintained by the solicitor
	
	  c) take out a special policy (this is expensive and may lead to 'double insurance' and disputes between insurance companies over liability)
	
	  d) seek agreement from a buyer or potential lender (eg: building society) to cover the risk
	
	  Note: lenders often prefer it if the buyer to whom they will lend the purchase price takes the risk rather than leaving it up to the seller

Occupation by the buyer prior to completion	*StC 5.2* sets out terms under which, with the seller's consent, the buyer may occupy the property prior to completion. If these terms are inappropriate, an alternative *SpC* should be drafted
Void conditions	Conditions will be void that: ➤ oblige a trustee to obtain consent from beneficiaries (*LPA s.42(1)*) ➤ restrict the buyer's choice of solicitor (*LPA s.48*) - this is also a breach of *SPR r.1* ➤ require the buyer to pay for the stamping of improperly stamped documents - this is the seller's responsibility (*SA 1891 s.117*)

Draft any other releases or documents which are necessary to accompany the contract.

➤ If a third party is in occupation, he or she should *either* be joined to the contract, *or* should sign a release:

'In consideration of the buyer entering this contract I, [..................], agree:

  a) to the sale of the property under this contract,

  b) that I will not register any rights over the property, whether under the *MHA 1983/FLA 1996* or otherwise, and I will ensure that any registrations made by me are removed before completion.'

III   Assemble the pre-contract package

Unregistered land	Registered land
Certified copies of documents which must be included in the title:	*LRA s.110:*
	a) Copy of Register entries
➤ Evidence of devolutions on death - death certificates, assents, grants of representation	b) Copy of file plan
➤ Evidence of any change of name of an estate owner - marriage certificate, deed poll, etc	➤ Evidence or an abstract if registered title is inconclusive on anything
➤ Discharges of any legal mortgages	➤ A copy or an abstract of any document mentioned on the Register
➤ Pre-root documents specifying restrictive covenants	*StC 4.2.1*
➤ Memoranda endorsed on documents of title, eg: sale of part, assent to a beneficiary, severance of a joint tenancy	➤ Requires Office Copy Entries (OCEs) rather than copies of the Registr entries
➤ Power of attorney (under which a document within the chain of title has been executed)	➤ a) and b) may *not* be excluded by a *Special Condition*

➤ **TWO** copies of the draft contract

➤ Evidence of any discharged equitable interests

➤ Details of equitable interests which will be overreached in the transaction

➤ Expired leases if the tenant is still in possession

➤ Other documents referred to in the contract, or in the seller's possession which may prove helpful to the buyer:

   ◆ copies of any relevant planning permission

   ◆ NHBC certificates if the property is a new building

   ◆ copies of any relevant insurance certificates or guarantees (eg: relating to roofing or dampcourse work)

   ◆ any necessary consents

   ◆ any plans

   ◆ copies of any searches which the seller has made (these should not be relied on by the buyer, but they can provide the buyer with comfort if a Bankruptcy search has been done against the seller (*Form K16*) showing the seller is not subject to insolvency proceedings)

Step 3	Buyer approves the contract

    I   Make pre-contract searches

    II   Check the title documents supplied

    III   Investigate each document

    IV   Check the terms of any restrictive covenants

    V   Ensure there are no planning difficulties

    VI   Commission a survey

    VII   Check and amend the contract

I   Make pre-contract searches

➤ For the searches necessary at this stage, see p.169.

II   Check the title documents supplied

➤ The documents required are set out on pp.163-168.

➤ Questions to ask:

- is the root as described in the contract?
- is the chain unbroken since the root?
- are there any defects in title adverse to the buyer's interest?

III   Investigate each document

A. Registered land

➤ Check that the OCEs are correct and that priority periods have not, or are not about to, expire.

➤ Check that any plans are accurate.

B. Unregistered land

➤ Start at the root, make written notes of omissions in the list of documents, and of errors in the documents.

- ◆ Check

  - ● **Compulsory registration:** do an Index Map search to ensure there has been no conveyance or sale since the area became subject to compulsory registration. Any unregistered conveyance on sale since the area became subject to registration is likely to be void at law (*LRA s.123* as amended *LRA 1997 s.1*).

  - ● **Searches:** were these done against *all* previous owners under the correct names for the correct periods? Will completion be within the priority period? (If the answer to either of these question is 'no', the buyer should do a fresh search.)

  - ● **Incumbrances:** what are they? Is there an unbroken chain of indemnity for covenants?

  - ● **Easements and rights:** do they follow the title? Are there additions or subtractions?

  - ● **Description of property:** is this accurate? Are plans provided where necessary?

  - ● **Dates:** do these form an unbroken chain from the root?

  - ● **Parties:** check the identities of the parties to conveyances (eg: their names may have altered due to marriage or divorce; if so ask for certificates to verify this).

  - ● **Receipt clause in a conveyance:** this is evidence that a seller's lien has been extinguished.

  - ● **Acknowledgement for the production of earlier deeds:** if needed, are the deeds present?

  - ● **Execution:** was this done by the correct parties in the correct form (ie: if positive covenants are present, did the buyers and the sellers both sign the conveyance)? Were any assents by deed (this imports consideration without which an assentee is not bound)?

  - ● **Power of attorney:** if one was used, was it valid? A copy of the grant should be supplied.

  - ● **Endorsements on deeds:** if needed, are these present? Are there adverse memoranda?

➤ Examine documents included in the abstract of title.

- ◆ Deeds must be in the correct form:

  BEFORE 31 JULY 1990

  - ● by an individual: signed, sealed, delivered as a deed. The seal must precede the signature. Delivery depends on intention; this is inferred from the signature and seal (*LPA s.73*).

  - ● by a company: sealed before a company secretary and a director (*LPA s.74*).

  AFTER 31 JULY 1990

  Clear on its face that it is a deed and delivered as a deed (*LP(MP)A 1989 s.1(2)(2)*):

  - ● by an individual: signed, signature witnessed and attested, or signed in his presence and at his command before 2 witnesses who attest the deed (*LP(MP)A 1989 s.1(2)(3)*).

  - ● by a company: execution by affixing a seal, *or* by a director and a company secretary's signature if the document is expressed to be executed by the company. Execution and delivery are presumed if it is clear on its face that the document was intended as a deed (*CA s.36A(5)*).

- ◆ There should be a 'Particulars Delivered' (PD) stamp from the Inland Revenue on:

  a) freehold conveyances, *and*

  b) grants or assignments of leases of 7 years or more (*FA 1931 s.28*).

- ◆ A conveyance should be stamped as evidence that duty has been paid at the correct rate unless it involved an instrument which is exempt from stamp duty and is certified as such (see pp.104-107).

IV   Check the terms of any restrictive covenants

1   Inform the buyer that the covenant exists.

2   Find out whether it:

    a)   affects the buyer's plans for the property, *or*

    b)   has been breached in the past (eg: by building work), *or*

    c)   adversely alters the property's value (a covenant preserving the character of the neighbourhood may actually enhance the value of a property, eg: if it was imposed by a developer and is rigorously enforced).

3   Does wording effectively annex the covenant to the land? If it does not, the covenant may be unenforceable.

4   If the covenant is post-1925, is it noted on the Charges Register, or as a Class D(ii) land charge?

    ➤   An unregistered covenant will be unenforceable.

5   If the covenant is valid, consider three options:

    a)   Insurance: the insurance company will normally need:

        ● a copy of the document imposing the covenant, or its exact wording, *and*

        ● details of past breaches, and a copy of planning permission for development, *and*

        ● the date of the covenant's imposition, *and*

        ● the date of the covenant's registration, *and*

        ● a description of the nature of the neighbourhood, *and*

        ● steps taken to trace whoever has benefit of the covenant.

    b)   Consent of the person with the benefit of the covenant.

    c)   An application to the Lands Tribunal (*LPA s.24*): this is slow and expensive.

V   Ensure there are no planning difficulties

Check ...

1   ... the date the property was originally built *and* the dates of subsequent additions or extensions.

2   ... that any alterations within the last 4 years *either* had planning permission *or* did not need it (and that any covenants in the lease have been complied with).

3   ... that any change of use over the last 10 years *either* did not need planning permission, *or* that it was granted (*and* that consent was granted by a landlord, if needed).

4   ... whether building regulation consent was gained *and* complied with for work done in the past year.

5   ... whether the property is a listed building *or* in a conservation area.

6   ... whether a Unitary Development Plan, or a Structural Development Plan affects the property.

Planning permission

1 **A 'development' requiring permission** (*TCPA 1990 s.55*) **involves *either*:**

a) 'building, engineering, mining, in, on, over or under the land', *or*

b) a 'material change' in use, (ie: not within same use class under *TCP(UC)O 1987*), *or*

c) an alteration of a listed building, or demolition in a conservation area (*P(LBCA)A 1990 s.74*).

2 **Limited permission to develop without permission is available** (*TCP(GPD)O 1995*) **for:**

a) maintenance work.

b) internal work not affecting the exterior.

c) use within the curtilage of a building for a purpose incidental to dwelling in the building.

d) change of use within a use class, *TCP(UC)O 1987*: Class A1, the majority of shops; Class A2, providing financial or professional services to the public; Class B1, use as an office outside A2.

e) development within a general development order, or under a local authority's *Article 4* direction.

3 **Applications for planning permission**

➤ An applicant need not own land, but must tell the owner (*TCPA 1990 s.66*); if a development order requires it, it will be necessary to advertise the application in the local press (*TCPA 1990 s.65*).

➤ There are two main types of permission.

a) **Outline permission:** matters which are 'reserved' must be approved within 3 years.

Work must usually start within 2 years from approval being granted for matters 'reserved', *or* 5 years from the original application, whichever is later (*TCPA 1990 s.91*).

b) **Full permission:** no matters 'reserved'; work must begin in 5 years (*TCPA 1990 s.92*).

➤ **Listed building consent**

This is required for altering listed buildings. It should only be granted after considering 'the building or its setting or any features of architectural or historic interest' (*P(LBCA)A 1990 s.72*).

➤ **Conservation area consent**

This is required to demolish a building in a conservation area. It should only be granted after considering 'preserving or enhancing the appearance of the area' (*P(LBCA)A 1990 s.66*).

4 **Penalties/enforcement**

➤ An enforcement notice may be served up to 4 years after a breach if there are unauthorised building operations, or an unauthorised change of use to a use as a single dwelling house. Otherwise, a notice may be served within 10 years of any other breach (*TCPA 1990 s.172*).

➤ The local authority may issue:

a) a stop notice (*TCPA 1990 s.183*): where an enforcement notice has been served, this compels builders to stop work or face criminal penalties.

b) a breach of condition notice (*TCPA 1990 s.187A*): to compel compliance with a condition.

c) a completion notice (*TCPA 1990 ss.94-96*): to compel the recipient to complete work.

d) a repair notice (*P(LBCA)A 1990 ss.47-48*): to protect a listed building; this can be a prelude to compulsory purchase.

e) a building preservation notice (*P(LBCA)A 1990 s.3*): to prevent demolition or alteration.

VI   Commission a survey

➤   There are 3 common types of 'survey' which a buyer can commission:

1   Valuation

✓   Cheap and fast.

✗   Very superficial, it only provides a guide as to whether, on the face of it, a price is fair in the present market.

2   Housebuyer's report and valuation

✓   This is more thorough than a valuation.

✗   The surveyor's duty is owed primarily to the building society. (With very 'low' priced property there is a duty to the buyer as well (*Smith v. Eric S. Bush* [1990] 1 AC 831).

✗   The building society is primarily concerned with ascertaining the property's resale value, so the survey will not give the buyer a clear idea of any major works which will need doing in the future.

3   Full structural survey

✓   This is always relatively expensive.

✓   A full structural survey always provides the most detailed information.

✓   If the property is unusual (eg: has its own drains in a remote location), the buyer can request special checks.

✓   The surveyor owes the buyer a duty of care, and may be held liable in contract and negligence.

◆   A survey is always advisable, but it should be considered particularly if:

● the property's construction is unconventional, *or*

● the property is in an unstable area, or it is likely to be a source of structural problems, *or*

● the property is not detached, *or*

● the property is of high value, *or*

● the property is under 100 years old, *or*

● a mortgage will provide only a small proportion (eg: under 75%) of the purchase price, *or*

● alterations or extensions are planned.

VII Check and amend the contract

Amending the contract

➤ Use red ink (and then green ink) to make amendments.

➤ Date alterations.

➤ Note on the contract 'Approved as drawn/amended on . . . [date].'

➤ **Questions to ask**

◆ Does the contract fulfil your client's instructions?

◆ Does it reflect what the buyer actually wants?

◆ Is it concise and unambiguous?

◆ Does it cater for the resolution of disputes?

◆ Does it describe the property accurately?

◆ Is a plan needed, and if so, is one supplied to an adequate scale?

◆ Is the seller offering full title guarantee, and if not, why not?

● If the answer to this final question is 'no', it is for the buyer to make a commercial judgment of the extent of liability, the risk involved in the circumstances, and the likely impact on the property's resale value.

| Step 4 | Preparations for exchange |

> I   Precautions regarding the parties
>
> II   Searches
>
> III   Deposit
>
> IV   Mortgage arrangements

I   Precautions regarding the parties

Undue influence

> The solicitor should ensure that the parties are not subject to undue influence:
>
> ◆ the price is fair.
>
> ◆ all the circumstances are known to any subordinate party (eg: an occupier).
>
> ◆ independent legal advice is available to all the parties, and they are all aware of this.

1   Minors

> Provided that there is no restriction on the Register, the buyer may assume the seller is over 18.

> If land is held on trust, and the trust instrument provides that a person should consent to any act of the trustees in relation to the land, *and* that person is a minor, then a buyer is not prejudiced if this consent is not obtained.

> ◆ The trustees are under a duty to obtain consent from the minor's parent or whoever has parental responsibility for him, or is his guardian (*TLATA 1996 s.10(3)*).

> A contract may be repudiated during a minority or in a reasonable time of majority (*MCA 1987*).

> ◆ A conveyance to a minor used to operate like a contract to convey (*SLA 1925 s.27(1)*), but from 1 January 1997, when the *TLATA 1996* came into force, a conveyance has operated as a declaration of trust over land in favour of the minor (a contract under *SLA 1925 s.27* now also operates as a trust) (*TLATA 1996 Schedule 1, para 1*).

2   Married couples

> If the seller is married, a spouse may have 'matrimonial home rights' (*MHA 1983 ss.1-2 / FLA 1996 ss.30-31*); these may be registered already *but* they can be registered at any time before completion, so the spouse should be asked to execute a release before exchange (see p.140).

> ◆ A right registered under *MHA/FLA* can be removed by submitting to the Registrar *either*
>
> • an application from the spouse benefiting from it, *or*
>
> • an official copy of a court decree stating that the marriage has been terminated, *or*
>
> • an official copy of a court order ending the spouse's matrimonial home rights, *or*
>
> • a death certificate (*MHA 1983 ss.1-2, FLA 1996 Sch. 4, paras 4(1)(a)-(c), 5(1)*).

> See also (3) overleaf for land held on trust for sale, or (after 1 January 1997) under a trust of land.

3 Land held on trust

➤ If land is held on trust, pay to all the trustees (being 2 or more) or a trust corporation(*LPA ss.2, 27*).

➤ If a sole owner is named as the proprietor on the Register: comply with any restriction to take free of any equitable interest.

➤ There may be a restriction on the Register regarding a joint tenancy.

◆ On the death of a tenant the legal estate vests in the survivor(s): *either* execute a vesting assent in favour of a fully entitled survivor, *or* insist on the appointment of another trustee and pay the purchase money to them both.

◆ If a joint tenant murders his fellow tenant, the property will not pass on survivorship.

◆ If there is no restriction, assume that joint tenants hold absolutely, so only a death certificate for the deceased tenant is usually needed (*LRR r.172*).

➤ From 1925, tenants-in-common and joint tenants held land under a trust for sale (under which they had a duty to sell land and a power to postpone sale). From 1 January 1997 when the *TLATA 1996* came into force land has been held by trustees under a trust of land (under which trustee have a power to sell land and a power to postpone sale) (consequential amendments to the *Land Registration Rules 1925* have been made by *LRR 1997*).

◆ Trustees of land are under a duty to 'as far as is practicable, consult the beneficiaries of full age and beneficially entitled to an interest in possession in the land' (*TLATA 1996 s.11(1)*), see further p.150.

● This duty only applies to trusts created by irrevocable deed. It does not apply to trusts which exclude this provision, nor to will trusts made or arising before *TLATA 1996* came into force (*TLATA 1996 ss.11(2)-11(4)*).

◆ A buyer of unregistered land who is not put on notice is not prejudiced by any limitation of the trustees' power to convey land, or their failure to consult beneficiaries (*TLATA 1996 s.16(1)*).

● A buyer who is on notice may take subject to the trust.

◆ A buyer of unregistered land is not (in any circumstances) prejudiced by any act of the trustees which contravenes any enactment or a rule of law or equity (*TLATA 1996 s.16(2)*).

◆ Trustees of unregistered land must, if the beneficiares are absolutely entitled and of full age, execute a deed declaring that they are discharged from the trust. If they fail to do so, a court may order them to do so. A buyer may rely on such a deed, provided he is not on notice that the trustees erred in making the conveyance to the beneficiaries (*TLATA 1996 ss.16(4)-(5)*).

4 PRs

➤ PRs may become registered as proprietors of registered land by submitting the grant of probate (*LRA s.41, LRR r.170*). If this happens, the buyer should comply with any restriction on the Register; otherwise the buyer should request a certified copy of a grant of probate and submit it with his application for registration.

➤ From 1 July 1995, one PR ceased to be able to bind the estate by contract. All the PRs who take a grant must be party to both the contract and the purchase deed (*LP(MP)A 1994 s.16*). Where there is a sole PR, the death certificate and the grant must be produced to show he acts alone.

➤ PRs do *not* need to seek consent from those interested in the administration of an estate before they sell land for the purposes of administration (*TLATA 1996 s.18*).

Overview of the powers and duties of trustees of land

➤ Trustees have power to sell land and power to postpone sale (*TLATA 1996 s.4*). They may also buy a legal estate in land (leasehold or freehold) anywhere in England or Wales, for investment, occupation by a beneficiary, or any other reason (*TLATA 1996 ss.6(3)-(4)*).

   ◆ This power can be expressly excluded or modified in the trust instrument or will (*TLATA 1996 s.8*).

➤ Trustees of land, when exercising 'any function' relating to the land subject to the trust must:

   a) 'as far as practicable' consult beneficiaries who are of full age and beneficially entitled to an interest in possession, *and*

   b) give effect to the beneficiaries' wishes, so far as is consistent with the general interest of the trust. If the beneficiaries dispute amongst themselves, the trustees should have regard to the wishes of the majority (by reference to the value of their combined interests under the trust) (*TLATA 1996 s.11(1)*).

   ● This does not apply either to trusts which expressly exclude this requirement *or* to will trusts which arose before 1 January 1997 (*TLATA 1996 s.11(2)*).

   ● This only applies to trusts created before 1 January 1997, if such of the settlor(s) who are still alive and of full capacity execute(s) a deed making an irrevocable election that it shall apply (*TLATA 1996 ss.11(3)-(4)*).

➤ If the beneficiares are of full age and absolutely entitled, the trustees may, having obtained their consent, partition land, convey it to them or mortgage it to pay the beneficiaries 'equality money' *(TLATA 1996 s.7)*.

   ◆ This power can be expressly excluded or modified in the trust instrument (*TLATA 1996 s.8*).

➤ If beneficiaries are of full age and absolutely entitled to an interest in possession, the trustees may delegate, by power of attorney, any of their functions as trustees which relate to the land (*TLATA 1996 s.9*).

➤ Trustees may not act so as to prevent *any* person occupying land from remaining in occupation, or so as to make it likely that *any* person might cease to occupy land, unless that person consents, or the trustees obtain a court order under *TLATA 1996 ss.14-15*).

➤ A beneficiary's interest under a trust is no longer subject to the 'doctrine of conversion' under which land given to a beneficiary under trust for sale was deemed to be a gift of the proceeds from the sale of the land, and a beneficiary of a trust of money to be invested in land had an interest in the land rather than the cash. Land is now be treated as land, and personal property as personal property (*TLATA 1996 s.3*).

   ◆ This only applies to will trusts when the testator died on or after 1 January 1997 (*TLATA 1996 s.18(3)*).

The rights of beneficiaries under trusts of land

➤ A beneficiary of a trust of land, who is absolutely entitled to an interest in possession under the trust may occupy the land if occupation is among the purposes of the trust, or the trustees hold the land so that it is available for occupation, provided the land is not unsuitable for occupation by that beneficiary (*TLATA 1996 s.12*).

➤ If 2 or more beneficiaries are entitled to occupy land held on trust, trustees may not:

◆ unreasably exclude a beneficiary's right to occupy land, or restrict it with regard to:

● the purposes for which the land is held,

● the settlor's intentions,

● each beneficiary's circumstances, *but*

◆ they may impose reasonable conditions on occupation, such as requiring a beneficiary to:

● pay outgoings or expenses in respect of the land, *or*

● assume any obligation in relation to the land or activities which take, or may take place on it (eg: comply with farming regulations, insure against a claim under the *OLA 1984*),

● pay compensation to other beneficiaries whose entitlement to occupy the land has been restricted or excluded, *and*

◆ forgo another benefit under the trust to which the beneficiary would otherwise have been entitled (*TLATA 1996 s.13*).

➤ These provisions of the *TLATA 1996* may *not* be excluded in the trust instrument and they apply to all trusts of land from 1 January 1997.

Trusts of land - a trap for the unwary

➤ *TLATA 1996* gives trustees and PRs wide powers to manage land and the proceeds of sale of the land where the trust or estate contain land (*TLATA 1996 s.17*). Therefore, if a trust is a trust of land, it remains a trust of land (with all the flexibility this entails) irrespective of whether or not it retains the original land.

➤ If a trust or estate does **not** contain land, but consists simply of personalty, *TLATA 1996* does not give trustees broad powers to deal with land as an 'absolute' owner (eg: selling it, retaining it, managing it, buying other land).

◆ Take care when drafting a will or trust deed to ensure that such trustees are expressly given all the powers they may need. (Note, for example, that with a trust of land the apportionment rules are automatically excluded - if the trust consists merely of personalty these rules must be specifically excluded).

◆ Trustees and PRs should check, on appointment, whether the trust has at any stage been a trust of land. If it has then irrespective of whether it still comprises land, they have the powers and duties of a trustee of land. Otherwise they do not.

5   Companies

> Lenders may insist that the Memorandum and Articles are checked to confirm that the company is acting within its powers, but a buyer should not be prejudiced if this is not done (*CA s.35A*).

> Limitations on the power to purchase may be contained in a restriction on the Register.

6   Charities

> If there is no restriction, no precautions are needed. Otherwise check:

   a)   whether the transaction was authorised by statute or the deed governing the charity.

   b)   whether the charity has been granted an exemption certificate under the *Charities Act 1992*.

   c)   if there is no exemption certificate, whether consent has been gained. This needs evidence that:

   ◆   the trustees are satisfied that the deal is a good one, *and*

   ◆   the land was advertised for a period, and in the way a surveyor advised, *and*

   ◆   there is a written report from a qualified surveyor approving the sale, *and*

   ◆   prescribed words have been inserted stating that:

   ●   the charity is not exempt, *and*

   ●   the land is subject to *CA 1992 s.32*, *and*

   ●   the land is held on trust for the charity, *and*

   ●   the requirements of *s.32* have been complied with.

7   Mental impairment

> A contract or conveyance for value is binding unless one of the parties is unaware of the other's disability (*Hart v. O'Connor* [1985] 2 All ER 880), in which case it is voidable.   A conveyance for no value involving someone of unsound mind is void.

> A receiver may deal with property with the court's consent (*MntHA 1983 s.99*); there will be no restriction on the Register unless the receiver is registered as the proprietor.

> If a trustee is mentally incapable of exercising his functions as a trustee, and all the beneficiaries are fully entitled and of full age, and nobody is willing and able to appoint a trustee to replace him under *TA 1925 s.36(1)*, the beneficiaries may issue a written direction to the trustee's receiver, his attorney under an enduring power of attorney, or a person authorised under *MntHA 1983 Part VII*, requesting that person to appoint a replacement trustee (*TLATA 1996 s.20*).

   ◆   A buyer should ask to see a certified copy of any such direction together with the deed of appointment.   Pre-contract enquiries should include a question as to whether a direction has been made, and requisitions on title could include a request for confirmation that none of the beneficiaries withdrew the direction before it was complied with under *TLATA 1996 s.21(1)*.

II   Searches

> The buyer should check that these are all correct, and that exchange will occur before priority periods expire.

III   Deposit

1   Where is the deposit coming from?

➤ Payment is by banker's draft or cheque drawn on cleared funds from client account (*StC 2.2.1*).

- ◆ If a client account cheque is used, the solicitor must be put in funds at least 5 working days in advance to ensure it clears (otherwise the *SARs 1991* may be breached).

➤ If payment is from a deposit account, ensure that notice of withdrawal is given sufficiently early to avoid incurring an interest penalty *and* to make certain that the money is released for exchange.

➤ If bridging finance is required, arrange this in good time.

- ✓ A loan may qualify for tax relief as a 'charge on income' (see p.170).

- ✗ A loan may be expensive.

- ✗ If the sale does not proceed liability must be discharged fast to prevent exorbitant interest payments.

2   How will the deposit be held?

➤ **As agent for the seller**

- ◆ This is the position under the general law, unless the parties agree otherwise (or an auctioneer holds the deposit, in which case the auctioneer holds as stakeholder).

- ◆ *StC 2.2.2* permits a seller to use the deposit, or part of it, as a deposit on the purchase of a property in England or Wales as his residence, if the related purchase contract is entered into before completion (ie: of the contract for the seller's sale) and that related contract contains similar provisions to *StC 2.2.2-2.2.3*.

- ◆ A trustee is under a duty not to lose control of money held on trust, so if the seller is a trustee, the seller's solicitor should hold the deposit as the seller's agent.

➤ **As stakeholder** (envisaged by *StC 2.2.3*).

- ◆ Unless the sellers are trustees, *or* the seller wishes to use the deposit to buy another property (in accordance with *StC 2.2.2*), the seller's solicitor holds the deposit as stakeholder and is obliged to pay it to the seller on completion, together with accrued interest.

3   Where will the deposit be held?

➤ In a deposit account? This depends on whether interest penalties are imposed for short-term deposits, and the feasibility of transferring money so it is available at need.

4   Interest on the deposit

➤ The solicitor must pay the client interest in accordance with the *SAR 1991 r.20*.

➤ Estate agents must account to their client for interest over £500 (*EA(A)R 1981 r.7*).

➤ If money is held as stakeholder, interest should be paid to the buyer on completion (*StC 2.2.3*).

5   Troubleshooting

➤ Deposit insurance: an insurance policy is advisable if it is feared the seller may run off with the deposit.

➤ Buyer's lien: this attaches to the house for the amount of any deposit.

- ◆ The buyer can protect it with a caution/notice (Registered land) or a C(iii) charge (Unregistered land).

➤ Estate agents must carry insurance against insolvency while holding a deposit (*EAA 1979 s.16*).

➤ If the cheque bounces, this breaches a condition of the contract: the seller can treat the breach as repudiatory (*StC 2.2.4*), or allow the contract to continue. In either case, he may sue for damages.

IV Mortgage arrangements

Types of mortgage		
Repayment	Endowment	Pension
The borrower makes monthly repayments of interest *and* capital

✗ On the borrower's death the debt falls due from the estate; if the estate is insolvent and property prices fall, the lender is left with a bad debt. A mortgage repayment policy insures against this occurring | The borrower makes repayments of interest only

An insurance policy is taken out on the borrower's life when the mortgage is granted, and this repays the capital when it matures

✓ When the policy matures any surplus is paid to the borrower

✓ The insurance policy on the borrower's life gives the lender extra security

✗ If the policy does not cover the loan, the borrower must make good the shortfall

✗ The mortgage cannot be transferred unless the whole sum is repaid - this is the negative equity trap

Note: this is an 'investment' under the *FSA 1986* | These are linked with pension arrangements

✓ Tax efficient for the self-employed on high salaries |

➤ Ensure that:

- ◆ the borrower is aware of the repayments and can afford them (even if interest rates rise).

- ◆ the borrower knows the overall cost of the mortgage (eg: the lender may insist the property is insured under its own block policy *and* that the borrower pays for this).

- ◆ the buyer has enough money in hand, after moving expenses, to proceed with the purchase.

- ◆ retentions for repair work are not such as to prevent the borrower meeting his financial obligations. if the lender retains some of the capital until specified repairs have been done, this may cause additional financing difficulties. Ensure that the borrower can meet these obligations.

  - ● The seller may allow the buyer access before completion to carry out work the lender requires. The lender will then release the whole of the loan to enable the buyer to complete.

- ◆ any conditions attached to the mortgage are not too onerous.   Explain the effect of any conditions to the client (eg: the mortgage may prohibit the borrower letting part of the property without the lender's consent).

- ◆ any guarantee premium which the lender demands is satisfactory.   Is this sufficient to protect the borrower if house prices fall?   Is the premium expensive?   (If acting for the lender, note that if the valuation is negligent, the lender will only be able to recover the difference between the correct valuation and the negligent one, *SAAMCO v. York Montague,* The Times 24 June 1996, HL.)

- ◆ there is no conflict if the lender instructs the buyer's solicitor. (Comply with *SPR r.6* (See p.3))

  - ● If a conflict of interest arises subsequently, the solicitor must cease acting, but he may not tell the other party the reason why as this would breach the duty of confidentiality.

- ◆ once a satisfactory offer has been made, the buyer accepts it within the time allowed.

- ◆ any arrangements with a mortgagee are co-ordinated with the rest of the transaction: with a repayment mortgage, mortgage insurance should be taken out so that the mortgage policy will be redeemed if the borrower dies.

Step 5	Exchange and its consequences

> I   Exchange
>
> II   Consequences of exchange

I   Exchange

➤ The contract is signed.

- ◆ *Either* both parties sign one contract *or* they each sign identical copies (*LP(MP)A 1989 s.2*). For a contract to be binding under *s.2*, documents containing the terms of the contract must actually be exchanged (*Commission for the New Towns v. Cooper (Great Britain) Limited* [1995] EG 26 129).

- ◆ The signatures need not be witnessed.

- ◆ A solicitor may sign, but should do so *either* under a power of attorney *or* with express written authority.

  - ● Failure to obtain the proper authority may be a breach of warranty of authority (*Suleman v. Shahisavari* [1989] 2 All ER 460).

➤ Do not exchange without a client's express written authority to do so.

➤ Exchange using either *Formula A, B, or C* (see box below) via:

- ◆ telephone (make a file note of the time of the exchange), *or*

- ◆ post, *or*

- ◆ personally (usually at the office of the seller's solicitors), *or*

- ◆ DX *(StC 2)*, *or*

- ◆ fax *(StC 1.3.3)*: this must be confirmed with hard copies as soon as possible.

Formula A	Formula B	Formula C
When one solicitor holds both contracts	When each solicitor holds their client's contract	For a 'chain' of transactions Each solicitor holds their client's contract and exchange is by telephone

II   Consequences of exchange

➤ Any subsequent variation to the contract which is agreed between the parties must comply with the *LP(MP)A 1989 s.2* (see previous page) (*McCausland and Another v. Duncan Lawrie Limited*, The Times, 18 June 1996, CA).

1   Consider whether to register the contract

➤ This is advisable if:

a) the seller's good faith is doubted, *or*

b) a dispute arises, *or*

c) there are more than 2 months between exchange and completion, *or*

d) the seller delays completion beyond the contractual date, *or*

e) the transaction is a sub-sale.

◆ Unregistered land: register the contract as a Class C(iv) land charge.

◆ Registered land: enter a caution/notice on the Register as a minor interest in the land.

2   Death of a party

➤ PRs are bound to complete a contract which the deceased entered. This can cause difficulties for the estate as the buyer's death may lead to a revocation of the mortgage offer.

3   Seller's bankruptcy

➤ The seller's trustee in bankruptcy may complete with a redrafted purchase deed (the bankrupt is not party to the deed), or the trustee may disclaim the contract (for a trustee's powers, see p.234).

4   Requisitions on title

➤ *StC 4.1.1*: these are made in writing within 6 working days of exchange, *or* when evidence of the seller's title is delivered to the buyer, whichever is later. The seller replies within 4 working days.

➤ Common law: the buyer accepts the seller's title on delivery of the draft purchase deed to the seller. Often the draft deed is submitted with requisitions on title. *StC 4.5.1.* preserves the buyer's right to raise requisitions.

Step 6	Buyer prepares the purchase deed

1 Procedure

➤ At least 12 working days before completion the buyer sends the seller a draft of the deed: 2 copies, one of which is engrossed (*StC 4.1.2*).

➤ The seller's solicitor replies with any queries within 4 working days of the draft being delivered to him (*StC 4.1.2*).

➤ The buyer must deliver an engrossment to the seller at least 5 days before completion (*StC 4.1.2*).

  ◆ *Protocol 7.1*: the draft deed and requisitions on title should be submitted as soon as possible after exchange, and within time limits set by the contract.

2 Form of the deed

➤ The deed should comply with the *LPA s.52* as amended by the *LP(MP)A 1989 s.1*.

➤ Registered land: the transfer should accord with the *LRR* and use standard wording, *or* use *Form 19* which HM Land Registry provides for convenience.

➤ Unregistered land: there is no prescribed form. A *Rule 72* transfer may be used.

3 Drafting

➤ The deed should reflect the terms of the contract.

➤ Consideration (*SA 1891 s.5*): exclude chattels; a separate receipt for these is given to the buyer on completion.

  ◆ VAT (if due) is included in the figure for consideration.

4 Parties

➤ All those whose consent to the transaction is necessary:

  ◆ a receiver or liquidator.

  ◆ a sub-purchaser on a sub-sale.

  ◆ a lender with a charge over unregistered land may *either* join a conveyance *or* give the buyer a separate deed of release.

    ● A lender with a charge over registered land will not do this as he will release the land using *Form 53*.

5 Signature

➤ The seller always signs the deed. The buyer signs the deed if it contains a covenant or a declaration on his behalf.

➤ If an individual is incapable of signing, the deed is read to him, and it can be signed on his behalf in the presence of 2 witnesses who attest his signature (*LP(MP)A 1989 s.1(2)(3)*).

➤ An attorney signs *either* 'O by his attorney P' *or* 'P as attorney on behalf of O'.

➤ A company may affix a seal in the presence of 2 directors who sign the deed. The seal is not essential, but the document must be a deed on its face (*CA s.36A*).

6   Plans

➤ Attach these to the deed.

➤ HM Land Registry requires parties to sign the plan if it is to accept its inclusion.

◆   Signing the plan is not compulsory for unregistered land, but it is advisable nonetheless.

◆   If a company seals the deed, it should seal the plan as well (this need not be witnessed).

7   Witnesses (where necessary)

➤ For evidential reasons an independent party is preferable.   A witness cannot be a party to the deed (*Seal v. Claridge* (1881) 7 QBD 516).

➤ 2 witnesses are required if a signature is by proxy.

8   Delivery

➤ A deed is usually held 'in escrow' (ie: conditional upon completion, signed but not dated).

➤ Delivery is presumed to be the date of execution unless the contrary is shown (*CA s.36A*).

➤ Receipt clause: this is sufficient discharge for the buyer (*LPA s.67*).

◆   A receipt clause authorises the buyer to pay consideration to the seller's solicitor (*LPA s.69*).

◆   A receipt is evidence, but not conclusive evidence, that the seller's lien over the property in respect of unpaid consideration is extinguished.

Step 7	Preparing for completion

1 **Send the seller (and the buyer if necessary) a letter with an engrossed purchase deed**

➤ Explain:

◆ the purpose and contents of the purchase deed.

◆ any instructions for executing the deed and the date by which the purchase deed should be returned to the solicitor.

◆ that the client should not date the purchase deed.

2 **Make final searches** (see p.169)

3 **Prepare and send completion statements to the clients**

➤ The seller's solicitor sends:

◆ the seller a statement of the sum due on completion, explaining how this was calculated, *and*

◆ the buyer 2 copies of the appropriate statement, together with any receipts if *either* the proceeds do not cover the price agreed *or* an apportionment is due (eg: in respect of a service charge).

➤ The buyer's solicitor sends the buyer a statement giving:

◆ the sum needed to complete, explaining how this was calculated, *and*

◆ a statement of the mortgage, mentioning how much will be advanced and retained, *and*

◆ the amount due in disbursements (eg: search fees, stamp duty, etc), *and*

◆ the solicitor's costs (plus VAT).

4 **Finalise arrangements with lender** (if acting for the lender)

➤ Buyer's solicitor ...

... sends the lender a report on the title and requests a cheque to cover the advance. Ensure that the cheque is paid in to client account at least 5 days before completion.

... prepares an engrossment of the mortgage deed.

... checks that all outstanding requisitions and enquires have been satisfactorily answered, and advises the client of any remaining difficulties.

➤ Seller's solicitor ...

... gives an undertaking to the lender to secure redemption of the mortgage insofar as monies come into the solicitor's hands, and seeks authority to act as the lender's agent to redeem the mortgage just before completion.

... verifies that the completion statement is correct.

... prepares a form of discharge of the mortgage, and if acting for a lender, checks their instructions as to completion.

5 **Settle arrangements for completion**

➤ Agree how the keys will be handed over. (Under the *Protocol*, the seller's solicitor releases them immediately after completion, and telephones the buyer to confirm that this has happened.)

➤ If completion is not personal, the buyer's solicitor instructs the seller's solicitor to act as his agent for completion and obtains an undertaking that he will hold any monies to his order pending completion.

Step 8	Completion

> The contract and the purchase deed do *not* merge on completion (*StC 7.4*).

   ◆ This ensures that an action in contract is preserved after completion.

1   Time

   > Completion takes place on the twentieth working day after exchange (*StC 6.1*), subject to any *SpC*.

   > If completion takes place after 2 pm, it is deemed to occur on the following working day (*StC 6.1.2*).

      ◆ Late completion on a Friday afternoon involves the buyer paying 3 days' interest.

2   Place

   > At the seller's office, or any place the seller may reasonably specify (*StC 6.2*).

3   Money

   > Legal tender (*StC 6.7(a)*).

   > Banker's draft: this is drawn on the bank's funds and is therefore secure (*StC 6.7(b)*).

   > Telegraphic transfer: this is a direct credit to an account which the seller nominates (*StC 6.7(c)*).

      Note: a) the deposit is released unconditionally by a stakeholder (*StC 6.7(d)*).

              b) telegraphic transfer from client account is made after a cheque clears, otherwise the *SARs* may be breached.

Usual methods of completion

Postal	Personal
Agree whether to use the Law Society's *Code for Completion by Post*. This is presumed to be adopted under the *Protocol 8.2*. Assuming it is adopted, the seller's solicitor confirms that he:	The buyer's solicitor:
◆ acts as the buyer's agent and will not charge a fee, *and*	◆ brings a banker's draft for the balance of the purchase price. (A cheque is not sufficient as only cash or an equivalent to cash is permitted by *StC 6.7*)
◆ will hold monies to the buyer's order, *and*	
◆ is authorised by a lender to discharge any mortgage of which the solicitor is aware	
The buyer's solicitor usually sends the balance of the completion monies to the seller's solicitor by telegraphic transfer early on the morning of completion, and gives the seller instructions on examining and endorsing documents of title	The seller's solicitor:
	◆ checks and signs 2 copies of the schedule of deeds (and retains one, giving the other to the buyer)
The seller completes the deed by inserting the date, before telephoning or faxing the buyer to confirm completion, and then posting the deed of transfer or conveyance by first class post or DX	

In all cases:

   ◆ the seller obtains discharges for any mortgages, or gives an undertaking to discharge any mortgages.

   ◆ the buyer (on a personal completion) or the seller (on a postal completion) checks the purchase deed.

   ◆ the seller gives a receipt for chattels.

For unregistered land: documents of title are checked against the epitome of title which the seller has supplied.

   ◆ If the seller sells as a PR, *or* on a conveyance of part, endorse a memorandum on the grant of representation or original conveyance of the whole respectively.

   ◆ If the seller will retain any of the documents (eg: sale of part, or trust instrument (*LPA s.45(9)*), the buyer's solicitor marks the abstract 'Examined against the originals at the office of .... on ...', and signs the abstract.

   ◆ If any of the documents of title are missing, the seller (or a fiduciary with custody of the relevant document) gives a written acknowledgement and undertaking, both of which are fulfilled at the seller's expense (*StC 4.5.4*).

Step 9	Post - completion

1 Seller's solicitor ...

... instructs the estate agents to release the keys. Under the *Protocol 8.3*, the solicitor should ensure the keys are released immediately and inform the buyer's solicitor when this has been done.

... deals with the proceeds of sale as instructed, and fulfils any undertakings (eg: to a mortgagee).

... redeems the mortgage and sends the appropriate receipt to the buyer:

- ◆ Registered land: obtain *Form 53*.

- ◆ Unregistered land: obtain a receipted mortgage deed.

... sends the client a letter, report and bill (for the rules regarding bills, see pp.14-15). Make it clear in this letter that the client is responsible for informing the water authority of the change in ownership (*Protocol 8.4*).

2 Buyer's solicitor ...

... completes the mortgage deed.

... fulfils any undertaking to repay bridging finance (eg: from a mortgage advance).

... ensures the purchase deed is stamped and *ad valorem* duty is paid at the correct rate (see p.105) (*FA 1993 s.201(1)(a)*). (He submits the purchase deed to HM Inland Revenue within 30 days for stamping if duty is payable.)

... obtains a Particulars Delivered stamp if a freehold interest (*FA 1930 s.28*) is being transferred. He applies to the District Land Registry if no stamp duty is payable, and if the land is registered or to be registered for the first time. Otherwise he submits *Form L(A)451* when paying stamp duty.

... registers the title and the mortgage deed, if appropriate (ie: on a grant or assignment of a lease with more than 21 years to run, or on a freehold transfer or a conveyance) (*LRA s.123*).

... if the buyer is a company, any fixed charge must be registered at Companies House within 21 days.

... makes a diary entry for the date when the Registry should return the land certificate or the charge certificate.

... discharges any entries which have been registered at the Registry or the Central Land Charges Department to protect the contract.

... if the Registry sends back a land certificate, retain it (subject to the client's instructions), *or* send the charge certificate to the lender.

... if the buyer has bought unregistered land from an attorney with a non-enduring power, or a power of attorney granted under *TLATA 1996 s.9*, he should advise the buyer to make a statutory declaration, as if the buyer dies without doing so there will be a defect in the title where statute does not offer protection.

Registration of a conveyance or transfer at HM Land Registry

1   Time limits for registration application

➤ Compulsory registration of dispositions of unregisterd land: register within 2 months of completion, *otherwise the conveyance is void at law* (but may take effect in equity) (*LRA ss.123A(4)* as inserted by *LRA 1997 s.1*).

   ◆ Entering a caution against first registration on *Form 13* (*LRA s.53, LRR r.64*):

      a) at the time of writing, protects a buyer of a freehold estate, *and*

      b) at the time of writing, protects a tenant taking a lease with more than 21 years to run, *and*

      c) will protect the person responsible for applying for registration under *LRA s.123A(2)* (ie: when *LRA 1997 s.1* is in force).

➤ Subsequent dealings: register within 30 working days (by 9.30am on the final day) (*LRR r.85*). Protection for this period is under a pre-completion search, otherwise another application may gain priority.

2   Method

➤ Send the following to HM Land Registry.

   ◆ On first registration:

      ● an application form, fee, documents, *Form A13*.

   ◆ On a transfer of registered land:

      ● *Form A4,* land or charge certificate and fee (see p.395), *plus* (as appropriate).

      ● a *Form 53*.

      ● if the disposition is in favour of a sole or last surviving trustee, an application for the registration of a restriction in *Form 62* (*LRR r.213(3)*).

      ● if the transfer of legal title is in favour of trustees of land, or PRs, whose powers under the trust are limited by virtue of *TLATA 1996 s.8* (see p.150), an application for a restriction in *Form 11A* or *11B* respectively (*LRR r.59A, 106A*).

      ● the new mortgage deed (and a certified copy).

      ● if the seller is a PR, a certified copy of the grant of representation.

      ● if the transfer was executed under a special power of attorney limited to the disposal the original power, *or* a certified copy of any other type of attorney.

      ● a PD form *LA(451P)*, if needed.

      ● a stamped addressed card for the District Registry to acknowledge the application.

Requirement for compulsory first registration

➤ When *LRA 1997 s.1* comes into force, which is expected to be 1 January 1998, the requirement for compulsory registration will apply to:

a) a 'qualifying' conveyance, grant (of term absolute of 21 or more years), assignment (of a term which has 21 or more years to run on the date of the assignment) (*LRA s.123(1)(a)-(b)*), *and*

   ◆ A 'qualifying disposition' is i) for consideration, *or* ii) by gift, *or* iii) by court order (*LRA s.123(6)*).

b) a disposition by way of assent or vesting deed of a freehold estate or a term absolute which has 21 or more years to run (*LRA s.123(1)(c)*), *and*

c) a legal mortgage of a freehold estate or a term of years absolute with 21 or more years to run (*LRA s.123(2)*).

➤ The Lord Chancellor may specify 'trigger events' (*LRA s.123(4)*) on which an application for first registration may be made at a reduced fee (*LRA s.1997 s.3*).

B   Checking title and making searches

I   Unregistered title

II   Registered title

III   Searches

I   Unregistered title

A. Freehold title

Root of title
A valid title has a 'root' which may be (*LPA s.44*):

either   a) a conveyance on sale, or legal mortgage at least 15 years old (this is preferable),

or   b) a voluntary assent or conveyance made after 1925,

and   it must be at the start of a chain which is uninterrupted up to the present day.

It is not necessary to look behind the root except for (*LPA s.45*):

➤ an abstract of a power of attorney under which an abstracted document was executed, *or*

➤ earlier documents referred to in an abstract, *or*

➤ a plan referred to in the abstract, *or*

➤ any limitation or trust over any part of property in an abstracted document, or any document of creation of trust, or any limitation relating to a document forming part of the epitome.

Documents capable of forming title

1   Conveyance by trustees to themselves

➤ This may be a breach of trust, and is voidable unless ...

a)   ... there is *either*:

i) a pre-existing contract to purchase land, or an option or right of pre-emption in favour of a trustee or PR,

or

ii) a PR is a beneficiary under a will or intestacy.

b)   ... the consent of the beneficiaries was obtained and all were *sui juris*.

c)   ... the conveyance was sanctioned by the trust instrument.

d)   ... the conveyance was executed under a court order.

2   Conveyance by trustees of land

➤ Prior to 1 January 1997 when *TLATA 1996* came into force land was held by PRs, trustees, tenants in common and joint tenants under a trust for sale.   Subsequently, such land has been held under a trust of land by trustees who have a power to postpone sale and a power to sell land (*TLATA 1996 s.4*).

➤ A buyer takes free of any interests under a trust if he pays to 2 or more trustees, or a trust corporation (*LPA ss.2, 27*).   A conveyance by an individual trustee needs further investigation.

➤ From 1 January 1997, a buyer of unregistered land does not take free of the trust (even if he pays to 2 trustees) if he is put on notice of any limitation of the trustees' power to convey *or* of their failure to take proper account of the beneficiaries' interests (*TLATA 1996 s.16*).

➤ Tenants in common

If only one tenant survives, the buyer should ask to see the death certificate, the grant of representation and the assent in favour of the tenant's successor under the will or intestacy.

➤ Joint tenants

A buyer can assume severance has not occurred if (*LP(JT)A 1964 s.1*):

a) no memorandum of severance is endorsed on the conveyance under which the joint tenants bought the property, *and*

b) no bankruptcy proceedings are registered against either joint tenant, *and*

c) the conveyance *either*:

   i)   contains a recital that the seller is solely and beneficially entitled, *or*

   ii) was executed pursuant to a contract for the sale of land dated before 1 July 1995, and the seller conveyed as 'beneficial owner'.

3   Conveyance by PRs

➤ If a grant is to 2 or more PRs, all must join the assent or conveyance.

➤ If only one PR survives, he can act alone.

   ◆ Check death certificates to ensure the other PRs were deceased at the time of the transfer.

➤ An assent passes the property to a beneficiary under a will. It should:

   ◆ be in writing, *and*

   ◆ be to the beneficiary named, *and*

   ◆ be signed by all the surviving PRs, *and*

   ◆ if covenants are contained, be by deed.

➤ An assentee or buyer should demand an endorsement on the grant, otherwise the trustees may subsequently defeat the assent by making a statement under the *AEA 1925 s.36* so that a subsequent buyer takes in priority to the assentee.

   ◆ A donee is not protected by statute against trustees defeating the assent in this manner.

4   Voluntary dispositions below full market value

➤ These may be revocable under *IA 1986* (see p.128) (see also *I(No 2)A 1994* for the position of a buyer who gives value to a seller where the seller has acquired land for a disposition which was below market value).

5 **Conveyance from an attorney**

➤ The buyer's position depends on the type of power of attorney which the seller has:

♦ ... if the seller's attorney has a *security power*, the buyer takes a clean title if he has no actual knowledge that the power has been revoked (*PAA 1971 s.4*).

♦ ... if the seller's attorney has a *non-enduring power*, the buyer takes a clean title if he acts in good faith without knowledge of revocation (death amounts to revocation) (*PAA 1971 s.4*).

● A buyer acquiring land from a seller under a non-enduring power, or an unregistered enduring power, is protected if (*PAA 1971 s.5(4), EPAA 1985 s.9(4)*) *either*:

a) the dealing between the attorney with the non-enduring power and the buyer occurred within 1 year of the power being granted, *or*

b) the buyer makes a statutory declaration within 3 months of completion that he was ignorant of the revocation of the power.

♦ ... if the seller's attorney is a beneficiary of a trust and has a power of attorney granted by a trustee under *TLATA 1996 s.9(1)*, the buyer is protected if he deals in good faith, having no knowledge of the power's revocation (eg: by the beneficiary ceasing to be entitled to an interest in possession (*TLATA 1996 s.9(4)*), and swears a statutory declaration to this effect within 3 months of the completion of the purchase (*TLATA 1996 s.9(2)*).

♦ ... if the seller's attorney has an *enduring power* of attorney, check the Court of Protection to ensure that the power was correctly registered under *EPAA 1985 s.6*.

● A trustee with an enduring power may act as attorney for a sole co-trustee (*EPAA 1985 s.3(3)*).

➤ Powers granted before 1 October 1971 are governed by *LPA ss.126-128*.

6 **Conveyance from a lender**

➤ Legal mortgages: if the lender sold under a power of sale there will be no receipt on deed.

♦ Valid receipt may be assumed if prescribed wording is present, signed by an authorised person (*BSA 1986, Schedule 4 para 2(3)*).

♦ For a building society mortgage receipted before 1 January 1987, or for a bank mortgage, ensure the receipt names the holder of the legal and equitable title as the payer of the debt. Otherwise, the receipt operates to transfer the mortgage (*LPA s.115*); so if a PR or a trustee redeems a mortgage, the receipt should state that no transfer is intended.

● If in doubt (or if the mortgage discharge post-dates the conveyance) make a land charge search against whoever bought from the borrower and ask for the title deeds from the lender/seller.

Documents retained by the seller

➤ If a seller has at any time retained documents of title (eg: the original conveyance on a sale of part, or a trust instrument on sale by trustees), a conveyance may include (*LPA s.64*):

a) an 'acknowledgement' entitling the buyer and any successor in title (but not a tenant paying rent) to demand whoever possesses the documents to produce them at the buyer's cost, *and*

b) an 'undertaking' giving the buyer and any successor in title (but not a tenant paying rent) a remedy in damages if the documents are mislaid, or perish due to fire or undue care.

Fiduciaries (eg: mortgagees, PRs, tenants for life, and trustees) are unlikely to have given an undertaking. If they have custody of documents, they may have given an acknowledgement.

Proving title

1   Produce a sound root of title at least 15 years old

➤ Include incumbrances not evidenced on the root, and which predate the root.

➤ A voluntary conveyance or assent will serve as a root provided it was made after 1925.

2   Ensure that the root is sound

➤ It should deal with *all* legal interests in the land.

➤ It should contain a recognisable description of the land.

➤ There are no elements which could cast doubt on the title.

3   Produce an abstract, or an epitome of the title

➤ List the documents comprising the root: these go to the buyer on completion *(StC 4.2.3)*.

B. Leasehold title

Proving title			
	Grant (lease)	Grant (sub lease)	Assignment
Open contract rules	Freehold title (as above). No title is given if the lease is under 15 years	*LPA s.44*: a head lease and title root going back at least 15 years	*LPA s.44*: the lease itself and all assignments going back at least 15 years
StC 8.2.4.	The seller provides everything necessary to give valid title (ie: an epitome going back at least 15 years)		
Effect of a *SpC*?		To exclude *StC 8.2.4* if the head tenant never asked to see the freehold	To enable the buyer to check that the lease was validly granted *if* it was granted under 15 years ago

---

II   Registered title

A. The 'Register'

The Register comprises three different registers.

1   Property Register *(LRR r.3)*

➤ Describes the property. The description does not exclude extraneous evidence from deeds, etc, unless the boundaries are 'fixed' by HM Land Registry at the proprietor's request.

➤ It gives details of:

♦ any mineral rights, *and*

♦ any rights from which the land benefits, *and*

♦ cross references to any related titles (eg: a lease, or head lease).

2   Proprietorship Register *(LRR r.9)*

➤ States the names and addresses of the proprietors, and gives the class of title. It notes:

♦ restrictions on the right of a sole proprietor (*Form 62*), trustees (*Form 11A*), PRs (*Form 11B*), a limited company or a charity to deal with land. To enter a restriction submit *Form 75* or *Form 76* (*LRA s.58, LRR rr.235-236*).

♦ inhibitions: if the proprietor is insolvent.

♦ personal covenants: such as indemnity covenants which do not run with the land.

3   Charges Register (*LRR r.7*)

➤ Charges (eg mortgages): the Register states the date of the mortgage and the lender's address.

➤ Minor interests:

◆   third party rights such as registrations under the *MHA 1983/FLA 1996*,

◆   estate contracts.

◆   equitable easements.

◆   restrictive covenants - the wording is usually in a schedule to the Charges Register.

◆   rights of beneficiaries under *TLATA 1996 s.6* or *s.8*.

➤ Notices of minor interests: these are placed on the Register with the proprietor's consent.

◆   Submit *Form A4* with the land or charge certificate. (For registration under *MHA 1983/FLA 1996* the proprietor's consent is not needed, so the land certificate need not be submitted.)

➤ Cautions: these are entered without the proprietor's consent.

◆   Submit *Form 63* with a statutory declaration on the back, or *Form 14*. The Registrar can warn off an applicant. After a limited period the right to prove the caution lapses.

Overriding interests

➤ These bind a buyer even if they are not entered on the Register (*LRA s.70(1)(a)-(k)*), eg:

◆   legal easements and profits predating first registration (*LRA s.70(1)(a)*) and rights excepted from first registration when the title is not absolute (*LRA s.70(1)(h)*).

◆   squatters' rights to land through adverse possession which have been acquired or are being acquired under *LA 1980* (*LRA s.70(1)(f)*).

◆   a right of anyone in occupation or receipt of rent except when there is no disclosure in response to enquiries by a buyer for value (*LRA s.70(1)(g)*).

◆   local land charges (eg: planning permission) (*LRA s.70(1)(i)*).

◆   legal leases of under 21 years (*LRA s.70(1)(k)*).

B. Freehold title

There are three classes of freehold title

1   Absolute title (*LRA s.5*)

➤ The State gives an indemnity if title is invalid, or is subject to incumbrances or minor interests (defined at *LRA s.3(xv)*) which the Register should show, but omits (*LRA s.83(2)* as amended by *LRA 1997 s.2*).

➤ Absolute title is (despite it's name) still subject to overriding interests, Register entries, beneficial interests of which the proprietor has notice and lease covenants (if relevant).

2   Possessory title (*LRA s.6*)

➤ This title is subject to adverse interests subsisting, or capable of subsisting at the date of first (or subsequent) registration.

3   Qualified title (*LRA s.7*)

➤ The State indemnity excludes a specified defect in the title.

The Registrar may upgrade a title after 12 years or when he is satisfied a different class of title is merited (eg: possessory title can be upgraded to absolute title (*LRA s.82*)). He may also rectify the Register if it is erroneous, and pay appropriate compensation (*LRA s.83(8)* as amended by *LRA 1997 s.2*).

Proving title

LRA s.110

> a) A copy of Register entries.
>
> b) A copy of the filed plan.

➤ Evidence or abstract if the Register is inconclusive.

➤ Copy or abstract of any document mentioned on the Register.

➤ Note that a) and b) may *not* be excluded by a *Special Condition*.

StC 4.2.1

➤ Requires OCEs rather than copies.

C. Leasehold title

There is a fourth class of title, 'Good leasehold' title   (*LRA ss.8, 10*).

➤ The freehold reversion is unregistered, so the Registrar guarantees the lease only insofar as the grantor acted within his rights in granting the lease.

Proving leasehold title

	Grant (lease)	Grant (sub lease)	Assignment
Open contract rules	*LRA s.110* does not apply. As the Register is a public document, it is possible to apply for OCEs		*LRA s.110* applies. Under *StC 4.2.1* the seller must supply OCEs rather than just copies
		There is *no* right to see the head lease.	
StC 8.2.4.	Imposes an obligation to apply for OCEs	Imposes an obligation on the seller to produce OCEs and a copy of the head lease	See OCEs which show absolute title

III   Searches

Checklist for making searches

1   Which searches are necessary?   Is the form being used the correct one?

2   If a plan is needed, are 2 correctly coloured copies attached, and is the scale sufficiently large?

3   Have any additional questions been correctly entered on the form? (ie: *CON29* Part II).

4   Is the correct fee included with the form (telephone first to confirm the rate)?

5   Are the addresses of the property and that for the answers to the search correct?

➤ Make a file note when the search request is despatched.

➤ Check the file, and chase up any late responses with the relevant authorities.

Pre-contract searches			
Type of search	**Information**	**Protection**	**Application**
In all cases			
Enquiries of seller	The *Protocol* provides a standard form on which the seller lists fixtures, fittings and chattels included in the sale	The seller can refuse to answer questions. Misrepresentation is the buyer's only protection	*Form SPIF* There is a supplementary form for a tenant to fill in if a lease is being assigned
Local land charges	Information statute makes local authorities keep	Yes (*LLCA 1975 s.10*)	*Form LLC1*
Local authority	Information *not* required by statute: ➤ adopted roads/sewers, *and* ➤ road schemes, *and* ➤ planning information, *and* ➤ smoke control orders, *and* ➤ imminent compulsory purchase orders	The authority is liable in negligence, subject to any exclusion clause on the search form	*Form CON29* **Part I:** for general queries **Part II and additional enquires:** for specific matters, a charge is usually made for each item queried
Coal search	Details of past, present and anticipated mineral extraction Check the Law Society's *Coal Mining Directory* for areas likely to be effected		*Form CON29M* is submitted to the surveyor at the Coals Authorities' head office
Commons registration	A registered common, or rights of common may: a) restrict planning permission, *or* b) subject land to third party rights (eg: grazing)		*Form CR1*
Company search	a) The company exists, *and* b) it has power to buy or sell land, *and* c) it is not in receivership, administration or liquidation, *and* d) that the land is not subject to a charge	None	Companies House search
Unregistered land			
Index Map	➤ Cautions against first registration ➤ Pending applications for registration ➤ Date when registration became compulsory	15 day priority period	*Form 96*
Central Land Charges Department	Incumbrances existing over unregistered land: a) easements and covenants affecting the land b) mortgages c) estate contracts d) occupation rights under *MHA 1983/FLA 1996*	15 day priority period	*Form K15* Search the names of all past and present title holders since 1926 (if known) for the period of their ownership of the estate Search against any owner who made a voluntary disposition in the last 5 years Search through pre-1973 counties as well as present day ones
Registered land			
OCEs	Details of title and incumbrances on HM Registry		*Form 94C* non-priority search
Index Map	Unregistered interests in registered land	15 day priority period	*Form 96*
Law Society Search Validation Insurance Scheme ➤ For properties selling up to £500,000 ➤ The scheme covers the difference between the original market price of the property and its value with the adverse entry			

Pre-completion searches		
Type of search	**Information**	**Application**
Unregistered land		
Land Charges Department	As above	
Registered land		
HM Land Registry search	As above. There is a 30 day priority period	*Form 94A* for whole of property *Form 94B* for part of property
Land Charges Department	Details of *unregistered freehold* if a lease has good leasehold title	*Form K15* search against landlord's name
If acting in particular circumstances		
With a company involved in the transaction	Use this to check that: a) the company is not in receivership, administration or liquidation, *and* b) that the land is not subject to a charge	Companies House search
For a lender	Bankruptcy search against the buyer	*Forms K15* and *K16*
	If making a priority search against the Register, do so in the lender's name and the buyer is also protected. Note that the lender is not protected if the search is done in the buyer's name	*Form 94A* for whole of property *Form 94B* for part of property There is a 30 day priority period
When a grant of probate (or a certified copy) are not available	Check that a grant has been issued to the party concerned and is still valid	Principal Probate Registry
When a party will complete using an enduring power of attorney	Check whether the power is registered, or whether registration is pending. a) If the power is registered *and* the grantor is still alive, the attorney may execute the deed b) If registration is pending, the attorney may only execute if the power falls within a limited category defined by *EPAA 1985*	Probate Registry *Form EP4*
If more than 3 months have passed since exchange	Repeat the Local Authority and Local Land Charges search	As above
If the contract is conditional on the results of subsequent searches		
House is under construction	Inspect the fabric to verify that it is satisfactory	Not applicable

---

Action if a pre-completion search shows an adverse entry

➤ Ascertain what the entry relates to.

➤ Contact the seller's solicitor and seek an undertaking that it will be removed prior to completion.

➤ If the search was at the Central Land Charges Department, apply for a copy of *Form 19* on which the entry was originally registered, to find out when (and by whom) it was registered.

➤ Keep client, lender and seller informed subject to the duty of confidentiality.

C Variations to the standard contract

> I   Conditional contracts
>
> II   Sale of part
>
> III   New buildings

I   Conditional contracts

➤ The terms and conditions must be clear and certain.

- ◆ If planning permission is needed:

  - ● decide, if conditions are attached, what would entitle the buyer to rescind. In particular, consider whether the buyer can rescind if the planning permission is not granted within a specified period *and* decide whether the buyer may rescind if a planning application is never submitted.

  - ● settle who pays the fee for the application.

  - ● agree whether the application for planning permission should be for outline, or for full consent, and the form of application.

➤ The contract should deal with all these issues and it must state unambiguously:

- ◆ the precise event on which the contract is conditional.

- ◆ by what time any conditions must be fulfilled.

- ◆ the exact terms on which the party with the benefit of the condition may rescind.

➤ Ensure there are no loopholes, except the single express condition enabling a party to rescind.

II   Sale of part

The transaction proceeds as normal, with these differences.

Step 1:   Taking instructions

> ➤ Obtain the consent of any lender with a charge over the land.

- ◆ Unregistered land: the lender executes a deed of release, or is joined to the conveyance.

- ◆ Registered land: the part to be sold is released from the mortgage by the lender completing *Form 53*, to which a plan will be attached.

Step 2: Seller prepares the pre-contract package

➤ There must be a scale plan, and a definition of the land sold and retained.

◆ Registered land: if the land is on a building site, use *Form 102* in lieu of a filed plan.

➤ Adapt the contract: draft any appropriate *Special Conditions*.

Protect the retained land from implied rights in favour of the plot disposed of	Ensure that the sale does not include: any easement of way, light, or air which might interfere with, or restrict the free use of the retained land, for building or any other purpose The transfer to the buyer should expressly exclude any such rights

Impose new covenants	These should be stated expressly Covenants which are negative in substance are advantageous as they will run with the land If covenants are to be enforceable against future owners they must be: a) expressly taken for the benefit of the retained land, *and* b) registered at HM Land Registry or the Central Land Charges Department

Grant any easements in favour of the plot over the retained land	These may be needed to gain access to the plot, or connect services to it

Step 6: Buyer prepares the purchase deed

➤ Unregistered land: a plan is advisable, though not essential.

◆ Include in the deed an acknowledgement that the seller has produced title deeds to the retained land and that they are in safe custody (*LPA s.64*, *StC 4.5.4*).

➤ Registered land: fill in the seller's title number on the purchase deed and attach a plan.

Step 7: Preparing for completion

➤ Registered land: make a pre-completion search on *Form 94B* attached to a plan.

◆ Before completion, deposit the land certificate at the Registry with *Form A15,* giving 'sale of part' as the reason for the deposit of the certificate.

Step 8: Completion

➤ Unregistered land

◆ The buyer marks the abstract or epitome as examined against the original. The seller also does this under the *Protocol.*

◆ A memorandum of sale is endorsed on the seller's most recent title deed (*LPA s.200*).

◆ The seller takes a note of any restrictive covenants which have been imposed, and keeps this with his documents of title.

III   New buildings

This is the same as for a freehold, with these additions:

Step 3: Buyer approves the contract

➤ The contract is likely to be in a standard form, which the developer wishes to use for the whole development.   It may be that the seller is consequently reluctant to negotiate terms which differ from the standard model.   Nonetheless, the buyer's solicitor must ensure that:

◆ any restrictive covenants do not unduly restrict the buyer's use of the property.

◆ the seller undertakes to remedy any minor defects which emerge after completion within a specified time (or that the buyer is protected by an NHBC 'Buildermark' insurance policy).

◆ the seller undertakes to leave the property in 'ship-shape and Bristol fashion' and will:

● landscape the development appropriately.

● hand the property over in a neat state and remove all builder's rubble.

● errect suitable boundary fences.

◆ extra payments for fixtures and fittings (jacuzzis, washing machines, etc) are quantified

◆ a plan, or *Form 102* is supplied with the contract and is accurate.

◆ a 'long stop' completion date is incorporated in the contract.   This should enable the buyer to rescind the contract if the work is unfinished after the time agreed.   The seller may ask for completion to take place a certain number of days after work on the site is finished, in which case the buyer's solicitor should ensure that:

● the period before completion is long enough for pre-completion searches and site inspections by the buyer and his lender.

● the buyer has alternative accommodation while waiting for completion.

● the buyer has access to bridging finance for this period of time, and that the buyer is given enough notice of the works being completed for the lender to put the buyer's solicitor in funds.

➤ If the seller offers a financing package, ensure that the buyer is properly (by a permitted third party, if appropriate - see p.19) advised on whether it is suitable for his needs.

➤ The seller may offer comfort in the form of an NHBC 'Buildermark' insurance policy, or a similar product.   A 'Buildermark' policy protects the buyer and his successors in title against structural defects for 10 years after completion.   The buyer is insured against the builder's default, including its insolvency, for 2 years after completion.

◆ A lender may insist on such insurance cover.

➤ Examine a copy of any agreement between the developer and the highway authority under which the developer will put in roads and street lighting, and the authority will adopt them at a later stage (these agreements are authorised under *HA 1980 s.38*).   Ensure the agreement is backed by an adequate bond, in case the developer becomes insolvent before completing its obligations.

◆ Similar considerations apply to drains and sewers, and agreements with the water authority under *WA 1991 s.104*.

Step 9: Post-completion

➤ Ensure the buyer receives the following documentation, and that it is kept with the title deeds:

◆ an NHBC pack (if appropriate).   Return the tear-off form to the NHBC.

◆ a 'final certificate' from the local authority confirming that planning consent and building regulations have been complied with.

➤ Before 2 year cover under a 'Buildermark' policy against the builder's default runs out, advise the buyer to carry out a full structural survey, to reveal any latent defects.

D Leases

I   Drafting a lease - outline points

1   **Definitions section**

2   **Grant**

➤ The premium, ie: the sum which the tenant pays the landlord for the grant of the lease.

➤ The term, ie: how long the lease lasts for.

➤ Starting date, ie: when the term runs from; this need *not* be the date of completion as the landlord may wish a batch of leases to start on the same day irrespective of when he finds tenants so as to ensure that the reversion dates are the same.

➤ Ground rent: this is often paid on the quarter days - Lady Day: 25 March; Midsummer Day: 24 June; Michaelmas: 29 September; Christmas Day: 25 December.

➤ Rent review: basis of calculation/frequency.

2   **Easements and reservations**

3   **Common parts**

➤ Identify these, provide for their maintenance and repair. This is usually done through a periodic service charge.

4   **Tenant's covenants**

➤ To pay rent, repair, not to make alterations or improvements, not to change user, or alienate the lease (eg: by subletting the property without the landlord's consent).

5   **Landlord's covenants: to insure, and keep common parts in repair**

6   **Insurance**

➤ This can be achieved in several ways, but contributions to a block policy taken out by the landlord (or management company) ensure tenants are covered for the same risks.

7   **Cesser of rent**

➤ A tenant may cease to pay rent if a building is burnt down, or on specified events.

8   **Forfeiture clause**

➤ This states in what circumstances the landlord may regain possession. A court order is needed for an occupied dwelling (*PEA 1977 s.2*). On breach of covenant, a notice is usually served under the *LPA s.146.*

Flats: common law presumptions

a) If the tenant is not responsible for something, then the landlord is presumed to be so.

b) External walls are included in the demise, even if the landlord is responsible for repairing them.

c) A flat includes ceiling, at least to the underside of the floor joists to which the ceiling is attached.

d) If the ownership of a roof is not expressly reserved by the landlord, the top floor tenant can occupy or alter it (eg: build extra stories).

e) There is *no* presumption that internal boundary walls divide flats from each other or from common parts; therefore an accurate plan marking the extent of the flat, common parts and rights of way is essential.

II   Management schemes

These schemes govern how an estate is maintained; there are three types of scheme commonly used.

1   The landlord manages the estate either directly, or through an agent

✘ The landlord cannot walk away and wash his hands of day to day administration.

✘ Tenants are not given the freedom to organise things as they wish.

✘ Tenants do not have a contractual right to ensure their neighbours comply with their covenants. They rely on the landlord to police covenants which he has with each tenant.

2   Tenants covenant with each other by deed of covenant

✘ There is no co-ordination or general oversight - each tenant is on his own.

✘ Enforcement can be haphazard and difficult.

3   A management company is set up

✔ Enforcement by the company is practicable.

✔ The landlord is freed from the burden of administration.

✔ The landlord retains his investment in the reversion.

➤ There are two ways of setting up a private company (see p.198): in both cases the landlord grants the lease and covenants to provide services. Then *either*:

a) at a later date, the management company can join the lease, and the landlord irrevocably instructs the tenant to pay the service charge to the company in consideration of the company undertaking the service obligations, *or*

b) the landlord grants the company a concurrent lease of the block (effectively leasing the reversion). During the lease, the company becomes the tenant's landlord and provides the services specified in the lease.

III   Procedure for granting a lease

This is the same as for a freehold conveyance, with these additions:

Step 2: Seller prepares the pre-contract package

➤ The landlord drafts the lease and the contract. He sends the buyer:

◆ proof of the freehold title (see pp.163, 166), *and*

◆ evidence that any lender with a charge over the land consents to the grant of the lease, *and*

◆ a draft contract and a draft lease.

Liability on covenants

➤ For leases granted on or after 1 January 1996 (other than under an agreement entered into, or a court order made before that date *and* assignments made by operation of law after that date) the tenant will be released from covenants on any subsequent assignment (*LT(C)A 1995 s.5*).

➤ The landlord can protect his position by inserting a covenant that the tenant shall:

a) secure adequate references from a future assignee.

b) enter into an 'authorised guarantee agreement' under which the tenant agrees to guarantee the performance of any covenants by the assignee until the assignee makes another assignment (or the tenancy is assigned by operation of law) (*LT(C)A 1995 s.16*).

Step 3: Buyer approves the contract

➤ The buyer checks the freehold title.

➤ The buyer checks the terms of the contract *and* the lease.

➤ The buyer should also discover whether the lease is sufficiently marketable and whether it will remain so if the buyer envisages assigning the term before the lease expires to secure a mortgage - banks and building societies are reluctant to lend money for leases of under 60 years.

Step 6: Landlord prepares the 'deed'

➤ The landlord sends a fair copy to the buyer at least 5 working days before completion (*StC 8.2.6*).

◆ A lease for less than 3 years does not need to be by deed (*LPA s.53*).

Step 9: Post-completion

➤ If the lease is granted for a term of more than 7 years, a PD stamp is needed.

➤ Stamp duty is payable, calculated by reference to the length of the term, the rent and the premium (see p.106).

IV   Procedure for assigning a lease

This is the same as for a freehold conveyance, with these additions:

Step 2: Seller (ie: assignor) prepares the pre-contract package

➤ The seller prepares evidence of the freehold title (*StC 8.2.4*).

➤ The seller should ensure that the contract contains an indemnity for the covenants.

◆ **Unregistered lease:** the burden of disclosing incumbrances is on a seller *for value* (*LPA s.77*).

◆ **Registered lease:** *LPA 1969 s.24* places the burden of disclosing incumbrances on the seller.

◆ *StC 4.5.3*: a purchase deed must contain an express indemnity where it is not implied by law.

➤ The seller sends the buyer (ie: the assignee):

◆ the landlord's licence(s) permitting assignment (in the past and consent this time), *and*

◆ proof of leasehold title (unregistered title, see p.163; registered title, see p.166), *and*

◆ a copy of the original lease, *and*

◆ a copy of the insurance policy, and a receipt for the last premium payment, *and*

◆ a copy of the receipt for the last payment of rent and the service charge.

Step 4: Preparations for exchange

➤ In addition to checking the lease, the contract, the consents and the seller's title, the buyer must ensure that:

◆ any references the landlord requires are prepared, *and*

◆ a surety is found (if required by the lease).

Step 6: Buyer prepares the purchase deed

➤ Registered land: use *Form 32*.

➤ Unregistered land: add a covenant for title mirroring *StC 8.1.4*.

Step 7: Preparing for completion

➤ The seller should take the necessary steps to obtain the landlord's consent, see p.199.

◆ The apportionment of rent or service charge should be checked (this is governed by *StC 6.3.5*). The buyer should ask to see service charge accounts for recent years.

Step 9: Post-completion

➤ Registered land: on registration, add to *Form A4* 'for the residue of the term granted by the lease'.

➤ Stamp duty is payable on the transfer or assignment of lease (see p.106).   A licence is not generally dutiable, provided that if it is by deed it has a certificate as required by the *SD(EI)R 1987*.

➤ A PD stamp is needed if the lease has more than 7 years to run (*FA 1930 s.28*).

V   Obtaining a landlord's consent to an assignment or transfer

---

Transfer of part - leases granted after 1 January 1996

➤ The general rule is that the tenant ceases to be liable for the covenants given by the tenant, or to be entitled to the benefits of covenants given by the landlord, in respect of the part of the premises which he assigns (*LT(C)A 1995 s.5(3)*).

➤ If the performance of a covenant is not attributable to the tenant or the assignee, the parties can agree to apportion liability (*LT(C)A 1995 s.9*) provided that within 4 weeks of the assigment the parties serve a notice on the landlord detailing the assignment, their agreement and their request that he should be bound by the apportionment.

   ◆ If the landlord does not serve a notice objecting to the apportionment within 4 weeks of service on him, he is bound (if he does object, the parties may apply to the County Court for a declaration that it is reasonable for the apportionment to bind him) (*LT(C)A 1995 s.10*).

   ● A notice should comply with the *LT(C)A(N)R 1995*.

---

1   Qualified covenants (ie: where the landlord covenants not to unreasonably withhold consent)

➤ Consent may not be unreasonably withheld (*LTA 1927 s.19*).

   ◆ For leases granted on or after 1 January 1996 (except those granted under an agreement or court order dated before that date) ...

   ... over property which is *not* let as a private residence, ...

   ... the landlord shall not be regarded as acting unreasonably if he refuses to grant consent, or agrees to grant it subject to conditions if the landlord cites a reason listed in an agreement with the tenant (eg: not to assign without securing for the landlord adequate references) (*LTA 1927 s.19A*).

➤ The landlord must respond within a 'reasonable' time, and must grant consent unless it is reasonable to withhold it (*International Drilling Fluids Ltd v. Louisville Investments (Uxbridge) Ltd* [1986] 1EGLR 39). The landlord must send the tenant a notice giving any conditions attached to the consent, and reasons for refusing it. (*LTA 1988 s.1(3)*).

➤ The seller is responsible for seeking consent and using 'all reasonable endeavours' to obtain it. If he fails, the buyer's remedy is recession (*StC 8.3.4*).

➤ The landlord does not usually charge a premium, but he may ask the tenant to pay a reasonable administrative charge to cover his expenses.

➤ The licence is written, but it is not by deed unless it contains a covenant by the buyer (assignee).

   ◆ The landlord sends the seller a licence and retains a copy with his deeds of title.

2   Absolute covenants prohibiting assignment

➤ Although the lease prevents assignment, a tenant who wishes to assign can persuade the landlord to:

   a) grant a deed of release from the covenant against assignment, *or*

   b) vary the lease, *or*

   c) give consent.

VI   Procedure for assigning a reversion

This is the same as for a freehold conveyance, with these additions:

Step 2: Assignor (ie: landlord) prepares the pre-contract package

➤ The seller discloses the leases which have been granted over the property, together with details of the service charge accounts.

Steps 4 to 9: Assignor and assignee comply with the requirements of *LT(C)A 1995*

➤ The landlord may apply to be released from his covenants under the tenancy (*LT(C)A 1995 s.6(2)*), and a former landlord who immediately before the assignment was bound by a covenant under that tenancy may also apply for release (*LT(C)A 1995 s.7(2)*).

◆ The procedure involves service on the tenant of a notice, and an opposition procedure operating over 4 weeks from the date of service, similar to that set out in the box on p.199 (*LT(C)A 1995 s.8*).

➤ Any release of liability in respect of the landlord's covenants is accompanied by a loss of the benefit of the tenant's covenants.

➤ If the landlord only assigns the reversion in part and wishes to apportion liability in respect of non-attributable covenants which the landlord is obliged to perform, a procedure similar to that for tenants assigning part of the demised premises should be followed (*LT(C)A 1995 s.9(2)*).

◆ For this procedure, see the box on p.179. The only difference is that the application for the apportionment to become binding is served on the tenant(s) of the premises.

E   Security of tenure

There are two classes of tenancy which, on a new grant of a leasehold interest, may qualify for security of tenure by virtue of statute.

I	Residential tenancies
II	Commercial tenancies

I   Residential tenancies

The main features of assured and assured shorthold tenancies
➤ The tenant has some security of tenure.   When the fixed term expires, a statutory periodic tenancy automatically arises (*HA 1988 s.5(2)*). Unlike the situation for commercial property under *LTA 1954 Part II*, the tenant does not have to serve a notice to obtain a new tenancy.
➤ The statutory periodic tenancy may be ended by:
a) a court order (*HA 1988 s.7*), *or*
b) action taken by a tenant at common law to end the tenancy (surrender, etc) (*HA 1988 s.5(2)*).
➤ A landlord may regain possession of property let on an assured shorthold tenancy by serving a notice under *s.21* of *HA 1988*.

1 Is the tenancy an assured tenancy, or an assured shorthold tenancy?	
Assured tenancy	**Assured shorthold tenancy**
	As for an assured tenancy plus (*HA 1988 s.20*):
Requirements (*HA 1988 s.1(1)*)	➤ fixed term, for a term certain,
➤ dwelling house	➤ the term starts not less than 6 months from the grant of the lease,
➤ let (ie: lease not a licence)	➤ no landlord's break clause in the first 6 months,
➤ as a separate dwelling (ie: at the time of the grant),	➤ for leases granted before 27 February 1997 a shorthold notice is given to the tenant before the lease is granted in the form of *Form 7* (*ATAO(F)R 1988*). From 28 February 1997 the onus is on the landlord to serve a notice if the tenancy is *not* to be an assured shorthold (*HA 1988 s.19A*). A tenant who does not receive a notice under *s.19A* will be entitled to request a written statement of the terms of the tenancy from the landlord (*HA 1988 s.20A*)
➤ to a tenant who is an individual (ie: not a company)	
Note: that a dwelling has been held to be somewhere where 'all the major activities of life, particularly sleeping, cooking and feeding ...' take place (*Wright v. Howell* (1947) 92 Sol Jo26, CA)	
Exclusions (outline)	
➤ Lease granted, or contract to grant a lease, dated before 15 January 1989	
➤ Student lettings	
➤ Lettings to homeless persons under *HA 1985 Part II*	
➤ Properties of a high rent or rateable value (eg: over £25,000 per annum if granted after 1 April 1990)	
➤ Low rent properties (eg: under £1000 per annum in the Greater London area if granted after 1 April 1990)	
➤ Tenancies within the scope of the *LTA 1954 Part II*, or (in respect of assured shorholds) *HA 1988 Schedule 2A*	

2   **Are there special terms which statute implies into the lease, or another statutory regulation?**

➤ There are controls on the calculation and payment of service charges (*LTA 1985 ss.18-30*).

    ◆ These controls were extended when *HA 1996 s.83(1)* (inserting *s.19(2A)-19(2C)* into *LTA 1985*) came into force. Tenants and landlords may ask a leasehold valuation tribunal to assess whether a service charge is 'reasonable' and whether work paid for by a service charge has been done to a 'reasonable standard'. *HA 1996 s.83(2)* allows the tenant to challenge the landlord's choice of insurer or excessive premiums.

      ● Note that the right to apply to a leasehold valuation tribunal under *HA 1996 s.83* does not apply if the tenant agrees to or admits the charge or insurance, *or* the tenant is a party to an arbitration agreement which covers the dispute.

    ◆ If a property is let as a 'dwelling', a landlord may not be able to re-enter the property or forfeit the lease for non-payment of a service charge, unless:

      ● the tenant agrees the amount of the service charge, *or*

      ● the amount is determined by a court or tribunal under an arbitration agreement (as defined by *AA 1996*) (*HA 1996 s.81*).

       ■ A notice served under *LPA 1925 s.146* is effective, provided it informs the tenant of his rights (in the form set out in the regulations) under *HA 1996 s.81*.

➤ Certain assured tenancies are subject to rent control provisions (*LTA 1988 s.22*).

➤ For *all* new residential leases of under 7 years granted to a new tenant (eg: not a former tenant or one in possession at the time of a grant), statute implies covenants that the landlord will:

   a) keep the exterior and structure in repair, *and*

   b) ensure installations for heating, water and space and those supplying water, gas, electricity and sanitation are kept in repair and proper working order (*LTA 1985 ss.11-14*).

3   **Can the landlord regain possession?**

➤ If the tenancy is an assured shorthold, the landlord will need to serve a notice under *s.21* of the *HA 1988* giving at least 2 months' clear notice of his intention to take possession.

➤ The landlord commences proceedings by serving a notice on the tenant stating the ground(s) upon which he intends to take possession of the property (*LTA 1988 s.8*). If *Ground 14A* (domestic violence) is relied on, the landlord's notice must meet additional requirements which are beyond the scope of this book (*LTA 1988 s.8A*).

    ◆ A notice under *HA 1988 ss.8-8A* may specify an earlier date for the commencement of proceedings if *Grounds 1,2,5,6,7,9,14* or *16* are relied upon by the landlord.

4   **Does the tenant have the right to buy the freehold, or to a lease extension?**

➤ The tenant may have the right to buy the freehold, or extend the lease by up to 90 years if the term of the lease exceeds 21 years (*LRA 1967, LRHUDA 1993* as amended by *HA 1996*).

➤ If, without 'reasonable excuse', a landlord fails to offer tenants first refusal on a disposal of his interest on or after 1 October 1996, he commits a criminal offence punishable by a fine of up to £5,000 (*HA 1996 Schedule 6*).

    ◆ This applies when premises contain 2 or more flats if more than half of those flats are rented (*LTA 1987*).

		Are there grounds for a court order for possession?	
		Assured tenancies	
Mandatory **1-8**	Ground 1*:	a)	at some time before the tenancy began the property was the landlord's principal home, *or*
		b)	the landlord seeks possession for himself or his spouse as a principal home *and* the reversion was not acquired for money or money's worth
	Ground 2*:	a mortgagee under a pre-existing mortgage is exercising a power of sale	
	Grounds 3-5*:	out of season holiday lettings, vacation lettings to students, lettings to ministers of religion	
	Ground 6:	the landlord 'intends to demolish or reconconstruct the whole or a substantial part of the dwelling, or carry out substantial building works ...', *and* the landlord did not acquire the reversion for money or money's worth *and* possession is essential for the works. (Varying the lease is unacceptable to the tenant or impractical)	
	Ground 7:	the death of a tenant. (A spouse's right to succession is not affected by this ground (*s.17*))	
	Ground 8:	rent arrears of 8 weeks if paid weekly, or 2 months if paid monthly, *when* notice is served *and* at the date of the hearing (plead Grounds 10 and 11 in the alternative) (amended by *HA 1996 s.101*)	
	*	The landlord must serve stating that possession may be sought under the appropriate ground. This must be given 'not later than the beginning of the tenancy'	
Discretionary **9-17**	Ground 9:	the landlord offers 'suitable' alternative accommodation as defined in *Schedule 2 Part III*	
	Ground 10:	less than 3 months' rent is in arrears	
	Ground 11:	persistent delay in paying rent	
	Ground 12:	breach of tenancy clause which does not relate to rent	
	Ground 13:	deterioration of the dwelling due to the tenant's neglect	
	Ground 14:	the tenant or a person residing in or visiting the dwelling:	
		a) is a nuisance or annoyance to anyone engaged in lawful activity in the vicinity, or b) is convicted for using the premises or allowing them to be used for illegal or immoral purposes, or c) commits an arrestable offence in the locality (as amended by *HA 1996 s.147*)	
	Ground 14A:	the occupiers are a married couple or living together as man and wife, one of the partners has left because of violence to themself or a child and is unlikely to return, and the landlord seeking possession is a 'registered social landlord' or a 'charitable housing trust' (inserted by *HA 1996 s.148*)	
	Ground 15:	deterioration of furniture due to the tenant's conduct	
	Ground 16:	the tenant's employment ends when the letting was a consequence of that employment	
	Ground 17:	tenant's false statement, made knowingly or recklessly, induced the landlord to grant the lease (*HA 1996 s.102*)	
		Assured shorthold tenancies	

➤ The grounds are the same as those for assured tenancies

➤ In addition, a notice can be served under *s.21* of the *HA 1988* giving the tenant not less than 2 months' notice that the landlord requires possession of the dwelling

II   Commercial tenancies

> ### Commercial property leases in England & Wales - Code of practice
>
> ➤ This code of good practice, endorsed by the Law Society and the British Property Federation, should be brought to the attention of landlords and tenants, especially if either are small businesses, before the grant of a lease.
>
> ➤ If the industry does not voluntarily implement the Code to make the market more transparent, the Government may legislate on the conduct of rent reviews and alternative dispute resolution.

The *LTA 1954 Part II* provides some security of tenure to tenants of commercial property by extending the term indefinitely after the date on which it would otherwise determine at common law (*LTA 1954 s.24(1)*).

1   Does the *LTA 1954* apply to the tenancy?

➤ If a lease to which the Act would otherwise apply is to be granted, the parties may wish to consider contracting out of the *LTA 1954*.

➤ If the parties wish to contact out, a copy of the lease and an originating application should be lodged at the County Court several weeks before the lease is granted.

> ### Tenancies protected by the *LTA 1954 Part II*
>
> ➤ A tenancy is protected if it (*LTA 1954 s.23*):
>
> a) is a tenancy (ie: not a licence), *and*
>
> b) is of premises, *and*
>
> c) is occupied at least in part by the tenant, *and*
>
> d) is for the purposes of a business (*Grayism Holdings Ltd v. P & O Property Holdings Ltd* 3 WLR [1995] 854, HL),
>
> ... provided that it is not excluded for any reason, eg:
>
> > i) the tenancy is 'contracted out' under *LTA 1954 s.38(4)*. An application to the County Court in the name of both the landlord and the tenant must be made before a lease is granted and the lease must be for a term certain, *or*
> >
> > ii) it is an agricultural holding (*LTA 1954 s.43(1)(a)*), *or*
> >
> > iii) it is granted by reason of employment (*LTA 1954 s.43(2)*), *or*
> >
> > iv) it is for a term certain not exceeding 6 months (*LTA 1954 s. 43(3)*).

2   If the *LTA 1954* applies, how can the landlord regain possession, or a new lease be granted under the *LTA 1954*?

➤ The *LTA 1954* operates a bureaucratic system of notices, which must be served correctly at the appropriate times.

➤ The procedural clock is set by reference to the 'termination date' of the lease. This date is set as follows:

◆ for a fixed term tenancy: not earlier than the date on which the tenancy would have expired at common law.

◆ for a periodic tenancy: not earlier than the earliest date on which the landlord could have served a notice to quit under *s.25(3)(a)*.

➤ A *s.25* notice is served by a landlord who wishes to regain possession. To be valid it must be:

♦ served not less than 6 months and not more than 1 year before the termination date, *and*

♦ given to the tenant, *and*

♦ specify the termination date, *and*

♦ demand action of the tenant (eg: vacate the premises, or enter negotiations for a new tenancy), *and*

♦ explain whether the landlord will oppose the grant of a new tenancy - there are 8 grounds on which the landlord may seek to end the tenancy (it is impossible to rely on grounds not cited in the *s.25* notice):

a) a breach of the tenant's repairing obligations.

b) persistent delay in paying rent.

c) other substantial breaches.

d) the landlord can provide suitable alternative accommodation.

e) the landlord needs possession for letting or disposing of the property as a whole.

f) the landlord intends to demolish or reconstruct the property.

g) the landlord intends to occupy the premises for his business or as his residence, *and*

♦ be in the correct form set out in the *Landlord and Tenant Act 1954 Part II (Notices) Regulations 1983*.

➤ A *s.26* request is served by a tenant who wants a new tenancy. This can only be served if the tenant has not indicated that he will leave *or* if he has received a *s.25* notice from the landlord. It must:

♦ specify a date for the new tenancy to begin, which is not more than 1 year and not less than 6 months after the date specified in the notice (which cannot be earlier than the termination date), *and*

♦ contain proposals for the new lease (the amount of detail depends on the tenant's negotiating tactics, eg: whether the tenant wishes to tell the landlord early on exactly what he wants), *and*

♦ demand action from the landlord, *and*

♦ be served by a tenant with an interest in the tenancy on a competent landlord, *and*

♦ be in the form set out in the *Landlord and Tenant Act 1954 Part II (Notices) Regulations 1983*.

3 Is the tenant entitled to any compensation on termination?

➤ If the landlord terminates the tenancy under grounds in *ss.30(1)(e)-(g)*, then generally the tenant will be entitled to compensation (*s.37*).

➤ If the tenant has made improvements to the property, he may be entitled to compensation under *LTA 1927 Part I*.

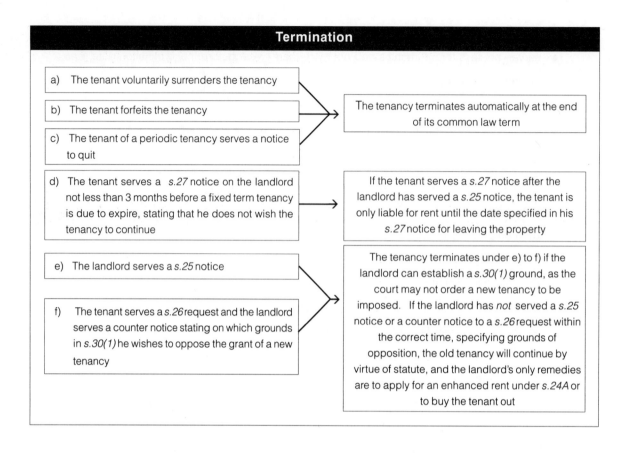

Termination

a) The tenant voluntarily surrenders the tenancy

b) The tenant forfeits the tenancy

c) The tenant of a periodic tenancy serves a notice to quit

→ The tenancy terminates automatically at the end of its common law term

d) The tenant serves a *s.27* notice on the landlord not less than 3 months before a fixed term tenancy is due to expire, stating that he does not wish the tenancy to continue

→ If the tenant serves a *s.27* notice after the landlord has served a *s.25* notice, the tenant is only liable for rent until the date specified in his *s.27* notice for leaving the property

e) The landlord serves a *s.25* notice

f) The tenant serves a *s.26* request and the landlord serves a counter notice stating on which grounds in *s.30(1)* he wishes to oppose the grant of a new tenancy

→ The tenancy terminates under e) to f) if the landlord can establish a *s.30(1)* ground, as the court may not order a new tenancy to be imposed. If the landlord has *not* served a *s.25* notice or a counter notice to a *s.26* request within the correct time, specifying grounds of opposition, the old tenancy will continue by virtue of statute, and the landlord's only remedies are to apply for an enhanced rent under *s.24A* or to buy the tenant out

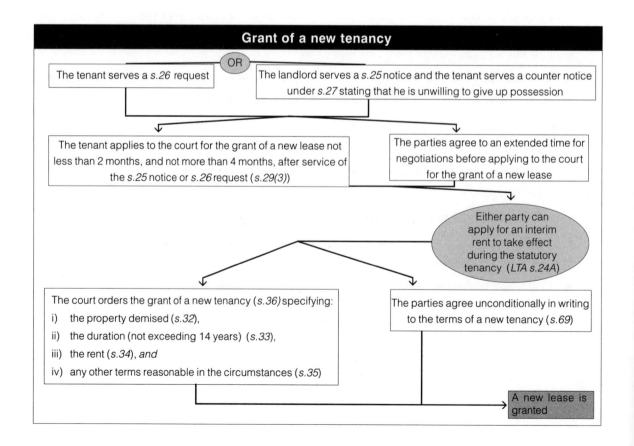

Grant of a new tenancy

The tenant serves a *s.26* request

OR

The landlord serves a *s.25* notice and the tenant serves a counter notice under *s.27* stating that he is unwilling to give up possession

The tenant applies to the court for the grant of a new lease not less than 2 months, and not more than 4 months, after service of the *s.25* notice or *s.26* request (*s.29(3)*)

The parties agree to an extended time for negotiations before applying to the court for the grant of a new lease

Either party can apply for an interim rent to take effect during the statutory tenancy (*LTA s.24A*)

The court orders the grant of a new tenancy (*s.36*) specifying:

i) the property demised (*s.32*),

ii) the duration (not exceeding 14 years) (*s.33*),

iii) the rent (*s.34*), *and*

iv) any other terms reasonable in the circumstances (*s.35*)

The parties agree unconditionally in writing to the terms of a new tenancy (*s.69*)

→ A new lease is granted

F   Remedies

I   Notice to complete

II   Compensation for delayed completion

III   Contractual remedies

Vendor and purchaser summons (*LPA s.49(1)*)

Under this section, either party may issue a summons to resolve disputes connected with the transation (but *not* one questioning the validity or existence of the contract itself).

The court has summary jurisdiction to resolve such matters as:

➤   the validity of a notice to complete.

➤   whether the buyer is taking a clean title as promised in the contract.

➤   whether a requisition on title is valid.

I   Notice to complete

➤   Initially time is not of the essence (*StC 6.1*), unless the contract is conditional.   It can be made of the essence if completion is delayed by serving a notice to complete.

➤   Time is 'of the essence' from the service of a notice to complete. Consequently, if completion does not occur when the notice specifies, the party at fault commits a breach of contract.

♦   The innocent party may choose to terminate the contract after this breach and/or sue for damages.

♦   If the party who served the notice defaults, the recipient of the notice has an action for breach. Consequently, a notice should only be served if you are sure you can complete.

1   At common law

➤ The notice must specify a 'reasonable' time for the new completion date.

➤ The party serving the notice must be ready, willing, and able to complete if the notice is to be valid.

2   *StC 6.8* displaces the common law rules

➤   The notice should state that it is served under this contractual provision.

➤   If a notice is served, the new completion date is set 10 clear days from the day of service.

➤   If the buyer has paid a deposit of under 10%, he must pay the full 10% on receipt of the notice.

➤   If the notice is ignored, the seller may rescind if he served the notice (*StC 7.5*), *or* the buyer may rescind if he served the notice (*StC 7.6*).

II   Compensation for delayed completion

---

1   Delay due to the seller's fault (at common law)

➤ The seller pays outgoings on the property during the period of delay.

➤ The seller retains *whichever is less of*:

   a)   the interest on the purchase price which the buyer pays at the general equitable rate, *or*

   b)   the net income on the property.

2   Delay due to the buyer's fault (at common law)

➤ The buyer pays outgoings on the property.

➤ The buyer retains any income from the property.

➤ The buyer pays the seller interest on the balance at the general equitable rate.

3   *StC 7.3* (this overrides the common law regime)

➤ Whichever party causes the greater period of delay pays the other compensation at the contract rate.

➤ The sum on which interest is paid depends on which party is liable to pay compensation.

   ◆ The buyer's interest is calculated on the balance of the purchase price outstanding (ie: the deposit is deducted).

   ◆ The seller's interest is calculated on the purchase price.

➤ Interest runs for whichever is the shorter of:

   a)   the time between the contractual completion date and actual completion, *or*

   b)   the length of time during which the party liable to pay compensation was in default.

   Note: compensation under *StC 7.3* is deducted from any damages a court subsequently awards.

III   Contractual remedies

Pre-completion	Post-completion
Action on the covenants for title	

For a list of the covenants implied by statute on, or after 1 July 1995, see p.139

Before 1 July 1995, *LPA s.76(1)* implied into conveyances or transfers of land for value covenants which depended on the seller's capacity (as 'beneficial owner', 'fiduciary' or 'settlor'), and whether the interest concerned was freehold or leasehold

➤   This action is *only* available *after* completion if the contract incorporates a non-merger clause similar to *StC 7.4*, otherwise the contract and the deed 'merge', removing the right to a remedy under the contract alone

Rescission

➤   This restores the parties to their original position

➤   The plaintiff may seek an indemnity in the contract for any loss incurred

➤   The plaintiff may seek damages if:

  a) he is claiming rescission under *MA 1967 s.2(1)*, *or*

  b) rescission is due to the defendant's breach, *or*

  c) the plaintiff is seeking a declaration from the court that the defendant has committed a repudiatory breach of contract

➤   The plaintiff may *not* seek damages where obtaining rescission is the purpose of the action

The *StC* expressly reserve the right to rescind if:

  a) the seller makes a misrepresentation (an error of fact upon which the buyer relies in entering the contract) (*StC 7.1*), *or*

  b) the landlord does not grant a licence to assign (*StC 8.3*), *or*

  c) the condition of the property alters substantially before completion (*StC 5.1*)

StC 7.2 lists rights on rescission *under the contract*:

  a) documents are returned to the seller, *and*

  b) the buyer pays for cancelling any entry on the Register to protect the contract, and regains the deposit plus interest

Damages for breach of contract	Rectification

➤ Calculated on the principle in *Hadley v. Baxendale* (1854) 9 Exch 341: all loss arising naturally from the breach which the parties could reasonably have foreseen on entering the contract would result from the breach	➤ This is an equitable remedy: the document is altered to reflect the party's original intentions
	
	Either the parties agree,
	
	or the court grants the remedy at its discretion if:
	
	  ◆ *both* parties were mistaken, *or*
	
	  ◆ *one* party was mistaken *and* the party 'in the know' was ...

Specific performance	

➤ An equitable remedy in the court's discretion
 	
➤ The court may award damages instead of granting specific performance (*SCA 1981 s.51*)
 	
➤ The court may award damages as well as specific performance (*Johnson v. Agnew* [1979] 1 All ER 883)
	a) aware of the error and so is estopped from resisting rectification, *or*
	
	  b) fraudulent, *or*
	
	  ◆ only one party is party to the document
	
	Note: if both rescission and rectification are available, the court may offer the plaintiff a choice, as *per* Lord Denning in *Solle v. Butcher* [1950] 1 KB 671

Business

This chapter examines:

All taxation aspects are dealt with together in the 'Taxation' section of this book.

Treaty of Rome - *Article 52*

The right to establish a business in any member state, provided that the requirements of national law regarding the running of that type of business are satisfied (ie: company, partnership, etc).

A Partnerships

I Formation of a partnership

➤ A partnership 'subsists between persons carrying on a *business in common* with a view to profit' (*PA s.1*) (our emphasis).

➤ A partnership can come into existence orally, *or* by an agreement, *or* through a course of conduct.

➤ 20 partners is the maximum permitted, except for partnerships consisting of members of certain professions (eg: solicitors, accountants) (*CA s.716*).

➤ However the partnership comes into existence, the *Business Names Act 1985* should be complied with.

Business Names Act 1985	
Section	**Content**
1	➤ If the name is the partners' surnames, either alone or with their initials, forenames or an 's' to show that there is more than one partner with a given name, then no restrictions apply.
2-3	➤ Words listed in the *Company and Business Names Regulations 1981 (amended in 1982, 1992 and 1995)* (eg: names suggesting a connection with HM Government or the royal family) require the approval of the President of the Board of Trade.
4	➤ Unless a name approved under *s.1* is used, then the names of partners and the address for service of documents must appear both: a) on letters, orders, invoices, receipts and written demands for payment, *and* b) at the place of business to which suppliers and customers have access. These details must also be given to anyone who requests such information. If a firm has more than 20 partners, it is sufficient to give the address of the main place of business where the addresses and names can be found.
5	➤ Fines may be imposed for non-compliance with the *Act*, and a contract with a third party who is prejudiced by the infringement will be unenforceable.
7	➤ Breach of the *Act* is a crime.

II A written agreement for a partnership

A written agreement is safest to effect a partnership. Various matters are highlighted below which the draftsman may wish to consider. References are to the *Partnership Act 1890*, unless otherwise stated, and the Act will apply if the partnership agreement is silent on a particular matter.

1   **Commencement date:** an objective test based on *s.1* - the date stated in the agreement is not conclusive.

2   **Name:** the firm's name (and its trading name if this is different). These must comply with *BNA 1985*.

3   **Financial input:** of each partner.

4   **Salaries:** if the agreement is silent, the partners will not be entitled to a salary (*s.24(6)*).

5   **Interest**
   ➤ Partners are entitled to interest at 5% on capital they advance in excess of their obligations under the terms of the partnership (*s.24(3)*).
   ➤ There is no entitlement to interest on capital until profits have been ascertained (*s.24(4)*).

6   **Capital profits or losses:** if the agreement is silent, these are shared equally (*s.24(1)*).

7   **Shares in profit derived from income:** if the agreement is silent, these are shared equally (*s.24(1)*).

8   **Drawings of money**

9   **Place and nature of business**

10   **Ownership of assets:** either i) by the partners privately, or ii) by partners on trust for all the partners.

11   **Work input**
   ➤ Full or part-time?
   ➤ Bar on the involvement of partners in other businesses during their membership of the partnership?

12   **Partners' roles**
   ➤ All the partners may manage the firm (*s.24(5)*), but this is inappropriate for 'sleeping' partners.

13   **Management**
   ➤ A simple majority prevails, unless otherwise stated (*s.24(8)*).
   ➤ Unanimity is required for i) changing the business (*s.24(8)*), ii) admitting new partners (*s.24(7)*).
   ➤ If unanimity is required for anything else, put it in the contract.

14   **Duration of the partnership**
   ➤ i) At will, or ii) for a fixed term, or iii) for as long as a minimum of two partners remain.
   ➤ *PA s.26* provides that if no date is given, then if a notice of dissolution is given, it is effective immediately. To prevent this occurring inadvertently, a notice period should be specified.

15   **Death/bankruptcy/retirement:** if the agreement is silent, these dissolve a partnership (*PA s.33*).

16   **Expulsion of partners:** this is impossible without an express provision in the agreement (*PA s.25*).

17   **Paying for an outgoing partner's share.** Consider:
   ➤ either i) an *option* for the remaining partners to purchase the share, *or* ii) an obligation on them to purchase it.
   ➤ a method for valuing the share. Provide for professional valuation if the partners do not agree.
   ➤ a date on which payment falls due (a grace period allows those remaining to find new equity).
   ➤ whether an indemnity is included in the valuation.

18   **Restraint of trade on outgoing partners:** the clause must be 'reasonable' to be enforceable at common law (ie: with regard to time, geographical area, and whether the activity competes with the partnership).

19   **Income tax**
   ➤ An outgoing partner may be obliged to join the others in sending a tax election to the Inland Revenue.
   ➤ An outgoing partner should be indemnified against additional liability resulting from his election.

20   **Arbitration:** name an arbitrator in case of disputes between the partners.

III   Obligations and liability of partners

A. Generally

➤   Partners are bound to each other:

1   **in contract:** in accordance with the terms of the partnership agreement, *and*

2   **under the *PA ss.28-30* and a century of case-law:** by a set of duties that can collectively be called a duty of utmost good faith:

  ◆   to divulge to each other all information relevant to the business, *and*

  ◆   to share any profit derived from the business or its property *and* to share any profit derived from a competing business.

B. Firm's liability

Recovery from the firm

➤   The firm is a group of persons who were partners at the time the cause of action arose (*PA ss.9,17*).

➤   Recovery is possible from the partnership assets and also from partners personally.

➤   The firm may be liable:

1   **in tort:** for a partner's act or omission in the ordinary course of business, *or* an act with a partner's authority (*PA s.10*).

2   **in contract:** for agreements made by a partner with, or with the partners', 'actual' or 'ostensible' authority.

  ◆   **Actual authority:** this can be expressly *or* impliedly given in the partnership agreement, or it may arise from a factual situation or a decision of the partners.

  ◆   **Ostensible authority:** 4 conditions must be satisfied (*PA ss.5-8*):

  subjective test
  - a) the third party knows or believes he is dealing with a partner, *and*
  - b) the third party is unaware that the partner was not actually authorised, *and*

  objective test
  - c) the partner would usually be expected to be authorised to enter into such a transaction, *and*
  - d) the firm's type of business is consistent with the nature of the transaction.

C. Personal liability of a partner

1   A partner to a third party

➤ A partner is personally liable in contract (if he or the firm are party to the contract) and in tort.

- Liability is without limit for debts incurred while a partner (*PA s.9*).

- Liability does *not* cease on leaving the firm in respect of obligations incurred while a partner (*PA s.17*).

2   A partner to a partner

➤ If a partner acts outside his authority, he can be liable to the other partners for breach of warranty of authority.

3   An ex-partner to a third party

➤ Any partner is liable for obligations incurred *after* his departure from the partnership if there is:

a) 'holding out' that the ex-partner is a partner (*PA s.14*) by:

   i)   a representation (oral/written/conduct) *either* by the ex-partner, *or* with his knowledge, *and*

   ii) reliance on this representation by a third party,

or b) failure to notify of leaving the partnership (*PA s.36*).

- An ex-partner is liable *unless* notice of the change:

   i)   is given to all who have dealt with the firm recently. This protects against claims from previous customers.

   ii) appears in the *London Gazette*. This protects against claims from future customers.

   Note: i) and ii) do not apply on death or bankruptcy, so an estate is not liable for a firm's subsequent acts.

4   A stranger to a third party

➤ A stranger will be liable for an obligation if he has been 'holding out' that he is a partner (*PA s.14*):

   i)   by making a representation (oral/written/conduct) that he is a partner, *and*

   ii) a third party relies on this representation.

D. Limitation of personal liability

1   By indemnity

a) No actual authority

Where a partner has acted without actual authority, the other partners are entitled to an indemnity for any loss they suffer as a result of the unauthorised act.

Note: i)   an indemnity will only protect the other partners if the indemnifier is solvent.

     ii) the other partners will only be entitled to any indemnity if they act to mitigate their loss.

b) Outgoing partner indemnity

An outgoing partner may negotiate an indemnity from the remaining partners to protect himself.

2   By novation

➤ A three-way agreement between a new partner, creditor and those continuing the partnership by which the new partner takes on the outgoing partner's liability. This is contractually binding on all who are party to it.

IV   Dissolution of a partnership

➤ The partnership agreement will usually make provisions for when a partnership may be dissolved. Where it does not (or there is no partnership agreement), the following list of defaults will apply.
(**Note:** number 5 below will apply even if a partnership agreement does deal with the situations listed in the agreement.)

➤ A partnership may be dissolved by ...

1   ... expiry

➤ A 'fixed term' partnership terminates at the end of its term (*PA s.32(a)*).

➤ A partnership intended to achieve a single undertaking ends when that undertaking is attained (*PA s.32(b)*).

◆ If the partners continue acting in concert the agreement continues, but as a 'partnership at will'.

2   ... notice

➤ This is when any partner gives notice to the other(s) of his intention to dissolve the partnership.

◆ Notice may be effective immediately, or after a specified period (*PA s.32(c)*).

◆ Notice does not need to be written unless the partnership agreement is by deed (*PA s.26(2)*).

3   ... illegality

➤ When an event occurs that makes it unlawful to continue in partnership (eg: loss of a licence which is required for running the business) (*PA s.34*).

4   ... court order under *PA s.35*

➤ Regardless of what a partnership agreement may provide, the court has discretion to dissolve a partnership on one of the following grounds:

Either when a partner, other than the partner applying to court ...

s.35(b)	is rendered 'permanently' incapable of carrying out obligations under the agreement, *or*
s.35(c)	engages in conduct prejudicial to the partnership's business, *or*
s.35(d)	wilfully breaches the partnership agreement, or behaves in such a way that it is not reasonably practical for the other partners to continue the business.
s.35(e)	Also, when the partnership can only be continued as a loss-making business, *or*
s.35(f)	when the court regards dissolution as 'just and equitable'.

5   ... court order under *Mental Health Act 1983* s.96(1)(g)

➤ This happens if a partner is a 'patient' (ie: mentally incapable of managing his affairs).

6   ... death, bankruptcy (*PA s.33(1)*), retirement (*PA s.26*) or expulsion (*PA s.25*) of a partner

➤ These events dissolve the partnership.

7   ... charging order

➤ If a partner's share in the partnership assets is subject to an order for payment of a private debt (*PA s.23*), a creditor can seek a court order for the asset's sale; when this sale takes place, a purchaser gains a share in the asset without becoming party to the partnership.

➤ When an order is made, the other partners may give notice of dissolution to prevent a third party purchaser gaining title to the asset (*PA s.33(2)*).

8   ... disposal

➤ A partner may insist on the sale of the business as a whole or in parts (*PA s.39*).

9   ... winding up

➤ Any partner, except a bankrupt, can apply to the court for the appointment of a receiver (*PA s.38*).

V   After dissolution - distribution of assets

➤   Partners all have continuing authority to act on behalf of the partnership after its dissolution (*PA s.38*).

➤   On dissolution, every partner has a right to insist that the partnership property is used to pay the firm's debts (*PA s.39*).

➤   If a dissolution occurs, the business may be sold:

◆   as a going concern, *or*

◆   by breaking up the business and selling off the assets.

➤   The assets (or proceeds from sale of the assets) are distributed in the following order (*PA s.44*):

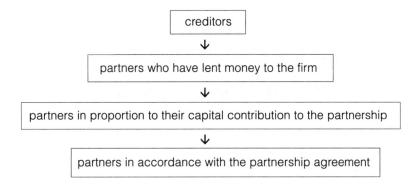

➤   When other partners continue the business, the outgoing partner is entitled to:

a) interest at 5% on that partner's share of the assets, or

b) whatever profit the court attributes to that partner's share of the partnership assets between the dissolution and the actual payment of his share (*PA s.42*).

➤   Where a partner dies, the entitlement under *s.42* to interest or ongoing profits is regarded as a debt owed to his estate from the date of his death (*PA s.43*).

VI   Taxation

➤   See the taxation chapter -Income tax - pp.72-74; CGT - pp.80-83; IHT - pp.85-88.

B   Private companies

References in this section apply to the Companies Act 1985, unless stated otherwise.

➤ From a procedural point of view, a solicitor's first task when dealing with a private company is the 'Establishment' of that company. Although theoretically owned by 'Shareholders' (also known as 'members'), and with all the conflicting interests that that implies, most often the day-to-day management of the company is carried out by the 'Directors'. However, the 'Shareholders' and 'Directors' may well often disagree as to how to make money for the company. The process of making money starts with 'Finance', and once this gets under way, the taxman will want to take his share - 'Taxation'.

I	Establishment
II	Shareholders
III	Directors
IV	Finance
V	Taxation - see 'Corporation tax' - pp.89-99

I   Establishment

A. Establishing the company

There are 2 ways of establishing a company as a vehicle through which to run a business.

1   From scratch

Steps

1   **Prepare:** 1) Statutory books, 2) *Form 10*, 3) *Form 12*, 4) Memorandum of Association,

5) Articles of Association, 6) Fee

2   **File:**   items 2) - 6) with the Registrar of Companies.

3   The Registrar incorporates the company if the documentation is in order (ie: the name does not need approval under *BNA 1985*). Incorporation occurs on the same day if everything is submitted to the Central Registry (Cardiff) before 3 pm. Regional branches (London, Birmingham, Leeds, Edinburgh) also offer same day service.

4   The Registrar issues the 'Certificate of Incorporation' which brings the company into existence as a legal person. Any pre-incorporation contract is voidable. The company can only participate in a pre-existing agreement through a contract of novation (ie: a new contract replacing the earlier contract).

2   Buy a 'shelf company'

➤ A shelf company has already been incorporated and 'sits on the shelf'.

➤ The existing directors of the shelf company resign and members complete a stock transfer form.

➤ This costs around £170 and it is fast and immediate. Changes may be needed for: a) directors, b) secretaries, c) shareholders, d) registered office, e) name, f) objects, g) articles, h) share capital.

➤ The purchased company comes with letters of resignation from the existing directors.

B. Company documentation

1 **Statutory books** (These must be updated throughout the company's life.)

   a) Register of Members,

   b) Register of Directors,

   c) Register of Company Secretaries,

   d) Register of Directors' Interests,

   e) Register of Charges (this is necessary even if the company does not take out any loans),

   f) Minute Books for board and general meetings,

   g) Accounting records (only after incorporation), *and*

   h) Copies of directors' service contracts (only after incorporation).

2 ***Form 10***

➤ This states the postal address of the company's registered office.

➤ It gives the details of the first directors and the company secretary who automatically take office on incorporation (see p.210 and p.216 for an explanation of what details of the officers are required).

➤ It is signed by the subscribers to the memorandum, or by a solicitor on their behalf.

Later alteration of a company's registered office
The registered country must stay the same for this method:
First: the board passes a resolution   →   **Second:** file *Form 287*

3 ***Form 12***

➤ This is a statutory declaration by a director, the company secretary, or a solicitor involved in the formation of the company that the *Companies Act*s have been complied with.

➤ It is sworn before a solicitor or commissioner for oaths.

4 **Memorandum of Association**

➤ The memorandum is printed and signed by at least one subscriber.

➤ It states the name, address, occupation of each subscriber, and the number of shares each will take on formation.

➤ It is dated and witnessed (one witness for both signatures is sufficient).

➤ It contains the following:

   a) Company name

     ◆ This must end with 'Limited' or 'Ltd' (*s.25*) unless the company is limited 'by guarantee' and conditions in *s.30* are fulfilled, limiting the company to humanitarian non-profit making activities.

        • A 'business name' is a trading name which a company may use in addition to the name under which it is incorporated. It need not end with 'Limited', but should comply with *BNA 1985* (see p.192):

As well as the business name...
...give the corporate name, and an address in the UK for serving documents:
a)   on all letters, orders, invoices, etc, *and*
b)   at all places of business to which customers have access, *and*
c)   to any member of the public who requests this information.

- An existing company name is not permitted (*s.26*). Search the Trademarks Index and at Companies House to check a name is not in use (there is no protection period after a search).
- Any offensive name, or any name suggesting a criminal offence, is also forbidden (*s.26*).
- The following require the President of the Board of Trade's written approval (*s.29*): any name suggesting HM Government, the royal family, local authorities or any word or expression contained in continually updated regulations.

Alteration of an existing company name
➤ A 'special resolution' alters the name (*s.28*). The change is advertised by the Registrar of Companies in the *London Gazette* (*s.711*); a third party is not fixed with notice until 15 days after the advertisement appears (*s.42*).
➤ The Registrar will issue a new certificate after payment of the fee.
➤ A change of name may become necessary if: a) the Registrar orders it because the name may harm or mislead the public (*s.32*), *or*   b) a third party's injunction prevents its use for appropriating good will ('passing off').

b) Country in which the registered office is situated *(s.2)*

- This cannot be altered.

c) Limitation of members' liability *(s.3)*

- This is frequently limited by 'share capital', unless stated otherwise.
- Alternatively, liability can be limited 'by guarantee', in which case the members are liable to the extent of the guarantee.

d) Nominal capital

- The maximum value of shares the company can issue. An ordinary shareholder resolution can alter this. (Such a resolution must be filed with the Registrar - see p.208.)

e) Objects of the company *(s.2)*

- The objects set out the purposes of the company and what it is allowed to do.
- *CA 1989* permits a description as a 'general commercial company'. This wording gives the company full freedom to do whatever it likes commercially, but it is unclear whether the company may perform actions which do not advance its business (eg: gifts to political parties or charitable donations).
- Old-style objects clauses may have a *Bell Houses* formula. This is wording as follows: The company is permitted to 'carry on any other trade or business whatsoever which can, in the opinion of the board ..., be advantageously carried on by the company in connection with, or ancillary to, any of the above businesses or the general business of the company' (*Bell Houses Ltd v. City Properties Ltd* [1966] 2 QB 656).
- Old clauses may also end with an 'independent objects' clause. This is done to avoid restrictive case law which in some instances reads 'lesser' objects clauses as subordinate to a 'main' object (ie: as powers of the company rather than an object). An independent objects clause says that each object is an independent object.

Alteration of objects
➤ A special resolution alters the objects (*s.4*).
➤ Minority shareholders can appeal to court within 21 days (*s.5*).

5   **Articles of Association** (the 'constitution' governing a company's internal workings)

➤ This is a contract between the company and its members, *governing members' rights in their capacity as members of the company (s.14)*.

➤ It is printed and signed by the subscribers to the memorandum, dated and witnessed.

➤ 'Table A' (see table below) is a model set of articles that will apply in the absence of other articles unless specifically excluded (*s.8*). However, it may need changes by including special articles, to:

◆ **empower directors to allot shares** (*s.80*).

◆ **empower directors to allot shares to whomever they wish:** lifting the statutory pre-emption rights of existing members to a pro rata allotment of newly issued shares (ie: in proportion to their existing holdings) without recourse to a general meeting (*s.89*).

◆ **enable directors to vote on issues in which they have a personal interest:** *Art.96* permits this in particular conditions; otherwise with a small company it can be difficult to achieve a quorum.

◆ **restrict members' right to transfer shares:** likely in a small family company where the members are anxious to retain control of membership. *Art.24* allows directors to refuse to transfer shares in certain limited circumstances.

◆ **prevent removal of directors:** likely in small company. If a director holds shares, a *Bushell v. Faith* clause is sensible as it multiplies his votes if a resolution proposes his removal. This provides some job security, but shareholders retain the right to remove directors by ordinary resolution (*s.303*).

Note: References in this chapter to Articles (Arts.) assume Table A applies.

➤ Articles can be altered by a special resolution if the change is *bona fide* and in the best interests of the company as a whole (*s.9*).

Summary of Table A

Articles	Subject matter	Articles	Subject matter
	Shares	72	Delegation of directors' powers
2-5	Share capital	73-80	Directors' appointment and retirement
6-7	Share certificates	81	Directors' disqualification and removal
8-11	Lien over shares	82	Directors' remuneration
12-22	Calls on shares and their forfeiture	83	Directors' expenses
23-28	Transfer of shares	84-86	Directors' appointments and interests
29-31	Transmission of shares	87	Directors' gratuities and pensions
32-34	Alteration of share capital	88-98	Directors' proceedings
35	Purchase of own shares		**General**
	Meetings	99	Secretary
36-37	General meetings	100	Minutes
38-39	Notice of general meetings	101	Company seal
40-53	Proceedings at general meetings	102-108	Dividends
54-63	Members' votes at general meetings	109	Accounts
	Directors	110	Capitalisation of profits
64	Number of directors	111-116	Notices
65-69	Alternate directors	117	Winding up
70-71	Directors' powers	118	Indemnity

54-63

First board meeting

Consideration may be given to the following:

1 Electing a chairman.

2 Approving the cost of formation: the company can reimburse the subscribers by a novation contract.

3 Adopting a business name.

4 Opening a bank account.

5 Ordering stationery complying with the requirements in *s.349*, to state:

   a) the company name, its place of registration and registered number (*s.351*), *and*

   b) the address of its registered office (*s.351*), *and*

   c) *either* the names of *all* its directors *or* none of their names (*s.305*).

   ◆ If a business name is used, the company's name and an address in Great Britain for the service of documents must be given.

   ◆ The information given in a) and b) demanded by *s.351* for stationery should also be displayed at any place where the company conducts business (*s.348*).

6 VAT registration with HM Customs and Excise (see p.100).

7 PAYE and National Insurance obligations: contact the local tax office.

8 Insurance.

   ◆ Ensure all the company's assets and necessary insurance policies (eg: see p.258) are in its own name.

9 Appointing an auditor.

10 The accounting reference date is fixed by statute as the last day of the month of incorporation (*CA(MAA)R 1996*). This may be changed later by submitting *Form 225*.

11 Adopting a company seal (*s.350*).

12 Awarding directors' service contracts.

   ◆ If the contract is for over 5 years, the board must resolve to seek shareholders' approval.

13 Allotting shares.

14 Whether to call a general meeting to obtain authority from shareholders to:

   ◆ award directors service contracts of longer than 5 years.

   ◆ allot shares (ordinary resolution *s.80*). Ensure that any pre-emption rights (*s.89*) do not restrict this.

   ◆ adopt an elective regime - see box at the base of this page.

15 Issuing debentures.

Elective resolutions

➤ These simplify the management of private companies by:

   a) giving the directors authority for any specified or indefinite period to allot shares (rather than being limited to 5 years) (*s.80A*).

   b) dispensing with the obligation to lay accounts and reports before an AGM (*s.252*).

   c) dispensing with the need to call AGMs automatically (but a member can still insist on one being called) (*s.366A*).

   d) reducing consent required to hold an EGM at short notice from 95% to a minimum of 90% (*s.369(4) and s.378(3)*).

   e) dispensing with the annual reappointment of auditors (*s.386*).

➤ These must be passed unanimously.

➤ Revocation of any of these is by ordinary resolution (*s.379A*).

II Shareholders

A. Joining a company (ie: becoming a member)

➤ The original subscribers to the memorandum are members automatically, regardless of whether they are entered on the Register of Members.

➤ Anyone can become a member of a company if he buys shares in that company.

◆ However, the directors must agree to write a person into the Register of Members, otherwise there are consequences which are listed below.

Register of Members

➤ This must state: the name, address and the number of shares held by each member, plus consideration for the shares, and the dates on which the shareholder's membership of the company begins and ceases (*s.352*).

➤ The details of new members must be entered within 2 months of acquisition, however they acquire their shares. Directors cannot refuse to enter a name unless the articles permit this - wrongful refusal can be overcome by applying to a court for rectification of the register.

➤ Between acquisition and registration, the prospective member is beneficially entitled to the shares. Dividends and voting rights of the existing registered member must be 'used' at the acquirer's direction.

➤ If a company has only one member, the register must state when this state of affairs begins and ends (otherwise there is a fine for the company and the responsible officer, plus a daily default fine).

➤ The court can order the register to be rectified if *either*:

   a) a name is 'without sufficient cause' entered incorrectly, or there is 'default ... or unnecessary delay' in entering a member's details (*s.359*), *or*

   b) it is 'just and equitable' to do so (*Burns v. Siemens Brothers Dynamo Works Ltd* [1919] 1 Ch 225).

Shareholders' agreement

➤ This binds members in matters beyond the scope of the articles and is used in practice to impose extra obligations on those concerned.

   ◆ It is a private document, and unlike the articles is not open to public inspection.

   ◆ It cannot be altered without the *unanimous* consent of all those who are party to it.

   ◆ It cannot override obligations under the articles or statute.

   ◆ It provides a remedy in breach of contract - via an injunction or damages.

   ◆ Possible uses include:

   • joining a director, who is not a shareholder, to the agreement to enhance his job security by obliging the other signatories not to vote for his dismissal.

   • binding the signatories to pursue a particular management policy - such matters are usually left to the board by the articles, and an agreement gives shareholders a direct influence on how the company is managed.

   • pre-emption rights, where enshrining this in the articles would be too public an act.

   • to allow a member to leave the company by obliging the other signatories to purchase the shares.

B. Shareholders' rights

➤ Obligations between shareholders and the company (or any combination of them) are governed by the memorandum and articles (*s.14*).

➤ For a summary of shareholders' rights, see the chart on the following page.

➤ If Table A is the articles, shareholders may *not* reverse management decisions made by the board (*Art.75*).

➤ **Voting:** a shareholder can generally vote as he sees fit *unless*:

 a) individually, or together with other directors, he holds 50% or more of the shares: this prevents his voting to permit an abuse of power in his capacity as a director, *or*

 b) a majority shareholder ignores 'equitable considerations'. The court may overrule a special resolution passed which disregards these 'equitable considerations' (*Clemens v. Clemens Brothers Ltd* [1976] 2 All ER 268).

➤ All members have a right to attend and vote at an Annual General Meeting ('AGM') of the company.

➤ All members have a right to attend and speak at a general meeting called at any other time - an Extraordinary General Meeting ('EGM').

➤ *The Minister for Company Affairs issued a consultative document on 16th April 1996, to seek views on:*

 ◆ *whether shareholders should have a right to circulate their own resolutions (if seconded by a certain number of shareholders).*

 ◆ *whether shareholders should have a right to appoint corporate representatives or proxies to speak for them at general meetings.*

 ◆ *whether shareholders should have expanded rights to ask questions at the AGM.*

 Note: None of these proposals are anywhere near becoming law at present but the Law Commission is expected to bring out a final report in September 1997.

All shareholders' rights		
Rights	**Notes**	**Statute**
Restrain an *ultra vires* act	Only before the act is done (thereafter the company is bound). Remedy is an injunction	*s.35(2)*
To a share certificate	Within 2 months of allotment or lodgement of transfer of shares. *Prima facie* evidence of title	*s.185*
To a copy of annual accounts	Applies even if an elective resolution dispensing with an AGM is in force	*s.240*
To have a say in removing or appointing a director		*s.303*
Name on Register of Members	Unless subject to a special article	*s.352*
To a dividend if one is declared	May not increase the sum recommended by directors, but may decrease it	*Arts.102-8*
To an AGM	This applies even if an elective resolution dispensing with the need to call an AGM is in force. Ultimately, a member may apply to the DTI which may convene a meeting for the purposes of which that member alone will represent a quorum (*CA s.367*)	*s.366* *s.366A*
To prevent an AGM being held on short notice		*s.369*
To receive notice of general meetings		*s.370*
To attend and vote at general meetings		*s.370*
Ask a court to call an EGM	If a members' boycott prevents a quorum, a court can reduce the quorum required to 1	*s.371*
To prevent the adoption of the elective regime		*s.379A*
To block a written resolution		*s.381A*
Inspect AGM/EGM minutes	Available at the registered office for consultation	*s.383*
Not to be unfairly prejudiced	Prejudice to rights as a member may be past, present, or future (see p.206)	*s.459*
Have a company wound up	Available if the member has a 'tangible interest'. The remedy is equitable	*IA1986* *s.122(g)*
Members with a minimum of 5% of the voting rights		
Place item on the agenda for an AGM	Written request to a company 6 weeks before an AGM with money to cover the company's expenses. (This may be refunded at the meeting.) If directors call an AGM within the 6 weeks, adequate notice is deemed to have been given	*s.376*
Circulate written statement	Written requisition deposited with company at least 1 week before a general meeting	*s.376*
Members with a minimum of 10% of the voting rights		
Call an EGM	May *not* be excluded by articles Members deposit at the registered office a written requisition which is signed by them all and states the reason for calling the meeting. If within 21 days, the directors do not call a meeting, to be held within 28 days of notice being sent out (ie: the maximum delay is 7 weeks from request), then members can call a meeting within 3 months and recover the cost from the company, which may deduct it from the directors' fees. Where members call the meeting they have an implied right to set the agenda (*s.368(3)*)	*s.368*
	This section, like *s.368*, allows members to call an EGM, but it differs in 3 respects: a) it applies to members with 10% or more of the *issued* (not the *paid up*) shares, *and* b) it permits the members themselves to summon the meeting, *and* c) it may be excluded by the articles	*s.370*
Prevent an EGM being held on short notice (unless an elective resolution is in force, in which case they can only do this with *greater than 10%* of the voting rights)		*s.369(3)(b)*
Demand a poll vote		*s.373* *Art. 46*

C. Safeguards for shareholders

➤ Members have a cause of action in contract to enforce rights as members of the company (*s.14*).

◆ Relevant rights include rights to:

a) a share of surplus capital on winding up.

b) a lawfully declared dividend.

c) vote at meetings.

◆ The liability of shareholders is limited to the amount invested in their shares.

Note: a company can use *s.14* to compel members to fulfil contractual obligations (eg: pay for shares).

1 Shareholders' common law actions

➤ General rule: members cannot sue in the company's name (*Foss v. Harbottle* (1843) 2 Hare 461).

➤ There are 4 exceptions to this rule (not dealt with in this book). If a member *does* succeed in bringing an action under these exceptions:

◆ the case is heard under *RSC Ord.15 rule 12A*.

◆ the action is 'derivative' as the plaintiff is pursuing a right which belongs to the company itself. *The company* is the plaintiff. If successful, *the company* is granted a remedy, not the member.

• There is a preliminary hearing to see whether the facts fall within one of the relevant exceptions. If so, this is followed by the main hearing, to determine liability.

2 Shareholders' statutory actions: 'unfair prejudice' (*s.459*)

➤ The member's rights as a shareholder include rights under statute, the memorandum, the articles and any shareholders' agreement.

➤ Whether or not there is unfair prejudice is an objective test, so prejudice is viewed from the perspective of the 'reasonable bystander' (*Re R. A. Noble (Clothing) Ltd* [1983] BCLC 273).

➤ The court can make 'any order it thinks fit' (*s.461(1)*) and a non-exhaustive list of powers is given (*s.461(2)*). These include:

◆ authorising a member to bring a civil action in a company's name.

◆ restraining a company from an act, or compelling it to act so as to avoid the 'unfair prejudice'.

◆ providing for a member's shares to be purchased by other members or a company at a fair price.

➤ An action brought under *s.459* is not derivative, as the plaintiff is suing in his own right. Consequently, *the plaintiff* will receive a remedy if his plea is successful.

Will the courts intervene?

➤ There is conflicting authority as to whether the courts will now intervene wherever it is equitable if there is no precedent for them to do so (*Heyting v. Dupont* [1964] 2 All ER 273, *Prudential Assurance Co. v. Newman Industries Ltd (No.2)* [1982] 1 All ER 354).

➤ Previous cases where the courts have granted a minority shareholder a remedy include where:

◆ the company acted illegally.

◆ the company passed an ordinary resolution when a special or extraordinary resolution is needed.

◆ the majority shareholders 'defrauded' a minority member (*Clemens v. Clemens Brothers* [1976] 2 All ER 268).

D. Shareholders' meetings

Extraordinary General Meetings ('EGMs')	Annual General Meetings ('AGMs')
➤ If Table A is applicable, then the board may call these at any time (*Art.37*), and in certain circumstances shareholders may do so (see p.205)	➤ No AGM need be held in the calendar year of incorporation or the following year, provided one is held within 18 months of incorporation (*s.366*) ➤ An AGM is called once every calendar year; the maximum gap between convening AGMs is 15 months (*s.366*) ➤ If an elective resolution is in force, then the need to call an AGM may be dispensed with (*s.366A*)

➤ There are **5** requirements for a meeting, discussed below:

1) a valid notice of the meeting must be sent out.
2) the correct form of resolution must be proposed.
3) the meeting must be quorate.
4) the correct formalities must be observed at the meeting itself.
5) the voting must be correctly carried out.

1 Notice of the meeting (*s.369, Art. 38*)

Meeting	Notice	Short notice	
AGM	21 clear days	If *all* the shareholders agree	An elective resolution is effective if less than 21 days notice is given, if all entitled to attend and vote at a meeting agree (*s.379A(2A)*)
EGM (generally, but see the box below)	14 clear days	If a majority holding 95% of the voting capital agrees NB: An elective resolution can reduce this to 90%	
EGM where: a) there are special or elective resolutions proposed, *or* b) there is a resolution to appoint a director, *or* c) (according to some interpretations of s.379, which is ambiguous), there is a resolution to remove a director (see p.211)	21 clear days		
	Invalid notice (the time given or the contents of the notice are incorrect)		
	General rule: in Table A, any resolution passed will be invalid (*Art.111*) *unless* the error in the notice is accidental (*Art.34*)		

a) Contents of the notice

➤ Name of company, date, time and place of meeting.

➤ State whether the meeting is an AGM or an EGM.

➤ The exact wording of special *or* extraordinary resolutions *or* resolutions requiring special notice.

➤ Ordinary resolutions *must* be given in sufficient detail for members to decide whether to attend.

➤ A proxy notice *must* be included (*s.372(3)*).

➤ Accidental errors may not invalidate the notice (see 'Invalid notice' in table above).

b) Recipients and service

➤ Notice is sent in writing to all members, directors, the auditor and all persons entitled to a share in consequence of death or bankruptcy of a member (*Art.38*), provided that:
  i) the member has a registered address in the UK (*Art.112*).
  ii) a PR or trustee in bankruptcy informs the company of their address, otherwise service is sufficient at the member's registered address (*Art.116*).

➤ Notice may be served personally, else it is deemed to be served 48 hours after posting (*Art.115*).

2   Resolutions to be proposed

➤ An ordinary resolution (more than 50%) is sufficient unless statute or the articles require otherwise. (For written resolutions, see below; for elective resolutions, see p.202.)

Note: directors may, at the company's expense, prepare a statement for circulation before the meeting.

Resolution	Type of meeting	Majority needed
Special	AGM or EGM	75% of those present and voting **NB:** more than 25% blocks these
Extraordinary	AGM or EGM	
Ordinary	AGM or EGM	More than 50% of those present and voting **NB:** 50% blocks these - this is 'negative control'
Elective	AGM or EGM	Unanimous consent of all who are entitled to vote

Shareholders' written resolutions (s.381A)

➤ A less cumbersome alternative to holding a general meeting.

➤ Where statute requires documents such as a director's service contract to be open to inspection, copies must be sent to members with the resolution.

➤ Written resolutions must be signed by *all* the members entitled to attend and vote at a general meeting, or on their behalf.

➤ The resolution is passed on the signature of the final member (*Art. 53*).

♦ The resolution must be sent to the auditors for checking at the time, or before the resolution is supplied to a member for signature (*s.381B*).

♦ If a director/the secretary does not ensure that this is done, the party responsible will be liable for a fine (*s.381B(2)*).

♦ If the resolution is not shown to the auditor, this does not affect the validity of the resolution (*s.381B(4)*).

➤ This procedure may *not* be used (according to *Schedule 15A*) to dismiss *either*:

♦ a director (*s.303*), *or*

♦ an auditor (*s.390*).

After a shareholders' resolution has been passed (s.380)

1   Resolutions should be filed with the Registrar at Companies House within 15 days if they are:

♦ special.

♦ extraordinary.

♦ ordinary, **but** only those that increase the authorised share capital, give or revoke *s.80* authority to allot shares, or revoke an elective resolution.

♦ elective.

♦ written.

2   Write up the minutes.

3   The board must meet and resolve to carry out any act which the shareholders have authorised *if* they wish to use this authority, but they are not compelled to do so.

3 Quorum

➤ The necessary quorum is 2, unless the company has 1 member (*s.370*).

➤ The articles can increase the minimum required (*s.370*).

➤ A member present through a third party proxy counts, provided the proxy is not a member in his own right as well.

➤ A quorum must be maintained throughout the meeting, else resolutions passed are invalid (*Art.41*).

4 Formalities at the meeting (proxies, minutes, sole members, chairman)

➤ The rights of proxies must be respected:

   ◆ a company may not require the deposit of a proxy more than 48 hours notice before a meeting (*s.372(5)*).

   ◆ a proxy may speak at the meeting (*s.372*).

➤ Minutes of the meeting should be kept (*s.382*).

➤ A sole member must provide the company with written notice of his resolution, otherwise although its validity is unaffected, he will be liable for a fine (*s.382B*).

➤ A chairman runs the meeting. He is usually the same individual as the chairman in a board meeting.

5 Voting

➤ Voting is *either* on a show of hands *or* by poll.

   ◆ **On a show of hands:** one vote per person, proxies are not counted.

     • This usually happens unless a poll vote is called.

   ◆ **A poll vote:** one vote for each share, proxies count.

     • A poll vote can be demanded by (*Art.46*) *either*:

       a) the chairman, *or*

       b) two members or proxies, *or*

       c) members or proxies with not less than 10% of the total voting rights or paid up capital.

     • The *CA 1985* provides a safeguard that articles may *not* be altered so as to raise the threshold above a top limit of *either* at most ...

       a) ... 5 members, *or*

       b) ... members with more than 10% of shares

       ... having the ability to request a poll (*s.373*).

➤ The chairman has a casting vote that can be used if votes are tied (*Art. 50*). It cannot be used to create a tie.

➤ If votes are equal, the negative view takes priority and a resolution is defeated (unless a chairman's casting vote is used).

III   Directors

A. Appointment

➤   The first directors are named on *Form 10,* and they take office on incorporation.

➤   Thereafter they are appointed by the board's resolution confirmed by ordinary resolution, or directly by ordinary resolution (*Arts.38,76-79*).

   ◆   A prospective director must sign a consent, *Form 288a*, which is filed at Companies House.

➤   A director will need to possess 'qualification shares' to join the board if a special article requires this.

➤   The director's name, occupation, and nationality must be entered on the Register of Directors.

➤   If necessary, the Register of Directors' Interests is also updated.

1   Number of directors

➤ There must be at least 2 directors (*Art.64*), but this can be altered by a special article.

2   Shadow director

➤ This is a person (ie: any legal person - this includes a parent company) who instructs the board or a governing majority of it and they are accustomed to follow that person's directions (*s.741* and *Re Unisoft Group Ltd (No.2)* [1994] BCC 766).

➤ This excludes a professional advisor.

3   Alternate director

➤ A director may appoint a fellow director as an alternate director, but the board must approve the appointment of a non-board member (*Art.65*).

➤ An alternate director is treated like the other directors and is given notice of board meetings (*Art.66*).

4   Remuneration of non-executive directors

➤ This is set by a general meeting (*Art.82*).

5   Service contracts

➤ When the board is about to discuss a director's contract, the director must declare his personal interest (*s.317*) (see p.213).

➤ The director concerned may not either vote *or* count in a quorum for this particular matter (*Arts.94-96*).

   ◆ In a small company, a special resolution could reduce the quorum in this instance, or an ordinary resolution could be used to the same end.

➤ Members must consent by ordinary resolution for contracts over 5 years, otherwise the fixed-term clause is void and the agreement becomes terminable at 'reasonable notice' (*s.319*).

   ◆ The contract must be available for inspection for 15 days before the members' meeting and at the meeting itself.

➤ All contracts with more than 1 year to run, and with a notice period of more than 1 year, must be permanently available for inspection by members at the registered office, the place where the Register of Members is kept, or the company's principal place of business *(s.318)*.

B. Loss of office

1   Events on loss of office

➤ A director may, depending on his contract, simultaneously lose any executive office.

◆ He may claim for wrongful or unfair dismissal, or redundancy.

◆ He may be entitled to compensation under his contract.

➤ The board and officers file *Form 288b* at Companies House, and delete the director's name from the Register of Directors and the Register of Directors' Interests.

2   Automatic removal

a)   *Articles 73-80*

➤ The directors (except the managing director) retire by rotation.

➤ All directors retire at the first AGM, but are automatically reappointed unless members pass a resolution to the contrary.

➤ Thereafter 1 in 3 directors must retire and be put forward for re-election. They must take turns to comprise this third. Those who retire are automatically re-elected unless members pass a resolution to the contrary.

➤ In a small company where membership and directorship go hand in hand, a special article can remove the requirement to retire every 3 years.

b)   *Companies Act 1985 s.303* - removal by members

Steps	
1	The members have the right to remove a director at any time by ordinary resolution.
2	Members contemplating seeking the dismissal of a director should check the director's service contract to ascertain what compensation may be due under it.
3	A member gives 'special notice', leaving a formal notice at the registered office at least 28 days before a general meeting. (If one is called in this period, notice is deemed to have been given.)
4	On receipt of the 'special notice', the company should immediately inform the director concerned.
5	If the board does not call a meeting the member can *either*:

    i)   if he owns at least 5% of the shares, request an AGM and put a resolution on the agenda, *or*

    ii) if he owns at least 10% of the shares, summon an EGM.

◆ Due to ambiguous drafting in *s.379*, it is better to give 21 days notice of the meeting (although depending on the clause's construction 14 days may be sufficient).

| 6 | The director can make a written representation to members and circulate a statement to them, as well as speak at the meeting (even if he is not a member). |
| 7 | If there is a *Bushell v. Faith* clause in the articles and the resolution concerns a director's employment, his votes will increase in proportion to the size of his shareholding. |

◆ Where the director has enough shares to defeat an ordinary resolution removing him from the board, consider passing a special resolution to remove this article.

3   **Disqualification**

a)   *Article 81*

➤ This article lists 5 circumstances in which a director will cease to be entitled to hold office:

a) the director ceases to be a director because of the *CA 1985* or otherwise by law.

b) the director is declared bankrupt.

c) the director becomes mentally ill.

d) the director resigns.

e) the director is absent from board meetings for more than 6 months without the board's permission, and the board resolves that he should cease to sit on the board.

b)   *Company Directors' Disqualification Act 1986*

➤ Disqualification may last from 2 to 15 years, depending on the director's previous conduct and the nature of the offence (*CDDA 1986* and *Re Sevenoaks Printers Ltd. [1991] Ch. 164*).

➤ Disqualification is imposed for *either*:

◆ general misconduct in relation to the company, *or*

◆ a criminal offence, *or*

◆ persistent default over filing with the Registrar of Companies, *or*

◆ fraudulent trading, *or*

◆ for a company which has gone insolvent, and the director's conduct during the insolvency makes him unfit to hold office.

4   **Protecting a director's position**

➤ To protect his position, a director might try to:

◆ insert a *Bushell v. Faith* clause in the articles. Where the director is also a shareholder, this multiplies the director's voting power at a general meeting at which his dismissal is on the agenda.

◆ pass a special article restricting the transfer of shares.

◆ replace the statutory pre-emption rights under *s.89* with a special article covering shares issued for any consideration.

◆ hold 25% of the voting shares for some, or over 50% to control the board's composition.

◆ hold a debenture which is conditional on the lender remaining a director.

◆ ensure damages are due under a service contract if the director is removed.

◆ remove the chairman's casting vote (especially if there are only 2 directors on the board).

◆ replace *Arts. 94 and 95* with a special article permitting directors to contribute to a quorum and to vote on resolutions which concern themselves.

◆ ensure the appointment of an alternate director to represent an absent director at board meetings.

C. Directors' duties and restrictions

Duty to declare personal interests

➤ Whenever the board is about to discuss a matter in which the director is personally interested, he must make a formal declaration of his interest (*s.317*).   **Failure to do so is a criminal offence.**

1 Fiduciary duty

a) A general duty of good faith owed to the company

➤ Power must be used for the benefit of the company *and* for the reason it was conferred.

➤ A breach entitles the company to seek loss from a director *or* to compel him to account for his profits.

Note: the articles, or service contract, may impose extra obligations.

b) Not to make a secret profit

➤ If a conflict of interest arises, a director must *either*:

i) make full disclosure of relevant facts and obt   ᵗʰe members' sanction with a resolution (impossible if the director is a majority sh?   ᵗʰis endorses a fraud on the minority), *or*

ii) account to the company for any profits   ᵗᵛ venture.

➤ *Art.85* permits personal interests if they a.   ⸍s not defrauding the company.

c) Not to exceed power under articles or abuse powers

➤ The director should not use powers for a purpose other than that ᵗu.

➤ An ordinary resolution can absolve a director of liability for a particular act, ᵃ ᵗᵒⁿᵍ ᵃˢ ᵗʰ⸍e is no fraud on the minority.

d) Duty to disclose information

➤ Service contracts: right to inspection by shareholders unless under 12 months long (see p.210).

2 Duty of skill and care

➤ **Skill** is a subjective test - ie: the competence reasonably expected of someone with a particular director's knowledge and experience.

➤ **Care** is an objective test - ie: the care a reasonable person would exercise on his own behalf.

➤ Unless extra duties are owed under a service contract, a director only owes a duty to attend board meetings and vote when he reasonably can.

3 Administrative duties

A director must comply with the following administrative duties in respect of company records:

a) Annual accounts (*s.226*)

➤ Duty to ensure these are compiled annually and sent to members and the Registrar within 10 months of the accounting reference date (*s.244*).

➤ These contain Profit and Loss account, Balance Sheet, Auditor's report, Directors' report (*s.248*), details of directors' emoluments and other benefits (*CA(DDE)R 1997*).

➤ Accounts can be less detailed for small/medium sized companies (*CA(ASMCMAA)R 1997*).

◆ An Auditor's report may not be necessary for certain companies (see p.216).

b) Director's report (*s.234*)

➤ Duty to submit this for each financial year.

c) **Annual return**

➤ Duty to submit this to the Registrar within 28 days of the 'return date' (*s.363*). (The 'return date' is fixed 1 year after incorporation, and thereafter 1 year after the last return.)

➤ This shows amongst other things, the address of the registered office, main business activities, details of directors and the company secretary, details of issued share capital, names of past and present members and details of any elective resolutions in force *(s.364)*.

d) **Register of Directors**

➤ Contains name, address, business occupation, date of birth, nationality, other directorships.

e) **Register of Directors' Interests in the company**

➤ Number of shares and debentures which directors, their spouses and children under 18 hold.

➤ Information must be given within 5 days of joining the board or gaining the interest.

➤ Company secretary updates it.

4 **Duty to consider the interests of employees** (*s.309*)

➤ Directors must consider employees' interests and balance these against members' interests.

➤ Employees do not have the right to enforce this.

5 **Duty to comply with rules on stationery** (*s.305*)

➤ All directors' names must appear, or none of them.

6 **Statutory restrictions**

The following topics have statutory restrictions where directors are concerned:

a) **Gratuitous compensation** (*s.312*)

➤ A 'golden handshake' must have prior approval of members by ordinary resolution (*s.312*).

➤ Rights to redundancy, compensation for unfair dismissal or breach of contract are unaffected.

b) **Service contracts** (*s.319*)

➤ These may not exceed 5 years, unless approved by members' ordinary resolution (see p.210).

c) **Substantial property transactions** (*s.320*)

➤ Directors' transactions with the company are forbidden if an asset is of 'requisite value':

a) over £100,000, *or*

b) between £2,000 and £100,000 *and* representing more than 10% of the company's net assets as shown in the latest accounts (or if there are no accounts, 10% of paid up share capital).

➤ BUT the transaction is permitted if members authorise it, by passing an ordinary resolution.

◆ If members' approval is not gained, the contract is voidable. Any director who authorised it must indemnify the company for any loss, and account to it for any profit.

d) **Contract with a sole member who is a director** (*s.322B*)

➤ The contract must be written, or the terms should be set out in a memorandum, or in the minutes of the first board meeting after the contract is made.

➤ The company and defaulting officers are liable to be fined if this is not done.

e) **Restriction on loans to directors** (*s.330*)

➤ These are forbidden, unless the amount concerned is very small.

➤ *s.330* does not make it a criminal offence to make such loans, and is often ignored in practice.

➤ *s.330* gives the company redress against the director who receives the loan and those directors who authorised it. This covers any profit or loss accruing to the company due to the transaction.

D. Board meetings

Board meetings

➤ A board meeting may be called by *any* director at *any* time (*Art.88*).

➤ Notice must be 'reasonable' and given to every director who is in the country. (Oral notice is sufficient.)

   ◆ What is 'reasonable' depends on the issue to be discussed and the make-up of the board.

1   Votes

➤ One per director.

➤ Resolutions are passed by a simple majority.

➤ *Art.88* gives the chairman a casting vote, but a special resolution may remove this, in which case the negative view takes precedence and a resolution is defeated.

➤ Personal interests may stop a director voting (*Art. 94*). A *s.317* declaration must be made to avoid criminal liability.

   ◆ Even a single director at a board meeting of one must make this declaration and note it in the minutes - *Neptune (Vehicle Washing Equipment) Ltd. v. Fitzgerald [1995] 3 All ER 811, Ch.D.*

➤ *Art.94* permits voting if the director is buying shares in the company or lending it money, otherwise it forbids him to vote if he has an interest, *unless* it comes within the 4 exceptions listed in *Art.94*.

➤ The board has powers of management (*Art.70*). In a deadlock, it should summon a general meeting.

2   Quorum

➤ 2 constitute a quorum, unless directors themselves or a special article dictate otherwise (*Art.89*).

➤ A director with a personal interest does not qualify as part of a quorum (*Art.95*).

3   Minutes

➤ Minutes must be kept of every board meeting (*Art.100, s.382(1)*).

4   Written resolutions

➤ Written resolutions avoid the need for a meeting, but consent must be unanimous (*Art.93*).

E. Company officers

1   Chairman

➤ The board elects a chairman and may remove the chairman at any time (*Art.91*).

➤ The chairman has a casting vote, but this is revocable by special article (*Art.88*).

➤ The casting vote can be used if directors' votes are tied, but it may *not* be used to create a tie.

➤ The chairman resolves disputes over whether a board meeting is quorate, and over voting rights.

2   Managing director

➤ The managing director is entrusted with the company's daily administration, but the board may alter or withdraw a managing director's powers at any time (*Art.72*).

➤ The managing director is a member of the board, but he does not need to retire by rotation at every third AGM as the other directors do (*Art.84*).

3   Company secretary

➤ It is compulsory to have a company secretary (*s.283*).

➤ The first secretary is named on *Form 10*.

➤ Subsequent secretaries are appointed by the board (*Art.99*).

➤ The board sets the terms of the appointment (*Art.99*).

➤ The secretary has ostensible authority (and probably actual authority) to act in administrative matters (*Panorama v. Fidelis* [1971] 2 QB 711). This includes keeping the statutory books.

➤ The board can remove the secretary at any time. Compensation depends on the terms of employment (*Art. 99*).

4   Auditor

The need for an auditor in a small company (*s.246 and s.249A*)				
Balance sheet	Over £1.4 million	£1.4 million or less		Shareholders holding at least 10% of shares can insist on an audit
Turnover	Any	Greater than £350,000	£350,000 or less	
Need for an auditor?	✓	✓	✗	

➤ Directors appoint an auditor before the first AGM.

◆ The auditor must be a certified or chartered accountant who is independent of the company.

➤ At the end of the first AGM, the auditor's office ends. The members decide who will act as auditor until the next AGM (*s.384*).

➤ Under the elective regime, the auditor is appointed within 28 days of the annual accounts being sent to members - he is deemed to be returned to office (*s.385A*).

➤ Members can remove the auditor at any time by an ordinary resolution at a general meeting (*s.391*). The procedure is the same as for the removal of a director (see p.211).

➤ The auditor may resign by sending a written notice to the company's registered office (*s.392*). This notice must state whether there are suspicious circumstances. This prevents an auditor abandoning members to a fraud (*s.394*).

F. Liability

1   Generally

A director is *not* personally liable, *except* if he ...

➤ ... **gives a personal guarantee.**

   ◆ This will occur in a small company where the banks insist on a personal guarantee to back loans.

➤ ... **acts while disqualified by court order.**

   ◆ He will be liable for all debts the company incurs during this period.

➤ ... **trades 'fraudulently' (*IA s.213*)** (see p.241).

   ◆ This means the director is knowingly party to fraudulent trading.

   ◆ An action under this section is only possible during liquidation when the liquidator may petition the court for the director to contribute to the company's assets.

➤ ... **trades 'wrongfully' (*IA s.214*)** (see p.241).

   ◆ The director knows or ought to know that the company's insolvency is likely, *and*

   ◆ The director fails to act to minimise the loss of creditors, *and*

   ◆ The director may be required to contribute to the company's assets during liquidation.

➤ ... **breaches a warranty of authority.**

   ◆ The director purports to act for the company, but acts *ultra vires*.

   ◆ If the director has ostensible authority, the company is bound.

➤ ... **delegates wrongfully.**

   ◆ A director delegates a function(s) to employees whom he should have known to be incompetent.

➤ ... **breaches a fiduciary/statutory duty** (see pp.213 - 214).

2   *Ultra vires* acts (ie: acts outside the objects clause of the company's memorandum)

   a)   Company acts *ultra vires* (s.35)

   ➤ The company is bound provided its agent had actual or ostensible authority to act (see p.252).

   ➤ The directors are liable for a breach of duty.

   ➤ Members can ratify a breach and indemnify directors by passing special resolutions.

   b)   Agent acts *ultra vires*, but within the company's power (s.35A)

   ➤ **Board of directors:** power to bind the company (and to authorise others to do so) is unfettered.

      ◆ Provided a third party acts in good faith the company will be bound.

      ◆ Members can ratify the directors' acts with an ordinary resolution.

   c)   Agent (eg: unauthorised director or company secretary)

   ➤ If the agent has 'ostensible' authority the company is bound.

   ➤ Members can ratify the act with an ordinary resolution.

Note:

➤ Although Companies House is a public register, third parties are not fixed with constructive notice of a company's constitution (*s.35B*).

➤ Members can seek an injunction to prevent an *ultra vires* act being committed (*s.35(2)*).

➤ Notwithstanding personal liability, an agent or director will not be subject to a penalty unless the company actually incurs a loss due to their actions.

IV   Finance

➤   This section examines 2 methods by which companies raise money: by loans and by shares.

A. Debentures

➤   Directors and a lender take the following steps to grant a debenture:

Steps	
1	Check whether the company has authority to borrow (this applies to the directors).
2	Make searches (this applies to the lender).
3	Agree the type of the security.
4	Agree the terms of the debenture.
5	Follow the procedure for granting the debenture.
6	Register the debenture.
7	Comprehend the lender's remedies.
8	Redeem the debenture.

> These steps are expanded below

1   Check whether the company has authority to borrow (this applies to the directors)

➤   A company may not borrow money unless it has the power under its memorandum or articles to do so.

 ◆   A 'general trading company' has implied authority, but the large City institutions prefer there to be actual authority in the articles.

➤   The directors should check they have power in the memorandum/articles to borrow.

 ◆   *Art. 70* gives directors the power to borrow.

2   Make searches (this applies to the lender)

➤   The lender should make a search of the Charges Register at Companies House which lists the date on which any charge was created, the amount of the security, the property subject to the charge and the holder of the charge.

 ◆   If these particulars are given incorrectly on the Register, then registration is void against an administrator, liquidator or purchaser for value.

➤   The lender should also check at Companies House to ensure that:

 ◆   the directors have power to borrow - he should inspect the memorandum and articles.

 ◆   the directors have been properly appointed - he should inspect *Form 10* and *Form 288a* which will confirm the authorisation of particular individuals to act on the company's behalf.

 ◆   the property is not already subject to a prior charge on the Charges Register.

   Note: the lender should ask the holder of a floating charge for a 'letter of non-crystallisation', stating that the charge has not crystallised.

➤   The lender should search HM Land Registry and the Land Charges Department. Both keep records of charges over land. A 'purchaser' for value is only fixed with notice of charges which appear on *these* registers, irrespective of whether the charge is also registered at Companies House.

3   Agree the type of security

a) **A fixed charge** is a charge over specified property. It prevents the company disposing of that asset without the debenture holder's agreement.

b) **A floating charge** hangs over a class of property. The company may dispose of the property in the class without the debenture holder's agreement. If an event specified in the debenture occurs, the charge 'crystallises' and the property in the class becomes 'fixed'. At this point the rules for a fixed charge apply. Examples of when a charge may crystallise include when:

- a winding up petition is presented to a court (*s.463*), *or*
- there is a members' resolution to voluntarily wind up the company (*s.463*), *or*
- a receiver is appointed by the court, or by a debenture holder under a power in the debenture, *or*
- any other event specified in the debenture occurs.

c) **A personal guarantee** may be required from the directors, in which case they will be personally liable if the company defaults.

- The director concerned must make a *s.317* declaration at the board meeting when the loan is discussed (see p.213).

4   Agree the terms of the debenture

➤ **Repayment date:** on a fixed date *or* on the occurrence of a specified event.

➤ **Interest:** when payable and how the rate will be calculated.

➤ **Conditions:** if the charge is a floating one, the lender will impose a condition preventing the subsequent creation of a fixed charge over the property as this would take priority over the floating charge on liquidation.

- The company is responsible for registering this prohibition.

➤ **Power to appoint a receiver:** to be exercised if the company defaults on interest or capital repayments.

- A receiver should be expressly empowered to:
    - sell assets, *and*
    - manage the company, *and*
    - take legal proceedings in its name.

➤ **Any other powers:** eg: power to sell the security, power to run the business, etc.

5   Follow the procedure for granting the debenture

➤ The board resolves to grant the debenture.

➤ 2 directors sign the debenture.

6   **Register the debenture as a charge** (*ss. 395-397*)

(NB: The Companies Act 1989 imposes a new regime for registration, but this is not yet in force. Below are the present rules that are still in force.)

➤ Register the charge at Companies House and, if appropriate with HM Land Registry or the Land Charges Department.

➤ It is the company's duty to register the charge, but anyone interested in it may do so.

◆ The security of an *un*registered charge is void against:

- an administrator,

- a liquidator,

- a creditor of the company - the creditor ranks as an unsecured creditor,

- a person who has registered a proprietary right or interest in the property subject to the charge.

➤ The debenture should be registered at Companies House within 21 days (*s.395*).

◆ The *Companies Act 1985* requires the registration of 'prescribed particulars' of the charge and the instrument of the charge at Companies House.

➤ Late registration

◆ Either seek leave of the court for late registration (*s.404*) or take out a fresh charge.

➤ Incorrect registration

◆ Corrupt entries on the register do not offer protection, so the lender should check a copy of the entry.

◆ Errors can be corrected (*s.404*). Although alterations are not retrospective, the court can order that the alteration should be valid if it does not prejudice a third party.

7   **Comprehend the lender's remedies**

➤ If remedies are required, then appoint an administrative receiver.

◆ An administrative receiver should notify the following of his appointment: the company, creditors and the Registrar (*IA s.46*).

8   **Redeem the debenture**

➤ The company sends a memorandum of discharge, usually *Form 403*, to the Registrar (*s.403*).

➤ The lender endorses a receipt for repayment on the debenture.

B. Shares

1   **Share capital**

Money from sale of shares
➤ The company can use the money raised from the sale of shares as it sees fit.
➤ If the company receives money for the shares above the nominal value, the extra consideration is paid into a share premium account (*s.130*).
➤ If the company receives money for the shares below the nominal value, the shareholder must pay the company a sum equal to the discount in the shares plus interest (*s.100*).

a)   Types of shares

➤ Fully paid: the shareholder has paid the company the share's nominal value.

➤ Partly paid: the shareholder has paid the company only part of the share's nominal value.

   ◆ If the company goes into liquidation, the shareholder will have to pay creditors whatever sum remains unpaid.

   ◆ Redeemable shares cannot be partly paid (*Art.3*).

b)   Issue of new shares

Steps	
1	A board meeting resolves to issue shares.
2	A general meeting is called to obtain shareholders' approval if:

a)   the authorised share capital needs to be increased. This can be done provided:

   ◆ the articles permit it (*Art.32* does), *and*
   ◆ the members pass an ordinary resolution.

b)   the directors lack valid authority to allot shares under *s.80*. This authority can be either granted:

   ◆ by an ordinary resolution (this must be filed with the Registrar). This lasts for a maximum of 5 years unless an elective resolution is in force - see p.202.
   ◆ by the articles (although an ordinary - ***not** a special* - resolution can revoke this).

c)   the directors wish to suspend pre-emption rights under *CA s.89*. This will be necessary where:

   ◆ the consideration is in cash, *or*
   ◆ the directors do not intend to offer existing members the chance to take up their pro rata entitlement (*either* because members are unlikely to do so, *or* because the directors wish to broaden the company's membership), *or*
   ◆ the directors do not wish to keep the share offer open for 21 days.

   Note: *s.89* authority is only valid provided that the *s.80* authority in force when the *s.89* authority was granted is still valid.

Suspending pre-emption rights - 3 methods
1   Insert a special article.
2   Pass a special resolution. A written circular to shareholders before the meeting must explain:
a) the reason for suspending *s.89* pre-emption rights,
b) the consideration for the shares,
c) a justification for the value of the consideration being asked for the shares.
3   Use a written resolution: the circular is the same as that for passing a special resolution.

Steps	
3	File with the Registrar the memorandum if this has been amended, *Form 123* (increase of share capital), any special resolutions and any ordinary resolutions that increase the authorised share capital, or that give or revoke *s.80* authority to allot shares.
4	The board resolves to issue shares. Any offer for those shares must come from a prospective shareholder, and must *not* be offered by the company to the public.
5	Payment need not be in cash, but if the consideration takes any other form, the written contract and *Form 88(2)* are filed with the Registrar.
	◆ Where the contract is oral, *Form 88(3)* is used.
6	The board resolves to seal share certificates.

2   Acquisition and transmission of shares

a)   Transfer of shares

Steps	
1	**The donor or vendor completes and signs a stock transfer form.**

➤ If the shares are partly paid, the transferee also signs the form.

➤ Unless the shares are a gift, stamp duty (0.5%) is due (*Finance Act 1986 s.64*).

2   The transferee sends the stock transfer form to the company.

3   The company amends the Register of Members and issues a certificate in the transferee's name within 2 months.

➤ Directors can refuse to transfer the shares if they are empowered to do so by a special article.

◆ Table A (*Art.24*) does *not* permit this if the shares are fully paid.

◆ Where shares are partly paid, the directors may refuse under *Art. 24* if *either*:

a) the company has a lien over them, *or*

b) there is a procedural irregularity such as:

● the transfer is not lodged at the registered office with the share certificate, *or*

● the transfer relates to more than one class of share, *or*

● the transfer is in favour of more than 4 transferees.

◆ The directors must act in good faith and decide within a reasonable time (under 2 months).

◆ If the directors refuse, and they are acting *ultra vires, or* the transferee shows they are acting in bad faith, the court will order the register to be rectified.

◆ If the directors validly refuse to transfer shares, this does not entitle the transferee to seek damages or recission of the contract to purchase the shares. In such a case:

● the transferor remains the legal owner of the shares and holds them on trust for the transferee.

● the transferor receives notice of general meetings, and he may both vote and receive dividends, but he must act as the transferee instructs.

4   If the transferee is a director:

➤ he must inform the company within 5 days, and the Register of Directors' Interests is amended.

5   The company records the transfer on the annual return.

b)   Transmission of shares

➤ Transmission of shares occurs when a member dies.

➤ Shares vest automatically in PRs or trustees in bankruptcy by operation of law. However, although the PRs or trustees control the beneficial interest, they are not members of the company and so cannot vote or receive dividends. They can *either*:

i) seek registration as members in their own right, *or*

ii) transfer the shares to a beneficiary or creditor who can then apply for registration as a member.

3   Reducing share capital - 3 methods

a)   Reduce share capital (*ss. 135-137*)

➤ This requires a special resolution and the court's consent.

➤ The company can:

◆ cancel further liability on partly paid shares, *or*

◆ repay to members surplus capital without reducing the capital available to repay creditors, *or*

◆ reduce the value of the shares in line with capital losses. (This does not prejudice creditors as it merely represents an admission of losses that have been incurred.)

b)   **Buy back its own ordinary shares which have been issued** (*s. 162*)

➤ Repurchased shares are effectively cancelled.

➤ It is only possible to buy back ordinary shares if:

◆ the articles permit it (*Art.35* does), *and*

◆ the members pass a special resolution, *and*

◆ the contract is available at the registered office for 15 days before a general meeting and 10 years after it (*s. 169(4)*), and is at the general meeting itself (*s. 164*), *and*

◆ the company has money available which will be from one of the following sources:

i)   distributable profits ('in reserves') (*s. 168*), *or*

ii)   an issue of shares (*s. 171*), *or*

iii)   capital (*s. 173*), but only if:

• there is no other possible source of finance, *and*

• shareholders pass a second special resolution, *and*

• creditors are notified, *and*

• the directors make a statutory declaration of the company's solvency for the next year.

NB: *Art. 35* in *Table A* specifically permits it (subject of course to the above).

➤ *Form 169* is sent to the Registrar. It states the number of shares bought and the nominal value of the shares.

➤ **Note:** a) if the directors make the statutory declaration erroneously, they may be liable together with the purchaser of the shares to compensate the company's creditors.

b) a vendor shareholder cannot vote at the meeting.

c)   Issue redeemable shares (*s. 159*)

➤ The company can buy back this type of share if:

i) the shares are fully paid up, *and*

ii) it has already issued non-redeemable shares.

➤ *Art. 3* permits the issue of redeemable shares in principle, but a special article must set out terms on which the shares are redeemable, eg: whether at the company's or a shareholder's behest.

➤ The members pass a special resolution to amend the articles, to state the terms and manner of the issue. *(NB: s. 159A is not yet in force, but will require all companies to state the terms and manner of such an issue in the articles.)*

➤ The members can approve an issue of redeemable shares by ordinary resolution.

Note on taxation (*TA 1988 ss.219-224*)

➤ Money received by an individual from the company is usually classified as a 'distribution' subject to income tax under Schedule F (see p.70).

➤ However, on a redemption, repayment or purchase of shares by a company, the individual is treated as having made a disposal for capital gains tax purposes rather than having received income under Schedule F if:

    a) the owner of the shares is domiciled, resident and ordinarily resident in the UK during the year of assessment in which the transaction occurs (*TA 1988 s.220(1)*), *and*

    b) has possessed the shares for 5 years (*TA 1988 s.220(5)*), *and*

    c) the sale 'substantially' reduces his holding or that of his associates (partners, close relatives, etc) (*TA 1988 s.222(1), s.224*),

    and the transaction was either:

        'wholly or mainly for the purposes of benefiting a trade carried on by the company' and not 'to enable the owner of the share to participate in a company's profits without receiving a dividend or for the avoidance of tax' (*TA 1988 s.219(1)(a)*)

    or

    i)   the money received is applied to pay IHT within 2 years of death, *and*

    ii) the IHT arises on death, *and*

    iii) undue hardship would arise if the company did not repurchase the shares.

---

4   **Prohibition on financial assistance for purchasing shares** *(s.151)*

➤ A company is prohibited from helping a third party to buy its shares.

➤ Such 'financial assistance' is defined by a list given in *s.152(1)*.

➤ A whole set of exceptions is listed in *s.153*, but many exceptions have been cut back due to recent case law. However, although a company is restricted by *s.151*, it *can* give financial assistance if it goes through the 'whitewash procedure' (*ss.155-158*). It can do this if:

    a) the articles permit it, *and*

    b) the directors make a statutory declaration that the company is solvent and will remain so over the next year, *and*

    c) the members consent by special resolution (within 1 week of the statutory declaration), *and*

    d) the auditor confirms the directors' statutory declaration.

Note: if the borrower is a director then a loan is forbidden by *s.330*. The *CA 1985* does not impose a criminal penalty, but it imposes an obligation on the directors who authorise the loan to indemnify the company for any resulting loss (see p.214).

➤ Although the House of Lords considered the application of *s.151* in considerable detail in *Brady v. Brady* [1989] AC 755, a pragmatic approach is to be found in a judgment of Hoffmann J in *Charterhouse Investment Trust Ltd v. Tempest Diesels Ltd* [1986] BCLC 1, where he emphasises that the 'commercial realities of each transaction' should be examined to determine if financial assistance is being given.

5   Dividends

➤ The directors consider the payment of a 'final' dividend after the accounts have been completed, and recommend it to a general meeting. The accounts for the calculation of a final 'dividend' must be the last set for the financial year, prepared in accordance with *s.226* (ie: audited, put before the members, filed with the Registrar, etc).

➤ At any time during an accounting period, the directors can decide to declare an 'interim' dividend if this appears 'justifiable by the profits of the company available for distribution' (*Art.103*). For the payment of an 'interim' dividend, the company can prepare 'interim' accounts.

➤ Dividends can only be paid if there are 'profits available' (*s.263*).

◆ There are 'profits available' if the undistributed trading profit which has accumulated during the past year and previous years exceeds the total amount of debts which have fallen due over the past year and previous years.

◆ In addition to the normal accountancy rules which are applied in working out the extent of profits and losses, there are some statutory rules (*s.263*):

• capitalised profit (ie: profit used to repay bonus shares or buy back shares) *is not* treated as profit.

• loss written off against a reduction of share capital *is not* treated as a loss.

• a provision against anticipated losses (ie: the reduction in the value of wasting assets) *is* treated as a loss (*s.275*).

➤ A general meeting votes upon whether to accept the directors' recommendation; it may not vote for a higher dividend than the directors propose (*Art.102*).

➤ Members can sue the company for unpaid 'final' dividends as a debt which is owed to them from the date when the dividend was declared. There is no debt action for unpaid 'interim' dividends as members may not expect these as of right until the money is actually paid to them.

➤ Members knowingly in receipt of dividends paid when there are insufficient 'profits available' must refund the money to the company (*s.277*).

◆ Directors are personally liable for breach of duty if any such sums are unrecovered after the company has paid a dividend without sufficient 'available profits'.

C. Comparison of shareholding and debenture holding

	Shareholder	Debenture holder
Management control	✔ The investor may attend general meetings and vote to influence how the company is run	✘ The lender usually has no right to vote at meetings
Income	✘ Dividends cannot be paid unless the company makes a profit	✔ The amount of interest and its payment dates are guaranteed. If insufficient profits are available, interest will have to be paid out of capital
Security	✘ The capital will not be repaid unless the company buys back its own shares or issues redeemable shares ✘ The value of the capital may fluctuate ✔ The capital may appreciate (It can also decline)	✔ The capital will be repaid on a predetermined date *or* when the debenture holder demands it ✔ The capital sum will normally remain set at the amount of the loan ✘ The capital sum will not appreciate
	✘ Capital is not returned if the company is insolvent on winding up	✔ Capital will be recovered on insolvency if the debenture is secured
Investment's marketability	✘ The articles may restrict the transfer of shares	✔ The debenture can be sold to anyone
Tax	✘ Dividends are not tax deductible, and advance corporation tax is due before mainstream corporation tax	✔ Interest on the loan may be deductible as a debit on a 'loan relationship' (see p.90)

Summary of company procedure

Transaction	Authority	Resolution	Internal procedures	External procedures
Appoint directors for at least 5 years	s.319	Ordinary	The contract is kept at the registered office for 15 days before the meeting and at the meeting itself	
Allot shares (if this power is not in the articles)	s. 80	Ordinary		File resolution. If consideration is in kind, file Form 88(2) and the contract, or Form 88(3) if the contract is oral
Remove statutory pre-emption rights	s. 95	Special		File resolution
Introduce elective regime	ss.379A-380	Elective		File resolution
Cancel elective regime	s.379A	Ordinary		File resolution
Change company name	s.28	Special	Alter memorandum	File amended memorandum and resolution
Select business name		Board resolution	Alter stationery as appropriate	
Increase nominal share capital	s.121	Ordinary		File resolution, Form 123 and amended memorandum
Change objects	s.4	Special		File amended memorandum and resolution
Change articles	s.5	Special		File amended articles and resolution
Remove a director	s.303	Ordinary	Complainant gives the board special notice 28 days before an EGM. The board gives a copy of this notice to the director. The board should resolve to call an EGM with 21 days' notice (arguably 14 is sufficient). A director can make a written representation which the board circulates to members. Alter the Register of Directors and the Register of Directors' Interests	File Form 288b
Remove an auditor	s.391	Ordinary	Special notice procedure as for the removal of a director	Give the Registrar notice within 14 days of the resolution
Alter minimum directors from 2	Art.64	Special		File resolution
Fix salary of non-executive director	Art.82	Ordinary		File resolution
Relax quorum requirement for a director voting on own service contract	Art.97	Alter articles by special resolution. Or temporarily relax rules under the Art.96 ordinary resolution procedure		File resolution if it is a special resolution
Reduce share capital	ss.135-137	Special		File resolution. Obtain the court's consent
Sanction a 'substantial property transaction'	s.320	Ordinary	After the transaction it may be necessary to alter the Register of Directors' Interests	

Transaction	Authority	Resolution	Internal procedures	External procedures
Gratuitous payment to a director	s.312	Ordinary		
Retirement by rotation		No resolution This is automatic (Art.76)		
Repurchase ordinary shares	s.162	Special	Update Register of Members, Register of Directors' Interests	Form 169 (stating number of shares and nominal value)
Financial assistance to buy shares	s.155	Special	Statutory declaration of solvency by the directors, confirmed by the auditor	File resolution and statutory declaration
Approve dividend	Art.102	Ordinary		
Absolve liability for ultra vires act		Special		File resolution
Grant indemnity for ultra vires act		Special		File resolution
Absolve liability for exceeding actual authority		Ordinary		
Issue of a debenture		Board resolution	The board resolves to take out the loan and to affix the company seal. 2 directors, or 1 director and the company secretary sign the agreement. Update Register of Charges	Registration at Companies House within 21 days (s.395). Charges over land should be registered with the Land Charges Department or HM Land Registry
Redemption of a debenture		Board resolution	Lender endorses receipt on the debenture Update Register of Charges	File statutory declaration and memorandum of satisfaction (Form 403) that the debt has been repaid
Voluntary winding up - company is insolvent	IA s.84 IA s.378	Extraordinary	see p.239	File the extraordinary resolution
Winding up - company is solvent	IA s.84	Special	see p.239	File the special resolution
Approve voluntary arrangement	Insolvency Rules	Ordinary (members) 75% by value (unsecured creditors)	see p.238	
Move registered office		Board resolution		File Form 287

Note:

a) these tables assume that Table A is in force and has not been amended

b) every members' resolution which is passed concerning the company's management will need a separate board resolution if it is to be executed

c) written resolutions are an acceptable alternative to members' resolutions passed at meetings in all cases except those listed on p.208

d) a complete list of which resolutions are to be filed can be found in s.380

C   Public companies

Advantages and extra stringencies associated with plcs

✓ Shares and debentures may be offered to the public.
(There is a criminal penalty for a private company which does this (*s.81*).)

✓ Prestige.

✓ The company may apply for listing of its securities if it has:
   ◆ traded for at least 3 years and at least 25% of its shares are held by the public.
   (Chapter 3 of the Listing Rules of the London Stock Exchange will apply.)

✗ Costs of changing name on memorandum *and* stationery.

✗ The rules of the City Code on Takeovers and Mergers will apply.   Rule 9 of the Code obliges anyone who alone, or in concert with others, acquires 30% of the shares to make a bid for all the share capital.

✗ Non-cash consideration for shares must be independently valued within 6 months (*s.44*).

✗ There is no elective regime.

✗ The prohibition on loans to directors (and associates) extends to quasi-loans and credit transactions (*ss.330-331*).

✗ Criminal penalties: loans to directors (*s.342*), giving unlawful financial assistance (*s.151*).

✗ There is an absolute bar on financial assistance to buy shares (*s.151*).

✗ The company must call an EGM if 'net assets' fall to 50% or less of the share capital (*s.142*).

✗ The company needs a special resolution, or article to disable statutory pre-emption rights (*s.95*).
(A private company may do this in its memorandum (*s.91*).)

✗ The dividend rules are more strict. A plc may only make a distribution when distributable profits equal accumulated realised profits less accumulated realised losses, plus the excess of unrealised losses over unrealised profits.

✗ A plc may not redeem or purchase shares from capital (*s.171*).

✗ 7 months to lay AGM accounts after accounting period ends (rather than 10 as for private companies) (*s.244*).

✗ Written resolutions are not available.

✗ Minimum of 2 directors (*s.282*).

✗ Directors may not be appointed over 70. They must leave office at the AGM after their 70th birthday, unless members agree otherwise (*s.293*).

✗ The directors' report must contain a statement of the company's policy and practice on the payment of its suppliers (*CA(DR)(SPP)R 1997*).

Conversion to a plc

Requirements

1   Issued share capital is a minimum of £50,000.
2   At least 25% (£12,500) of the share capital is fully paid to the nominal value and the whole of any premium (*s.45*).

Procedure

Steps

1   Special resolutions to (a) re-register as a plc, *and* (b) alter the memorandum, adding 'plc' to the company's name.

2   Apply for registration as a plc.

3   Adopt a new memorandum and articles suitable for a public company.

4   Send to the Registrar (*s.43*):
   ◆ a printed copy of the new memorandum and articles,
   ◆ a copy of the latest balance sheet,
   ◆ an auditor's report that the company's net assets are not less than its capital balance sheet,
   ◆ a statutory declaration made by a company secretary or director that the net asset value in the auditor's report is accurate and that the requirements of the *Companies Acts* have been complied with.

5   The Registrar issues a certificate of incorporation as a plc.

D Converting businesses

Converting sole trader to partnership	Converting a partnership to a company
Formalities	

➤ Draw up a partnership agreement
➤ Decide on the ownership of capital assets, which can be:
  ◆ leased or licensed to the firm
  ◆ owned by the partners jointly - this requires a transfer or conveyance
  ◆ held on trust by a partner for all the partners
➤ Comply with *BNA 1985*
	➤ Purchase or create a company
	➤ Observe the formalities for board and shareholder meetings
	➤ Draw up a contract for sale of the business:
	  ◆ listing the assets being sold, consideration and method of payment
	  ◆ stating the company's acceptance of the seller's title to assets
	  ◆ recording the company's acceptance of stock in its current condition
	  ◆ apportioning the value of assets
	  ◆ providing an indemnity from the company in respect of business liabilities.
	➤ Comply with *BNA 1985*, and *CA ss.25-30* (see p.192 and p.199)

Income tax	
	➤ The seller may incur a 'balancing charge' on the sale of capital assets under Schedule D Case VI. Provided the ex-partners are controlling shareholders, then the company may elect to inherit the business's writing down allowance (it has 2 years to make this election) (*CAA 1990 s.77*) If the company makes this election, no 'balancing charge' is deemed to arise on the discontinuance of trade by the partnership (*CAA 1990 s.78*) ➤ Unrelieved trading losses can be carried forward and offset against any salary or dividends paid by the company to the vendor, as long as shares in the company provided most of the consideration for the sale (*TA 1988 s.386*)
Capital taxation	

➤ A sole trader going into partnership may be disposing of chargeable assets.
Consider:
  ◆ annual exemption
  ◆ hold-over relief on a *gift* to a partner
  ◆ retirement relief
	➤ Insofar as shares are consideration for the transfer of assets, gains can be 'rolled-over' into shares on condition that all the business's assets (except cash) are sold to the company (*TCGA 1992 s.164A-N*). This has disadvantages:
	  ◆ any subsequent gain may be liable to double taxation
	  ◆ assets transferred to the company are available to creditors if it becomes insolvent, and so might not be recoverable

Stamp duty	
➤ Stamp duty is less likely to be applicable as title to assets may not be not be transferred unless goodwill is assigned, etc	➤ Stamp duty may be due on an instrument transfering or agreeing to transfer an interest in certain property, see pp.104-109
VAT	
➤ If the company is not registered *before the sale,* the seller must charge VAT unless the business is transferred as a going concern (*VATA s.49*)	
Employees	
Transfer of Undertakings (Protection of Employment) Regulations 1981 ➤ When the business is taken over, the employees retain all the rights they enjoyed previously	

E   Choice of business medium

➤ The choice of business medium determines how the business is financed and run. The principal issue concerning clients is often the different liabilities assumed by sole traders or partners (as opposed to shareholders). The choice made also affects the amount of statutory control over the business, and in particular, how easily profits may be extracted from the business. Moreover, clients are most concerned, not only to work out what tax is payable by the business, but to work out the tax payable by the individuals involved. This will of course depend on whether they are sole traders, directors or shareholders.

	Sole trader or partnership	Company
	General matters	
Personal liability for debts	✘ A partner and a sole trader are personally liable for debts the business incurs **Note:** A novation agreement or an indemnity only provide protection if the guarantor is solvent **NB:** Under the self assessment regime, partners are in most cases no longer jointly and severally liable for income tax	✔ Shareholders are only liable to the extent of the fully paid up value of the shares ➤ Directors are not personally liable *unless* they: ◆ give a personal guarantee ◆ breach their fiduciary duty to the company ◆ trade wrongfully or fraudulently (*IA 1986 ss.213-214*) ◆ breach certain statutory administrative requirements ◆ sign a document which gives the company's name incorrectly
Finance	✘ Can only create fixed charges ✘ A new partner is liable for future debts	✔ A company can create a floating charge ✔ A new investor in shares only incurs limited liability
Management	✔ Flexibility: the business can be organised as the participants wish ✘ All partners have apparent authority to bind the firm	✔ Management is largely divorced from capital investment ✔ Shareholders have no authority to act for the company
Status		✔ Often seen by clients as more substantial and 'solid'
Setting-up	✔ Theoretically this need cost nothing as acting in a certain way is enough to start a partnership ✘ For a partnership, an agreement ought to be drawn up, so in practice this is not a viable 'short-cut'	✘ Many statutory requirements must be fulfilled
Statutory control	✔ This is minimal	✘ The inconvenience of maintaining the required registers, minutes, annual returns, etc ✘ The expense of professional advice to ensure compliance with statutory requirements ✘ Restrictions on certain activities: ◆ purchase and redemption of its own shares ◆ paying dividends solely out of 'available' profit as defined by *s.263* of the *Companies Act 1985*
Publicity	✔ Need reveal only the partners' names and their addresses for the service of documents	✘ Information filed at Companies House is open to public inspection. This includes annual accounts, but with a 'small company' a profit and loss account does not have to be filed, and smaller companies do not need audits (see p.216)

Sole trader or partnership	Company	Director
Income tax / National insurance contributions		
✔ Expenses are more generous: anything 'wholly and exclusively for the purposes of the trade'		✔ Expenses: 'wholly, exclusively *and necessarily* in the performance of an employee's duties'
£0-£4,100 at 20% £4,101 - £26,100 at 23% £26,100+ at 40% ✘ Profit £26,100+ at 40% rather than 21-33.5%	£0-£300,000 at 21% £300,001- £1,500,000 at 33.5% £1,500,000+ at 31% ✔ Reinvestment of profits is easier if they are taxed in the 23% band	£0-£4,100 at 20% £4,101 - £26,100 at 23% £26,100+ at 40%
✔ Start-up relief over first 4 years ✔ Losses can be set against an individual's income or gains from other sources		
A sole trader/partner pays Class 4 contributions related to profit and Class 2 contributions at a flat rate ✔ From 1996/97 neither qualify for tax relief, but the overall burden is less ✘ Benefits are poorer than for employees	✔ A company has tax relief on secondary national insurance contributions and there is room for planning (eg: through payment in kind using goods not traded on a recognised investment exchange)	✘ No tax relief on national insurance contributions ✔ Benefits are more generous than for a self-employed person
✔ Interest on a loan to buy into a partnership may be set against income tax as a 'charge on income' (*TA 1988 s.362*)	✔ Interest on a loan to buy shares may be a 'charge on income' (see p.70)	

Sole trader or partner	Director/Shareholder	Company
Capital gains tax		**Corporation tax**
✔ Annual CGT exemption		✘
✔ Roll-over relief on the replacement of 'qualifying assets'	✔ Roll-over relief on replacement of 'qualifying assets' *if* the company is a personal trading company	✔
✔ Retirement relief	✔ Retirement relief *if* the company is a personal trading company *and* a shareholder has worked full-time *and* the company owns the asset (*STI 27 June 1996*)	✘
✔ Hold-over relief on a gift of business assets	✔ Hold-over relief on a disposal of assets used by the company (other than shares) not at arm's length provided the company is a personal trading company	✘
Double taxation		
✔ A trader or partner only pays CGT once	✘ A shareholder may be taxed twice: the company pays corporation tax on gains and a shareholder pays capital gains tax on corresponding rises in share value ✔ This can be alleviated or prevented if a company distributes capital profit, although see pp.95-97 for further information on the imputation system. ✘ If a shareholder owns assets and licenses/leases them to the company he is only taxed once, but retirement relief may not be available	
Inheritance tax		
✔ Business property relief ✔ The instalment option is always available on business assets	✘ Business property relief is not always available, see p.87 ✘ The instalment option is only available if *either* the transfer concerns a controlling holding *or* other conditions are satisfied	✘

F   Insolvency

All references in this section are to the Insolvency Act 1986, unless stated otherwise.

> I   Personal insolvency
>
> II   Partnership insolvency
>
> III   Corporate insolvency

I Personal insolvency

A. Voluntary arrangement

✓ Avoids stigma and disability of bankruptcy.

✓ Cheaper and quicker.

✓ Creditors retain the option of petitioning the court if a debtor defaults.

✗ The supervisor of the voluntary arrangement does *not* have power to set aside transactions.

➤ This is commonly referred to as an 'IVA'.

➤ There is a moratorium which prevents creditors starting bankruptcy proceedings or seizing assets, in return for which the debtor agrees to a voluntary repayment plan.

➤ A resolution for a voluntary arrangement must be passed by a majority of at least 75% (by value) of the creditors present in person or by proxy. The resolution binds every person who had notice of, and was entitled to vote at the meeting, or is a party to the arrangement.

➤ A debtor may enter a voluntary arrangement at any time before a bankruptcy petition by the debtor is pending (*s.253(5)*).

➤ A voluntary arrangement may take the form of a 'composition', ie: the creditor and debtor agree the payment of a lesser sum in full satisfaction of the claim. Alternatively, it can take the form of a 'scheme of arrangement' which can be on any terms acceptable to the parties (eg: sale of assets, etc).

Steps	
1	The debtor appoints an insolvency practitioner known as a 'nominee' to investigate his finances.
2	The debtor prepares a proposal for the intended nominee setting out, inter alia, i) the terms of the IVA , and ii) a statement of affairs containing particulars of his creditors, debts, other liabilities, assets and other information as may be prescribed.
3	The proposal is sent to the intended nominee, who then decides whether to act as nominee.
4	If he agrees to act as nominee, he prepares a report on the proposal to the court.
5	The debtor may apply for an intermediate order. This usually lasts for 14 days but can be extended (*ss.255(6), 256(4)*).
6	The nominee reports to the court and the court considers whether, based on the nominee's recommendation, a creditors' meeting is necessary to obtain their approval (*s.258*).

♦ If a meeting is necessary, then during the period of the interim order, creditors can examine the proposed voluntary arrangement.

♦ 75% (by value) of creditors at the meeting must agree to the IVA (*Insolvency Rules*).

Steps cont.

7

Provided that consent is obtained, a bankruptcy order is avoided, and the nominee is appointed as the debtor's 'supervisor' to ensure the IVA is carried out in accordance with its terms (*s.263*).

B. Bankruptcy

Steps

1

A petition is made to the High Court or a County Court with insolvency jurisdiction, by any of the following:

a) **Creditor (1)** (*s.267*) ...

   i)   ... who is owed £750 or more, *and*

   ii) the debt is for a liquidated sum payable now, or at a certain future time, and is unsecured, *and*

   iii) the debtor is unable to pay or has no reasonable prospect of doing so.

   ♦ The evidence for this is:
   - 1) there is evidence of the debtor's failure to comply with a statutory demand within 3 weeks, *and*
   - 2) there is no outstanding application to set aside a statutory demand.

   or ● the debtor has failed to satisfy execution of a judgment debt.

b) **Creditor (2)** ...

   ... who is bound by a voluntary arrangement where the debtor has not complied with the arrangement, or the debtor has entered the scheme giving misleading information.

c) **Debtor** ... with a statement of affairs showing that he is unable to pay his debts (*s.272*).

2

A bankruptcy order is made at a court hearing (at least 14 days must elapse between service of the petition and the hearing), or the court may appoint an insolvency practitioner to investigate the possibility of an IVA.

3

An official receiver is appointed by the court (*s.287*) - pending vesting of the bankrupt's estate in the trustee in bankruptcy.

♦ If a creditor began the action, the debtor has 21 days to submit a statement of affairs (*s.288*).

4

A creditors' meeting is held at the official receiver's discretion *or* if 25% of creditors (by value) request it (*s.294*).

5

A trustee in bankruptcy is appointed by the creditors at the meeting, *or* if no meeting is called or no appointment is made by creditors, the official receiver will act as the trustee in bankruptcy (*s.293*).

6

The bankrupt's property vests in the trustee (see chart overleaf '*Property vesting in the trustee*') (*s.306*).

7

The function of the trustee is to get in, realise, and distribute the bankrupt's estate to satisfy the creditors (see chart overleaf for '*Trustee's powers to gather assets*').

8

The bankruptcy order is discharged, usually after 3 years, although this may be delayed if the bankrupt has not co-operated, or where the bankrupt has been an undischarged bankrupt at any time within the preceding 15 years (*s.279*).

Property vesting in the trustee in bankruptcy

Property retained by the bankrupt	Property vesting in the trustee
➤ Any right which is purely personal, rather than proprietary ➤ Tools of a trade, vehicle (*s.283(2)*) ➤ Bankrupt's and family's furniture, bedding and clothing (*s.283(2)*) **Note:** the above might be replaced by functional cheaper versions	➤ All other property **Note:** If the debtor only partly owns his house, the trustee in bankruptcy will need an order for sale from the court (*LPA 1925 s.30*)

➤ Initially the bankrupt can usually continue to occupy the family home *if either:* (*ss.336-338*)
   a) a spouse has a right of occupation under the *MHA/FLA, or*
   b) the bankrupt is living with minors and therefore has a right of occupation under the *MHA/FLA*
➤ During the first year a possession order is unlikely to be granted as the needs of the children are paramount
➤ *After 1 year, an order for possession will probably be granted as the creditors' interests now become paramount*

Trustee's powers to gather assets

Transaction	Time of transaction	Defence	Effect
At an undervalue (*ss.339, 341*)	With an unconnected person ➤ Within 5 years prior to bankruptcy, *and* the debtor is insolvent at the time or became so as a result of the transaction		All such property is 're-claimed' under a court order by the trustee, and distributed to the creditors
	With an associate ➤ Within 2 years prior to bankruptcy	a) The debtor was not insolvent at the time, *or* b) the debtor did not become insolvent as a result of the transaction	
To create a preference (*ss.340, 341*)	With an unconnected person ➤ Within 6 months prior to bankruptcy, *and* the debtor was insolvent at the time or became so as a result of the transaction, *and* the debtor intended to prefer, *and* the creditor was thus put in a better position	The debtor did not intend to prefer, or pressure was exerted to prefer	
	With an 'associate': ➤ Within 2 years prior to bankruptcy, *and* the debtor was insolvent at the time or became so due to this transaction (presumed), *and* the creditor was put in a better position as a result (presumed)	a) The debtor was not insolvent at the time, *or* b) the debtor did not become insolvent as a result of the transaction The debtor did not intend to prefer, or pressure was exerted to prefer	
At an undervalue to defraud creditors (*s.423*)	No time limit		

➤ 'Onerous' contracts or property - if an interested third party serves notice, a trustee must disclaim the contract or property within 28 days, otherwise he loses this right to disclaim and will be deemed to have adopted any contract (*s.316*).
   ◆ Third parties who lose from a disclaimed contract claim loss from the bankrupt's estate

➤ Any disposition made between the day of presentation of the petition and the vesting of the bankrupt's estate in the trustee is void unless the court consents (*s.284*)

A trustee is *not* entitled to pursue:
➤ sale proceeds from a fully enforced judgment order obtained before the bankruptcy order was made (*s.346*)
➤ goods which, before a bankruptcy order was made, a landlord has distrained for up to 6 months arrears of rent (*s.347*)

Disabilities (ie: things the bankrupt may not do)

➤ Take credit above £250 without disclosing his bankruptcy - this is a criminal offence (*s.360*).

➤ Trade under a non-bankrupt name without disclosing the bankrupt name - this is a criminal offence (*s.360*).

➤ Retain membership of a partnership - consequences depend on the partnership agreement (see p.193).

➤ Retain directorships - *Art. 81* of Table A provides for this, and *CDDA 1986 s.11* requires it.

➤ Perform any of the the following occupations:

   i)   barrister.

   ii) solicitor.

   iii) Justice of the Peace.

   iv) Member of Parliament.

   v) local authority member.

   vi) insolvency practitioner.

   vii) company secretary.

Order of distribution

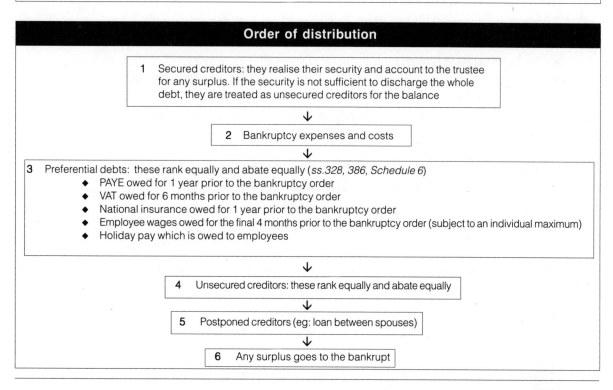

1 Secured creditors: they realise their security and account to the trustee for any surplus. If the security is not sufficient to discharge the whole debt, they are treated as unsecured creditors for the balance

↓

2 Bankruptcy expenses and costs

↓

3 Preferential debts: these rank equally and abate equally (*ss.328, 386, Schedule 6*)
- ◆ PAYE owed for 1 year prior to the bankruptcy order
- ◆ VAT owed for 6 months prior to the bankruptcy order
- ◆ National insurance owed for 1 year prior to the bankruptcy order
- ◆ Employee wages owed for the final 4 months prior to the bankruptcy order (subject to an individual maximum)
- ◆ Holiday pay which is owed to employees

↓

4 Unsecured creditors: these rank equally and abate equally

↓

5 Postponed creditors (eg: loan between spouses)

↓

6 Any surplus goes to the bankrupt

II   Partnership insolvency

Insolvent Partnerships Order 1994, Insolvency Act 1986

➤ The provisions of the *IA* regarding company voluntary arrangements apply to partnerships.

➤ The provisions of the *IA* regarding administration orders apply to partnerships.

➤ The partnership is treated as an unregistered company even though a partnership is not a legal person in its own right. There are different treatments for:

   a) creditors' winding up petitions.

   b) members' winding up petitions.

➤ The law of bankruptcy does not apply to the firm, but individual partners may be subject to bankruptcy orders, whereupon the official receiver becomes trustee.

III   Corporate insolvency

A.   Alternatives to liquidation

There are 4 alternatives:

1   The company is declared defunct.

2   An administrative receiver, or receiver, is appointed by a debenture holder.

3   An administration order is made.

4   A voluntary arrangement is made.

1   The company is declared defunct (*CA ss.652-653*)

➤ The company has ceased trading.

➤ The Registrar of Companies can act on his own initiative to strike off the company.

➤ The Registrar must advertise his intention to strike off the company.

➤ For up to 20 years, a member or creditor who is prejudiced may apply for the company's restoration to the register.

➤ The liability of every director, managing officer and member of the company continues, and may be enforced as if the company had not been dissolved (*s.652(6)(a)*).

2   An administrative receiver, or receiver, is appointed by a debenture holder

Most debentures allow a debenture holder to appoint an **administrative** receiver in the event that he is not paid sums he is owed under the debenture, provided that the holder has security (floating charge or a fixed and floating charge) over all, or substantially the whole of the assets of the company. (If he does not have such security, he might still appoint a receiver - different from an administrative receiver.)

The *aim* of a receiver is **to recover the debenture holder's debt, interest and his own costs though he is the agent of** *the company.*

➤ Only an insolvency practitioner can be appointed as an administrative receiver. His powers are laid down under statute but are generally augmented in the debenture.

Steps	
1	The debenture holder appoints the administrative receiver, who must formally accept.
2	The administrative receiver must notify the company, the Registrar of Companies and known creditors of his appointment (*s.46*).
3	Floating charges crystallise, preventing the company from dealing with the assets concerned.
	◆ The receiver must cede priority to fixed chargees and preferential creditors (if security is by way of a floating charge).
4	The directors give the administrative receiver a statement about the company's affairs.
5	The administrative receiver can *only* set aside transactions that were used to defraud creditors.
6	The administrative receiver produces final reports and accounts.
7	The court can remove an administrative receiver, or he can resign (*s.45*), but the debenture holder cannot dismiss him.

3   An administration order is made

The *aim* of an administration order is **to avoid or postpone the liquidation or receivership of a company.**

Steps	
1	Petition: the directors, members, creditors or the supervisor of a voluntary arrangement, may petition the court for an administration order (*s.9*).
2	Notice is given to any person entitled to appoint an administrative receiver. If an administrative receiver is validly appointed at this stage, the petition will be dismissed.
3	If the court is satisfied that grounds exist and that no administrative receiver has yet been appointed, an administration order is made appointing an insolvency practitioner to act as administrator of the company.
4	The directors give the administrator a statement of the company's affairs.
5	The administrator (within 3 months of the order) draws up proposals based on the statement.
6	A meeting of the company's unsecured creditors must approve the proposals by more than 50%.
7	The administrator manages the company accordingly, and may set aside transactions to defraud creditors, transactions at an undervalue, and preferences.
8	If the administrator achieves the aims of the order, or if he realises that it is impossible, he can ask the court to discharge the order (*s.18*).

a)   **From the time of the petition there is a moratorium preventing** (*s.10*):

   i)   the company being put into liquidation (by the court or voluntarily).

   ii)   the enforcement, without the court's consent, of any security against the company's property, including repossession of goods held under hire purchase agreements and goods supplied under retention of title clauses.

   iii)   any legal proceedings being commenced or continued without the court's consent.

   NB: However, a debenture holder entitled to appoint an administrative receiver (see p.236) has the right to appoint an administrative receiver after the petition for the order, but before the order is granted - this generally requires the petition to be dismissed and so means that the debenture holder can veto the granting of an administration order.

b)   **Grounds for an order** (*s.8*)

   ➤   If the court is satisfied that the company is insolvent, or on the verge of insolvency, and the making of the order is likely to achieve one or more of the following:

   i)   the survival of the company, and the whole or any part of its undertaking, as a going concern, *or*

   ii)   the approval of a company voluntary arrangement, or

   iii)   the sanctioning under *CA s.425* of a compromise or arrangement, or

   iv)   a better realisation of the company's assets than would be achieved on liquidation.

c)   **Consequences of the order** (*s.11*)

   ➤   On making the order:

   i)   any outstanding petitions for winding up the company are dismissed, *and*

   ii)   any administrative receiver of the company immediately vacates his office, *and*

   iii)   a receiver who is not an administrative receiver stays in office unless the administrator requires him to vacate.

➤ While the order is in force:

    i) no resolution can be passed, or order made, to wind up the company, *and*

    ii) no administrative receiver may be appointed, *and*

    iii) no steps may be taken to enforce any security over the company's property or to repossess goods held under a hire purchase agreement, or supplied on retention of title terms, without the consent of the administrator or leave of the court, *and*

    iv) no other proceedings and no distress, execution or other legal process may be commenced or continued against the company without the consent of the administrator or leave of court (ie: a moratorium is imposed in respect of creditors seeking to enforce their claims against the company).

d) **Role of the administrator who is appointed**

➤ The administrator acts in the company's name as the company's agent. He is there to manage the company, investigate its affairs and draw up proposals. He has a liquidator's powers (see 'Liquidator's powers to recover assets', p.241) to set aside:

- preferences,
- transactions at an undervalue,
- floating charges, and.
- unregistered charges.

➤ The directors remain in office, unless the administrator removes them, but cannot use their powers in a manner which would interfere with the administrator.

4 **A voluntary arrangement is made** (*ss.1-7*)

The *aim* of a company voluntary arrangement ('CVA') is **for the company to agree on a binding plan to repay debts whereby the company can survive and continue trading.**

Steps	
1	The directors draft a proposal for a composition or scheme of arrangement.
2	An insolvency practitioner, called a 'nominee', submits a report to the court, stating whether meetings of shareholders and creditors should be held to consider his proposals. Unless the court directs otherwise, meetings of shareholders and creditors are held.
	• Consent must be obtained from 50% or more of the members who are present and voting, and 75% (by value) of the unsecured creditors who are present and voting.
3	If approved, this approval is reported to the court.
4	The 'nominee' now becomes the 'supervisor' and carries out the CVA.

➤ Consequences:

- A voluntary arrangement is binding on every creditor who had notice of, and was entitled to attend and vote at the meeting.

- It is *not* binding on secured creditors *unless* they agree to be bound by the arrangement.

- If the company defaults, creditors or members can petition to have the company wound up.

Note: Unlike IVA's there is *no* interim order imposing a moratorium to protect the company while the CVA is being proposed. *The Minister for Company Affairs, on 27th November, 1995, indicated that he intended to introduce legislation for* **small companies** *(as defined in CA s.247) so that there would be a 28 day moratorium on action by creditors in order to give a struggling company time to get on its feet. The Insolvency Services Policy Unit has, as of 4 July 1997, confirmed that this is still the government's intention.*

B. Liquidation

1   Voluntary liquidation

Sometimes a company may be wound up following criteria laid down in the articles (eg: to enable the shareholders to extract their capital, or to facilitate restructuring of a group of companies). Otherwise it may be wound up after a special resolution has been passed to wind up the company, or after an extraordinary resolution has been passed due to its perceived liabilities.

Steps	
1	The directors prepare a statement of affairs.
2	*Either*:

a) the company is **solvent**. This is known as a members' voluntary liquidation since the members will control the winding up of the company.

The directors make a statutory declaration that the company will be able to pay its debts, including interest, within a period not exceeding 1 year (and this must be done within 5 weeks prior to passing a resolution to wind up the company) (*s.89*). They summon a general meeting (*s.89*) at which the members may:

i)   pass a special resolution to wind up the company (*s.84*), and advertise the fact in the *London Gazette* within 14 days of the resolution being passed (*s.85*), *and*

ii)   pass an ordinary resolution to appoint a liquidator (*s.91*).

or:

b)   the company is **insolvent**. This is known as a creditors' voluntary liquidation. It is not a remedy available to creditors, but rather it is a procedure supervised by creditors.

The members pass an extraordinary resolution to wind up the company (*s.84, CA s.378*), and the resolution is advertised in the *London Gazette* (*s.85*). Separate meetings are held for creditors and members to appoint a liquidator - generally all meetings are held on the same day.

◆   The creditors should meet within 14 days of the members' general meeting (*s.98*), where they are shown a statement of affairs by the directors (*s.99*).

◆   The creditors may appoint a liquidator.

◆   The creditors' choice of liquidator takes priority over that of the members (*s.100*).

3	The liquidator advertises his appointment and notifies the Registrar of Companies (*s.109*).
4	The liquidator has the same powers and duties as in the case of a compulsory insolvency (see p.241).
5	After the company's assets have been distributed, the liquidator makes final reports prior to dissolution to a meeting of members (members' voluntary winding up)(*s.94*), *or* to meetings of members and creditors (creditors' voluntary liquidation)(*s.106*).
6	The liquidator sends the final return to the Registrar of Companies (*ss.94(3),106(3)*).
7	The Registrar dissolves the company 3 months after receiving the liquidator's final return (*s.201*).

2 Compulsory liquidation

Generally, the creditor is unsecured as there are more specific remedies for secured creditors, such as appointing an administrative receiver or receiver.

Steps	
1	A creditor *or* the company petitions the Chancery Division of the High Court on one of 7 statutory grounds (*ss.122 (a)-(g)*) (eg: the company is unable to pay its debts or the company has passed a special resolution to wind itself up).

- The company is *presumed* to be unable to pay its debts if:
  - a statutory demand has been served by a creditor (minimum debt of £750) and is outstanding for 3 weeks, *or*
  - execution has been issued for an unsatisfied judgment debt.
- If this presumption does not arise, insolvency must be shown to the court by taking into account actual, prospective and contingent liabilities.

2	The court has discretion to grant a winding up order (*s.125*).
3	An official receiver is appointed by the court who will be the liquidator until another is appointed (*s.136*).

The official receiver:

- takes the board's powers and is obliged to alter the company's notepaper so that the insolvency is apparent to third parties (*s.188*).
- advertises his appointment in the *London Gazette* and the local paper.
- notifies the Registrar of Companies and the company itself of his appointment.

4	The directors present a statement of affairs to the official receiver (or liquidator) within 14 days of the order. He reports to the court on the reasons and causes for the failure, and generally the position, dealings, etc, of the company, and any suspicious circumstances (*ss.131-132*).
5	The receiver calls separate members' and creditors' meetings, and may nominate an alternative liquidator to the official receiver (*s.136(5)*).

- The official receiver *must* call a creditors' meeting if 25% (by value) request it (*s.136(5)*).
- The creditors' nomination as liquidator takes priority.

6	The liquidator:

- takes the board's powers
- collects in all property of the company (see chart overleaf for '*Liquidator's powers to recover assets*'). The powers of a liquidator are listed in *Schedule 4* of the *IA*.

7	The liquidator distributes assets (see p.242 for the '*Order of distribution*').
8	After distribution, the liquidator notifies the Registrar of Companies, who dissolves the company 3 months later (*s.202*).
9	The liquidator makes a final report to the creditors' and the members' meetings (*s.146*).

Liquidator's (and administrator's for *ss. 238, 239, 423*) powers to recover assets

Transaction	Requirements	Defence	Effect
At an undervalue (*s.238*)	Within 2 years prior to the insolvency + the company was insolvent at the time or became so as a result of this transaction (presumed if with a connected person)	A bad bargain was: ➤ in good faith ➤ on reasonable grounds ➤ for genuine commercial reasons	He can set aside the transaction. (It is actually more complicated than this, but it holds true in general terms)
To create a preference (*s.239*)	Within 6 months prior to the onset of insolvency + the company was insolvent at the time or became so as a result of this transaction + voluntary act + desire to prefer + creditor put in a better position as a result		
	Within 2 years prior to the onset of insolvency for a transaction with a 'connected person' + insolvent at the time or became so as a result of this transaction + voluntary act + creditor put in a better position as a result	Pressure was exerted on the company (no desire to prefer)	
At an undervalue to defraud creditors (*s.423*)	An attempt to put assets beyond the reach of the person making, or who at some time, may make a claim, or otherwise prejudicing the interests of such a person	None	
Fraudulent trading (*s.213*)* Criminal offence *CA s.458*	➤ A positive act ➤ The business has been carried on with intent to defraud creditors or for any fraudulent purpose	No such intention	The court will require an offender to contribute to the company's assets insofar as it thinks it proper in the circumstances
Wrongful trading (*s.214*)*	➤ A director knew, or ought to have concluded that there was no reasonable prospect of the company avoiding insolvency; and ➤ did not take every step he ought to have taken to minimise loss to creditors	On becoming aware, he took every step that a reasonably diligent person would have, to minimise loss to creditors	

* The liquidator alone can seek an order under these sections

Charges

Fixed charge: void against the liquidator if unregistered (or registered after 21 days of creation of charge) *(CA s.395)*

Floating charge is:	void against the liquidator if:
	◆ unregistered (or registered after 21 days of creation of the charge) *(CA s.395), or*
	◆ (except to the extent of the value of consideration provided to the company in money or money's worth at the same time, or after the creation of the charge):
	  ● (if in favour of a connected person) the charge was created within 2 years of liquidation, *or*
	  ● (if in favour of an unconnected person):
	    i) the charge was created within 1 year of liquidation, *and*
	    ii) the charge was created at a time when the company was insolvent or became insolvent as a result *(IA s.245)*.

Note:	there are proposed changes to the registration requirements by the *CA 1989,* see p.220

A liquidator may not pursue sale proceeds of a fully enforced judgment order obtained before the bankruptcy order. If the order is not fully enforced, the sheriff will transfer any seized goods to the liquidator (*s.183*)

A liquidator may set aside 'onerous contracts', or disclaim 'onerous property', provided he replies to any inquiry by an interested third party within 28 days (*s.178*). 'Onerous' means that it is a drain on the company's assets or cash flow

Distribution

➤ Property does NOT vest in the liquidator as he is only the agent of the company, but he is under a duty to take it all into his possession.

➤ Legal proceedings against the company cannot proceed without leave of court. Leave will be refused, for example, if the effect would be to give the plaintiff a chance to 'promote' himself from an unsecured position.

Order of distribution

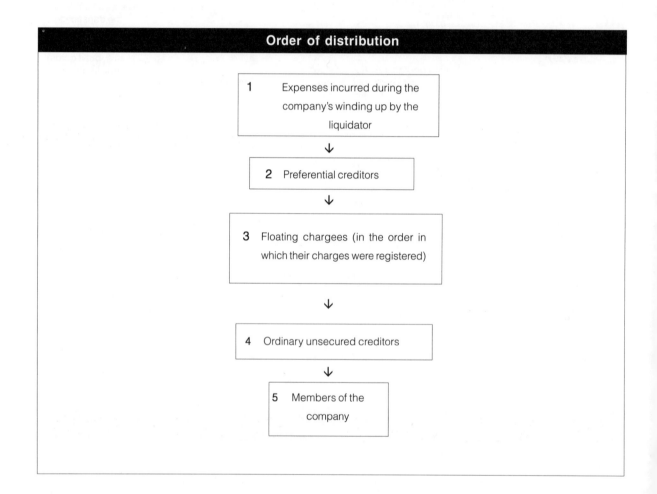

| 1 | Expenses incurred during the company's winding up by the liquidator |

↓

| 2 | Preferential creditors |

↓

| 3 | Floating chargees (in the order in which their charges were registered) |

↓

| 4 | Ordinary unsecured creditors |

↓

| 5 | Members of the company |

G Trading

Any business buying supplies, or selling products, will enter into contracts. A solicitor must be able to draft, negotiate and advise on enforceability. Businesses should comply with the following legislative regimes:

I   **EU competition law - enforcement,** *Article 86, Article 85* **of the Treaty of Rome** (For UK legislation, see *Commercial Agreements,* p.251)

II   **Free movement of goods -** *Articles 30-36* **of the Treaty of Rome**

III   **Contracts for the sale of goods and supply of services (UK law)**

I   EU competition law

Enforcement *of EU competition law (Regulation 17/62)*

➤ The European Commission ('Commission') may *request* information informally or formally.

◆ Non co-operation is punishable by a fine.

➤ The Commission can *investigate* informally or formally ('dawn raids' on premises).

◆ Obstruction of an investigation is punishable by fine. BUT the Commission has to hold a hearing to consider the merits of a case before imposing a fine.

➤ Fines for infringements of EU competition law may be up to 1 million ECU, or a greater sum up to 10% of an undertaking's worldwide turnover during the preceding year (*Regulation 17/62, Art.15(2)*).

◆ The amount depends on the seriousness of the abuse, the party's position in the market, the size of the offender, and any mitigating factors such as co-operation with the Commission.

◆ An undertaking may appeal against the Commission's ruling. This appeal is to the Court of First Instance for a 'preliminary' ruling, but the European Court of Justice (ECJ) itself is the final authority.

➤ The remedies obtainable in UK courts are uncertain. Cases have stated that injunctions or damages for breach of statutory duty may be available.

Article 86

➤ This article prohibits abuse by one or more undertakings of a dominant position ...

◆ ... within the EC or a substantial part of it ...

◆ ... which may affect trade between member states.

➤ A market share of 40% and more is a good indication that an undertaking is dominant in that market.

◆ Markets can be defined widely or narrowly (eg: passenger aircraft or commuter aircraft).

◆ A market is evaluated:

• geographically, *and*

• by product market: the test is 'what other product, if any, can be substituted for the product in question, given the nature of it, its price and its intended use?' (*United Brands v. Commission* [1978] ECR 207).

Avoiding infringement of *Article 86*

➤ If dominant in the market, an undertaking should not abuse its position.

➤ The Commission can grant negative clearance. This is a declaration that an agreement does not contravene *Article 86* - this is the only option open to an undertaking to avoid infringement.

Article 85

➤ This article prohibits agreements, decisions and concerted practices ...

- ◆ ... between undertakings or associations of undertakings ...
- ◆ ... which have as their object *or* effect ...
- ◆ ... prevention, restriction or distortion of competition within the EU.

➤ Such agreements are void, although *Article 85(2)* permits severance of an offending term if national law permits this. UK law does permit this.

Avoiding infringement of *Article 85*

➤ **Agencies** (Commission Announcement 24 December 1962) - there is no infringement if:

a) the principal and agent are pursuing the same economic interest, *and*

b) the agent does not take the financial risk, and does not act independently of the principal.

➤ **Agreements between parents and subsidiaries**

- ◆ These are *usually* treated as one 'undertaking', and therefore are not caught by *Article 85*.

➤ **Agreements of 'minor importance'**

- ◆ Agreements that fall within this Commission Notice do not infringe *Art. 85*. In such agreements:

  a) the parties' share of the relevant market is under 5% of the total market in the area covered by the agreement, *and*

  b) their combined turnover does not exceed 300 million ECU.

- ◆ The Commission is not bound by the Notice, but compliance with it will avoid heavy fines.

➤ **Block exemptions**

These allow parties to certain types of agreements (see below) to include provisions in their agreements which, strictly speaking, are anti-competitive or would infringe *Article 85*. They will nevertheless be permitted, provided that the agreement is drafted strictly in accordance with one of the block exemptions. Block exemptions give guidance as to the forbidden 'black' clauses (eg: export bans) (which must be avoided) and permitted 'white' clauses (eg: certain territorial restrictions).

- ◆ The block exemptions of most relevance are:

Regulation 1983/83	-	exclusive Distribution agreements.
Regulation 1984/84	-	exclusive Purchasing agreements.
Regulation 4087/88	-	franchising agreements.
Regulation 240/96	-	new technology transfer.

➤ **Notifying the Commission:** this protects against fines in respect of the period from the date of notification until the Commission's 'first adverse reaction' (ie: possibly before its final ruling).

- ◆ The Commission then has 3 options:

  a) **Negative clearance:** a declaration that *Article 85* is not infringed.

  b) **Individual exemption:** granted under *Article 85(3)* if the agreement can be justified on the basis that it will 'contribute to the improvement of production or distribution of goods, or to promoting technical or economic progress, while allowing consumers a fair share of the resulting benefit'. An exemption binds the Commission, but few are granted and the process is lengthy.

  c) **Comfort letter:** an informal (non-binding) reassurance that *either Article 85* is not infringed, *or* a block exemption covers the agreement, *or* the Commission is closing its files for the moment.

II Free movement of goods

Treaty of Rome - *Article 30*

➤ *Article 30* prohibits: 'quantitative restrictions on imports and all measures having equivalent effect.'

◆ 'Equivalent effect' means 'all trading rules enacted by member states that are capable of hindering, directly, or indirectly, actually or potentially, intra-community trade' (*Procureur du Roi v. Dassonville* [1974] ECR 837).

◆ *Article 30* applies not only to the official laws of the state, but also when the state acts through another undertaking or 'bodies established or approved by an official authority' (*Re Peter Vriend* [1980] ECR 327, *Commission v. Ireland* [1982] ECR 4005).

◆ The effect can be indirect and need not be the main purpose of the legislation (*Torfaen Borough Council v. B & Q plc* [1989] ECR 765) (one of the Sunday trading cases), and it includes bureaucratic procedures (*Rewe-Zentralfinanz GmbH v. Landwirtschafiskammer* [1975] ECR 843).

◆ Discrimination against national goods is allowed since *Article 30* is not meant to give a level playing-field, but rather to avoid discrimination against imports (*Nederlandse Bakkerij Stichting v. Edah BV* [1986] ECR 3359).

Two classes of exception to *Article 30*

1   Rule of reason (if both domestic and imported products are affected)

➤ National legislation for 'fiscal supervision, the protection of public health, the fairness of commercial transactions and the defence of the consumer' (*Rewe-Zentral AG v. Bundesmonopolverwaltung fur Branntwein (Re Cassis de Dijon)* [1979] ECR 649), and the protection of the environment *(Commission v. Denmark* [1989] CMLR 619) will not infringe *Article 30*.

➤ The 'rule of reason' test. Is the restriction ...

a) ... justifiable under EU law, *and* ...

b) ... in proportion to its declared aim? (This involves considering whether the effect is 'direct, indirect or merely speculative' and whether it 'impedes the marketing of imported products more than the marketing of national products' (*Stoke-on-Trent City Council v. B & Q plc* [1993] 1 All ER 481)).

2   *Article 36*

➤ Certain laws will escape the prohibition of *Article 30*. They must be:

◆ to uphold the public morality practised in that state (*R. v. Henn & Darby* [1979] ECR 3795 (pornography imports)), *or*

◆ on grounds of public policy, *or*

◆ to maintain public security (internal and external), *or*

◆ to protect public health, *or*

◆ to protect national treasures, *or*

◆ to protect intellectual property rights.

➤ **But** they must not *either:*

a) constitute a means of arbitrary discrimination, or

b) represent a disguised restriction on trade between member states.

III   Contracts for the sale of goods and supply of services (UK law)

A. Terms implied by statute

➤   In the absence of express terms dealing with certain matters (*SGA s.55*), terms are implied by statute concerning those matters into a contract for sale or supply of goods and/or services. The table below gives a useful index to the 3 statutes concerned, in order to check whether particular terms are relevant.

Term	SGA 1979 amended by *SSGA* 1994/5	SGSA 1982 amended by *SSGA1994*		Contract for services	SG(IT)A 1973	When a term is implied into a contract *and* a few details as to the nature of the term
	Contract for sale of goods	Contract for hire	Contract for transfer of goods		Contract for hire purchase	
			Contract for work and materials			
Description	*s.13*	*s.8*	*s.3*		*s.9*	Goods/services must correspond with their description
Satisfactory quality	*s.14(2)* *s.14(2A)*	*s.9(2)* *s.9(3)*	*s.4(2)* *s.4(3)*		*s. 10(2)*	Implied when dealing in the course of seller's business. Not applicable to: a) defects shown to the customer, *or* b) defects which the customer's examination ought to have revealed
Fitness for purpose	*s.14(3)*	*s.9(4)* *s.9(5)*	*s.4(4)* *s.4(5)* *s.4(6)*		*s. 10(3)*	Implied when dealing in the course of seller's business, except where defects are specifically drawn to the attention of the customer, or the customer examines the goods
Title	*s. 12*	*s.7* (Possession)	*s.2*		*s.8*	Always implied
Price	*s.8*					See p.247
Payment	*s.10*					See p.247
Ownership	*ss. 16-18*					See p.247
Risk	*s.20*					See p.248
Delivery	*s.29*					See p.248
Sample	*s.15*	*s.10*	*s.5*		*s.11*	Always implied on a sale by sample
Reasonable care and skill				*s.13*		Implied when dealing in the course of the seller's business
Within reasonable time				*s.14*		Implied when dealing in the course of the seller's business. Not applicable if the time is fixed by contract, or is left to be agreed in the manner set out in the contract, *or* is determined by a course of dealing between the parties
Reasonable charge				*s.15*		Always implied. Not applicable if charge is fixed by contract, or is left to be agreed in the manner set out in the contract, *or* is determined by a course of dealing between the parties

B. *Sale of Goods Act 1979* (as amended 1994 and 1995)

➤ When a sale of goods contract is formed, sometimes not all terms that are supposed to be included, are in fact included. *The following defaults only apply where the contract does **not** make provision.*

Sale of Goods Act 1979		
s.	**Area**	**Content**
Formation of the contract		
2	Definition	A contract for sale of goods is a contract by which the seller (**S**) transfers or agrees to transfer the property in goods to the buyer (**B**) for a money consideration, called the price
8	Price	Where price is not agreed, or determined by fact, B must pay a reasonable price
10	Time of payment	Not of the essence **Note:** other stipulations as to time depend on the terms of the contract
15	Sale by sample	2 implied terms: ◆ the bulk corresponds with the sample in quality ◆ the goods are free from any defect not apparent on a reasonable examination of the sample
Effect of the contract		
16 17 18	Ownership	Ownership passes when the parties intend it to pass ◆ If the parties do not express an intention as to when ownership passes, the time it does pass depends on the type of contract: See table below

Type of contract	**Ownership passes**
Unconditional contract for specific goods	When the contract is made
Contract for specific goods to be put into a deliverable state	When they are in a deliverable state and B is told of this
Contract for specific goods where something must be done to ascertain the price	When the price is set and B is told what it is
Goods on approval for sale and return	When *either:* ◆ B indicates his acceptance of the goods to S, *or* ◆ B's conduct implies that he accepts the sale transaction *or* ◆ B retains the goods beyond a reasonable period (or agreed time) without rejecting them
Unascertained goods	When goods are available and unconditionally appropriated to the contract (ie: ascertained)

Specific goods are 'goods identified and agreed on at the time the contract of sale is made' (*SGA s.61(1)*)

| 19

Note: *the importance of retention of title clauses is manifest on insolvency; their purpose is either to recover goods when a business becomes insolvent, or failing that, to put the debtor in a strong position in negotiations with the receiver* | Reservation of title | ◆ S may reserve title to 'specific goods' or those 'appropriated to the contract' by a 'retention of title clause'
◆ There are 3 types of these clauses, known collectively (and confusingly!) as '*Romalpa*' clauses.
  a) Retention of title clause: title is reserved until payment is received
  b) 'All moneys clause': title does not pass until *all* moneys owing to S, whether under this contract or any other contract, are paid
  c) A true '*Romalpa*' clause: title is retained in the goods, and S is permitted to trace the purchase price into the hands of a third party to whom the goods are sold
  • a) and b) are generally upheld by the courts
  • c) only succeeded on particular facts once when a fiduciary relationship was found to exist between S and B (*Aluminium Industrie v. Romalpa Aluminium Ltd* [1976] 2 All ER 552). Attempts to emulate it have failed and the courts construe c) as an unregistered (ie: void) charge
◆ To stand a chance of being effective a clause should:
  • reserve full *legal* title to the goods (equitable and/or beneficial title are insufficient), *and*
  • entitle the seller to enter the buyer's property to inspect and repossess the goods, *and*
  • oblige the buyer to store the goods separately, or label them, so they can be identified as being appropriated to the contract |

	**Sale of Goods Act 1979 (cont.)**

s.	Area	Content
	**Effect of the contract (cont.)**
20	Risk	◆ Goods are at the risk of S unless property is transferred to B ◆ Once property has been transferred to B, goods are at B's risk whether delivery has been made or not ◆ If goods are delayed due the fault of one party, the goods are at the risk of the party at fault
20A	Undivided shares in bulk	When goods within a bulk become identified *and* the price has been paid for the goods in the bulk, *then* ◆ property in undivided share is transferred to B, *and* ◆ B becomes an owner in common of the bulk
21	Capacity to pass property	One cannot give what one does not have - *nemo dat quod non habet.* (Exceptions include factors, S in possession after sale, and motor vehicles (*Hire Purchase Act 1964 s.27(5)(a)*))
	**Performance of the contract**
27 28	Duties	S must deliver the goods and B must accept and pay for the goods Delivery and payment are concurrent (ie: cash on delivery)
29 31	Delivery	**Place of delivery:** S's place of business (or if not, his residence) Note: if the goods are specific goods and they are known to be at another place, delivery is at that other place Note: delivery to an independent carrier is counted as delivery to B **Delivery time:** S must send the goods within a reasonable time and at a reasonable hour
30	Wrong quantity delivered	**Smaller quantity than expected:** B may reject all the goods (unless he is not a consumer and the shortfall is only slight) B may accept all the goods. If so, he must pay for them at the contract rate **Larger quantity than expected:** B may accept the right quantity and reject the excess B may reject the whole (unless he is not a consumer and the excess is only slight) B may accept all the goods. If so, he must pay for them at the contract rate
31 34 35 35A 36	Acceptance ?	**B accepts the goods by:** ◆ intimating to S that he accepts, *or* ◆ after the goods have been delivered, acting in a manner inconsistent with the ownership of S **B rejects the goods:** ◆ B has a right to reject the goods if he has not had a reasonable opportunity to examine the goods (this cannot be waived if B is a consumer) ◆ B has a right to reject part of the goods ◆ B is not bound to return rejected goods ◆ B does not have to accept the goods if they unexpectedly arrive in instalments
41 42 44 45	Unpaid seller	**An unpaid seller, if he has received no payment, or tender of payment may:** ◆ have a lien on the goods or part of them for the price, *or* ◆ (if B is insolvent) stop the goods in transport, *or* ◆ (if the goods are perishable and S informs B he has not been paid) re-sell the goods
	**Remedies**
49 50 15A	Things go wrong	**Remedies for S** ◆ **Property has passed and S has received no payment** - S sues for the price ◆ **Property has passed and payment time has passed without payment** - S sues for the price ◆ **B wrongfully refuses to accept the goods** - S sues for damages and losses 'directly and naturally' flowing from B's breach of contract **Remedies for B** ◆ **S does not deliver** - B sues for damages and losses 'directly and naturally' flowing from S's breach of contract ◆ **S breaches a warranty** - S sues for damages Note: if S breaches *ss.13-15* (see p.246) and B is a non-consumer, and the breach is slight, this may be treated as a breach of warranty.

C. Exclusion clauses

➤ A clause which attempts to exclude or limit liability must comply with common law and statutory hurdles if it is to be effective:

1 Common law rules

➤ **Incorporation:** the clause must be properly incorporated into the contract (ie: reasonable steps must be taken to draw the term to the promisee's attention).

➤ **Construction:** the clause must cover the breach which occurs. There are certain restrictive rules (eg: to exclude negligence, this must be specifically and clearly stated for an exclusion to apply).

➤ **Particular common law rules:** the *'contra proferentem'* rule - any ambiguity in a term of the contract is interpreted against the party attempting to rely on the exclusion.

2 Statutory rules - background

➤ *Unfair Contract Terms Act ('UCTA')* has been UK law since 1977.

➤ *Unfair Terms in Consumer Contracts Regulations 1994 ('UTCC')* has been grafted into UK law from a European directive.

➤ There are 3 problems with having two sources of legislation:

a) There is a degree of overlap because:

◆ *UCTA* deals with exclusion and limitation of liability clauses in business and consumer contracts.

◆ *UTCC* deals with any unfair terms which may include exclusion clauses, but only in consumer contracts.

Thus, where there is a **consumer contract** containing an **unfair exemption clause,** there will be an overlap between the two. In such a case both *UCTA* and *UTCC* must be checked against the contract terms.

b) Key concepts such as 'consumer' are defined differently in both pieces of legislation.

c) The list of contracts exempted from each legislative regime is different and must be checked.

➤ Procedure

Steps	
1	Check definitions of *UCTA*.
2	Check contents of *UCTA* (see box overleaf).
3	Tighten up the contract to comply with *UCTA*.
4	Check definitions of *UTCC*.
5	Check contents of *UTCC* if it is a consumer contract (see box overleaf).
6	Tighten up the contract to comply with *UTCC*.

(Step 2) - *Unfair Contract Terms Act 1977* - contents	
Attempted exclusion	Effect
s.2 a) The common law duty of care, *or* b) liability under the *Occupiers Liability Act 1957*	Void for death *or* personal injury Valid for other loss if the clause satisfies the 'requirement of reasonableness'
s.3 General exclusion of liability NB: This section is only applicable if one party 'deals as a consumer' and/or uses the other's standard written terms ➤ Covers 2 parties dealing in business ➤ Not applicable to implied terms	Entitles the promisor to offer performance of the contract 'substantially different from that which was reasonably expected of him', subject to the 'requirement of reasonableness'
s.6 *SGA* or *SG(IT)A* implied terms: ◆ Description, satisfactory quality, fitness for purpose, sample ◆ Title	Exclusion is void against purchaser 'dealing as a consumer', but otherwise it is valid if it satisfies the 'requirement of reasonableness' ─────────────── Always void
s.7 Where possession or ownership of goods passes under a contract which is not a sale of goods or hire purchase contract, ◆ any term is implied by law, *or* ◆ s.2 of the *SGSA* (Title), *or* ◆ right to transfer goods	◆ Exclusion is void if a party is dealing as a consumer, otherwise a clause is valid subject to satisfying the 'requirement of reasonableness' ◆ s.2 *SGSA* (Title) is not excludable ◆ Subject to 'reasonableness'

Requirement of reasonableness (*s.11*) is ...
'...a fair and reasonable [term] ... having regard to the circumstances which were, or ought reasonably to have been, known to or in the contemplation of the parties when the contract was made'   ➤ Although the guidelines exist in *Schedule 2* to define reasonableness, they are only obligatory for *ss.6-7*. Nevertheless, the courts frequently use them in other cases too. They include: ◆ the customer's knowledge   ◆ the bargaining position of the parties   ◆ whether the contract involved the customer making a special order

(Step 5) - *Unfair Terms in Consumer Contracts Regulations 1994* - contents	
Section	Breakdown of the section
s.2	Interpretation clause. Includes the definition of: ◆ business, and ◆ consumer (different definition to *UCTA*)
s.3	Regulations apply to any contract where any term has not been individually negotiated **but** subject matter of the contract and price are not tested for fairness
s.4	Key concept of an 'unfair term' which is a term 'contrary to . . . good faith [which] causes a significant imbalance in . . . rights . . . to the detriment of the consumer'
s.5	Any unfair term is not binding on the consumer
s.6	Terms must be in plain language; if not, the term will be construed in the consumer's favour
Schedule 1	Excluded contracts, eg: employment contracts
Schedule 2	'Definition' of 'good faith'
Schedule 3	Examples of unfair terms

➤ The Office of Fair Trading (OFT) has published a bulletin covering the following topics:
     ◆ the most common unfair terms in consumer contracts
         ● eg:
            ■ entire agreement clauses
            ■ penalty clauses
            ■ variation of price clauses
     ◆ terms that have been successfully excluded after OFT intervention
         ● eg: 'The Council accepts no liabiliity for loss or damage to cars parked in this car park ... howsoever caused.'

H Commercial agreements

Clients wishing to join commercial ventures with other businesses (eg: for the sale of their products in unfamiliar areas) may seek advice on 'Agency agreements' or 'Distribution agreements'. These should be carefully drafted. Particular care needs to be taken to 'choose the right form of agreement' for an individual client.

I Agency agreements

II Distribution agreements

III Choosing the right type of agreement
(Agency, Distribution, Franchise or Licence?)

Note: in this section
P=Principal
A = Agent
C=Customer

I Agency agreements

A. 3 types of agency

Three types of agency		
Classical sales agency	P authorises A to enter into contracts with C on behalf of P	P → A ↖ ↓ C
Marketing agency	P authorises A to introduce customers (C) to P	P → A ↖ ↓ C
Note: a del credere agent guarantee's C's performance for an additional commission		

B. Legislative rules

Commercial Agents (Council Directive) Regulations 1993	
Effect - on all commercial agents operating in the UK after 1 January 1994	*Regulation*
◆ oblige the principal and the agent to exchange certain information	*3-4*
◆ govern the amount of commission paid to an agent and the method of payment	*6-12*

◆ provide for compensation to be paid to the agent on termination especially where:
   a) the agent has been deprived of commission which proper performance of his duties would have procured forhim, while the principal retains substantial benefits linked to the agent's activities, *or*
   b) the agent has been unable to amortise the costs and expenses that he had incurred in the perfomance of the contract on the prinipal's advice
 	
 ◆ give the parties a choice between an indemnity or compensatory arrangement on termination
   • Where no preference is expressed, the agent will be entitled to compensation (*rr. 17-18*)
   • The right to damages, as well as an indemnity (linked to the fruits of the agent's efforts), is preserved
	13-19

◆ renders any attempt to restrain an agent's trade after termination void, unless it:
   a) is contained in a written agreement
   b) defines a geographical area where the agency operates *or* the area in which customers are situated
   c) ceases no more than 2 years after termination
	20

Note a) agencies in other EU member states may be governed by a version of the *Regulations* enacted in accordance with that state's laws. Complicated questions of jurisdiction and applicable law determine which courts (UK or foreign) will enforce which set of legislation (UK, local state or EU directive) b) certain classes of agent, such as unpaid agents, insolvency practitioners and those whose 'activities as agents are considered to be secondary' are excluded from the *Regulations*	

C. The law of agency - basic principles

➤ An agency agreement can be oral or written, express or implied.

1   Authority

➤ **Actual authority:** this can be given expressly *or* impliedly.

➤ **Ostensible authority.** Four conditions must be satisfied (*PA ss.5-8*):

subjective ⎡ a) C knows or believes he is dealing with A, *and*

test   ⎣ b) C is unaware that 'A' is not actually authorised, *and*

objective ⎡ c) 'A' would usually be expected to be authorised to enter into such a transaction, *and*

test   ⎣ d) P's type of business is consistent with the nature of the transaction.

2   Liability

➤ **When A is authorised to act**

◆ P is liable for A's acts.

◆ A is not liable unless the contrary is agreed, expressly or implicitly, by A and P *or* A and C.

➤ **When A is *un*authorised to act**

◆ Generally, P is not liable to C for A's acts.

◆ If A has ostensible authority, but has exceeded his actual authority, P will be liable and A may be liable to P and C for breach of warranty of authority.

3   Ratification of A's acts

➤ **P can 'ratify'** (ie: agree to be bound by) **a contract by an unauthorised A if:**

a) C could identify P when the contract was agreed, *and*

b) P has contractual capacity at the date of the contract and the date of ratification, *and*

c) the act is capable of ratification (ie: not illegal), *and*

d) ratification occurs within a reasonable time.

4   Non-disclosure of agency

➤ **If A does not disclose his agency, P can always intervene *unless*:**

a) the contract between A and C, expressly or impliedly excludes an agency, *or*

b) C wished to contract with A, *or*

c) the 'personality' of the parties is central to the contract.

5   Termination

➤ The agency agreement can be terminated by *either* A *or* P at any time subject to the contract.

➤ If P who is a debtor gives a creditor authority to act as an agent, then while the debt remains outstanding, the agency is irrevocable (*Greer v. Downs Supply Co* [1927] 2 KB 28).

➤ The contract is terminated by the death or mental incapacity of A or P, but A is protected if he acts in ignorance of P's incapacity (*PAA 1971 s.5(1)*).

6   Payment

➤ Payment to A by C does not discharge a debt owed to P by C unless *either* A has authority (actual or apparent) to receive the payment, *or* P is undisclosed.

➤ Payment by P to A does not discharge a debt owing to C unless C misleads P into thinking that the money is to reimburse A for money already paid to C.

II   Distribution agreements

➤ There are several types of distribution agreement:

1 Exclusive distribution - the distributor alone may distribute the supplier's goods in a particular territory, but the supplier may still make passive sales in the territory.

2 Sole distribution - as in 1, but the supplier can actively sell within the 'exclusive territory'.

3 Selective distribution - the supplier attempts to retain control over the sales that his distributor makes.

4 Exclusive purchasing - the distributor promises to buy goods from a sole supplier, for an 'exclusive territory' .

1   Relevant EU law

➤ Any distribution agreement may infringe European competition law, if it contains anti-competitive provisions. Unless the agreement is one of 'minor importance', it should be drafted to come within a block exemption (see p.244). If there is no relevant block exemption, anti-competitive practices should be avoided. The block exemption covering exclusive distribution agreements is *Regulation 1983/83*. It permits clauses which:

- ◆ prevent the distributor manufacturing or distributing competing goods, *or*
- ◆ forbid the distributor *actively* to seek customers for goods outside the exclusive territory, *or*
- ◆ forbid the supplier *actively* to seek customers for goods from within the exclusive territory.
  Note: both parties must be permitted to make *passive* sales to preserve a free market.
- ◆ oblige the distributor to buy minimum quantities and take complete ranges of goods.
- ◆ compel the distributor to resell goods in the supplier's packaging with the supplier's trademark.
- ◆ oblige the distributor to keep a stock of the goods.
- ◆ compel the distributor to advertise and promote the goods, and provide after-sales support.

2   Relevant UK law

a) *Restrictive Trade Practices Act 1976* NB: *The new government wishes to replace this with EU-style competition law legislation.*

➤ This applies where 2 parties both accept restrictions which may restrict competition.

➤ Parties to agreements which are affected must lodge the agreements within 3 months with the Office of Fair Trading ('OFT') which will put them on a public register (unless confidentiality is requested and the DTI grant it) and may refer them to the Restrictive Trade Practices Court.

➤ Agreements between parties whose aggregate UK turnover does not exceed £20 million and that are exempt from *Article 85(1)* by a block exemption (see p.244), need not be registered.

➤ Restrictions in unregistered agreements, and those not notified to the OFT within 3 months, are void. It is a criminal offence to attempt to enforce an unregistered restriction. The parties may be sued for breach of statutory duty, by third parties who are prejudiced.

➤ The *Act* can be circumvented by careful drafting to bring the agreement within an exemption as follows (*Associated Dairies Ltd v. Baines,* [1995] ICR 296):

i) *Exclusive dealing exemption*: the supplier is restricted only by the obligation to supply specified goods to particular persons, *and* the distributor only acknowledges a restriction to buy specified goods from particular suppliers.

ii) *Export exemption*: the restrictions apply only to overseas trade.

b) *Resale Prices Act 1976*

➤ Agreements which attempt to fix minimum prices for the sale of goods by a distributor are void.

III   Choosing the right type of agreement

	Agency agreement	Distribution agreement
Supervision	This depends on the type of agency: **classical sales agency:** requires more supervision over the agreement **marketing agency:** requires less supervision over the agreement	There is no need for day to day supervision, and the principal specifies any detailed requirements in the agreement. These are preferable if the principal wishes to deal in a new geographical market with minimum expense and inconvenience
Goods	Suitable for goods which are ordered on a 'one-off' basis to a customer's individual specification	Suitable for standard ranges of goods which do not require specialist after-sales support
Prices	➤ The supplier sells directly to the retailer ➤ The supplier controls the price ➤ The agent takes commission	➤ The supplier sells to the distributor who marks up the resale price ➤ The supplier can 'recommend', but cannot control the price as *Article 85* and the *Resale Prices Act 1976* prohibit price-fixing
Marketing	The supplier retains tight control over marketing	The supplier has less say; the distributor has more freedom of action
Enforcing contracts	This is difficult as the supplier sells to many customers	This is straightforward as there is only one buyer - the distributor
Liability	This depends on the type of agency: **classical sales agency:** the principal is directly liable in contract to customers **marketing agency:** the agent has no actual authority to act on the principal's behalf	The principal is only liable in contract to the distributor The principal may be liable to consumers under the *CPA 1987* or *GPSR 1994*
Protection of a territory	As a principal and agent are separate undertakings, the agent can be given an 'exclusive territory'	**Passive sales** cannot be banned (*either* those by a distributor outside his territory, *or* by a supplier within the territory) **Active sales** by either party in contravention of an 'exclusive territory' can usually be banned
Article 85 problems	Usually non-applicable as principal and agent are counted as one undertaking	This can be a problem, unless use is made of a block exemption
Taxation	An overseas business trading through an agency in the UK may be subject to corporation tax	This depends on the agreement's wording, and the extent of the principal's presence in the UK
Compensation	The agent may seek compensation for termination under *CA(CD)R 1993*	The only remedies are those usually available in contract and tort

Franchise

➤ These are suitable vehicles for exploiting a 'business format' (eg: Pizza Hut). There is a block exemption (*Regulation 4087/88*) from *Article 85*

  ◆ The franchisor can control closely many aspects of the product, and thus protect and foster his goodwill without incurring the capital costs of expanding in new markets
  ◆ The franchisee also benefits from the accumulated goodwill. He contributes his own capital. His freedom to innovate is rather limited by the franchise

Licence

➤ These enable the exploitation of intellectual property rights by permitting a third party to use a process, or manufacture a product

  ◆ The licensor is spared the difficulties and capital investment involved in manufacture
  ◆ A licence (possibly combined with a distribution agreement) may be vital where national laws insist that products are manufactured within a given area

I Employment

Employers, employees, or self-employed businessmen will need to be aware of 'free movement of workers' and of 'residence rights' in EU member states.   Both employers and employees may seek advice on the 'rights to equal treatment of workers' and on 'UK employment legislation'. Finally, with the state reducing its retirement provisions, clients should receive advice on 'pensions in the UK'.

I	Free movement of workers (EU law)
II	Residence rights (EU law)
III	Rights of workers to equal treatment (EU law)
IV	UK employment legislation
V	Employment-related factors to consider when starting a business
VI	Pensions in the UK

I Free movement of workers (EU law)

Treaty of Rome - *Article 48*

➤ This article prohibits discrimination based on nationality between workers of member states, for employment, or remuneration and other conditions of work and employment.

Derogation and exclusions *(Article 48(3)-(4))*

➤ *Article 48(3)* allows a member state to refuse to comply with the rights set out in *Article 48* on the grounds of public policy, public security or public health. The state must show that the individual's personal conduct presents a current threat in one of these respects. *Directive 64/221* says that derogation on these grounds must be based 'exclusively on the personal conduct of the individual concerned' and 'shall not be invoked to serve economic ends.'

➤ *Article 48(4)* excludes jobs in the public service 'involving the exercise of official authority and functions relating to safeguarding the general interests of the state' (*Commission v. Belgium* [1980] ECR 3881). The term 'public service' cannot be interpreted widely so as to erode the principle of freedom of movement for workers (*Commission v. France* [1984] ECR 307).

II Residence rights (EU law)

1 If employed

➤ A citizen of a member state has an absolute right of residence in any other member state where he is employed on a full or part-time basis (*Levin v. Staatssecrestaris van Justitie* [1982] ECR 1035).

➤ Notwithstanding an involuntary loss of work, an EU citizen is entitled to a 5 year residence permit (*Directive 68/360*), and his right of residence is unimpaired by incapacity due to disability or reaching the retirement age, subject to certain criteria (*Regulation 1251/70*).

2 If 'voluntarily' unemployed

➤ A citizen of a member state has a right of residence for as long as the individual and the members of his family are not a burden on the social assistance system of the host state (*Directive 90/364*).

III Rights of workers to equal treatment (EU law)

1 To enter to look for work

➤ *Article 48* extends to the right to move freely in search of employment.

➤ Deportation is allowed if someone is jobless after 6 months and cannot support himself, unless he can show he had genuine chances of being engaged (*R. v. Immigration Appeal Tribunal, ex parte Antonissen* [1991] 2 CMLR 373).

2 Conditions of work: there must be no discrimination against citizens of other member states for:

➤ **employment, dismissal, social and taxation status, training, and union membership** (*Regulation 1612/68*): the right to these must be the same as for any citizen of the host state.

➤ **social security benefits:** entitlement is the same as for a national of the host state subject to the individual having made contributions to similar schemes in other member states (*Regulation 1408/71*).

3 Right to bring a family

➤ A spouse, children under 21 and dependant relatives may enter *with a worker* (*Regulation 1612/68*).

➤ A spouse, children up to 21 and dependants can enter *with a self-employed person* who provides 'services' (*Directive 73/148*).

➤ The right to bring a family is only lost if *Article 48(3)* permits a member state to exclude the worker himself, or if the couple divorce (*Diatta v. Land Berlin* [1985] ECR 567).

➤ A returning national may bring a spouse that he/she married in another member state notwithstanding any obstacles to this in national law (*R. v. Immigration Tribunal and Surinder Singh, ex parte Home Secretary* [1982] 3 All ER 798).

4 Mutual recognition of qualifications

➤ A diploma after 3 years' higher professional education or training is accepted in all member states. If national criteria differ substantially, the individual can submit to an aptitude test *or* an 'adaptation' period of up to 3 years (*Directive 89/48*).

5 Recipients of services

➤ Recipients of services have a right to seek services from another member state (*Article 59* and *Luisi v. Ministero del Tesoro* [1984] ECR 377). This embraces the right to vocational training at no extra fee due to nationality (*Gravier v. City of Liege* [1985] ECR 593).

IV   UK employment legislation

A. Statutory rights

a)   *Equal Pay Act 1970*

➤ This places a duty on an employer to provide equal pay for men and women employed to do the same or comparable work.

b)   *Sex Discrimination Act 1975, Sex Discrimination Act 1986, Race Relations Act 1976*

➤ These place a duty on an employer not to discriminate directly or indirectly on grounds of sex, race, or marital status.

c)   *Disability Discrimination Act 1995*

➤ It is unlawful (unless justified) to discriminate against disabled employees or potential employees, whether in recruitment, working conditions or promotion prospects. There is also a duty to take reasonable steps to prevent a disabled person being disadvantaged by the employer's working arrangements or physical features of the work premises. (NB: this latter duty is limited to certain sizes of business).

d)   *Employment Rights Act 1996 s.1*

➤ The employer must provide the employee with a written statement within 2 months of employment commencing. The statement must contain certain particulars as follows:

Statement of employment	
◆ the name of the employer ◆ the name of the employee ◆ the date that employment began ◆ the period of 'continuous employment' for statutory purposes ◆ pay and how the pay is timed ◆ the hours of work ◆ holiday time (and any holiday pay) ◆ sickness time (and any sickness pay)	◆ pensions ◆ notice periods ◆ job title ◆ place of work ◆ any collective agreements ◆ certain details if the employee must work outside the UK for more than 1 month ◆ disciplinary procedures ◆ complaints procedures

e)   *Health and Safety at Work Act 1974 (and the common law duty to take reasonable care for the health and safety of the employee at work)*

➤ The employer has a duty to provide the employee with a safe place of work, safe equipment and to provide a Health and Safety policy. Breach leads to criminal prosecution.

➤ The employee can sue for damages for breach of common law duty *and* breach of statutory duty.

f)   *Transfer of Undertakings (Protection of Employment) Regulations 1981*

➤ These regulations apply when a business is transferred as a 'going concern'.

◆ The contract of employment of any employee employed by the seller of a business immediately before the transfer is not ended by the transfer.

◆ The employer's liability and obligations under the contract are transferred to the seller.

g)   *Collective Redundancies and Transfer of Undertakings (Protection of Employment) (Amendment) Regulations 1995*

➤ All business transfers and certain redundancies oblige an employer to consult with employees.

h)   *Trade Union and Labour Relations (Consolidation) Act 1992*

i)   *Asylum and Immigration Act 1996 (s.8)*

➤ It is a criminal offence for an employer to employ a person who either has not been granted leave to remain in the UK or whose leave is not 'valid and subsisting'.

B. Some rights before and on being made redundant

a) **Notice rights (*ERA 1996 ss.86-93*)**

> ➤ This means the employer has failed to give the employee the necessary period of notice.

> ➤ The employee can claim damages.

> ➤ The contract will normally stipulate the correct notice period that should have been given.

>> ◆ There is a statutory minimum period of notice which is: 1 week of notice for every year of continuous employment up to a limit of 12 weeks.

b) **Unfair dismissal (*ERA 1996 ss.94-134*)**

> ➤ This means the employer has dismissed the employee for an unfair reason (after a minimum of 2 years' continuous service).

> ➤ The employee can claim:

>> ◆ reinstatement, *or*

>> ◆ re-engagement in the service of the employer, *or*

>> ◆ compensation made up of:

>>> • a basic award. (The formula used is set out in the *ERA 1996 ss.119-122* and *s.126,* and is not related to the loss of the employee), *and*

>>> • a compensatory award. (The formula used is set out in the *ERA 1996 ss.123, 124, 126, 127.* It is an award that an industrial tribunal makes (subject to a maximum) if it is 'just and equitable' for losses caused to the employee *consequent* to the dismissal.)

c) **Redundancy (*ERA 1996 ss.135-181*)**

> ➤ This means that the employee is made redundant after 2 years of qualifying service.

> ➤ The employee can claim a redundancy payment calculated by a statutory formula. (The calculation is made using the employee's final week's pay, his length of service and his age.)

V   Employment-related factors to consider when starting a business

---

> ➤ The following are some employment-related factors to consider when starting a business:

>> ◆ the number of employees and the responsibility for them.

>> ◆ the terms of any contracts of employment.

>> ◆ employment legislation (see the previous and this page).

>> ◆ health and safety legislation.

>> ◆ insurance legislation.

>>> • This will include the statutory duties to obtain and display a certificate of insurance in respect of employees and accidents.

>>> • This may include motor insurance.

>> ◆ allowing employees time off to perform statutory duties including:

>>> • public duties (eg: jury service or acting as a magistrate).

>>> • trade union duties.

>> ◆ the need to provide personnel services (sometimes called human resources) for employees.

>> ◆ the need to deal with payroll and the implementation of PAYE machinery (see p.69).

VI Pensions in the UK

Pensions - general points

➤ Pensions can be provided via an Inland Revenue approved arrangement, or an unapproved arrangement.

➤ Pension schemes (both employer-operated and personal schemes) can elect to contract out of the State Earnings Related Pension Scheme (SERPS).

A. Rules for directors and employees

➤ Of the various options available, an 'exempt approved retirement benefits scheme' is one of the most popular. These are approved by the Inland Revenue Superannuation Funds Office.

➤ A qualifying scheme benefits as follows (*TA ss.590-612*):

a) an employee can deduct annual contributions from *Schedule E*, *and*

b) an employer's contributions may be deducted from profits under *Schedule D Cases I and II*, *and*

c) income on the scheme's investments and deposits is not subject to income tax, *and*

d) pensions/annuities under the scheme are charged under *Schedule E* and deducted through PAYE.

➤ If an employer does not operate an occupational scheme, or an individual desires to have another pension in respect of earnings not earned from an employer, he can make provision as an individual.

➤ Individuals who have made national insurance contributions for 90% of their working life with an employer who has not contracted out of the government scheme, are eligible for a state pension.

B. Rules for sole traders and partners

1   **Personal pensions** (begun after 1 July 1988)

➤ A contributor under the age of 36 is given tax relief up to 17.5% of his 'net' earnings. If aged 36 or over, the relief increases proportionately with the passing years up to 40% for those aged 61 or more (*s.640*).

➤ For pension schemes begun before 27 July 1989, a lump sum payment to a pensioner may not exceed £150,000. For subsequent schemes, the limit is set at 25% of the total benefit provided and the value of rights protected by the *Pensions Schemes Act 1993* (*s.635*).

➤ Lump sum death benefits must be payable before the member reaches the age of 75 (*s.637*).

➤ Contributions can be carried back (*s.641*) or forward (*s.642*) utilising relief from one year to another.

2   **Annuity contracts** (created on, or before, 29 June 1988 and which are still effective (*s.618(1)*))

➤ Contributors under the age of 51 are entitled to tax relief at 17.5% of their net relevant earnings (*s.619*); the rate of relief for older contributors rises to a maximum of 27.5% (*s.626*).

➤ The annuity is liable to income tax. Capital gains tax is not payable on a lump sum on retirement, but this must not exceed triple the value of the annuity payable after the lump sum has been deducted, and, is subject to a ceiling of £150,000 (*s.618(2)*).

3   **Partnership annuities** (*s.628*)

➤ A partnership may agree to pay an annuity to a partner, his spouse or dependants. This is paid net of basic rate tax. A partner can set the payment off against his 'Total Income' as a 'Charge on Income'.

➤ As an alternative to paying an annuity, the partnership may appoint a retiring partner as a 'consultant'. This retains the value of goodwill the partner has acquired, so his fees would be a 'deductible expense'.

4   **State pensions**

➤ Unless an individual or an employer's scheme contracts out of SERPS, the individual will receive a state pension in respect of his past national insurance contributions.

Civil Litigation

This chapter examines:

Rules of the court

➤ Rules of High Court procedure are governed by the **Rules of the Supreme Court 1965 (RSC)**. These are collected, together with commentary, in 'The Supreme Court Practice' known as the 'White Book'.

➤ Rules of County Courts' procedure are governed by the **County Court Rules 1981 (CCR)**. These are collected together with commentary, in 'The County Court Practice' known as the 'Green Book'.

➤ *Note: CCA 1984 s.76 says that general principles of practice in the High Court may be adopted in the County Court where the CCRs are silent.*

Civil Procedure Act 1997

➤ The Civil Procedure Act 1997 sets up a Civil Procedure Rules Committee to make Civil Procedure Rules. This is a preliminary step to implement the Woolf report (see p.329).

◆ Practice directions will also be more widely used.

A First steps

I   Is the claim viable?

II   Are there any alternatives to starting proceedings in the UK courts?

III How will the client finance the action?

I Is the claim viable?

Contract	Tort		
	Negligence	**Personal injury**	**Latent damage**
**1 Is the defendant worthy of attention?**			

1 Is the defendant worthy of attention?

Is the defendant i) traceable and ii) solvent?

2 How strong is the plaintiff's case?

Does the evidence i) show all the elements required in law, *and* ii) prove these elements on the balance of probabilities?

3 Has the limitation period expired? (*LA 1980*)

Contract	Negligence	Personal injury	Latent damage

6 years from the breach of contract (*s.5*)	6 years from when the damage occurs (*s.2*)	3 years from (*s.11*):
		a) the date of the accident, *or*
		b) the date of knowledge that (*s.14*):
		  i) the injury is significant enough for proceedings +
		  ii) an injury is due to the defendant's fault +
		  iii) the defendant's identity becomes known
			Either:
			a) 6 years from the date on which the cause of action accrues (*s.14A*), *or*
			b) (if later than a)), 3 years from the date that a plaintiff could start proceedings because a plaintiff now has:
			  i) the knowledge* required for bringing an action, *and*
			  ii) a right to bring such an action (ie: recovery from a defendant seems realistic)
			(NB: it must not be more than 15 years from the date of the breach)

For death and personal injury, the court has discretion to override the limitation period (*s.33*)

If the cause of action belongs to a minor, the limitation period runs from the child's majority at 18

4 What damages are available?

Contract	Negligence	Personal injury	Latent damage

Generally
Loss which flows naturally from the breach
 	
Loss which was within the reasonable contemplation of the parties at the time the contract was made
 	
There is a duty to mitigate loss
 	
Debt claims
If the action is a claim for debt, the one claiming the sum outstanding does not have the duty to mitigate his loss, which applies to all other types of damages
	Direct loss and consequential loss which is a reasonably foreseeable consequence of the negligence
	
	Note: Usually, it is impossible to recover pure economic loss, but recent cases now cast doubt
		a) **Special damages**: liquidated claims for actual financial loss up to the date of the trial
		b) **General damages**: unliquidated, compensating for:
		  i) past and future non-financial loss, *and*
		  ii) future financial loss
		c) *From 1 October 1997 (SS(RB)A 1997)*: if the plaintiff receives state benefits then:
		  i) the defendant obtains a certificate of recoverable benefits from the Department of Social Security (DSS) Compensation Recovery Unit (CRU).
		  ii) the defendant is obliged to pay to the CRU the *full* amount of certain benefits listed which have been paid to the injured person.
		  iii) where part of the compensation payment itself from the defendant to the plaintiff is in respect of a particular kind of loss, (loss of earnings, cost of care, loss of mobility) and benefits have been paid to the plaintiff for this kind of loss, the defendant may deduct the benefits concerned from the compensation payment ie:the plaintiff is paid damages net, minus the sum due to the DSS which the defendant forwards to the CRU within 14 days of the plaintiff receiving compensation
		NB: No deductions are possible for pain and suffering ie: the victim keeps all the damages for pain and suffering
			i) the knowledge* required for bringing an action, *and*
			ii) a right to bring such an action (ie: recovery from a defendant seems realistic)
			
			(NB: it must not be more than 15 years from the date of the breach)
			
			*Knowledge means knowledge of the facts such that an action may be brought, eg: the identity of the defendant and that the damage was due to the defendant's fault, etc

5 Does the claim carry interest?

Contract	Negligence	Personal injury	Latent damage
Interest is given from: i) the date when the action arose to judgment *or* ii) date of payment (if sooner) *either* a) at the contract rate, *or* b) at a court's discretion (unlikely to exceed the judgment debt rate) **Debt claims**(*JD(RI)O 1993*) *High Court:* 8% from final judgment date *County Court:* 8% if £5,000 or more	At the court's discretion	Judgment for a sum ... a) ...**over £200**: a court must award interest (but will not do so if it has a special reason) (*SCA1981s.35A*) b) ...**£200 or less**: at the court's discretion **The rate is usually:** i) 0% for future loss of earnings ii) 2% from the service of the writ to the trial, for pain, suffering and loss of amenity iii) half the court's average Special Account average rate from the accident to the start of trial for 'special damages'	At the court's discretion

6 What other remedies are possible?

Eg: possession orders (*RSC Ord. 45 r.3, CCR Ord. 26 r.17*), injunctions (*SCA 1981 s.37(1), CCA 1984 s.38*), etc

II Are there any alternatives to starting proceedings in the UK courts?

1 **Negotiation**	6 **Criminal Injuries Compensation Board**
2 **Trade schemes**	7 **Criminal compensation order**
3 **Alternative dispute resolution**	8 **Application in a foreign jurisdiction**
4 **Motor Insurers' Bureau**	9 **Statutory demand (see p.233)**
5 **Insurance (motor accidents)**	10 **Arbitration in the County Court**
	11 **Arbitration under** *Arbitration Act 1996*

1 Negotiation

➤ This is always better than litigation and should normally be conducted 'without prejudice'.

2 Trade schemes

➤ These are operated by various trade and professional bodies and include:

   ♦ Royal Institute of Chartered Surveyors (RICS).

   ♦ Association of British Travel Agents (ABTA).

   ♦ British Association of Removers.

3 Alternative dispute resolution (mediation) (ADR)

➤ A third party mediates and the mediation may or may *not* be binding.

   ♦ If no binding agreement is reached, then arbitration or litigation is possible later.

➤ The procedure is quicker, cheaper and less destructive of the parties' relationship than litigation.

➤ ADR is becoming increasingly important and the Woolf report (see p.329) takes the lead from the US in putting a duty on solicitors to resolve disputes by trying ADR first. Practice directions are already beginning to reflect this new approach.

4 Motor Insurers' Bureau ('MIB')

➤ There are 2 schemes:

Victims of *uninsured* drivers	Victims of *untraced* drivers
Commence proceedings ↓ Notify the MIB within 7 days of commencing proceedings ↓ If 7 days after final judgment against the defendant driver the claim is not satisfied, the MIB will meet the claim together with costs ↓ Judgment must be assigned to the MIB so they may try and recover from the insured driver	The death or injury must not have been caused deliberately by the untraced driver ↓ Notify the MIB by letter within 3 years of the accident ↓ The MID itself investigates the merit of the claim ↓ Negligence *must* be proved ↓ The MIB will cover death, bodily injury or emergency hospital treatment, and there is no need to prove these costs
The first £175 of property damage is not covered	Property damage is *not* recoverable
	Queen's Counsel hears appeals against the amount of damages by way of arbitration
	There is an accelerated process for claims up to £50,000. This allows the claimant and the MIB to reach a compromise, but there is no full investigation and no right of appeal

5   Insurance (motor accidents)

➤ The decision how to claim depends on the type of insurance policy concerned:

    a) **Compulsory risks** (required by *RTA 1988*). Such insurance covers ...

       ◆ ... death or injury to any other person, *and*

       ◆ ... property damage up to £250,000, excluding damage to the insured vehicle and its contents, *and*

       ◆ ... the cost of emergency hospital treatment.

    b) **Third party, fire and theft.** Such insurance additionally covers...

       ◆ ... the insured against these risks.

    c) **Comprehensive.** Such insurance additionally covers...

       ◆ ... damage to the insured's vehicle and limited compensation for a driver's injuries.

➤ Claims against the insured's own insurance (*only* if the policy is 'comprehensive').

    ◆ A 'no-claims' bonus may be lost, increasing the premium payable on the policy in the future.

    ◆ The insured may have to pay an 'excess' as a contribution to damages.

    ◆ The insurance company may insist that the insured lends their name to any legal proceedings.

    ◆ If the other party has 'comprehensive' insurance, the companies may agree between themselves to cover the costs of their own insured - the claimant has no control over the settlement they reach. This is called 'knock for knock'.

    ◆ The claimant may also choose to proceed against the other party or their insurer's for any *uninsured* losses, eg: the amount of the excess *or* loss of any discount given by a no claims bonus.

➤ Claims against the other party's insurance.

    ◆ Provided the plaintiff serves a notice on the defendant's insurers within 7 days of commencing proceedings, he can recover damages from them, even if they are entitled to avoid *or* cancel the policy (*ss.151-152 RTA 1988*).

➤ Insurance is not necessarily an alternative to proceedings in the courts because of subrogation of rights - the insurer may still bring the action, leading to litigation.

6   Criminal Injuries Compensation Board

➤ The Criminal Injuries Compensation Board is a body that was set up under the Royal Prerogative in 1964 to award, *ex gratia*, small amounts of compensation to the victims of crime.

➤ There is a fixed scale of awards (see *CICA 1995*).

7   Criminal compensation order (*PCCA 1973 ss.35-38*)

➤ This is available for personal injury losses or damage following a criminal offence (other than loss due to accident arising out of there being a personal motor vehicle on a road). Compensation may be payable for damage which is not covered by the MIB.

    ◆ Magistrates' Court: fine up to £5,000 for each offence.

    ◆ Crown Court: fine unlimited, taking account of the defendant's means.

8   Application in a foreign jurisdiction - (*CJJA 1982 & PIL(MP)A 1995*)

➤ A person domiciled in the UK, or a company based in the UK, may sue in the UK.

➤ But a UK plaintiff may sue abroad if:

    ◆ for contractual claims: *either* the defendant is domiciled abroad, *or* the cause of action arose abroad, *or* a foreign law or jurisdiction is stipulated in the contract.

    ◆ for tortious claims: *either* the tort occurred abroad, *or* the damage was suffered abroad.

    NB: Consider the costs and remedies, and the likelihood of enforcement in foreign jurisdictions.

10   **Arbitration in the County Court (ie: the 'small claims court')** (*CCR Ord.19*)

11   **Arbitration under *Arbitration Act 1996***

➤ This is often a cheaper and faster option than litigation. It is binding and appeal lies to the courts. The procedures are governed by Arbritration Act 1996 (not dealt with here).

Small claims arbitration
Advantages (✓) and Disadvantages (✗)

✓ Quicker and less formal than a court hearing ✓ The remedies are more flexible and the parties are bound by the ruling	✗ Legal aid is *not* available and there is less investigation ✗ Less right of appeal ✓ and ✗ Less costs available

Reference to arbitration

➤ **Automatic reference:** a reference to arbitration is automatic when a defence is filed in the County Court in respect of a claim worth £3,000 or less (unless it is a personal injury claim, in which case the claim must be worth £1,000 or less) ➤ If there is a dispute about the amount claimed, a district judge will hold a hearing to determine the amount being claimed	➤ **Voluntary reference:** even if a claim is worth more than £3,000, any party may apply to the court for the case to go to arbitration. If so, the procedure is exactly the same as for 'small claims' arbitration but the 'no costs' rule (see below) does not apply and costs are awarded as at a normal trial

Procedure (*CCR Ord.19 r.6*)

Automatic directions apply:

Steps

1   The district judge gives at least 21 days notice of the hearing to both parties
2   At least 14 days before the hearing, the parties exchange documents
3   At least 7 days before the hearing, the parties exchange:

   ◆ the experts' reports they will rely upon, *and*

   ◆ a list of witnesses to be called at the hearing

4   The actual hearing is informal and is held in private. Strict rules of evidence do not apply

The 'no costs' rule (*CCR Ord.19 r.4*)

➤ *Only* the costs of enforcing the award, and those stated on the summons, and costs due to the unreasonable conduct of the other party are recoverable

Setting aside a reference to arbitration (*CCR Ord.19 r.3*)

➤ If there is:
   a) alleged fraud, *or*
   b) complexity of law or fact, *or*
   c) the parties agree that a trial in court would be preferable, *or* →
   d) arbitration is unreasonable due to:
      i) the subject matter, *or*
      ii) the size of any counterclaim, *or*
      iii) the circumstances of the parties, *or*
      iv) the interests of a third party

> *THEN* either party may apply for the reference to arbitration to be rescinded. If this happens, then the case is referred to the County Court for trial (ignoring the claim's monetary value)

III   How will the client finance the action?

➤ The client may be eligible for legal aid (see p.7). If not, the solicitor should:

a) explain that the client is responsible for all the solicitor's costs and that if the case is lost he may have to pay the other side's costs. Even if the client is successful, costs are at the court's discretion and will not be awarded to the client automatically. Although some costs may be recovered from the other side, the client will have to meet any shortfall (see p.318 for taxation), *and*

b) ask the client for a 'payment on account' to finance preparatory work, expert's reports, etc.

After the first client meeting

1   Write to the client confirming instructions (give information required by *SPR 1990 r.15*, see p.4).

2   Take general statements from the client and witnesses.

3   Make a site visit, if relevant, as soon as possible and take appropriate photographs, etc.

4   Commission any expert reports.

5   Research any relevant law.

6   **Road traffic accident cases only**
   ◆ Write to the Chief Superintendent requesting a copy of the police accident report.
   ◆ Obtain a certificate of conviction from the court (if appropriate).
   ◆ Serve a *s.151/s.152* notice on the defendant's insurers before issuing proceedings or within 7 days after issuing proceedings.

7   **Personal injury cases only:**
   ◆ Write to the client's employer for details of gross and net salary over the 26 weeks prior to the accident, the employee's prospects and details of the employment contract.
   ◆ Write to the Inland Revenue to claim a tax rebate (if appropriate).
   ◆ Notify the Compensation Recovery Unit within 14 days of receiving a letter before action.

8   Send a letter before action to the defendant stating:
   a) for whom the solicitors are acting.
   b) the factual circumstances by which the claim has arisen.
   c) the action the solicitors are preparing to take.
   d) brief details of any loss, injury or damage.
   ◆ The letter should demand either settlement *or* a response within 7 to 14 days, failing which proceedings will be issued. The letter should warn that any claim will include interest and costs.

9   Negotiate?
   ◆ Before proceedings are issued the solicitor has no implied authority to settle.
   ◆ After proceedings have been issued the solicitor has implied authority to settle; however, the client's express authority should always be sought (ideally in writing).
   ◆ Negotiations should normally be conducted 'without prejudice' so that nothing in the negotiations will be admissible in court.

10   Draw up formal 'Instructions to Counsel' and arrange any necessary conferences with counsel.

11   Pre-action discovery (*RSC Ord.24 r.7A, CCR Ord.13 r.7*)
   a) In claims for personal injuries or death:
   ◆ ask the defendant to co-operate by letter. This should save the plaintiff costs.
   ◆ lodge an originating summons (High Court) or an application on notice (County Court) with an affidavit:
      i)   giving the factual basis of a likely claim, *and*
      ii) stating what documents are needed, and why, and that the defendant possesses them.
   ◆ at the hearing, the court will make an order for discovery now, rather than at the pre-trial stage, if this is absolutely essential. (This is not limited to personal injury cases.)
   b) Apply for an order for discovery against someone who is likely to be a party to the proceedings.

12   Pre-action inspection (*RSC ord.29 r.7A, CCR Ord. 13 r.7*)
   ◆ The procedure is the same as for pre-action discovery (see above).
   ◆ An order can be made against *anyone* who holds property central to the case.
   ◆ An order may permit: photography, detention and custody, inspection, testing, and sampling. (Any or all of these may be necessary to preserve or procure evidence.)

B   Starting proceedings

I   Identifying the parties (and extra procedural points that result)
II   Selecting the court
III   Starting the action

I   Identifying the parties (and extra procedural points that result)

1   Joint plaintiffs or defendants (*RSC Ord.15 r.4, CCR Ord.5 r.2*)

➤ *No* leave of the court is needed if there is a common question of law or fact, and if the claim arises from the same transaction or series of transactions. Otherwise leave of the court must be sought.

➤ In the High Court, a co-plaintiff must obtain the written consent of other co-plaintiffs to commence the action. (Co-defendants obviously do not need this consent.)

➤ Co-plaintiffs cannot make allegations inconsistent with those of other co-plaintiffs.

2   Joinder of causes of action (*RSC Ord. 15 r.1, CCR Ord. 5 r.1*)

➤ A plaintiff does not need leave of the court to join causes of action unless he is suing in two capacities (eg: if he is suing the same defendant both personally *and* as personal representative).

3   Sole trader (*CCR Ord.5 r.10*)

➤ Plaintiff: must sue in his own name.

➤ Defendant: may be sued in his own name *or* in his business name.

4   Partnership (*RSC Ord.81, CCR Ord.5 r.9*)

➤ A partnership can sue or be sued in:

   ◆ the firm's name, *or*

   ◆ the names of all the individual partners.

➤ Suing partners in their firm name:

   ✓ makes service easier, *but*

   ✗ leave is needed for enforcing judgment against the individual partners' own assets.

5   Company

➤ Company as plaintiff: can sue in its own name.

➤ Company as defendant: can be sued in its own name - verify the company's details with a company search.

➤ High Court: a company must appoint a solicitor (*RSC Ord.5 r.6*).

6   Plaintiff is a minor (ie: under 18) *(RSC Ord.80, CCR Ord.10)*

➤ A minor plaintiff will need someone to protect him, called his 'next friend'.

➤ The plaintiff acts through a next friend whose name is added to the title of the action - 'M (minor) by B (his brother and next friend)'.

➤ The next friend is personally liable for costs, but is usually indemnified for these by the minor.

➤ The next friend has authority to agree all agreements or settlements. Where money is claimed on behalf of a minor, the court must approve any settlement or compromise, whereupon any money won by the minor will usually be paid into court until the minor is 18 (although sums may be drawn earlier for reasons such as schooling, holidays or medical expenses).

➤ The minor may adopt or repudiate proceedings on coming of age during the proceedings.

➤ High Court: file with the writ or summons a) the next friend's consent to act, *and* b) a solicitor's certificate that there is no conflict of interest between the next friend and the minor. The next friend must appoint a solicitor.

➤ County Court: file with the summons an undertaking by the next friend to pay costs for which the minor might be liable. (The next friend has a right of indemnity against the minor.)

7   Defendant is a minor (ie: under 18) *(RSC Ord.80, CCR Ord.10)*

➤ A minor defendant will need someone to protect him, who is called his 'guardian *ad litem*'.

➤ Proceedings are served on a guardian *ad litem* whose name is added to the title of the action - 'M (minor) by B (his guardian *ad litem*)'.

➤ The guardian *ad litem* is only liable for costs due to his personal negligence or misconduct.

➤ The court must approve any settlement or compromise.

➤ The guardian *ad litem* has authority to agree procedural matters.

➤ High Court: supply with the acknowledgement of service a) a consent to act, and b) a solicitor's certificate that there is no conflict of interest between the guardian *ad litem* and the minor. The guardian *ad litem* must appoint a solicitor.

➤ County Court: supply with the admission, defence and/or counterclaim, a certificate that the guardian *ad litem* is a fit and proper person to act, and has no conflicting interest with those of the minor.

8   Insurers

➤ If the client is the plaintiff, he must send a *s.151/152 RTA 1988* notice to the defendant's insurers within 7 days of issuing proceedings. This enables the defendant's insurers to defend the claim, and for the plaintiff to claim against them if he wins.

II Selecting the court

A. Courts Generally

High Court	County Court
There is **one** High Court divided into: **Chancery Division** (includes: ◆ Patent Court ◆ Companies Court) **Family Division** **Queens Bench Division** (includes: ◆ Commercial Court ◆ Admiralty Court) Used for: landlord and tenant disputes, trusts, contentious probate, partnership actions, intellectual property actions and actions requesting equitable remedies Used for: claiming damages in contract actions and tort actions	There are **many** County Courts ◆ The Central London County Court Business List is sometimes used for certain business/commercial transactions up to £200,000 in value (*CCR Ord. 48C*) ◆ The Central London Civil Trial Centre has now opened at the Central London County Court. More complex County Court cases are heard here, especially those expected to last for more than 1 day. Cases may be referred here by any London County Court
The jurisdiction of the High Court is governed by royal prerogative	The jurisdiction of the County Court is governed by statute

➤ All trials are heard by a High Court judge
➤ All interlocutory applications are heard by:
  ◆ in the Central Office - a Master
  ◆ in a District Registry - a district judge
	➤ All trials are heard by:
	  ◆ over £5,000 - a circuit judge
	  ◆ £5,000 or less - a district judge
	    NB: A district judge may also try a case here:
	    • all parties and the judge consent, *or*
	    • the case is undefended
	➤ All interlocutory applications are heard by a district judge

B. Commencement of an action

➤ An action can be commenced in the High court or a County Court.

➤ The County Court chosen will be the one in the district where the defendant resides/carries on business or where the cause of action arose. However, for a default action (ie: an action for a liquidated sum), the action can begin in any County Court. It will then be transferred to the defendant's local court if he puts in a defence (unless the plaintiff asks the court to exercise its discretion).

➤ A case may commence in the High Court or the County Court depending on the jurisdiction of each:

The jurisdiction of the courts is set out in *CCA 1984* and *SI 1991/724*	
The following cases are heard in the High Court	The following cases are heard in the County Court
Tort actions over £25,000 (Note the overlap with the County Court)	Tort actions up to £50,000 (*CCA 1984 s.15*)
Contract actions over £25,000 (Note the overlap with the County Court)	Contract actions up to £50,000 (*CCA 1984 s.15*)
Personal injury actions worth £50,000 or over	Personal injury actions worth under £50,000 (*SI 1991/724*)
Libel	Equitable interests and land charges disputes where the property has a value of £30,000 or less (*CCA 1984 s.23*)
Anton Piller order (authorises a party to search for documents or property at their opponent's premises)	Taxation of a solicitor's bill if (*SA 1974 s.69(3)*): ◆ it only relates to work done in the County Court, *and*
Slander	◆ it is for £5,000 or less
Judicial review	**Note:** claims under £3,000 (except personal injury when the figure is under £1,000) are referred to the small claims court - see p.265
Mareva injunctions (to freeze assets)	

C. Trial of an action

➤ If and when a case comes to trial, the action usually carries on in the court in which it was commenced.

➤ However, in certain cases the trial can be transferred to a different court and the rules set out below on this page govern when this happens (*High Court and County Courts Jurisdiction Order 1991*).

1   High Court transfer to County Court

➤ The High Court can transfer whatever it wants to the County Court (*CCA 1984 s.40*).

➤ This might occur in the following types of cases:

a) cases that *could* only be started in the High Court, eg: slander, libel.

b) cases that *should* never have started in the High Court *must* be moved to the County Court (*CCA 1984 s.40*), eg: a personal injury action worth less than £50,000.

c) cases that can be heard in either court.

➤ A case will automatically be transferred to the County Court unless a 'statement of value' showing the action is worth at least £25,000 (or a statement saying why the action ought to be heard in the High Court) is delivered:

a) before a summons for directions is heard, *and*

b) on setting down, *and*

c) on seeking leave to defend at an application for summary judgment.

2   High Court transfer to County Court and County Court transfer to High Court

➤ Generally, the High Court has power to transfer cases to the County Court and the County Court has power to transfer cases to the High Court.

➤ In deciding whether to transfer, a court must look at the elements of each case. The more serious the case, the more likely that it will be heard in the High Court. The following 4 factors are used to gauge this:

Factors used to gauge 'seriousness'

1   **Value of the claim** (including any counterclaim):

➤ for claims below £25,000, the trial of the action is likely to be in the County Court (except for personal injury where the County Court will hear claims for up to £50,000).

➤ for claims over £50,000, the trial of the action is likely to be in the High Court.

➤ for claims between £25,000 and £50,000, the trial may be in either court.

2   **Importance of the case:**   to the public generally or to any interested third parties. ✳

3   **Complexity:**   matters of law, fact, procedure or remedies.

4   **Speed:**   which court can despatch the business quicker
(NB: This factor is not sufficient on its own to justify a transfer.)

➤ The following are usually considered important under factor 2 in the practice box on the previous page, and so would usually be heard in the High Court (*Practice Direction (County Court: Transfer of Actions) [1991] 1 WLR 643*):

- ◆ professional negligence.

- ◆ fatal accident.

- ◆ fraud/

- ◆ undue influence.

- ◆ defamation.

- ◆ malicious prosecution.

- ◆ false imprisonment.

- ◆ claims against the police.

Value of a claim

➤ The value of an action for a sum of money, whether specified or not, is the amount which the plaintiff reasonably expects to recover.

➤ Where the action is for a specified relief other than money (such as an injunction) then the test used is the value equivalent to the 'financial worth of the claim'.

➤ The following are ignored in calculating value:

a) unspecified or further relief, *and*

b) interest, unless it is due under a contract, *and*

c) costs, *and*

d) contributory negligence unless the plaintiff admits it.

➤ In personal injury cases, sums that will be due to the Department of Social Security under *SS(RB)A 1997* (see p.xxx) are included in the value at this stage (seep.262).

➤ Any debt the plaintiff admits he owes to the defendant is deducted from the value of the claim.

➤ If there is a counterclaim, the value is the aggregate of the claims (ie: add them together).

➤ If there is more than one plaintiff, then the value is the aggregate of the claims.

D. Striking out an action - wrong court

➤ The High Court and the County Court may both strike out any action where the plaintiff either knew, or ought to have known, that the proceedings should have been brought in the other court.

III Starting the action

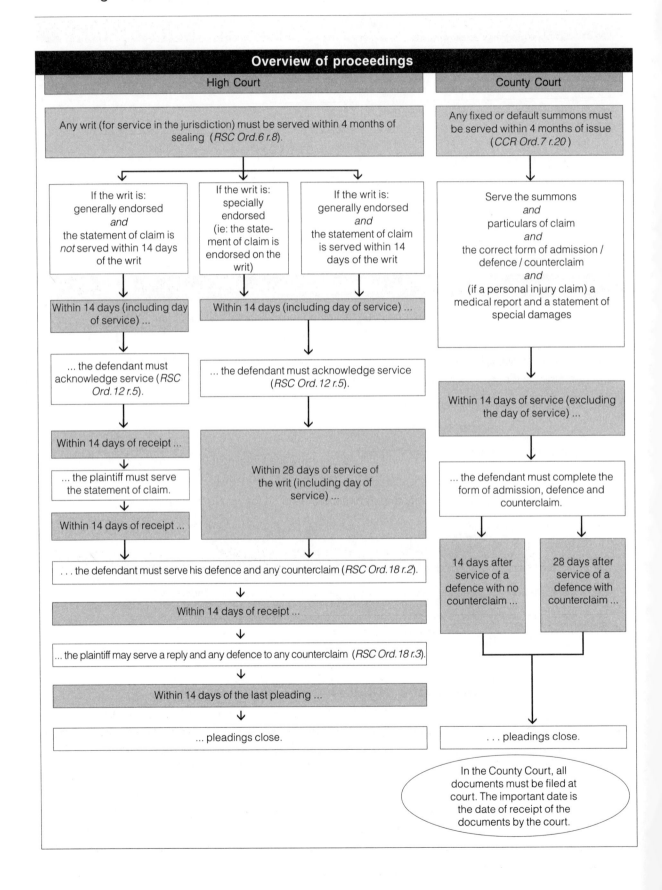

Overview of proceedings

High Court

Any writ (for service in the jurisdiction) must be served within 4 months of sealing (*RSC Ord.6 r.8*).

| If the writ is: generally endorsed *and* the statement of claim is *not* served within 14 days of the writ | If the writ is: specially endorsed (ie: the statement of claim is endorsed on the writ) | If the writ is: generally endorsed *and* the statement of claim is served within 14 days of the writ |

Within 14 days (including day of service) ...

Within 14 days (including day of service) ...

... the defendant must acknowledge service (*RSC Ord.12 r.5*).

... the defendant must acknowledge service (*RSC Ord.12 r.5*).

Within 14 days of receipt ...

... the plaintiff must serve the statement of claim.

Within 14 days of receipt ...

Within 28 days of service of the writ (including day of service) ...

... the defendant must serve his defence and any counterclaim (*RSC Ord.18 r.2*).

Within 14 days of receipt ...

... the plaintiff may serve a reply and any defence to any counterclaim (*RSC Ord.18 r.3*).

Within 14 days of the last pleading ...

... pleadings close.

County Court

Any fixed or default summons must be served within 4 months of issue (*CCR Ord.7 r.20*)

Serve the summons *and* particulars of claim *and* the correct form of admission / defence / counterclaim *and* (if a personal injury claim) a medical report and a statement of special damages

Within 14 days of service (excluding the day of service) ...

... the defendant must complete the form of admission, defence and counterclaim.

| 14 days after service of a defence with no counterclaim ... | 28 days after service of a defence with counterclaim ... |

... pleadings close.

In the County Court, all documents must be filed at court. The important date is the date of receipt of the documents by the court.

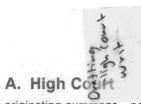

A. High Court

1 Drafting - an action is started by writ (or originating summons - not dealt with here).

Drafting a High Court Writ (*RSC Ords. 5 and 6*)

➤ Drafting the writ can be done on the appropriate pre-printed form (*Appendix A No.1 - White Book*) but this is not essential.

Front page of the writ

1   Registry
   - ➤ If the writ is to be issued out of the Central Office or Chancery Chambers, strike out the reference to the District Registry.
   - ➤ If the writ is to be issued out of a District Registry then insert the Registry's name.

2   Number
   - ➤ Fill in the year of issue and add the first letter of the plaintiff's name (eg: 1997M). The court completes the rest.

3   Parties
   - ➤ Check the details of a company by carrying out a search at Companies House.
   - ➤ Insert the full names of the plaintiff and the defendant (or as much of the name as is known).

4   Defendant's details
   - ➤ Insert the name after the words 'To the Defendant', and his/her address after the word 'of'.
   - ➤ For a company, this address is its registered office (revealed by a company search).

5   Registry
   - ➤ At the foot of the page insert the name of the issuing Registry or Central Office or Chancery Chambers.

6   Date of issue
   - ➤ There is a space for the date of issue - the court will complete this.

Reverse of the writ

➤ The reverse is used for various endorsements: (Note: a) and d) below are completed in all cases.)

a) Either:

   i)   A 'full' endorsement: this contains a full 'statement of claim' and is usually only completed for straightforward debt claims. This is called a 'specially endorsed' writ, *or*

   ii) A 'general' endorsement: this is used, for example, when the statement of claim is not yet ready, or where privacy is required (since a writ is a public document and the statement of claim may contain sensitive details). This is called a 'generally endorsed writ'. A separate statement of claim must be served subsequently. A general endorsement should state the nature of the claim and the relief or remedy required and may include:

Note: See Section C - Pleadings for drafting a statement of claim (p.279)

Breach of contract	Personal injury
1 ➤ The plaintiff's claim (ie: damages) ➤ The plaintiff's claim (ie: breach) ➤ The form of agreement (eg: oral) ➤ The agreement date ➤ The parties to the contract ➤ The contract's subject matter	1 ➤ The plaintiff's claim (ie: damages for personal injury) ➤ The type of tort (ie: negligence) ➤ The party committing the (alleged) tort (ie: defendant) ➤ The location of the accident ➤ The date of the accident
2 ➤ A claim for interest	2 ➤ A claim for interest

b) A 'fixed costs' endorsement: this is completed if the action concerns a debt/liquidated sum and is obtained from court tables (it depends on the amount of the principal sum + interest claimed). This informs the defendant that if the figure is paid within 14 days, the defendant will not be liable for any further sums and proceedings will be stayed.

c) A 'cause of action' endorsement: if the writ is issued out of a District Registry this prevents a transfer to the Central Office or another Registry. It is used if one of the causes of action arose wholly or partly in the area of a Registry.

d) A service endorsement: *either* the plaintiff's address where the plaintiff sues in person, *or* where the plaintiff sues by a solicitor, that of his solicitor.

e) A certificate of value endorsement: for personal injury actions worth over £50,000. Wording:
   'This writ includes a claim for personal injury but may be commenced in the High Court because the value of the action for the purposes of *Article 5* of the High Court & County Courts Jurisdiction Order 1991 exceeds £50,000' (*RSC Ord.6(2(1)(f)*).

2 **Issue of proceedings**

➤ The plaintiff's solicitors should:

Steps	
1	prepare at least 3 copies of the writ and all documents accompanying it (see steps 4 and 5 below), for the plaintiff, each defendant and the court (see chart on p.277).
2	sign one of the copies (the court will keep this copy).
3	prepare the acknowledgement of service.
4	if the plaintiff is legally aided, prepare the legal aid certificate.
5	if the plaintiff is a minor, prepare the next friend documents, the next friend's consent to act, and the solicitor's certificate of 'no-conflict' (see p.268).
6	if proceedings are to be issued by post, prepare a stamped addressed envelope ('SAE')
7	prepare the court fee.
8	take, or send (include the SAE if so), the writ, the acknowledgement of service and any of the above documents to the court, together with the court fee.
9	The court will issue an action number, seal the documents, keep one copy and send the rest (now sealed) back to the plaintiff. The copy marked 'ORIGINAL' by the court is for the plaintiff to keep.

3 **Service of the writ**

➤ The writ, the acknowledgement of service form and any other documents which the court sealed must be served within 4 calendar months starting with the date of its issue. Although there is no need for the statement of claim to be served now, it is usually served anyway.

➤ The plaintiff serves the writ *and* acknowledgement of service form by one of the following methods:

a) **postal service:** relevant documents are sent by first class post to the defendant's address (residential or business) and service is presumed to be effective 7 days later (*RSC Ord. 10 r. 1*).
   Note: second class post is not permitted (*RSC Ord. 10 r. 1*).

b) **letter box service:** documents may be served by putting a writ through the letter box at the defendant's residential/ business address. Service is presumed to be effective 7 days later (*RSC Ord. 10 r. 1*).

c) **personal service:** documents are served by leaving the writ with the defendant. This is effective immediately. If he is uncooperative, it is sufficient to leave it in his presence (*RSC Ord. 65 rr. 1-2*).

d) **substituted service:** this is an ex parte application to permit service on a third party. The court will have to be satisfied that it is not practicable to serve the relevant documents in the usual way, and that the defendant will receive the writ from the third party (*RSC Ord. 65 r. 4*).

➤ **Service on a limited company:** see chart on p.278.

4 **Service on the defendant's solicitor**

➤ If the defendant's solicitor is authorised to accept service, one of the above methods may be used on him.

➤ The defendant's solicitor endorses the plaintiff's writ when acknowledging its receipt, and service is deemed to take place on the day of the endorsement (*RSC Ord. 10 r. 1(4)*).

5 **Defendant is difficult to serve**

➤ If it proves difficult to serve a writ on an individual defendant (eg: he cannot be located) the plaintiff may apply to the court for an order that the court should allow a 'substituted service'. In this case, the writ is served on a third party on the assumption that the third party will be able, and will in fact, bring the writ to the attention of the defendant.

6 **Time of service**

➤ a) Service is presumed to occur on the day the defendant acknowledges service, but this is rebuttable (*RSC Ord. 10 r. 1(5)*), *or*

b) the plaintiff's solicitor swears an affidavit of service to indicate when service occurred.

B. County Court

1   **Drafting** - an action is started by a summons *or* a petition (eg: for bankrutcy or divorce) (not dealt with here) *or* originating application (eg: certain landlord & tenant applications) (not dealt with here).

Drafting a County Court summons (*CCR Ords. 3 and 6*)

There are 2 main categories of County Court summons (there are others not dealt with here):

1   **Default summons**

➤ This is used for default actions which are claims for money and nothing else, eg: debt and damages.

➤ Actions are commenced by lodging at court a default summons and particulars of claim.

➤ Use *either:*

a) *Form N1* for fixed claims, *or*

b) *Form N2* for claims where damages are not fixed.

◆ When completed, *Form N1* specifies the amount of the debt claimed, the court fee paid on issuing the summons and the amount of fixed costs payable in the event of the plaintiff obtaining a default judgment *or* the defendant conceding the claim.

2   **Fixed date summons**

➤ This is issued in claims for any other relief (even if it also includes money), ie: it is used for all actions excluded from the definition of default actions such as an injunction.

◆ Both the summons served on the defendant and the 'plaint note' sent by the court to the plaintiff have a fixed date endorsed which is either for the hearing or for a pre-trial review.

For both of the above categories, it is a matter of filling in the correct form and drafting any particulars of claim in a similar way to the statement of claim on a writ (where relevant)	(***Note:*** *See Section C - Drafting particulars of claim (p.279)*)

---

2   **Issue of proceedings**

➤ The plaintiff's solicitors should:

Steps	
1	check the correct venue (see box overleaf).
2	a) i) prepare a formal request to the court so that the court will issue the summons, *or* ii) prepare at least 2 copies of the summons, *and* b) prepare also the correct form of admission, defence or counterclaim.
3	if the plaintiff is legally aided, prepare the legal aid certificate and at least 2 copies of the notice of issue of the certificate, for each defendant and the court.
4	if the plaintiff is a minor, prepare the next friend's undertaking to pay costs (see p.268).
5	if the plaintiff has a personal injury action, prepare a medical report and statement of special damages.
6	if proceedings are to be issued by post, prepare a stamped addressed envelope ('SAE').
7	prepare the court fee - cheques are payable to 'HM Paymaster General'.
8	take, or send the summons or request and any of the above documents to the court, together with the SAE and the court fee.
9	The court will issue an action number, seal the summons (or prepare one if a request was sent) and prepare it for service.

County Court venue

Venue for starting proceedings

Except with default actions, proceedings are commenced *either.*
  a) in the district where the defendant resides or carries on business, *or*
  b) in the district where the course of action arose in whole or in part.
    ◆ Default actions may be commenced in any court (ie: at the plaintiff's convenience).

Venue for hearings

➤ Claims for liquidated sums are automatically transferred to a court with jurisdiction over the address of the defendant given in the summons where the defendant files a defence, *but* the plaintiff may apply for a transfer back to the plaintiff's jurisdiction if there is a good reason for this.

➤ In the case of an action for unlimited damages, the plaintiff has an unrestricted choice of court in which to issue proceedings. However, either party may apply under *CCR Ord.16* for transfer to a more convenient court.

---

3   Service of the summons

➤ After the relevant documents have been issued, the summons, particulars of claim, form of defence admission and counterclaim, and any other documents which the court sealed, must be served within 4 months of the claim being issued.

  ◆ If the claim is for a liquidated sum, the correct forms of admission, defence and counterclaim are *N9A* and *N9B.*

  ◆ If the claim is for an unliquidated sum, the correct form of admission, defence and counterclaim is *N9.*

➤ Usually the court serves the summons by methods a) or b) below. However, any of the following methods will work:

  a) postal service: as for the High Court (*CCR Ord.7 r.10*), *or*

  b) personal service: this is done by the bailiff and there is an extra fee for this (otherwise the rules are as for the High Court above (*CCR Ord.7 r.10*)), *or*

  c) the plaintiff's solicitor may serve the documents personally (*CCR Ord.7 r.10*), *or*

  d) in personal injury actions only, the plaintiff's solicitor can serve the summons by post (*CCR Ord.7 r.10A*).

➤ **Service on a limited company:** see chart on p.278.

4   Service on the defendant's solicitor

➤ As for the High Court (see p.274)

5   Defendant is difficult to serve

➤ As for the High Court (see p.274)

6   Time of service

➤ *Either:*

  a) service is presumed to occur on the day that the defendant returns the form of admission, defence and counterclaim, but this presumption is rebuttable (*CCR Ord.7 r.12*), *or*

  b) if the court has served the documents, it supplies a certificate called a 'plaint note' to the plaintiffs stating the date of service and the title and number of the case, *or*

  c) if the plaintiff's solicitor has served the documents, he may swear an affidavit of service.

Summary of documents needed to commence proceedings

High Court — Documents	No. needed	Who are the copies for?	County Court — Documents	No. needed	Who are the copies for?
Writ	Minimum 3	1 for the plaintiff 1 for the court 1 for each defendant	Summons	Minimum 2	1 for the court 1 for each defendant
Statement of claim (unless the writ is specifically endorsed, this can follow within 14 days of the writ being served)	Minimum 3	1 for the plaintiff 1 for the court 1 for each defendant	Particulars of claim (this *must* accompany the summons) if not endorsed on the summons	Minimum 2	1 for the court 1 for each defendant
Plaintiff is on legal aid: any legal aid certificate and notice of issue together with any amendments and notice (*LA(G)R 1980 r.51*)	Minimum 3	1 for the plaintiff 1 for the court 1 for each defendant	**Plaintiff is on legal aid:** any legal aid certificate and notice of issue together with any amendments and notice (*LA(G)R 1980 r.51*)	Minimum 2	1 for the court 1 for each defendant
Acknowledgement of service	Minimum 1	1 for each defendant	Form of admission, defence and counterclaim	Minimum 1	1 for each defendant
Fee	1	1 for the court	Fee	1	1 for the court
Personal injury actions: ▶ Statement of special damages ▶ Medical report High Court rules do not *require* that these should be sent with the statement of claim	Minimum 3	1 for the plaintiff 1 for the court 1 for each defendant	**Personal injury actions:** ▶ Statement of special damages ▶ Medical report (The court may grant an order lifting this requirement if injuries are light) ◆ If this is omitted, the court can stay proceedings, or refuse to issue them	Minimum 2 Minimum 2	1 for the court 1 for each defendant
Plaintiff is a minor: ▶ Next friend's consent to act ▶ Solicitor's certificate that there is no conflict of interest	Minimum 3	1 for the plaintiff 1 for the court 1 for each defendant	**Plaintiff is a minor:** ▶ Next friend's undertaking as to costs	Minimum 2	1 for the court 1 for each defendant

If the proceedings are being issued through the post, a stamped addressed envelope is needed

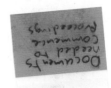

Documents needed to commence proceedings

277

Summary of service of documents of originating process

Originating process (writ in the High Court)			(Fixed date/Default summons in the County Court)			
Method of service	Authority	When service takes effect	Method of service	By	Authority	When service takes effect
High Court			**County Court**			
On an individual defendant			**On an individual defendant**			
Personal	RSC Ord.10 r.1	Same day	Personal	Anyone	CCR Ord.7 r.10	Same day
First class post	RSC Ord.10 r.1	Seventh day after posting	First class post NB: This is done by a court officer automatically unless personal service is requested	A court officer, or the plaintiff (in personal injury actions only)	CCR Ord.7 r.10 CCR Ord.7 r.10A	Seventh day after posting
Leaving in letter box	RSC Ord.10 r.1	Seventh day after insertion				
On a partnership/sole trader			**On a partnership/sole trader**			
a) Personal service on one or more partners, *or* b) at the principal place of business on a person who (at the time) has control and management	RSC Ord.81 r.3	Same day	a) Personal service on a partner, *or* b) at the principal place of business on a person who (at the time) has control and management	Anyone	CCR Ord. 7 r.13	Same day
First class post on a) or b) in the box above	RSC Ord.81 r.3	Seventh day after posting	First class post on a) or b) in the box above. NB: This is done by a court officer automatically unless personal service is requested	A court officer	CCR Ord. 7 r.13	Seventh day after posting
Through the letter box of an **individual partner**	RSC Ord.81 r.3	Seventh day after posting	Through the letter box of an **individual partner**	Anyone	CCR Ord. 7 r.13	Seventh day after posting
On a limited company			**On a limited company**			
Leaving at the registered office	RSC Ord.65 r.3	Same day	Leaving at: a) the registered office, *or* b) any place of business that has a *real* connection with the matter in issue	Anyone	CCR Ord. 7 r.14	Same day
First class post	CA s.725 IA 1978 s.7	Second working day after posting	First class post to: a) the registered office, *or* b) any place of business that has a *real* connection with the matter at issue	Anyone	CCR Ord.7 r.14 CA s.725 IA 1978 s.7	Second working day after posting
Second class post	CA s.725 IA 1978 s.7	Fourth working day after posting	Second class post	Anyone	CCR Ord.7 r.14 CA s.725 IA 1978 s.7	Fourth working day after posting

C   Pleadings

A. Pleadings generally

Pleadings

➤ Pleadings are documents that all the parties produce, which contain formal statements of a party's case.

➤ Pleadings focus the parties and the court on the pertinent issues.

➤ Time limits for service of pleadings are often (and usually) extended by agreement between the parties.

➤ **High Court**

   ◆ The order of pleadings is:

   • statement of claim.

   • defence (and counterclaim if necessary).

   • reply (and defence to counterclaim, if necessary).

   • certain other rare pleadings (not dealt with here).

   ◆ Pleadings 'close' 14 days after delivery of the last pleading.

➤ **County Court**

   ◆ The order of pleadings is:

   • particulars of claim.

   • defence (and any counterclaim).

   ◆ Pleadings 'close':

   • 14 days after delivery of a defence with no counterclaim, *or*

   • 28 days after delivery of a defence with a counterclaim.

B. Drafting the statement / particulars of claim

Statement / Particulars of claim

➤ In the High Court, the pleadings are commenced by the 'statement of claim' (see p.277).

   ◆ This is *either* endorsed on the writ *or* may be sent separately later.

➤ In the County Court, the pleadings are commenced by the 'particulars of claim' (see p.277).

   ◆ This is sent with the summons (and is usually endorsed on the summons).

Four cardinal rules (*RSC Ord. 18, CCR Ord. 6*)

1   Plead facts, not law.
   ◆ Foreign law is treated as a matter of fact.
2   Plead facts, not evidence (*RSC Ord.18 r.7*).   This rule will be strictly enforced (*Practice Direction (Civil Litigation: Case Management) 1995*).
   ◆ The exception to this rule is criminal convictions, which may be pleaded as evidence that the party committed the offence (*RSC Ord.18 r.7A*) (and see p.309).
3   Plead facts relevant to the action.
4   Plead all material facts.

➤ For dates, sums and other numbers, use figures not words (*RSC Ord.18 r.6(3)*).

➤ A pleading must be endorsed with the name (or firm name) and address of the solicitor who serves the pleading, and also, (if the solicitor is the agent of another) the name (or firm name) and address of his principal, or the party's name and address (*RSC Ord.18 r.6(4)*).

➤ A pleading must be signed by counsel, a solicitor or the party (if he acts for himself) (*RSC Ord.18 r.6(5)*).

➤ The contents of a pleading ought to deal with matters in the box below:

		Breach of contract		Goods sold and delivered		Personal injury
Claim	1	◆ Whether it is an oral or written contract ◆ Date of + parties to the contract ◆ Purpose of the agreement ◆ Consideration (unless under seal)	1	◆ The price of the goods	1	◆ The date of the accident ◆ The location of the accident ◆ The names of those involved in the accident
	2	◆ The term breached	2	◆ The date the goods were sold ◆ The date delivery was due	2	◆ The allegation of negligence (with 'particulars of negligence')
	3	◆ The alleged breach of term	3	◆ Particulars of goods	3	◆ The injuries suffered
	4	◆ The losses flowing from the breach	4	◆ The price of the goods	4	◆ The losses suffered (with a schedule of special damages and a medical report (*RSC Ord.18 r.12(1A)*))
	5	◆ Special damages (if relevant)			5	◆ Interest
Prayer for relief	6	◆ Damages sought (ie: the loss the plaintiff has suffered)	5	◆ Damages sought (ie: the debt outstanding)	6	◆ Damages sought
	7	◆ Interest	7	◆ Interest	7	◆ Interest

Note:

➤ In the High Court interest is sought under *SCA 1981 s.35A*.

➤ In the County Court interest is sought under *CCA 1984 s.69*.

➤ For debt actions, interest may accrue at a rate set by an agreement between the parties - if the agreement is silent then the rate is set by statutory instrument (currently 8%) (see p.262). The pleading should state the total interest accrued up to the date of issue and the daily rate at which it runs thereafter (ie: until the judgment or sooner payment).

➤ It is necessary to plead specifically for:

a) special damages, *and*

b) interest, *and*

c) any relevant limitation statute.

➤ There is no need to plead costs as these are at the court's discretion.

➤ The prayer for relief at the end is headed 'AND THE PLAINTIFF CLAIMS' and goes on to specify exactly what the plaintiff wants the court to order.

C. Amending writs and pleadings

Practice tips

➤ Amendments generally take effect retrospectively from the date of the original document.

➤ If the limitation period has expired, only certain amendments are allowed (see d below).

➤ Successive amendments should be typed in red, green, purple, yellow, brown.

a) Amending a writ *without leave* (*RSC Ord. 20 r.1*)

➤ A plaintiff may amend a writ *once*, without leave of the court, before pleadings close.

➤ The nature of the alteration allowed depends on whether the writ has been served.

Before service (but after issue)	After service
◆ The nature of the alteration is irrelevant - any change can be made **Steps** **1** A note must appear on the writ 'Amended [date] pursuant to *RSC Ord. 20, Rule 1*' **2** The court seals the original writ and returns it to the plaintiff **3** The plaintiff files the amended writ at court **4** The amended writ is served on the defendant following the rules for original service of the writ	◆ It is *not* possible to: i) add, omit, substitute a party to an action, or alter a party's capacity; *or* ii) add, or substitute a new cause of action ◆ The amended writ is served on the defendant following the rules for ordinary service

b) Amending a pleading *without leave* (*RSC Ord. 20 r.3, CCR Ord.15 r.2*)

High Court	County Court

➤ Any party may amend a pleading *once* without leave before the pleadings close
➤ A note must appear on the pleading: 'Amended [date] pursuant to *RSC Ord. 20, Rule 3*'
➤ The amended pleading must be served on the opposing parties
➤ Another party has 14 days after service during which it can *either*:
  a) make consequential amendments, *or*
  b) apply to the court to disallow the amendments if leave would have been refused had it been applied for (*RSC Ord. 20 r.4*)
	➤ The pleading can be amended at any time before pre-trial review, or at the trial itself if automatic directions apply
	  ◆ Any amendment to the parties of the action, if performed after the summons has been served, requires leave of the court
	➤ The amended pleading must be served on the opposing party and filed at court
	➤ The court has discretion to disallow amended pleadings

c) Amending a pleading *by agreement* (*RSC Ord. 20 r.12, CCR Ord.15 r.2*)

➤ This can be done at any time during proceedings, provided the parties are not altered.

➤ **High Court:** there must be an agreement, made in writing, and then the amendment is made as normal.

➤ **County Court:** the amended pleading is filed, with an endorsement of consent by all the parties.

d) Amending a writ or pleading *with leave* (*RSC Ord. 20 r.5, CCR Ord.15 r.1*)

➤ This can be done at any time during proceedings.

➤ Before a trial, the amending party seeks leave by an interlocutory application. During a trial, the amending party must apply to the judge for leave.

◆ Leave is granted *unless* the amendment causes injustice to the other party; the applicant will normally have to meet the costs resulting from the changes as it would not be just for the other party to bear them.

➤ The amending party notes on the writ/pleading: 'Amended [date] pursuant to leave of Master [name] given on [date]'.

➤ After a limitation period has expired, alterations are *only* allowed to:

a) correct the name of a party, if the mistake was genuine and the identity of the party was never in doubt, *or*

b) alter the capacity in which a party sues, provided the party acquired this capacity on the day proceedings were issued or since proceedings began, *or*

c) add or substitute a new cause of action, if the facts are substantially the same as those already pleaded.

➤ The amended writ/pleading is served normally, unless the court lifts the service obligation.

Summary of service of documents of *non*-originating process

Other documents - *non* originating process					
Method of service	Authority	When service takes effect	Method of service	Authority	When service takes effect
High Court			**County Court**		
Personal	*RSC Ord.65 r.5*	Same day	**When acting in person**		
Delivery at address			Personal	*CCR Ord.7 r.1*	Same day
First class post	*RSC Ord.65 r.5 IA 1978 s.7*	Second working day after posting	First class post		Second working day after posting
Second class post		Fourth working day after posting	Second class post		Fourth working day after posting
Leaving at a document exchange (DX)	*RSC Ord.65 r.5(2A)*	Second business day following day it is left	**When acting by a solicitor**		
Fax sent before 4 pm	*RSC Ord.65 r.5(2B)*	Same day	Delivery at the address	*CCR Ord.7 r.1*	Same day
Fax sent after 4 pm		Next business day	First class post		Second working day after posting
			Leaving at a document exchange (DX)		Second business day following the day it is left

➤ If there is no proper address for service use:
a) the business address of any solicitor acting, *or*
b) (for an individual) his usual or last known address, *or*
c) (for a company) the registered or principal office, *or*
d) (for a firm) the principal or last known place of business

➤ A document can only be sent by DX if:
a) the other party has a DX number on his notepaper, *and*
b) the other party has not indicated that he is unwilling to accept service by DX

➤ A fax can only be sent if:
a) both parties act by solicitor, *and*
b) the party being served has his fax number on his notepaper, *and*
c) a copy of the summons is delivered by another method (or else it is deemed never to have been served)

➤ If there is no address for service:
a) deliver to the defendant's residence, *or*
b) send by first class post to the defendant's last known residence

NB: All County Court documents must be filed in court at the same time as they are served on the other party

D   Defendant's responses

I   High Court

1   **Acknowledgement of service form - 3 options**

> ### Acknowledgement of service form (*RSC Ord.12 r.3*)
>
> ➤ The defendant must return an acknowledgement of service within 14 days of service of the writ indicating whether or not he will defend the action.
>
> **Note:** there is no equivalent to this in the County Court.

a)   Concede the claim

>   ➤ i)   To concede the whole claim, the defendant should use the acknowledgement of service form. He should tick 'No' in paragraph 2, indicating that he does not intend to defend.
>
>   ii) To concede only part of the claim the defendant must serve a defence indicating which parts are admitted and which are not (see 3 on p.285).
>
> ➤ The plaintiff must now obtain judgment in full under i) or for the part admitted under ii). The plaintiff takes the original writ and 2 forms of the judgment to the court. There is no hearing. The court grants judgment by sealing the copies and returning one to the plaintiff (there is no need to serve one on the defendant).
>
>   ♦ If the claim is liquidated, judgment is final.
>
>   ♦ If the claim is unliquidated, the judgment is interlocutory and there must be a later hearing to determine quantum and costs.

b)   Obtain time to pay

> ➤ If the defendant needs time to pay an amount that he admits, he should tick 'Yes' in paragraph 3 of the acknowledgement of service form.
>
> ➤ Within 14 days from service of the acknowledgement of service form, the defendant must issue an interlocutory application for a stay of execution. This must be accompanied by a supporting affidavit of means. At the hearing, the Master or district judge may order payment by instalments.
>
>   ♦ If no application is issued by the defendant within the 14 days, the plaintiff can apply for judgment and can have this enforced.

c)   Transfer proceedings to another District Registry or the Central Office in London *only*

> ➤ This happens automatically if the defendant ticks the correct box in paragraph 4 of the acknowledgement of service.
>
>   ♦ He can tick this if:
>
>   i)   the writ was issued out of a District Registry, *and*
>
>   ii) the defendant's residence/place of business is not in the district of the issuing registry, *and*
>
>   iii) there is no endorsement on the writ (by the plaintiff) that the cause of action arose in the issuing district.
>
>   ♦ If the defendant does not tick this box, he may *not* later seek to have the case transferred.
>
> ➤ The plaintiff may object to transfer within 8 days of receiving the acknowledgement of service and a district judge decides whether the objection should be upheld.

2   Transfer proceedings to a more convenient court *(RSC Ord. 4 r.5(3))*

> ➤ This may be done at any time as in 1c) above, by issuing an interlocutory application but in addition to the transfers in 1c above, the application may be heard before a Master to transfer the action from the Central Office to a District Registry.

3   Draft a defence or partial defence (and counterclaim if appropriate) *(RSC Ord. 18 r.12)*

a)   Drafting a defence

> ➤ If the statement of claim is too vague for a defence to be drafted, the defendant can seek 'further and better particulars' (see p.291).

> ➤ The 'four cardinal rules' of drafting apply (see p.279).

> ➤ The 'rule of implied admissions' applies, ie: the defence is taken to admit anything it does not deny *(RSC Ord. 18 r.13)*.

> ➤ The defence has two aims:

>> i)   to deny *every* allegation which the defendant disputes, *and*

>> ii) to plead all facts on which it wishes to rely and which are not in the plaintiff's pleading.

> ➤ The following must be pleaded specifically:

>> i)   any defence under the *Limitation Act 1980*, *and*

>> ii) facts which are relevant to mitigation of damages, *and*

>> iii) contributory negligence.

> ➤ There are 2 approaches to drafting a defence:

>> *either* i)   chronologically, giving the defendant's version of events, and with a 'seriatim clause':
>> 'Save as in hereto specifically admitted each and every allegation in the statement of claim is denied as if each allegation were set out herein and specifically denied'.

>> *or*   ii) answering the plaintiff's allegations paragraph by paragraph.

b)   Drafting a counterclaim

> ➤ The defendant may make a counterclaim, whether or not it relates to the plaintiff's action.

> ➤ The counterclaim is pleaded in the same way as a statement of claim (see pp.279-280).

> ➤ The counterclaim may state that it repeats paragraphs from the defence.

> ➤ The counterclaim *must* seek a specific remedy.

c)   Serving the defence (and counterclaim)

> ➤ The time limits within which this must done depend on the type of writ.

>> i)   **Specially endorsed writ:** the defendant has 28 days from the service of the writ.

>> ii) **Generally endorsed writ:** the defendant has 14 days from when the statement of claim is served on him.

> ➤ The rules for service are the ordinary service rules that apply to documents of non-originating process (see p.282).

4 - 10   *See 'Interlocutory applications', p.289.*

II County Court

1   **Admission, defence and counterclaim - 2 options**

    a)   Concede the claim or part of the claim

➤ Fill in the appropriate forms sent with the summons (*CCR Ord.9*) (ie: *Form N9* for an unliquidated claim; *Form N9A* and *Form N9B* for a liquidated claim).

    i)   The defendant might want to pay the amount.

      ◆ For a liquidated sum, he will return *Form N9A* to the plaintiff.

        • The plaintiff will then produce *Form N9A* to the court and obtain final judgment.

      ◆ For an unliquidated sum, he will return *Form N9* to the court. The court will send a copy to the plaintiff.

        • The plaintiff will then apply for judgment which will be for liability only. A hearing on quantum and costs will be held at a later date.

    ii)   To admit part of the claim and/or to counterclaim, the defendant should return to the court *Form N9A and Form N9B* (liquidated claim) or *Form N9* (unliquidated claim), within 14 days of the summons being served. The court send copies to the plaintiff.

      ◆ If the plaintiff does not accept the part admitted in satisfaction of his whole claim, he must notify the court. The court will then fix a date for a pre-trial review.

    b)   Obtain time to pay

➤ To admit the claim in full, but to request more time to pay, the defendant should return *Form N9A* (liquidated claim) to the plaintiff within 14 days of the summons being served. He should include a statement of means if periodic payments are requested.

➤ The plaintiff may choose whether or not to accept the offer of repayment.

    ◆ The plaintiff must notify the court of his decision on *Form N205A*.

    ◆ The court then decides (without a hearing) the methods of payment.

➤ If the court suggests a payment scheme, the parties have 14 days to appeal if they are dissatisfied, whereupon the case is transferred to the defendant's home court and a district judge holds a hearing to fix a suitable repayment rate.

2   **Transfer proceedings to a more convenient court**

➤ Claims for debts and liquidated sums are automatically transferred to a court with jurisdiction over the address of the defendant given in the summons, but the plaintiff may apply for a transfer back to the plaintiff's court if there is good reason for this.

➤ All other actions are heard at the court which issues the summons *unless* the defendant applies successfully for a transfer to a County Court near where he resides.

3 **Draft a defence or partial defence (and counterclaim if appropriate)**

a) Drafting a defence

➤ Either:

i) complete the form of admission, defence and counterclaim, *or*

ii) the defendant or his solicitor may want to draft a new separate document (ie: not *Form N9* or *N9A*). If so, see the High Court defence drafting points (p.285).

➤ The rule of implied admissions does not apply according to the *CCR*, but in practice it is observed.

➤ The rules of specific pleadings of limitation, facts concerning mitigation of damages, and facts concerning contributory negligence, do not strictly apply in the County Court, but are usually complied with anyway.

b) Drafting a counterclaim

➤ Either:

i) complete *Form N9B* (liquidated claim) or *Form N9* (unliquidated claim), *or*

ii) the defendant or his solicitor may want to draft a new separate document. If so, see the High Court counterclaim drafting points (p.285).

c) Serving the defence (and counterclaim)

➤ Within 14 days of the summons being served, return to the court the form of admissions, defence and counterclaim, or the separately drafted form.

4 - 10 ***See 'Interlocutory applications', p.289.***

E   Plaintiff's responses

1   **Obtain judgment after the defendant indicates he will not defend** (see p.284 and p.286)

2 Reply and defence to counterclaim	
High Court	County Court
The reply: the plaintiff may reply to the defence within 14 days of the service on him of that defence. Note that he does not *need* to reply and if he does not, he is automatically assumed to deny the defence (*RSC Ord.18 r.14*) **The defence to the counterclaim:** the plaintiff must respond to a counterclaim within 14 days of the service on him of the defence, or the defendant may seek a default judgment (*RSC Ord.18 r.18*). **Reply *and* defence to counterclaim:** if the plaintiff wishes to respond with both, they must be in the same document (*RSC Ord.18 r.3*)	There is no need for the plaintiff to serve a reply and defence to counterclaim, as the defendant may not seek default judgment on a counterclaim. The *CCRs* do not provide for a reply or defence to counterclaim, but the plaintiff may wish to do so anyway as he is likely to be asked to provide one at the pre-trial review. Time limits are as for the High Court but, here, in addition to service on the other party, a copy of the reply and/or defence to counter-claim must be filed at the court.

3 Discontinuance (*RSC Ord.21, CCR Ord.18*)	
High Court	County Court
Discontinuance halts the action, and the defendant is entitled to taxed costs to date for the part of the proceedings that are discontinued (*RSC Ord.62 r.5(3), CCR Ord.18 r.2*)	
Within 14 days of service of the defence, the plaintiff may notify the defendant of discontinuance without seeking leave. Thereafter, leave is needed or all the parties must consent. The defendant is entitled to taxed costs unless leave has been sought, in which case the court has a discretion as to costs	At any stage in the proceedings the plaintiff may file a notice of discontinuance with the court, discontinuing the action. The defendant is entitled to costs

4   **Join a third party to the proceedings** (for 'third party notices', see p.292) (*RSC Ord.16, CCR Ord.12*)

> ➤ When a defendant begins third party proceedings, a plaintiff may wish to join a third party to the original action. If the third party is later found liable, the plaintiff may then seek a remedy against it.

> ➤ A third party who is joined to proceedings becomes a co-defendant.

5 - 12 See 'Interlocutory applications', p.289.

F Interlocutory applications

A. Making an interlocutory application

High Court (*RSC Ord.32*) - 4 methods	County Court (*CCR 1981 Ord.13*) - 2 methods
Method 1 - Ex parte application	**Method 1 - Ex parte application**
Used when no notice is given to the other party (eg: in cases of secrecy or urgency)	*Used when no notice is given to the other party (eg: in cases of secrecy or urgency)*

High Court — Method 1 Steps

1. The applicant sends an application and (usually) a supporting affidavit to the court office
2. The Master or district judge looks at it and decides if a hearing should be held
3. If there is to be a hearing, the hearing is held
4. Whether a hearing is held or not, the order is granted or refused
5. The decision is noted on the affidavit
6. The applicant draws up the order and serves it on the other party

County Court — Method 1 Steps

1. The applicant sends 2 signed copies of the application and (usually) supporting evidence to the court office
2. The district judge looks at it and decides whether a hearing should be held
3. If there is to be a hearing, the hearing is held
4. Whether a hearing is held or not, the order is granted or refused
5. The decision is noted
6. The order is drawn up and served on the other party

Method 2 - Application by summons inter partes

Used when notice is given to the other party so that they may attend the hearing. This is the most usual of the 4 methods used.

(NB: There is a slightly different procedure for the Queens Bench Division and the Chancery Division. What follows is a generalisation)

Steps

1. The applicant must send to the court office:
   i)   2 copies of a summons setting out the order sought, *and*
   ii) 2 copies of an affidavit, *and*
   iii) a fee, *and*
   iv) an estimate of the length of the hearing

2. The court issues the summons, which is stamped with the court seal, and then sends back to the applicant the summons and a copy of the affidavit
   (The 'return day' (ie: the day the hearing will take place) is fixed and written on the summons)

3. The applicant must serve (by ordinary service) the summons and a copy of the affidavit on the other party. For most applications (see p.240 for some exceptions), this must be (*RSC Ord. 32 r.3*):
   i)   a minimum of 2 clear days before the return day, *and*
   ii) (usually but not always) within 14 days of issue, *and*
   iii) the affidavit *must* be served with the summons

4. The hearing is held in chambers

5. The Master or district judge notes the decision on the copy of the summons on the court file. The parties should also make a written note

6. The successful party must draw up the order and lodge 2 copies at the court office (*RSC Ord.42 r.4*)

7. The court staff check the order, seal it and send a copy to the party that lodged it. They also keep a copy on the court file if it is the Chancery Division.

8. The lodger must serve a copy of the sealed order on the other party/ parties by ordinary service

Method 2 - On notice applications (ie: on notice to the other party)

Used when notice is given to the other party so that they may attend the hearing. This is the more usual of the 2 methods.

Steps

1. The applicant must send to the court office:
   i)   3 copies of the application, *and*
   ii) an original sworn affidavit, *and*
   iii) a fee, *and*
   iv) an estimate of the length of the hearing

2. The court issues the documents, which are stamped with the court seal, and sends back to the applicant all but one copy of the application and affidavit (this one copy is kept on the court file)
   (The 'return day' (ie: the day the hearing will take place) is fixed and written on the summons)

3. A minimum of 2 days before the return day, the applicant must serve each respondent with:
   i)   1 copy of the application, *and*
   ii) 1 copy of the affidavit

4. The hearing is held

5. The district judge notes the decision on the copy of the application on the court file. The parties should also make a written note

6. The court draws up the order

7. The court serves a copy of the order on all parties by post

---

Method 3 - Application by notice under summons for directions - see p. 304

Method 4 - Application by motion - *This is a hearing before a judge in open court and is used for urgent motions*

Steps

1. The applicant applies to the judge on any day of the week giving minimum 2 clear days' notice to his opponent
2. The applicant files at court 2 copies of the motion and the writ and an estimate of the length of the hearing
3. The motion is listed for the day on which it is to be heard

Interlocutory applications - general

➤ An interlocutory application:

♦ is an application to the court at any time *after* the originating writ/summons has been issued but *before* the trial, *and*

♦ does not determine the final rights of the parties.

➤ Time for service

♦ High Court

• Summons for extension or abridgment of time: must be served the day before the day of the hearing.

• Any other interlocutory summons (except *Ord.14* or *25* summons) must be served (*RSC Ord.32 r.3*):

a) not less than 2 days before the day of the hearing of the application, *and*

b) within 14 days of issue, *and*

c) evidence in reliance (eg: affidavits) must be served with the summons.

♦ County Court

• A notice of application must be served a minimum of 2 days before the hearing of the application.

B. Interlocutory applications

➤ There are many interlocutory applications that may be made. The following list shows those that are covered in the following pages

1. Security for costs

Purpose: to order the plaintiff to give security (in any form the court may direct) for the costs incurred by the defendant in the action or in other proceedings

	High Court (*RSC Ord.23*)	County Court (*CCR Ord.13 r.8*)
Procedure	Summons supported by affidavit, at any stage in proceedings	Notice of application supported by affidavit, at any stage in proceedings
Grounds	a) The plaintiff is ordinarily resident outside the jurisdiction, *or* b) the plaintiff is merely a nominee (not suing in a representative capacity) and there is reason to believe he may not be able to pay costs, *or* c) the plaintiff's address is not as stated on the writ, *or* d) the plaintiff has changed address during proceedings to evade the consequences of litigation (*Ord.23 r.1*), *or* e) the plaintiff is a limited company whose solvency is doubtful (*CA s.726(1)*) *AND* the court thinks it is just to make an order, having regard to all the circumstances of the case	a) The plaintiff is resident outside the jurisdiction, *or* b) the plaintiff is a company of dubious solvency (*CA s.726*)

2. Striking out

Purpose: to delete all or part of a particular pleading, called 'striking out'

	High Court (*RSC Ord.19*)	County Court (*CCR Ord.13 r.5*)

Grounds	The pleading:
	    a) discloses no reasonable course of action or defence, *or*
	    b) is scandalous, frivolous or vexatious, *or*
	    c) may prejudice, embarrass or delay the fair trial of the action, *or*
	    d) is an abuse of the process of the court	

Procedure	Summons, usually with an affidavit (Note: an affidavit is not admissible under ground a))	Notice of application with affidavit
Time	At any time before the close of pleadings, but preferably as soon as the offending pleading is served	

3. Further and better particulars

Purpose: to obtain material facts on which a party relies and which are omitted from pleadings, or pleadings are vague or too brief. It is used to request the facts *not* evidence

	High Court (*RSC Ord.18 r.12(3)-(6)*)	County Court (*CCR Ord.6 r.7*)
Format of request	Specify the information sought on a formal request for further and better particulars Note: the request has no effect on the date of service on the next pleading	
Format of reply	A point by point reply to the request For each point repeat the request verbatim and provide a reply The reply becomes part of the formal proceedings and must be served on all necessary parties (**NB:** In the County Court, the reply must also be filed at court)	
Court application	If the other side does not reply, issue a summons	If the other side does not reply, issue a notice of application

4. Judgment on admissions

Purpose: to reduce the expense of a trial by resolving agreed issues beforehand

	High Court (*RSC Ord.27 r.3*)	County Court (*CCR Ord.17 r.6*)
Grounds	The defendant makes an admission - it can be formal *or* informal, written *or* oral The admission *must* be a full admission of a cause of action	
Procedure	Summons or motion with an affidavit which: a) identifies the words and circumstances in which admissions were made, *and* b) shows that the admission concedes the cause of action concerned	Use *Form N9*

5. Third party proceedings

Purpose: A defendant issues third party proceedings rather than separate proceedings. There is a consistent result and costs are saved. The defendant may claim a remedy similar to that claimed by the plaintiff arising from the same facts

	High Court (*RSC Ord. 16*)	County Court (*CRR Ord. 12*)
Leave	A third party notice may be issued without leave before the defence is served on the plaintiff (*r. 1*). Otherwise leave is required An *ex parte* application to court for leave to issue a notice is supported by an affidavit. There is no hearing and the Master's leave is endorsed on the affidavit (*r. 2(1)*)	A notice may be issued without leave before the close of pleadings Leave is needed in a) a fixed date action, b) a default action when a date has been fixed for hearing or pre-trial review, c) when pleadings have closed (*r. 1(2)*) Application for leave is by way of interlocutory application
Affidavit	The affidavit contains details of: a) the nature of the plaintiff's claim, *and* b) the stage the main proceedings have reached, *and* c) the nature of the defendant's claim against the third party, or the issue plus (in both cases) the relevant facts, *and* d) the name and address of the third party (*r. 2(2)*)	None, but the notice states the nature and grounds of the claim or the issue to be settled
Service	As a writ: serve on the third party (*r. 3*): a) the third party notice, *and* b) the writ or originating summons, *and* c) the pleadings to date, *and* d) a form of acknowledgement of service Send a copy of the notice to the plaintiff	As a summons: send the court at least 3 copies of the notice (1 for the plaintiff, 1 for the defendant and 1 for the court) and serve: a) the third party notice b) the summons, *and* c) particulars of claim, *and* d) any defence filed

Response / Effect	a) The third party must acknowledge service within 14 days (inclusive) by returning the acknowledgement of service to court to say whether or not proceedings will be contested
	b) If the third party does send back notice of intention to defend or (if ordered to serve a defence) he sends back a defence:
	  i) he is deemed to admit any claim stated in the notice and is bound by any judgment in the action relevant to anything in the notice, *and*
	  ii) if judgment in default is given against the defendant, after the judgment is satisfied and with leave of court, he may enter judgment against the third party for the relief claimed in the notice
		The third party should serve a defence, admission or counterclaim within 14 days (*r. 2*)
		
		If this does not happen, an order to serve a defence may be made at pre-trial review
		
		The plaintiff may not enter judgment in default and a pre-trial review is compulsory (*r. 1(7)*)
		
		If the third party is absent at the trial, he is taken to admit the claim and is bound by any judgment (*r. 3(3)*)

Third party directions	The defendant must take out a summons for third party directions. If the defendant does not do so within 7 days of the acknowledgement of service / notice of intention to defend, the third party may do so. The defendant must serve the summons on the plaintiff and on the third party. At the hearing, the court has wide discretion including power to (*r. 4*): a) dismiss the third party proceedings b) order judgment to be entered against the third party c) order any claim or issue to be tried d) permit the third party to defend e) grant the third party leave to appear at the trial f) give any directions that appear just and that are enforceable g) determine the extent by which the third party will be bound by a judgment in the action h) give directions after judgment has been entered against the plaintiff	A pre-trial review date is set on issue of the notice and endorsed on the third party notice (*r. 1(5)*) ↓ The court gives any necessary directions at pre-trial review

6. Summary judgment

Purpose: The plaintiff seeks judgment quickly and cheaply without the expense and delay associated with a trial

	High Court (*RSC Ord.14*)	County Court (*CCR Ord.9 r.14*)
Grounds	There is no defence to the claim made in the writ, or a part of that claim (*r.1*)	There is (*r.1A, 1(5)*): a) no defence to the claim, *and* b) no reason to proceed to trial
Time	Any time after notice of intention to defend has been served on the plaintiff, *provided* that the statement of claim has been served on the defendant (*r.1*) The defence may be served at any time until the application for summary judgment is heard (*r.4*)	Any time after a defendant delivers to the court a document purporting to be a defence. (Summary judgment is not available in cases referred to arbitration under *CCR Ord.19* or where the claim concerns the possession of land or libel)

Plaintiff
 	
↓
	Serves on the defendant a minimum of 10 clear days before the hearing (*r.2*):
	a) the summons, *and*
	b) a statement of value (if the claim is over over £25,000) (*r.6(3)(b)*, and
	c) an affidavit which:
	  ◆ verifies the facts on which the claim is based, *and*
	  ◆ states the deponent's belief that there is no defence (or none except for the amount of damages)
		Serves on the defendant a minimum of 7 clear days before the hearing (*r.(1)-(3)*):
		a) a notice of application, *and*
		b) an affidavit (as in the High Court)

Defendant ↓ Plaintiff	May file with the court an affidavit in response up to 3 clear days before the hearing (*r.4*)	
Plaintiff	May file and serve a reply at any time. If it is served too close to the hearing, he may be penalised in costs	

		Usual costs order

Orders	*Either* (*r.3*):
	  a) judgment for the plaintiff. This is granted if:
	    ◆ the plaintiff can provide clear proof of his case *and* the defendant i) has no bona fide defence and ii) cannot raise a triable issue (unliquidated claims require a further hearing to settle quantum and costs)
		→ Fixed

	or b) unconditional leave to defend: This is granted if:
	    ◆ there is a triable issue, *or*
	    ◆ there is some reason for a trial (a direction to serve an amended defence is often given)
		→ Costs in the cause

	or c) conditional leave to defend. This is granted if: ◆ the court doubts whether the defence is genuine or valid (it may order a payment into court funds or the giving of security, failing which the plaintiff gets judgment - this is *not* the same as a payment into court)	→ Costs in the cause
	d) dismissal of the summons (*r.7*)	→ Defendant's costs in any event
Directions	The judge now gives directions. In personal injury cases, although automatic directions apply, the judge asks the parties if they want additional directions (*r.6*)	Although automatic directions will always apply, the judge asks if the parties want additional directions

7. Dismissal because of delay

Purpose: The defendant wishes to have the action dismissed for want of a prosecution or default in complying with the *Rules of Court* or an order of the court

	High Court	County Court

Grounds	There are 2 possible grounds (*Birkett v. James* [1978] AC 297):
	  a) 'intentional and contumelious delay': a deliberate failure to comply with a court order (usually an 'unless' order - see p.297), *or* conduct abusing the process of the court
	or b) delay which is:
	    i) inordinate: relative to the length of proceedings, not just since the last step (ie: years, not months), +
	    ii) inexcusable: if this is due to a solicitor, this is not a good reason to seek a remedy against a solicitor, +
	    iii) prejudicial to the fair trial of the action, eg: evidence is less cogent due to the lapse of time
	AND
	    the limitation period has expired (otherwise the plaintiff could issue fresh proceedings)
	Note: a) the defendant must not actively acquiesce in the delay. He has no duty to jog the plaintiff's memory, but is more likely to obtain a dismissal if he does so as the court looks at the conduct of both parties
	    b) the defendant, for his part, must not be in default	

Procedure	Summons with affidavit giving facts about the delay	Notice of application + affidavit with facts about delay
Plaintiff	May file a reply (ie: an affidavit) before the hearing of the application	

8. Payment into court

Purpose: the defendant wishes to stay proceedings and cap his costs, as a plaintiff who refuses to accept the payment, takes the risk of having to pay both parties' costs from the date the payment is made (see below 'Non-acceptance')

	High Court (*RSC Ord.22*)	County Court (*CCR Ord.11*)
Time	After service of a writ for debt or damages (*r.1*)	After the summons is served on the defendant
	An increase in the amount offered may be made at any time	
Amount to pay in	3 points to consider: 1 **Interest:** calculate interest accrued to date and include it in the payment-in 2 **Counterclaims:** the notice should state whether any counterclaim is included, and whether acceptance will also stay those proceedings (*r.3(5)*) 3 **Plaintiff in receipt of state benefits:** withhold the sum stated in the certificate of recoverable benefit supplied by the DSS; the defendant should supply the court with a copy of the certificate and mention the deduction on the notice. If the payment is accepted, the defendant pays this sum to the CRU (*SS(RB)A 1997*) (see p.262)	
Inform the court (and any other defendant)	Submit to the court **i)** a request for lodgement, **ii)** a cheque, **iii)** defendant's sealed copy of the writ and **iv)** a notice of payment-in. The court returns the sealed writ with a receipt	Submit to the court **i)** a form of payment-in, **ii)** a cheque, and **iii)** a notice stating the payment is in satisfaction of the plaintiff's cause of action. (If this notice is not included, the money is treated as a payment on account and is paid to the plaintiff)(*r.1*)
Serve the plaintiff	The defendant serves the notice of payment-in on the plaintiff who must acknowledge receipt within 3 days (*r.1(2)*)	If time permits, the court notifies the plaintiff (and every party to the action) of the payment-in (*r.1(10)*)
Acceptance	**For payments made before the trial begins** the plaintiff has 21 days to accept **For payments made after the trial has begun** he has 2 days (*r.3*) to accept by: ◆ serving notice of acceptance on every defendant in the action, *and* ◆ filing a copy of the notice at court	**Before the hearing begins,** the plaintiff should (usually) accept within 21 days of receiving the notice of payment-in and in any event must accept not less than 3 days before the hearing begins (*r.3(1)*). The plaintiff accepts by sending a notice of acceptance to the court and the defendant. **When the hearing has begun,** the plaintiff has 14 days after receipt of the notice of payment-in to accept the payment and must accept before judgment is given *r.3(2)*)
	Acceptance stays proceedings (*r.4*): the plaintiff is entitled to the money paid in (*r.3(6)*) and to taxed costs up to the date of the notice of acceptance	
Non-acceptance	The plaintiff need not take any action. The court invests the funds and any interest automatically belongs to the defendant. The trial judge is *not* told of the payment until after liability and quantum have been established (*RSC Ord.22 r.7, CCR Ord.11 r.7*). Costs at the end of the action depend on the plaintiff's damages (*RSC Ord. 62 r.9(1)(b)*): a) if damages *exceed* the payment-in, the plaintiff is awarded costs in the cause, *but* b) if they *are lower than, or equal to* the payment-in, the usual order is that the plaintiff pays the defendant's costs from the date of the payment-in	

Leave to obtain payment-out

This is not necessary except when (*RSC Ord. 22 rr.4-5, CCR Ord.11 r.7(4-5)*):
a) **notice of acceptance is late** (ie: outside the 21 day limit): alternatively, the parties may agree to a consent order, *or*
b) **payment-in is made by one of several defendants:** an interlocutory application is made, *or*
c) **the claim is under the** *Fatal Accidents Act 1976* **or the** *Law Reform (Miscellaneous Provisions) Act 1934, or*
d) **the plaintiff is under a disability** (*RSC Ord.80 r.11, CCR Ord.10 r.11*). The following is needed - an interlocutory application and affidavit giving:
    i) the state of proceedings, *and*
    ii) up-to-date medical evidence, *and*
    iii) counsel's advice on liability or quantum

Note: if the plaintiff is a minor, the court will *not* release money until the minor comes of age, so the affidavit may contain advice to the court on investment; a parent or guardian may apply for funds if the minor has specific needs. (NB: These need not be connected with the action, or the plaintiff)

The court may *either*   ◆ accept an application and give directions for investment, *or*
                       ◆ adjourn and send the parties away to negotiate, *or*
                       ◆ dismiss the application and give directions for the future conduct of the action

9. Default judgment

Purpose: The plaintiff wants to obtain judgment when the defendant (*rr. 1-6*):
    a) has failed to return a notice of intention to defend, *or*
    b) has failed to deliver a defence after delivery of a notice of intention to defend

	High Court (*RSC Ord. 13*)	County Court (*CCR Ord.9 r.6*)
	Judgment in default of notice of intention to defend	

Grounds	The writ has been properly served and the defendant *either* (*r. 1*):
	♦ has not acknowledged the writ within 14 days of service (including the day of service), *or*
	♦ refuses to defend
	
	The plaintiff must prove that the writ was properly served *and* that the time for acknowledging service has expired.
	
	NB:
	  a) Judgment is not granted if a guardian *ad litem* is to be appointed
	  b) If the defendant concedes the claim and seeks a stay of execution, the plaintiff may not enforce the judgment for 14 days
		If the defendant *either*:
		♦ does not pay the plaintiff within 14 days of service of the summons, *or*
		♦ admits the claim and does not counterclaim, *or*
		♦ does not deliver an appropriate response to the plaintiff's claim (eg: form of acknowledgement with defence, counterclaim or admission)
		
		NB:
		a) Judgment is not granted if a guardian *ad litem* has not yet been appointed (*Ord. 10 r.6*)
		b) A defendant may not apply for a default judgment on a counterclaim

Procedure	Take to the court: i) 2 copies of the form of judgment, *and* ii) the writ and proof that the writ has been served (ie: an affidavit of service) (*r. 7*) **Judgment is entered with no hearing** The court grants judgment by sealing the copies and returning 1 to the plaintiff (there is no need to serve one on the defendant) **Liquidated claim:** judgment is final **Unliquidated claim:** judgment is interlocutory and there must be a subsequent hearing to settle quantum and costs	The plaintiff must produce to the court (*r. 1A*): i) a request for judgment (*Form N14*), *and* ii) if the claim is liquidated, a statement that the plaintiff has not received a response from the defendant, *and* iii) a certificate stating what payment (if any) has been received from the defendant, *and* iv) if necessary, *Form N234* (request for damages to be assessed) **Judgment is entered with no hearing**

High Court - Judgment in default of pleadings (No County Court equivalent) (*RSC Ord.19*)

Grounds	♦ **The defendant** has not served a defence within the required time following the return of the acknowledgement of service (*rr.2-7*) - see table on p. 272 for time limit details, *or* ♦ **The plaintiff** has not served a statement of claim within the required time (*r. 1*)
Procedure	The same as for *RSC Ord. 13* (see top of this box) BUT: a) no affidavit of service of the writ is needed, *and* b) if a plaintiff is applying, his solicitor should endorse on the back of the form of judgment, a certificate stating that no defence has been served (*Practice Direction (Judgment by Default)* [1979] 1 WLR 851) The procedure and grounds for having the judgment set aside are the same as *RSC Ord. 13*.

	High Court	County Court
	Setting aside a judgment in default	
Procedure	Summons and supporting affidavit to seek an order (*Ord. 13 r.9*): a) setting the judgment aside, *and* b) granting leave to defend, *and* c) giving directions for the future conduct of the action	*Either:* a) on notice with an affidavit in support, *or* b) the court may do so on its own motion
Grounds	On application by the defendant or an interested third party. *Either:* a) the service of proceedings was irregular. Judgment will be set aside as of right and costs in the cause will usually be awarded, *or* b) there is a defence to the claim on the merits and the court will also consider the defendant's excuse as to why the procedural default occurred.	Not stated, so it is assumed that these are the same as in the High Court (see p.261)

10. Interim payments in respect of claims for damages

Purpose: The plaintiff wants an advance from the defendant against a debt or damages

Note:
  a) before applying to court, it is wise to negotiate with an insurance company for a voluntary payment
  b) if resolving the case takes longer than expected, the plaintiff can make additional applications to court

	High Court (*RSC Ord.29 Part II*)	County Court (*CCR Ord.13 r.12*)
Grounds	There are 3 possible grounds (*r.11(1)*). *Either:* a) the defendant has admitted liability for the plaintiff's damages, *or* b) the plaintiff already has judgment for damages to be assessed, *or* c) at trial the plaintiff would gain substantial damages against a defendant	
Requirements	For personal injuries claims the defendant *must* (*r.11(2)*): a) be insured in respect of the plaintiff's claim, *or* b) be a public authority, *or* c) have the means and resources to make an interim payment	As in the High Court, but this order is *not* available if the claim is referred automatically to arbitration under *CCR Ord.19 (r.2)*
Amount	A 'reasonable proportion of the damages' which 'the court considers just' taking account of (*r.11(1)*): a) the sum likely to be recovered by the plaintiff, *and* b) any contributory negligence, *and* c) any counterclaim or set-off on which the defendant is likely to rely **Personal injury:** small amounts may be awarded from general damages, but an award will not exceed the total of special damages claimed	
Legal aid	Interim payments are paid directly to the plaintiff - they are *not* subject to the statutory charge (see p.10)	
Time	After the writ has been served and the time for acknowledging service expires (ie: 14 days after service of writ) (*r.10*)	When a defence has been filed at court

Plaintiff	Files at court:
	a) a summons, or he includes a request on a summons for summary judgment under *RSC Ord 14* (*r.10(2)*), *and*
	b) an affidavit which (*r.10(3)*):
	  i) states the grounds for the application, *and*
	  ii) outlines the nature of the claim by reference to pleadings, *and*
	  iii) verifies the amount at stake, *and*
	  iv) states the amount of special damages which have accrued to date, *and if appropriate*
	  v) explains why the plaintiff needs the money (this is not vital, but it can be helpful), *and*
	  vi) states, in a personal injury action, that *r.11(2)* requirements are met (see '**Requirements**' above)
	c) exhibits: a medical report or statement of special damages
	
	Service: on the defendant a minimum of 10 clear days before the hearing
		Files:
		a) a notice of application (*Ord.13 r.1*), *and*
		b) an affidavit as in the High Court
		
		Service: on the defendant a minimum of 7 days before the hearing (*r.12(2)*)

Defendant	May serve an affidavit in reply disputing the grounds for an order	
Conse-quences	1) The judge considers the need for directions on the future conduct of the case - normally automatic directions suffice, but in the High Court an action for breach of contract proceeds as a summons for directions 2) The secrecy rule applies - the trial judge is not told until liability and quantum are resolved, unless the defendant consents (*r.15*) 3) Any subsequent 'notice of payment into court' must state whether an interim payment has been taken into account (*RSC Ord.22 r.1*) 4) The plaintiff needs leave of court or the consent of all the other parties to discontinue proceedings once an interim payment has been made 5) The plaintiff repays the defendant (with interest) any surplus if the final award exceeds the payment into court	

C. Three types of Order

1. 'Unless' order

➤ Purpose

◆ If one party has obtained an interlocutory order, and the other party has not complied with that order, the aggrieved party may apply for an 'unless' order.

➤ Procedure

◆ The aggrieved party issues a summons requesting that 'UNLESS' the original court order is complied with within a certain time, the claim/defence of the other side will be struck out and the action will be ended.

2. Consent order

➤ Purpose

◆ To obtain a court order without a hearing, thus saving time and costs.

➤ Procedure

◆ The parties agree on the terms of the order, draft it and sign it. As long as it is says 'By Consent', the court will seal it.

3. Tomlin order

➤ Purpose

◆ To stay the action by consent of both parties on terms set out in a schedule to a court order.

➤ Procedure

◆ Both parties submit a consent order. The agreement terms are set out in a schedule to the order.

◆ If enforcement is necessary, an application can be made to court for specific performance or an injunction.

➤ Any payment to be made under an order is *not* treated as being paid under a judgment, so statutory interest is not available as it is on judgments under *JA 1838 s.17*.

D. Tactics - The Calderbank offer

Calderbank offer

➤ This is used where a payment into court is not suitable to resolve a claim (eg: one of several co-defendants wishes to settle the claim with the plaintiff in respect of his own liability or when a claim is valued no higher than the CRU figure (see p.262) so a payment into court is not possible) (*Calderbank v. Calderbank* [1975] All ER 333).

➤ Procedure

◆ The defendant makes a written offer 'without prejudice save as to costs'.

◆ If the offer is not accepted, the offer letter remains secret from the trial judge until liability and quantum are resolved.

◆ If the damages offered in the letter are not exceeded by the judgment, then the judge may ask the plaintiff to pay both sides' costs from the date of the offer.

G Discovery and inspection

I Documents for discovery
II Privileged material
III Discovery
IV Problems with disclosure
V Interlocutory applications associated with discovery

I Documents for discovery

➤ Discovery is the advance disclosure of a party's documentary evidence.

➤ All relevant 'documents' must be disclosed.

Relevant documents for discovery (*RSC Ord. 24 r.1*)

◆ Material created before or after an event in question, which is pertinent to liability or quantum.

◆ Both items that help *or* hinder a party's case must be disclosed.

◆ Anything on which information is recorded - tape recordings, disks, photographs, micro-filmed records, documents, etc.

◆ Items held by the party itself, or in its custody or power (ie: by its bailee, agent or employee).

II Privileged material

Privileged material

➤ Some documents are called 'privileged'. These are documents that are 'relevant documents' (see above) and must be disclosed. However, they do not have to be turned over for inspection. The following are the categories of privileged documents:

1 **Solicitor-client correspondence,** for the purpose of legal advice.

2 **Solicitor-third party correspondence,** if created after litigation is commenced, or if created with a view to starting litigation or to obtain evidence or advice.

3 **Client-third party correspondence,** if the primary purpose was to see if legal advice should be obtained for potential litigation.

4 **'Without prejudice' evidence of negotiations** (unless as evidence of a settlement which was reached where the dispute is whether any settlement was reached at all!).

5 **Public policy material,** eg: defence, NSPCC, social work and probation records.

6 **Material incriminating a party to the proceedings** (in UK criminal or penal proceedings).

➤ Secondary evidence of a privileged document is admissible, unless prevented by an injunction (but see 'Professional ethics' p.21 and see also p.301).

➤ Privilege belongs to the client, so the solicitor may not waive it without the client's authority.

III   Discovery

A. High Court procedure (*RSC Ord.24*)

1   Automatic discovery (*RSC Ord.24 r.2(1)*)

➤ Automatic discovery always applies *except:*

   a) in third party proceedings (*RSC Ord.16*), *or*

   b) to a defendant in a road accident case (*RSC Ord.24 r.2(2)*). Automatic discovery still applies to a plaintiff, *or*

   c) if the court otherwise orders (*RSC Ord.24(r.2(5))*).

➤ Discovery takes place within 14 days after the close of pleadings, but this time may be extended by agreement.

2   Discovery against third parties (not parties to the action)

➤ Normally, discovery only applies to parties involved in the action (*RSC Ord.24 r.1(1)*).

➤ However, for personal injury or proceedings concerning a death, or where a non-party has facilitated the wrongful acts of another (albeit innocently) (*Norwich Pharmacal Co. v. Commissioners for Customs & Excise* [1974] AC 133), discovery is allowed against third parties (*RSC Ord.24 r.7A*).

➤ The side seeking discovery should serve an interlocutory application on all parties to the proceedings and the person against whom the order is sought.

➤ An affidavit must describe the documents sought, their relevance, and it must also state that the person is likely to have them.

3   Format of discovery

➤ A list must be produced in the following format:

Schedule 1 Part 1	All documents which are discoverable and not privileged. These documents are open for inspection ◆ Item number, description, date - in date order
Schedule 1 Part 2	All documents which are discoverable but for which privilege is claimed ◆ Dates and the names of their makers need not be mentioned, merely the class of document and the ground(s) for opposing inspection
Schedule 2	All documents no longer in the party's possession, custody or power ◆ When the documents were last in the party's possession, what has become of them and who possesses them now

4   Inspection

➤ Service of the list of documents is also accompanied by a notice stating a place and time for inspection within 7 days of the notice being served (*RSC Ord.24 r.9*).

➤ A party entitled to inspect documents serves a notice requiring copies to be supplied and undertakes to pay reasonable charges for this (*RSC Ord.24 r.11A*).

➤ Copies (and an account of the expense of copying) are tendered within 7 days (*RSC Ord.24 r.11A*).

➤ A party need not permit copying of documents which cannot be photocopied (eg: video and audio tapes or floppy disks).

B. County Court procedure *(CCR Ord.14)*

1   Automatic discovery

> ➤ Most County Court actions have automatic directions (see p.307):

> ◆ one direction is that 28 days after the close of pleadings (14 days after a defence is served, or 28 days if a counterclaim is served), document lists should be exchanged.

> ◆ another direction says that documents must be inspected 7 days after the list is served.

> ➤ Format of the list and inspection procedure is the same as in the High Court (see p.299).

2   Non-automatic discovery

> ➤ Where automatic directions do *not* apply (see p.307) a court order is usually made for discovery at the pre-trial review.

> ◆ An order may be applied for by interlocutory application to a district judge on notice. If the case proceeds to pre-trial review, the application should be made then.

> ◆ It is usually prudent to seek voluntary disclosure rather than waiting for a court order.

3   Discovery against third parties (not parties to the action)

> ➤ Procedure is as in the High Court (see p.299).

IV   Problems with disclosure

1   Erroneous inclusion of privileged documents in *Schedule Part 1 (see also p.21)*

> ➤ If one party accidentally gives the other party privileged documents, it should notify the recipient party in writing of the documents sent in error and the grounds for claiming privilege.

> ➤ If the notification happens after inspection, the 'privileged' documents may be used by the party that received them in error as secondary evidence, but may have to cease to act on ethical grounds.

2   Unusual situations

a) A party gives no discovery

Steps

1   The aggrieved party should send a reminder of the time limit, and should request compliance with discovery by a fixed deadline.

2   If there is no result, the aggrieved party should seek a court order by interlocutory application, requesting compliance with the rules of court.

3   If there is still no result, the aggrieved party should make an interlocutory application for an order *either* dismissing the claim against a defendant, *or* striking out the defence and entering judgment for the plaintiff - depending on who is the aggrieved party.

4   If there is still no result, the aggrieved party should make an interlocutory application requiring compliance within a specified time limit. The court is likely to make an 'unless' order, ie: unless the plaintiff/defendant complies, the claim/defence will be dismissed/struck out.

5   Further disobedience leads to committal for contempt (*RSC Ord.24 r.16(2), CCR Ord.14 r.10(2)*).

b) A party is not required to give discovery, but has relevant documents

> ➤ The party seeking discovery should write inviting voluntary disclosure and threaten to apply for an order for discovery. Tactics are part of a solicitor's skills! If there is no voluntary compliance, an interloctuory application for discovery should be made.

c) A party does not disclose fully. There are *four* alternatives:

i) **write to the other party asking for more documents.** This should be tried first.

ii) **serve a notice requiring a 'verifying affidavit'** (*RSC Ord.24 r.2(7)*). The recipient has 14 days to comply. The complainant files the notice with the court and serves a copy on the other party. If the affidavit is not supplied and filed in court, then the complainant can make an interlocutory application for an order compelling the other party to provide it.

Note: A false affidavit is perjury or contempt.

iii) **interlocutory application for a 'further and better list'** (*RSC Ord.24 r.3, CCR Ord.14 r.1*). This can be applied for on one of 4 grounds:

◆ a schedule is missing or inappropriate privilege is claimed, *or*

◆ a list is internally inconsistent, referring to documents which are not included, *or*

◆ the party made an admission, eg: in the pleadings, *or*

◆ if the party had understood its obligations it would have disclosed, but it did not.

iv) **interlocutory application for discovery of particular documents** (*RSC Ord.24 r.7, CCR Ord.14 r.2*). The party applying should swear an affidavit that describes and explains:

◆ the documents or class of documents, *and*

◆ why they are believed to be in the other party's possession, custody or power, *and*

◆ the relevance of the documents to the matter in question.

V   Interlocutory applications associated with discovery

➤ The following applications can be made before discovery, but they are most likely to prove useful at this stage to help the parties reduce the issues to be resolved at trial, and therefore to save costs.

11. Detention, custody, preservation or inspection of property.

12. Notice to admit facts.

13. Interrogatories.

11. Detention, custody, preservation or inspection of property		
Purpose: to safeguard, gain access to, or preserve certain property		
	High Court (*RSC Ord.29 r.2*)	County Court (*CCR Ord.13 r.7(1)(b)*)
Property	Any property which is the subject matter of the action, *or* about which a question may arise ◆ Photographs, disks, etc.	
Procedure	*Either:* a) ◆ the plaintiff can apply for an interlocutory application any time after proceedings have commenced ◆ the defendant can only apply after he has given notice of intention to defend unless the court otherwise directs. NB: A supporting affidavit is needed in either case, *or* b) by notice under the summons for directions (see p.304)	*Either:* a) ◆ the plaintiff can apply for an interlocutory application any time after proceedings have commenced ◆ the defendant can only apply after he has filed a defence unless the court otherwise directs NB: A supporting affidavit is needed in either case *or* b) at pre-trial review

12. Notice to admit facts		
Purpose: to obtain certain facts which remain at issue and which the other side is 'unreasaonbly' denying or refusing to admit		
	High Court (*RSC Ord.27 r.2*)	County Court (*CCR Ord.20 r.2*)
Procedure	Serve a notice to admit facts *not* later than 21 days after an action is set down for trial If the other party does not admit facts within *14 days,* if he has been 'unreasonable', he bears the costs of proving those facts	Serve a notice to admit facts *not* later than 14 days before the trial or hearing Same sanction as in the High Court if there is no compliance within *7 days*

13. Interrogatories

Purpose: to obtain admissions from the opponent by putting to the opponent a list of questions which he may be called upon to answer on oath

➤ **Drafting:** use plain language, capable of being answered by recipient - 'fishing' is not allowed.
➤ **Interrogatories should** (*Ord. 26 r.1*):
  a) 'relate to the matter in question':
     ◆ they may do so *in*directly (eg: handwriting on documents unconnected with the case can be used to check authorship of documents connected with the case)
     ◆ they:
        i)   may not seek information as to a witness's credit, *or* their opinion, *and*
        ii) may not probe to discover what evidence a party intends to call, *and*
        iii) should not go to the opponent's evidence, *and*
        iv) should not be oppressive, *and*
        v)   should not be such that they will be disallowed under the court's discretion
  and b) be 'necessary either for disposing fairly of the cause or matter or for saving costs'
     ◆ they may *not* seek to obtain an admission of fact *either* from a witness who will be called anyway, *or* if an admission is clearly unlikely

➤ **A note should be made at the end of the interrogatories stating:**
     ◆ the time within which an answer is expected (at least 28 days), *and*
     ◆ if served on a company, the name of the company officer on whom the interrogatories should be served, *and*
     ◆ if served on two or more parties, who should answer which question (eg: which servant or agent of a party should answer), *and*
     ◆ in the County Court the note must state that the opponent can apply within 14 days of service to have the interrogatories varied or withdrawn

High Court *and* County Court procedure (*RSC Ord.26 r.3, CCR Ord.14 r.11*)	

Interrogatories *without* a court order
 	
NB: Interrogatories may not be served on the Crown without a court order
	➤ Interrogatories can be served on a party *twice* without a court order
	➤ The recipient may:
	  a) answer within the specified time (answer on affidavit)
	    ◆ Objections on grounds of privilege are also made on affidavit
	  or b) apply to court within 14 days for their withdrawal or modification
	➤ **Insufficient answer:** the court may order a further answer
	➤ **Recipient takes no action:** the other party can apply for judgment in default. The court may:
	  a) dismiss the action or order the defence to be struck out, *or*
	  b) (most likely) give a further time limit and then make an 'unless' order, *or*
	  c) refuse to make an order if the interrogatories are unfair *or* unnecessary

Interrogatories *with* a court order	➤ A summons *and* a copy of the proposed interrogatories are filed at court and served on the other party ➤ The court considers any offer to supply information by other means

H Directions

Summons for directions

➤ A summons for directions is made:
  ◆ to obtain directions from the court so that the action goes to trial speedily *and*
  ◆ to allow the parties to consider the issues.

A. High Court (*RSC Ord.25*)

1 Non-personal injury cases

Steps

1 The plaintiff, within 1 month of the close of pleadings, must take out a 'summons for directions'.

  ◆ If the plaintiff does not do so, the defendant may seek an order that the action be struck out, or he may take out the summons for directions himself.

  ◆ If the time for automatic discovery is extended (by consent or court order), a summons for directions must be issued within 14 days of the close of the extended time.

2 On receiving the summons, a defendant may within 7 days of the directions hearing, serve the plaintiff a notice listing directions *he* seeks.

3 A minimum of 1 day before the hearing, the plaintiff (or defendant if there is only a counterclaim proceeding) must file at court a statement saying *either:*

a) that the value of the action is not less than £25,000, *or*

b) explaining why High Court proceedings are necessary.

Note: if this is not done, the case is automatically transferred to the County Court (see p.270).

4 If the parties agree, a summons for directions is granted by consent. Both parties send letters of consent in advance to the court, or one party attends court with a letter of consent from the other party. If there is no consent, the parties attend court on the appointed day.

5 The duty of the court at the hearing

➤ To consider independently all the matters which the summons should deal with.

  ◆ Since pleadings are not filed at court, the parties should provide copies at the hearing.

6 Order for directions

➤ The plaintiff draws up the appropriately amended standard form order, immediately after the summons has been heard.

➤ The matters on the facing page should be considered and the appropriate orders made. (Strike out the number of any direction which is not wanted.)

In the High Court in London, a Practice Direction for medical negligence cases has been given. As a result, such cases will be run using rules that are half-way between existing rules and the Woolf proposals.

Directions
High Court

A list of matters to consider on a summons for directions	
Order	Comment
1 Consolidation of actions	Grounds: a) a common question of law or fact, *or* rights to relief arise from the same transaction(s), *or* b) it is desirable for any other reason ◆ The main purpose is to save time and costs If the plaintiffs and defendants in various actions differ, consolidation is possible provided that the plaintiff in one action is *not* a defendant in another. Parties should agree on which solicitors will act for them. Instead of consolidating the actions, the court may order simultaneous trials, or trials in succession
2 Trial by official referee	Complicated questions of fact may need to be resolved by a specialist (eg: building disputes)
3 Transfer to County Court	Grounds: a) the financial substance of action, its importance to other parties, complexity, *or* b) a transfer would be likely to speed up trial of the action, *or* c) other reasons (see p.270)
4 Amend writ or summons	Leave is needed to do this at this stage in the proceedings
5 Amend pleadings	Leave is needed to do this at this stage in the proceedings
6 Further / better particulars	An order may be required to achieve this
7 Discovery	This should have already happened. If unsatisfactory, take appropriate action (see p.301)
8 Inspection	This should have already happened. If not, an order may be required
9 Retention, preservation, & inspection of property	This order will usually have been applied for already
10 Expert reports	These are inadmissible, unless before the trial takes place, the court has determined whether the substance of a report should be disclosed at trial. ◆ The court will order the parties to disclose expert evidence to each other within a specified time period ◆ The court may: a) limit the number of experts - often to 2, *and/or* b) order a 'without prejudice' experts meeting to identify issues between them ● This saves preparatory work, promotes a settlement, and may reduce costs
11 Witness statements	◆ An order is usually made to serve within a period specified (usually 14 weeks) written statements of evidence which the parties intend to introduce for examination-in-chief, instead of oral evidence ◆ Leave or consent is needed to adduce evidence not included in the exchange of statements ◆ A court will now substitute a statement for examination-in-chief as a matter of course ◆ A party introducing hearsay evidence should (as the law is now) include a *CEA 1968 ss.23-25* notice and, if needed, seek an extension for exchange. (It must be simultaneous)
12 Other directions	The plaintiff may apply for any extra direction he desires (eg: permitting the use of photographs)
13 Directions for trial	**Place where the case will be heard** **Mode:** judge alone or judge and jury **Category:** A = case of great substance or difficulty or public importance B = a case of substance or difficulty C = other cases **Estimated length of the trial** **Setting down:** the number of days it takes for the case to be set down **Costs of the summons for directions**

305

2 **Personal injury cases - automatic directions** *(RSC Ord.25 r.8)*

➤ In personal injury cases, no summons for directions is required.

➤ Automatic directions apply and there is therefore no need to draw up an 'order for directions'.

➤ A party may apply for further or different directions where appropriate via interlocutory application.

➤ The automatic directions are:

a) **Discovery**

- Discovery is within 14 days of the close of pleadings, and inspection is during the next 7 days.

- If liability is admitted, *or* the action arises from a road accident, only the plaintiff is bound by discovery and this discovery is limited to documents relating to special damages.

b) **Expert evidence**

- Within 14 weeks of the close of pleadings, the substance of expert evidence must be disclosed in a written report.

- Any medical report which has been updated since the statement of claim must be disclosed, together with an updated statement of special damages.

   Note: the report attached to the statement of claim need not be disclosed.

- Simultaneous exchange of expert evidence is mandatory: agreement on evidence should be sought if possible.

- Normally, each party is only permitted reports from 2 medical experts and 1 from another expert.

c) **Other oral evidence**

- Both parties must serve written statements within 14 weeks of the close of pleadings.

d) **Photographs, plans, police accident report**

- These are admissible at trial and should be agreed if possible.

e) **Place of trial:** is where the action is proceeding or elsewhere if the parties agree.

f) **Time of trial**

- The action must be set down within 6 months.

g) **Category of case**

- This is set at category 'B' (see p.305).

h) **Mode of trial**

- This is set as trial by judge alone.

i) **Estimate of length of the trial:** this is set by certain rules (not dealt with here).

B. County Court (*CCR Ord.17*)

1 Automatic directions

➤ Automatic directions apply on close of pleadings *except* when there is/are:

- ◆ proceedings that are referred to small claims arbitration, *or*
- ◆ an action for delivery of goods, *or*
- ◆ a partnership action, *or*
- ◆ an action where there is an admission of part of the plaintiff's claim, *or*
- ◆ an action where a third party notice has been issued, *or*
- ◆ a tort action between husband and wife, *or*
- ◆ an action on the Central London County Court Business List (see p.269).

➤ The following automatic directions take effect on the close of pleadings:

Automatic directions in the County Court		
	Non-personal injury	**Personal injury**
Discovery and Inspection	Discovery must take place within 28 days after the close of pleadings, and inspection within the next 7 days (see p.300 for the rules) NB: If the defendant is a defendant in a road accident case (see p.306), he does not need to disclose documents other than documents relating to damages	
Evidence	◆ Written experts' reports must be disclosed within 10 weeks of the close of pleadings, else leave of court or consent is needed to use the report ◆ A maximum of 2 experts (leave or consent is needed for more, unless all parties agree) ◆ Written statements of oral evidence must be served on the other parties within 10 weeks ◆ Photographs and plans should be agreed if possible, and are admissible at trial	◆ Written experts' reports must be disclosed within 10 weeks of the close of pleadings, else leave of court or consent is needed to use the report ◆ A maximum of 2 medical experts and 1 other expert witness ◆ Written statments of oral evidence must be served within 10 weeks ◆ Photographs, plans and a police accident report should be agreed if possible, and are admissible at trial ◆ No further medical report need be disclosed if the plaintiff is relying on the one with the particulars of claim, but if a new one is used, it must have a statement of special damages attached
Hearing length and trial length	**Within 6 months** of the close of pleadings, the plaintiff must ask the court for the date of the trial, and must state the anticipated trial length and the number of witnesses **Within 15 months** of the close of pleadings (or 9 months from any deadline fixed by the court), the court will automatically strike out the action if the plaintiff does not request a hearing date ◆ The County Court may reinstate the action if the plaintiff shows he has acted with due diligence	
Amendments	Automatic directions may be varied or amended by making an application to a district judge to explain the reasons	

2 No automatic directions - pre-trial review

➤ Where automatic directions do *not* apply, a pre-trial review is held.

➤ The court should consider the same matters as in the High Court at a summons for directions hearing (and one or two in addition, such as whether the claim is suitable for the small claims court - see p.265)

➤ The court sends notice of the date to all the parties, and subsequently draws up and serves any order which is made at the hearing.

I   Admissibility of evidence

    I   Opinion

    II   Documents

    III   Hearsay

    IV   Children's evidence

I   Opinion

➤ A witness may only testify as to matters actually observed by him and may not give his *opinion* about those matters.

➤ Opinion 'evidence' is inadmissible unless it is:

  1   **expert opinion (*CEA 1972 s.3(1)*).**

     ◆ This is opinion on any relevant matter on which the expert is qualified to give expert evidence.

  2   **perception (*CEA 1972 s.3(2)*).**

     ◆ The witness conveys relevant facts personally perceived by him. The reason for this relaxation is that it is not always possible to separate facts from inferences.

II   Documents

➤ A document at trial is *deemed* to be authentic unless the other party objects (*RSC Ord.27 r.4*).

➤ Authenticity does *not* go to proof of contents.

➤ If authenticity is at issue *either*:

  a) a witness can give supporting evidence orally (eg: calling the writer of the document to prove his handwriting or signature), *or*

  b) the party disputing authenticity must serve a notice to admit authenticity on his opponents requiring that it should be proved authentic.

A notice to admit authenticity (*RSC Ord.27 r.5, CCR Ord.20 r.3*)	
High Court	County Court
A party may serve a notice to admit authenticity within 21 days after the action is set down for trial	A party may serve a notice to admit authenticity not later than 14 days before trial
Where the objection is unreasonable, the objector pays the costs of proving authenticity	

➤ A party is deemed to be on notice to produce all documents in discovery lists (*RSC Ord.27 r.4(3)*).

  ◆ If that party does not do so, it may be necessary to serve a notice to produce documents.

A notice to produce documents (*RSC Ord.27 r.5, CCR Ord.20 r.3*)
High Court *and* County Court
◆ There is no time limit for service of the notice, but it must be a reasonable period before trial (*George v. Thompson* (1835) 4 Dowl. 656). ◆ There is no obligation to produce the documents following the notice.

◆ If the notice is disregarded:
  ● any secondary evidence (copies) may be introduced as evidence, *and*
  ● the court may draw adverse inferences at trial.

III Hearsay

Hearsay - a statutory meaning

➤ Hearsay is 'a statement made by someone *other* than the person *now* giving evidence, intended to prove the truth of the matter stated' whether first hand hearsay (ie: reported directly from a source) or multiple hearsay (coming from a source via intermediaries).

Hearsay - a plain English (!) meaning

➤ Hearsay is an assertion, other than one made by a person while giving oral evidence in the proceedings, if the assertion is used to prove the truth of what it asserts.

➤ The law used to be that hearsay was *in*admissible *unless* the evidence fell within these 6 categories:

1. **Public records**
2. **Admissions** (Statements against a party's interest, made by that party, are admissible.)
3. **Published works dealing with matters of a public nature** eg: dictionaries, maps.
4. **Public documents**
5. **Statements establishing reputation or family tradition**
6. **Criminal convictions**

➤ Under *CEA 1995* these 6 (although being hearsay) are now admissible.

Hearsay procedure

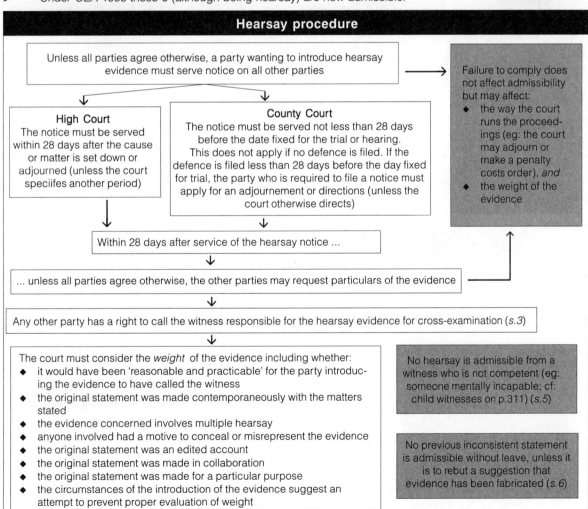

Unless all parties agree otherwise, a party wanting to introduce hearsay evidence must serve notice on all other parties

High Court
The notice must be served within 28 days after the cause or matter is set down or adjourned (unless the court speciifes another period)

County Court
The notice must be served not less than 28 days before the date fixed for the trial or hearing. This does not apply if no defence is filed. If the defence is filed less than 28 days before the day fixed for trial, the party who is required to file a notice must apply for an adjournment or directions (unless the court otherwise directs)

Failure to comply does not affect admissibility but may affect:
♦ the way the court runs the proceedings (eg: the court may adjourn or make a penalty costs order), *and*
♦ the weight of the evidence

Within 28 days after service of the hearsay notice ...

... unless all parties agree otherwise, the other parties may request particulars of the evidence

Any other party has a right to call the witness responsible for the hearsay evidence for cross-examination (*s.3*)

The court must consider the *weight* of the evidence including whether:
♦ it would have been 'reasonable and practicable' for the party introducing the evidence to have called the witness
♦ the original statement was made contemporaneously with the matters stated
♦ the evidence concerned involves multiple hearsay
♦ anyone involved had a motive to conceal or misrepresent the evidence
♦ the original statement was an edited account
♦ the original statement was made in collaboration
♦ the original statement was made for a particular purpose
♦ the circumstances of the introduction of the evidence suggest an attempt to prevent proper evaluation of weight

No hearsay is admissible from a witness who is not competent (eg: someone mentally incapable; cf: child witnesses on p.311) (*s.5*)

No previous inconsistent statement is admissible without leave, unless it is to rebut a suggestion that evidence has been fabricated (*s.6*)

Contents of a hearsay notice

➤ The rules about what is in a hearsay notice are given by:

- ◆ High Court: *RSC Ord. 38 rr.20-24*
- ◆ County Court: *CCR Ord. 20 rr.14-17*

➤ A hearsay notice must state:

a) it is a hearsay notice, *and*

b) what the hearsay evidence consists of, *and*

c) the identity of the person who made the statement, *and*

d) that that person will (or may) be called to give oral evidence, *and*

e) if it refers to hearsay in a witness statement, it must refer to the part of the statement where the hearsay is set out.

➤ 1 notice may deal with more than 1 witness.

➤ No notice is needed for affidavit evidence.

Business records

➤ Although hearsay, business records are admissible in evidence (*CEA 1995 s.9(1)*).

- ◆ To be accepted as a business record, a document must be certified by an officer of the business (*CEA 1995 s.9(2)*).

- ◆ Computerised statements are also prima facie admissible as hearsay (*CEA 1995 s.1-2*)

IV   Children's evidence

➤   A child is anyone under the age of 18.

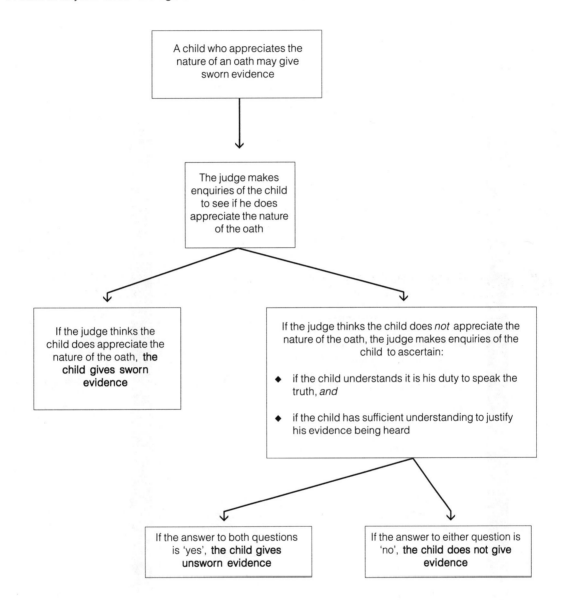

J Trial preparations

I   Setting down (check the availability of witnesses before setting down)
II   Instructing counsel
III   Ensuring attendance of witnesses

I   Setting down

	High Court (*RSC Ord.34*)	County Court (*CCR Ord.17*)
Setting down the initial bundle (*RSC Ord.34 r.3*)	**Steps** **1** Check where the trial will be (not every court has trial jurisdiction) **2** It is the plaintiff's responsibility to set the action down for trial within the dates specified on the summons for directions. If he does not (*RSC Ord.34 r.2*): ◆ the defendant may set it down for trial, *or* ◆ the court may dismiss the action, *or* ◆ the court may make such an order as it thinks just **3** A pre-trial check list must be lodged at the court at least 2 months before the trial (*Practice Direction (Civil Litigation: Case Managment)* [1995] 1 WLR 262) **4** A pre-trial review is now mandatory 4 to 8 weeks before trial: (*Practice Direction (Civil Litigation: Case Managment) 1995* [1995] 1 WLR 26): ◆ to check procedure *and* ◆ to see how the size and complexity of the trial can be contained, *and* ◆ to encourage settlements and reduce costs **5** The solicitor sends the court 2 bundles, which are paginated and bound on the left-hand side. A fee is payable and the bundle is accompanied by a letter requesting setting down for trial. The bundles contain: ◆ the writ ◆ the pleadings ◆ a request for further and better particulars and reply ◆ any interrogatories and answers ◆ any interlocutory orders ◆ a statement of value ◆ a note on the expected length of the trial ◆ a notice of issue of any legal aid certificate ◆ if outside London, a statement that directions have been complied with and details of solicitors and counsel for each party **6** The solicitor notifies the other parties within 24 hours after setting down (*RSC Ord.34 r.8*) **Personal injury cases:** exchange both sides' experts' reports as soon as practicable after setting down	**Steps** **1** Within 6 months of the close of pleadings, the plaintiff requests a hearing date, sending the court a note giving the estimated trial length (*CCR Ord.17 r.11(3)(d)*) **2** The defendant tells the plaintiff which documents he wishes to be included in the bundle at least 14 days before trial (*CCR Ord.17 r.12*) **3** The plaintiff files, at least 7 days before the trial, 1 paginated and indexed bundle, on which either party intends to rely, or which either party wishes to have before the court, together with 2 copies of: ◆ a request for further and better particulars and answers, ◆ answers to interrogatories, ◆ witness statements that have been exchanged, ◆ experts' reports which have been disclosed with an indication of areas which are agreed, ◆ notice of an issue of any legal aid certificate
↓ **The queue** ↓	The court places the case in the queue until it enters the 'warned list'	The court fixes the date for the hearing (unless it operates a 'warned list')
The trial bundle (*RSC Ord.34 r.10*)	**At least 14 days** before trial, the defendant tells the plaintiff which documents are central to his case, and which should be included in the trial bundle **At least 2 days** before the trial, the plaintiff lodges at court 2 bundles containing: ◆ witness statements that have been exchanged ◆ any experts' reports which were disclosed, and an indication of whether the documents are agreed ◆ any documents the defendant wishes to include, and those central to the plaintiff's case ◆ if ordered at directions, a note summarising issues, legal propositions, a list of authorities and a chronology of events	There is no equivalent at this stage! *The relevant documents have already been deposited in the setting down bundle (see above).*

Personal injury actions		
In a personal injury action, where special damages have not been agreed between the parties (a situation that is unusual in practice), then the plaintiff must serve a schedule of special damages on the defendant before trial. This lists special damages already incurred *and* an estimate of future expenses or losses		
	High Court (*RSC Ord.34*)	**County Court** (*CCR Ord.17*)
	Special damages for personal injury cases (*Practice Note* [1984] 1 WLR 1127)	
District Registry	◆ The plaintiff serves a schedule of special damages on the defendant on lodging at court a notice confirming compliance with directions	There is no mandatory equivalent, *but* it is good practice to follow the High Court procedure
In London	◆ The defendant has 14 days to respond ◆ The plaintiff serves a schedule of damages within 7 days of the appearance of the case on the 'warned list' ◆ The defendant has 7 days to respond	

Defendant	◆ The defendant replies, explaining:
	  • which items are agreed, *and*
	  • why other items are contested, *and*
	  • any counter-proposals	

II   Instructing counsel

Steps	
1	**A brief - always needed**
2	**A conference may be necessary**
3	**The barrister's fee**

1.   A brief - always needed

➤ A brief is the traditional presentation of the case to the barrister who will appear at the hearing.

➤ It is traditionally typed on 'brief-sized' paper (A3), but this is optional.

➤ The brief should include:

  ◆ the heading of the action.

  ◆ a list of enclosures being forwarded to counsel (eg: client's statement, witness statements, pleadings, any legal aid certificate, experts' reports, *relevant* correspondence, pleadings, setting down bundle, trial bundle, counsel's earlier advice, etc).

➤ It should then:

  ◆ identify the client.

  ◆ set out *both* sides of the case.

  ◆ indicate the solicitor's view, and draw attention to where advice is specifically needed.

  ◆ formally request counsel to carry out the task required.

➤ The back sheet should be endorsed with:

  ◆ the title of the action.

  ◆ a definition of what the instructions are.

  ◆ counsel's name and that of his chambers.

  ◆ the solicitor's firm's name, address and reference.

  ◆ if relevant, the legal aid reference number.

Note: the third person is traditionally used in writing to counsel.

2   **A conference may be necessary**

➤ This is useful if the facts are complex, or if counsel wishes to assess a client as a witness, or to fully comprehend and assess his injuries.

◆ The solicitor should arrange this with the counsel's clerk if it is thought necessary.

➤ A written opinion should be specifically requested.

◆ Costs will not be allowed unless the court judges the need to hold the conference to be reasonable.

3   **The barrister's fee**

➤ The Legal Aid Board will pay the fee, if the legal aid certificate covers it.

➤ A solicitor negotiates on behalf of a private client. The solicitor is liable to counsel for the fee, so a solicitor should ensure that he has been put in funds by a client before the barrister is instructed.

◆ The fee is payable once the brief is delivered, but it is usually waived or reduced if the action settles before the hearing.

◆ The fee covers 1 day, unless otherwise agreed. A 'refresher' is due on subsequent days.

III   Ensuring attendance of witnesses

➤ The solicitor must check the availability of witnesses.

➤ Sometimes witnesses may not attend court voluntarily and it is necessary to compel them to do so.

➤ There are 2 types of subpoena for the High Court and 1 type of witness summons for the County Court. The 2 types of subpoena are:

1 A *subpoena ad testificandum* - this requires a witness to come to court to give oral evidence.

2 A *subpoena duces tecum* - this requires a witness to come to court to give evidence and to bring documentation with him.

➤ **Expert witnesses:** may prefer to be summonsed as the obligation helps break appointments.

➤ **Police officers:** *must* be summonsed, as they will not otherwise give evidence in a civil matter.

Subpoena/Summons	
High Court	County Court
The request for a subpoena must be obtained by lodging a praecipe with the completed subpoena	The request for a witness summons must be filed at court
The *subpoena* must be served in person	The witness summons may be served by post
Non-appearance is contempt which is punishable by a fine and imprisonment	Non-appearance is punishable by a fine
The solicitor must: ◆ provide for conduct money (eg: travel expenses). (Salary loss can be claimed later) ◆ include instructions to bring any relevant document(s)	

K   The trial

1

The plaintiff's side makes the opening speech

➤ This involves taking the judge through the pleadings and introducing agreed exhibits.

2

The plaintiff gives evidence

➤ This is done by oral examination, but examination-in-chief is conducted by using the witness statement exchanged previously, unless the court decides otherwise. This is a recent change in practice.

➤ The sequence of questioning is:

◆ examination-in-chief by the plaintiff's side,

◆ cross-examination by the defendant's side,

◆ re-examination (on points arising from the cross-examination) by the plaintiff's side.

➤ The defendant's case must be put to the plaintiff during cross-examination.

➤ Each side should check the admissibility rules (see p.308 et seq).

3

The plaintiff's side presents evidence

➤ This is done by oral examination of the witnesses.

➤ The sequence of questioning is:

◆ examination-in-chief by the plaintiff's side. (This is conducted by using the witness statements ex-changed previously, unless the court decides otherwise. This is a recent change in practice.)

◆ cross-examination by the defendant's side,

◆ re-examination (on points arising from the cross-examination) by the plaintiff's side.

➤ The defendant's case must be put to the witness.

➤ Each side should check the admissibility rules (see p.308 et seq).

➤ If a witness gives consistently unfavourable or adverse answers to the surprise of the plaintiff, the plaintiff's side should ask the judge to declare the witness hostile.

◆ If the judge does so, previously inconsistent statements can be put to the witness (see the new law on hearsay p.309).

4

The defendant's side makes its opening speech

➤ In the High Court, the defendant's side may make an opening speech.

➤ In the County Court, *if the defendant's side makes an opening speech*, the rule is that the defendant's side will not be able to make a closing speech without leave of the court.

Steps cont.

5

The defendant gives evidence

➤ This is done by oral examination, but examination-in-chief is conducted by using the witness statement exchanged previously, unless the court decides otherwise. This is a recent change in practice.

➤ The sequence of questioning is:

♦ examination-in-chief by the defendant's side,

♦ cross-examination by the plaintiff's side,

♦ re-examination (on points arising from the cross-examination) by the defendant's side.

➤ The plaintiff's case should be put to the defendant.

➤ Each side should check the admissibility rules (see p.308 et seq).

6

The defendant's side presents the evidence

➤ This is done by oral examination of the witnesses.

➤ The sequence of questioning is:

♦ examination-in-chief by the defendant's side. (This is conducted by using the witness statements exchanged previously, unless the court decides otherwise. This is a recent change in practice.)

♦ cross-examination by the plaintiff's side,

♦ re-examination (on points arising from the cross-examination) by the defendant's side.

➤ The plaintiff's case must be put to the witness.

➤ Each side should check the admissibility rules (see p.308 et seq).

➤ If a witness gives consistently unfavourable or adverse answers to the surprise of the defendant, the defendant's side should ask the judge to declare the witness hostile.

♦ If the judge does so, previously inconsistent statements can be put to the witness (see the new law on hearsay p.309).

7

The defendant's side's closing speech

➤ In the County Court, if the defendant made an opening speech, he now needs leave to make a closing one.

8

The plaintiff's side's closing speech

9

Judgment is given and any necessary orders are made

Are leading questions allowed?		
Examination-in-chief	✗	(except to obtain a denial of the other party's case)
Cross examination	✓	
Re-examination	✗	(except to obtain a denial of the other party's case)

L Costs

I   Costs generally
II   The costs order as between the parties
III Solicitor and own client costs
IV   Legal aid costs

I   Costs generally

➤   There are two bases upon which costs may be awarded (the choice is up to the judge):

1   Standard basis (most usual) (*RSC Ord.62 r.12(1)*)

◆   The winner is awarded a '*reasonable* amount in respect of all costs *reasonably* incurred'.

◆   Doubts over what is 'reasonable' are resolved in favour of the paying party.

2   Indemnity basis (rare) (*RSC Ord.62 r.15*)

◆   All costs are allowed unless the amount is *unreasonable,* or they were *unreasonably* incurred.

◆   Doubts over what is reasonable are resolved in favour of the receiving party.

II   The costs order as between the parties

➤ A costs order between the parties is made following a hearing, early termination, settlement or at the conclusion of case when liability and quantum have been settled.

➤ In the High Court there is a single scale of costs.

➤ In the County Court there are 3 scales of costs:

Costs scales used in the County Court (*CCR Ord.38 rr.3,5,6*)		
Amount	Scale	Comments
Over £25, but not exceeding £100	Lower scale	Such cases are usually referred to arbitration where the 'no costs' rule applies. This scale is therefore rarely used in practice
£100 to £3,000	Scale 1	A sum is set for each of 14 specific aspects of an action (eg: each interlocutory hearing). The court has discretion to award a greater amount than the scale allows, but the more the scale is exceeded, the more reluctant the court is to exercise discretion. The amount allowed for expert witnesses is often insufficient to cover their costs; the client will have to make up any shortfall
Over £3,000	Scale 2	This follows the High Court scale. At the court's discretion - as much as is 'reasonable'

➤ The 'amount' above is calculated as follows:
◆ for costs of the plaintiff, it depends on the sum recovered or accepted (ie: *not* the value of the claim)
◆ for costs of the defendant, it depends on the sum claimed by the plaintiff
◆ for costs of a third party, it depends on the amount claimed against him
◆ for costs payable by a third party, it depends on the amount recovered by him

➤ Costs may be decided on by five different methods as follows:

1 Costs are agreed

2 Costs are fixed

- ◆ This occurs when there is a debt case which finishes before trial.
  - Costs are fixed according to tables for both the High Court and the County Court.
  - Fixed costs will have been listed on the debt claim.
  - Defendants who settled within 14 days will only be liable for costs associated with service of the writ/summons.
  - Costs are fixed according to tables for summary and default judgments.

3 Costs are to be assessed

- ◆ This means that costs are to be assessed at the end of the present hearing by the judge.
  - Costs *must* be assessed if:
    - a) they are on the County Court lower scale, *or*
    - b) they are on the County Court scale 1 and the solicitor to be paid requests that the costs be assessed (*CCR Ord. 38 r.17(3)*).
  - Assessed costs are particularly appropriate in the County Court, if the defendant's circumstances make recovery of costs unlikely (eg: a landlord's action for possession).
  - Assessed costs are payable immediately.
- ✓ Assessed costs avoid the delay and labour of drawing up a bill of costs.
- ✗ The sum will be lower than that which would be awarded on a full taxation.

4 Costs are to be taxed (unless agreed)   (This is most usual)

- ◆ Taxation is the term used when inter partes costs are checked by special court procedure.
- ◆ Taxation procedure:

Steps

1   **Draft the bill**
  - ◆ Heading of the action.
  - ◆ Authority to tax, date of the authority to tax (ie: of the costs order).
  - ◆ Number of any legal aid certificate.
  - ◆ Succinct summary of subject of case.
  - ◆ Level of fee earner who did the work.
  - ◆ Fee earner's rate.
  - ◆ Chronological list, itemising the action taken, up to and including work on the taxation.

2   **Lodge the bill** (*RSC Ord. 62 r.29, CCR Ord.38 r.20*)
  - ◆ This must be done within 3 months of the final order (6 months for matrimonial cases), otherwise the party may be penalised for the delay (*RSC Ord. 62 r.28(4)(b)*).
  - ◆ Lodge at court (*RSC Ord.62 App.1*):
    - the bill, *and*
    - the solicitor's file which should be properly collated in thematic bundles (correspondence, attendance notes, counsel's fee notes and receipts for disbursements, instructions to counsel, pleadings, experts' reports, etc), *and*
    - the order authorising taxation, *and*
    - notice of discharge of the legal aid certificate and any other certificates.

Steps cont.	
3	**Serve the bill**
	◆ In an inter partes taxation, the bill must be served on the paying party.
	◆ In a legal aid taxation, the bill must be served on a legally aided client with a financial interest in the outcome (ie: he is paying a contribution to the costs of the action).
	◆ In the County Court, the party receiving the bill must state within 14 days if he wishes to be heard on the taxation (*CCR Ord. 38 r.20*). (In the County Court, taxation is usually without a hearing.)
4	**Provisional taxation** (*RSC Ord.62 r.31, CCR Ord.38 r.20*)
	◆ There might be a provisional taxation (disallowing 'unreasonable' items).
	◆ All have 14 days to object. If they do so, a hearing date is fixed for final taxation.
5	**Taxation hearing**
	◆ Where there is no provisional hearing, then as soon as documents are lodged, a date is fixed for the final taxation.
	◆ Interested parties may attend if they wish.
	◆ The taxation officer has a duty to safeguard the interests of the Legal Aid Board, otherwise he acts as a neutral arbiter on whatever issues the parties themselves raise.
6	**Review** (*RSC Ord. 62 rr.33,34,CCR Ord.38 r.24*)
	◆ Parties may request a review within 21 days (High Court) or 14 days (County Court).
	◆ The Officer reconsiders the taxation and gives his reasons.
	◆ If parties are still dissatisfied, they have 14 days to appeal to a judge (who sits accompanied by two assessors).

5   Costs after a hearing for an interlocutory application

◆ The costs of the interlocutory application are at the discretion of whoever is presiding. There are 7 possible orders:

Note:
Costs may be payable earlier than at trial but not against a legally aided party (*RSC Ord. 62 r.8; CCR Ord. 38 r.1*)

NB: This order cannot be made against a legally aided party (*RSC Ord. 62 r.8, CCR Ord.38 r.1*)

Order	Reasoning of judge at interlocutory stage	Trial winner (ie: claims costs of trial)	Trial loser (ie: pays costs of trial)
Named party pays costs in any event	Loser's conduct is unreasonable *or* costs relate to a collateral issue	The named party claims costs of the application from the non-named party whatever the outcome of the trial	
Costs Thrown Away	Loser's conduct is unreasonable *or* costs relate to a collateral issue	The winner of an interlocutory order which is later rendered ineffective is entitled to costs	
Named party's costs in the cause	Loser's conduct is unreasonable. Named party's conduct is only considered reasonable if he succeeds later at trial	If the trial winner is the named party, he claims the costs of the application. If he is not the named party, then there is no effect	If the trial loser is not the named party then there is no effect. If he is the named party, he pays the costs of the application
Costs in the Cause	Costs are preliminary to trial and conduct of both parties is reasonable	Trial winner claims costs of interlocutory application	Trial loser pays costs of interlocutory application
Costs Reserved	It is not yet possible to make a decision on the reasonableness of either party's conduct	Trial judge decides. If he does not decide, trial winner claims costs of the application	Trial judge decides. If he does not decide, trial loser pays costs of the application
No order	Merits (or lack of merits) of both sides are equal	Each party bears his own costs of the interlocutory application	
Costs forthwith	Costs are unusually heavy or loser's conduct is unreasonable and the court wishes to express disapproval	*The interlocutory winner* is entitled to claim costs from the *interlocutory loser* and may tax these immediately. The costs of *the interlocutory loser* are not recoverable	

III   Solicitor and own client costs

➤   See 'Disputed bills' (see p.15)

IV   Legal aid costs (*LAA 1988, LA(G)R 1989*)

➤   The solicitor cannot claim remuneration from the assisted person.

➤   The solicitor should ensure that the court grants an order after taxation of the legally aided party's costs (but it is not fatal if this is not done).

➤   **Assessment:**

◆   Any legal aid costs claimed from legal aid will be assessed by the Legal Aid Board rather than the court, if costs do not exceed £1000 (*regs 105,106*).

➤   **Taxation:**

◆   Legal aid will be taxed on the basis of prescribed rates for particular types of work.

Legally aided party is the...	
...winner	**...loser**

The costs of the winner's solicitor:
i) there is a legal aid taxation on the winner's 'solicitor and own client costs'
Inter partes costs:
ii) there is an order for inter partes costs 'to be taxed if not agreed' (ie: 'inter partes taxation')
  ◆ If a taxation occurs, the winner's solicitor submits a bill of costs at 2 rates:
  i) at the prescribed rate, *and*
  ii) at a 'private individual's rate'
  ◆ That which is paid by the other side will be at the 'private individual's rate'
  ◆ That which is paid by the Legal Aid Board will be at the prescribed rate
	The costs of the loser's solicitor:
	i) the loser's solicitor can claim these costs from the Legal Aid Board at the prescribed rates (and following the '**Assessment**' procedure above if appropriate)
	Inter partes costs:
	ii) there is an order for inter partes costs 'to be taxed if not agreed' (ie: 'inter partes taxation'), *but* this is restricted by *LAA 1988 s.17* which states that:
	'costs cannot exceed the amount it is reasonable for him to pay having regard to all the circumstances including the means of all the parties and their conduct in connection with the dispute'

Usually, money recoverable through recovery of inter partes costs (ii) above) will pay for the costs of the winner's solicitor (i) above). However, if there is: ◆ a shortfall, a contribution may be requested from the winner ◆ a surplus, it may be subject to a statutory charge	If the legally aided loser is also the plaintiff, and the non-legally aided defendant is the winner, then the Legal Aid Board can pay some of the defendant's costs if it is just and equitable to do so *and* the defendant will suffer severe financial hardship unless such an order is made (*LAA 1988 s.18*)

M Enforcing judgments

I   Reciprocal enforcement
II Investigating the debtor's means
III Interest on judgment debts
IV Methods of enforcement (extracting the
    judgment debt from an unwilling debtor)

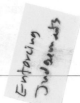

I   Reciprocal enforcement (*RSC Ord. 71, CCR Ord.35*)

1   Enforcing a foreign judgment in England and Wales

➤ A judgment from an EU member state, and from certain other European countries, may be registered in an English court and enforced normally *(CJJA 1982)*.

➤ A judgment from certain other countries may be registered and enforced normally (*AJA 1920, FJ(ER)A 1933*).

2   Enforcing an English judgment outside the jurisdiction

➤ An English judgment may be registered and enforced elsewhere in the UK (eg: Jersey), the EU member states and certain other European countries (*CJJA 1982*).

➤ There is provision for reciprocal enforcement of some other foreign judgments (*AJA 1920, FJ(ER)A 1933*).

➤ If a country is not covered, fresh proceedings should be started there.

II   Investigating the debtor's means

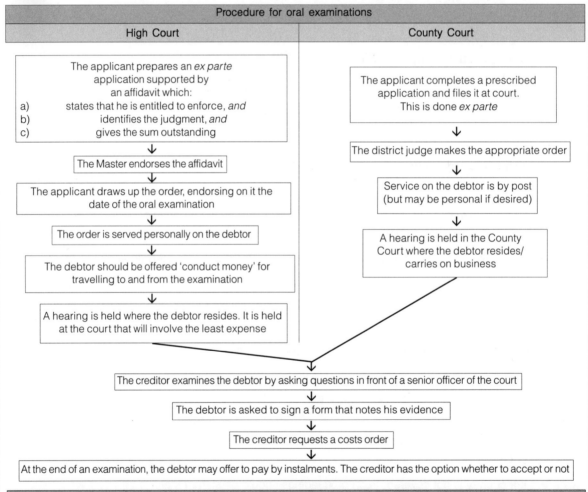

Investigating and tracing a debtor

Steps

1   Use an enquiry agent
- ◆ This is to investigate and trace a debtor (set a cost ceiling to limit the expense).
- ✓ This is relatively fast and may unearth more than an oral examination will.
- ✗ It is more expensive than an oral examination.

2   Oral examination (*RSC Ord.48 r.1, CCR Ord.25 r.3*)
- ◆ This is an examination of the means of a debtor while he is under oath.

Procedure for oral examinations

High Court	County Court
The applicant prepares an *ex parte* application supported by an affidavit which: a) states that he is entitled to enforce, *and* b) identifies the judgment, *and* c) gives the sum outstanding	The applicant completes a prescribed application and files it at court. This is done *ex parte*

High Court:
The Master endorses the affidavit
↓
The applicant draws up the order, endorsing on it the date of the oral examination
↓
The order is served personally on the debtor
↓
The debtor should be offered 'conduct money' for travelling to and from the examination
↓
A hearing is held where the debtor resides. It is held at the court that will involve the least expense

County Court:
The district judge makes the appropriate order
↓
Service on the debtor is by post (but may be personal if desired)
↓
A hearing is held in the County Court where the debtor resides/ carries on business

↓

The creditor examines the debtor by asking questions in front of a senior officer of the court
↓
The debtor is asked to sign a form that notes his evidence
↓
The creditor requests a costs order
↓
At the end of an examination, the debtor may offer to pay by instalments. The creditor has the option whether to accept or not

Failure to attend

High Court	County Court
Failure to attend results in an order for committal to prison Note: orders for committal to prison, are usually 'suspended' when they are issued for the first time	Failure to attend leads to an adjournment Notice of adjournment is served personally on the debtor and 'conduct money' should be offered Failure to attend the adjourned hearing results in a date being set for a new hearing Failure to attend the new hearing will result in an order for committal to prison

III   Interest on judgment debts *(Judgment Act 1838 s.17)*

Interest on judgment debts *(Judgment Act 1838 s.17)*

➤ **High Court:** all judgment debts currently carry interest at 8% (see p.262) from the date the judgment is entered until final payment, regardless of whether the sum represents damages or costs.

➤ **County Court:** *(County Court (Interest on Judgment Debts) Order 1991)*

a) all judgments over £5,000 carry interest at 8% (see p.262) from the date judgment is entered until final payment.

b) when enforcement proceedings begin, interest ceases to run *unless* the proceedings produce no payment.

◆ If anything at all is recovered, then the balance of the debt becomes interest-free.

c) An application to enforce interest must be made. This must be done with a certificate setting out:

◆ the amount of interest claimed, *and*

◆ the sum on which the interest is claimed, *and*

◆ the dates to and from which interest has accrued, *and*

◆ the rate of interest.

➤ If an interlocutory judgment leaves quantum to be assessed, interest runs from the date of final judgment (*Thomas v. Bunn* [1991] 1 AC 362).

➤ On a costs order, interest runs from the judgment date, not the date of the certificate of taxation (*Hunt v. R.M. Douglas (Roofing) Ltd.* [1990] 1 AC 398).

➤ Interest does *not* accrue on instalments (or judgment for deferred sums), until the instalment falls due.

IV Methods of enforcement

Methods of enforcement	Assets available
1. Bankruptcy (individual) or winding up (company)	Various
2. Execution of the judgment against goods	Goods and chattels
3. Charging order over land	Land
4. Charging order over securities	Securities
5. Attachment of earnings order	Earnings
6. Garnishee proceedings	Money held on the debtor's behalf by others

1. Bankruptcy (individual) or winding up (company)

Steps

1 If no execution has so far been levied, issue a statutory demand.

2 If execution has been levied but is unsatisfied, see the procedures for bankruptcy/winding up on pp.232-242.

2. Execution against goods
(HCCJO 1991 Art.8, HCCJ(A)O 1996, RSC Ord.45 r.1, Ord.47, CCR Ord.26)

	High Court	County Court
What judgments are enforceable and where?	High Court judgments County Court judgments if £1,000 or over	County Court judgments under £5,000 (unless proceedings are under *CCA 1974*)
	◆ County Court judgments between £1,000 and £5,000 are better brought in the High Court as interest is payable there (see p.323) ◆ If a debt is payable by instalments, the writ/summons can be issued for an instalment or the whole amount due	
Procedure	The creditor completes: a) 2 copies of the writ of *fieri facias, and* b) a *praecipe* for a writ of *fieri facias.* He sends these to the court office together with the judgment and taxation certificate (if costs are involved)	The creditor completes a form of request for a warrant of execution. He files it at the court with a fee
Execution	The court seals the writ, returns one copy to the creditor who forwards it to the under-sheriff for the county where the debtor resides or carries on his business. The under-sheriff sends it to an officer for execution	The bailiff for the district where the debtor resides or carries on business executes the warrant

The creditor should tell the officer about all seizable items of which he knows, eg: the type and registration number of a car. The relevant court officer seizes the goods and auctions them off to pay the debt and expenses

Items exempt from seizure (*Law of Distress (Amendment) Act 1888 s.4, AJA 1956 s.37*)

◆ Goods on hire or hire-purchase

◆ Tools, books, vehicles and items necessary for the debtor's personal use in his job or business. A vehicle will be seized unless the debtor satisfies the officer that no reasonable alternative transport is possible and that mobility is essential to him

◆ Clothing, bedding, furniture, provisions and household equipment for the basic domestic needs of the debtor and his family. Microwaves (when a conventional oven is present), a stereo, a TV and video are *not* regarded as being vital for domestic survival!!!

Methods of seizure

◆ The following are forbidden for the court officer:
  a) forcible entry to premises, *or*
  b) taking goods from the debtor's person

◆ 'Walking possession' is a method by which the sheriff or bailiff agrees not to remove items if the debtor agrees not to dispose of them or permit them to be moved. (This gives the debtor an extra chance to meet the claim, or oppose seizure)

◆ The debtor may apply for suspension of execution. If he succeeds, the writ of *fieri facias* is suspended conditionally on payment by specified instalments

3. Charging order over land (*Charging Orders Act 1979, RSC Ord.50, CCR Ord.31*)

	High Court	County Court
Preliminary matters	Do an index map search to discover if the land is registered. Search for prior incumbrances and give written notice of the order to prior chargees, to prevent tacking of later advances	
	The court will not make an order if the debtor is up-to-date with instalments	
Which judgments are enforceable and where?	High Court judgments for over £5,000 County Court judgments for over £5,000	All High Court judgments All County Court judgments
Procedure	File at court: a) an affidavit giving: ◆ the name and address of the debtor and of other known creditors, *and* ◆ the amount due, *and* ◆ identification of the land, *and* ◆ verification that the interest is beneficially owned by the debtor b) a draft charging order *nisi*.	
	The district judge considers the application in private and makes a charging order *nisi* if he sees fit	
Register the order *nisi* (if possible)	Register the order with Land Charges Department or HM Land Registry, provided the land is *not* jointly owned. If the land is jointly owned, the order attaches to the debtor's beneficial interest alone, as the debtor's only interest is under a trust, rather than an interest in the land itself. Such an order is not registrable	
Preparation for the hearing for the order absolute	The *nisi* order is endorsed with a hearing date. It is served personally on the debtor, together with a copy of the supporting affidavit at least 7 days before the return day	Same as in the High Court, but service may be personal *or* by post
The hearing for the order absolute	The order absolute is made at the hearing unless the debtor shows cause otherwise. The creditor is granted a charge enforceable by sale	
Enforcement (ie: getting the money)	By sale of the property. This is achieved by fresh proceedings commenced in the Chancery Division	By sale of the property: this is achieved by applying for an order for sale from the County Court only if the debt remaining does *not* exceed £30,000

4. Charging order over securities

The procedure is similar to that for granting an order over land (see above box) but applies to securities instead of land

5. Attachment of earnings order (*Attachment of Earnings Act 1971, CCR Ord.27*)

County Court only - High Court proceedings are transferred to the County Court

Conditions	The debtor is employed (not self-employed or unemployed). The sum due exceeds £50
Application	File an application form ↓ The court informs the debtor of the application and asks him to: ◆ pay the sum due, *or* ◆ file a statement of means form

If the debtor replies

Steps	
1	The court makes a diary entry when the form is returned
2	The court then fixes repayment according to the following 2 guidelines: a) 'normal deduction rate' (this is the amount of money to be deducted), *and* b) 'protected earnings rate' (this is an amount the debtor must be left with - a 'safety net' for the debtor)
3	The order is served on the debtor and the employer by first class post and a copy sent to the creditor
4	The employer must forward to the court: a) the deduction, *and* b) up to £1 for himself for administrative expenses on each deduction under the order (*AtEA 1971 s.7*)
5	If either party objects or the court staff consider that the statement of means has insufficient information, a judge hears the matter, but meanwhile the employer complies with the order unless it is varied
6	If the debtor informs the court of his unemployment or self-employment, the application is dismissed

If the debtor *does not* reply

Steps	
1	The court automatically issues an order to produce a statement of means
2	The bailiff serves this personally on the debtor (If the creditor provides the employer's name and address, the court may ask the employer for a statement of earnings)
3	If the debtor does not respond at all, the court automatically issues a 'notice to show cause' which the bailiff serves
4	Failure to attend a subsequent hearing before a district judge will ultimately lead to committal to prison

6. Garnishee proceedings (*RSC Ord.49, CCR Ord. 30*)

	High Court	County Court
Which judgments are enforceable and where?	Judgment for £50 or more	Judgment for £50 or more Apply to the court which passed judgment
Conditions	A third party (the 'garnishee') owes money to the judgment debtor, who in turn owes money to the creditor. The debt *must* belong to the judgment debtor solely and beneficially. The garnishee must be within the jurisdiction of UK courts	

Application	File at court:
	◆ an affidavit giving:
	  ● the name and last known address of the debtor, *and*
	  ● details of the date and amount of the judgment, *and*
	  ● the sum outstanding *and* details of the garnishee
	◆ a draft garnishee order *nisi*
	↓
	The district judge considers the application *ex parte* and endorses the hearing date on the order. This is the order *nisi*	

Service of the order	◆ There must be personal service on the garnishee, at least 15 days before the day fixed for consideration of the order absolute ◆ The garnishee is bound on service to retain money in his possession until the court ruling ◆ There must be ordinary service on the debtor at least 7 days *after* service on the garnishee and at least 7 days before the hearing date	The same rules apply as in the High Court, but service on the garnishee may be by post. (A garnishee who admits the debt after service may pay the amount into court, whereupon the application for decree absolute is stayed)
The hearing	The district judge has discretion as to whether to make the order absolute. He will usually do so unless liability is disputed	
Costs	**For a successful application:** costs are retained by the creditor, from the money received from the garnishee in priority to the judgment debt **For a failed application:** the court has discretion as to costs and as to whether to award these against the debtor or the judgment creditor	
Special rules for seeking a garnishee order against deposit taking institutions		
Affidavit	In addition to the details above, the affidavit should state the branch where the account is held and the account number	
Service	Service is to the institution's registered head office *and* to the branch where the account is held	
Hearing	The institution usually complies by a letter sent to the court instead of appearing personally. If the institution claims not to hold any money for the debtor, proceedings are stayed unless the creditor disputes this	
Administration	The institution can deduct up to £30 from the repayment, to cover administrative expenses	

N   Appeals

A very simplified table of possible Appeal Courts

Appeal to:	Appeal from:	Leave needed?	Powers on Appeal
County Court (Circuit Judge)	a District Judge in a County Court for interlocutory matters (*CCR Ord.13 r.1(10)*)	No	◆ To set aside judgment ◆ To vary judgment ◆ To remit to the District Judge ◆ To give another judgment ◆ To order a new trial
	a District Judge in a County Court for judgment or final order (*CCR Ord.37 r.6*)		
	a District Judge in a County Court for taxation (*CCR Ord.38 r.24*)		
High Court (Single Judge)	a Master (*RSC Ord.58 r.1(1) Ord. 44 r.12(1)*)	No (*SCA 1981 s.18(1)(f)*)	◆ The court holds a rehearing of the case
	a District Judge in Chambers (*RSC Ord. 58 r.1(1), Ord. 44 r.12(1)*)		
	a Taxing Master (*RSC Ord. 62 r.35*)		
Court of Appeal (*SCA 1981 ss.15-18*)	The High Court	No	◆ To set aside the order of the court ◆ To vary the order of the court ◆ The court has all the powers of the High Court to affirm a judgment or to order a new trial
	a Master or a District Judge exercising trial jurisdiction, eg: for assessment of damages	Yes, third party if bound Yes, if case comes under *RSC Ord.89 r.1B*	
	County Court	This depends (*County Court Appeals Order 1991*)	
House of Lords	Court of Appeal	Yes	
	High Court under the *AJA 1969* 'leap-frog' procedure		
European Court of Justice	Court of Appeal (*RSC Ord.114*)	Any reference is up to the national court	◆ The court can make a ruling on any matter in the Treaty of Rome 1957
European Court of Human Rights	High Court (*RSC Ord.114*)		
	Crown Court		

> **Note:** judicial review as an 'appeal' against decisions is not dealt with in this table

Area of detail - appeal against an interlocutory order (*RSC Ord. 58, CCR Ord.13*)

High Court or County Court

Steps	
1	File a notice of appeal at the court.
2	Within 5 days of the interlocutory order being made, serve the notice on the other parties.
3	The appeal must be heard at least 2 days after service of the notice.
4	There is a rehearing of the application by a judge in chambers.

O The future - the Woolf Report

➤ The Woolf Report proposes a radical upheaval of the entire civil litigation machine.

➤ One of the primary aims of the report is to transfer litigation management from clients and their advisers to the courts.

➤ As yet unimplemented proposals include:

◆ moves to encourage settlement, including greater encouragement for parties to use Alternative Dispute Resolution and mediation (see p.263).

◆ a fast-track justice system for cases under £10,000 with fixed costs (to be heard in the County Court).

◆ a multi-track justice system for other cases.

◆ increased scope for summary judgment.

◆ case management by judges.

◆ timetables for every type of case.

• The value of a case will be inversely proportional to the rigidity of the timetable.

◆ a new post of 'Head of Civil Justice' to be created.

◆ more specialist judges.

◆ far greater use of information technology in the courts.

◆ greater training for judges.

◆ pleadings to be overhauled.

◆ courts to have complete control over expert evidence.

◆ amount of discovery to be set at different levels depending on the complexity of the case.

◆ cross-examination to be by leave of the judge only.

◆ 'payments into court' to be replaced by 'offers of settlement' before the commencement of a claim.

◆ greater use to be made of systems of fixed fees.

◆ changes to rules of costs for successful unassisted litigants against unsuccessful assisted litigants.

◆ mobile courts for rural areas.

◆ larger towns to contain permanent advice centres for civil litigation.

◆ encouragement of the retail sector to appoint more ombudsmen, who would have powers to transfer cases to court. The court would have a power to transfer cases to ombudsmen.

➤ Implemented proposals include:

◆ new limits for small claims arbitration (now generally £3,000 as opposed to the old £1,000 - see p.265).

➤ Sir Richard Scott V-C in a letter to judges pointed out that although the rules in the White Book and the Green Book constrained judges until the advent of the new civil litigation procedure rules from the Civil Procedure Rules Committee (see p.261), judges should interpret the existing rules with the Woolf proposals in mind.

◆ He said that judges should particularly take account of the 4 cornerstones of the new proposed rules - equality, economy, proportionality and expedition.

Criminal Litigation

This chapter examines:

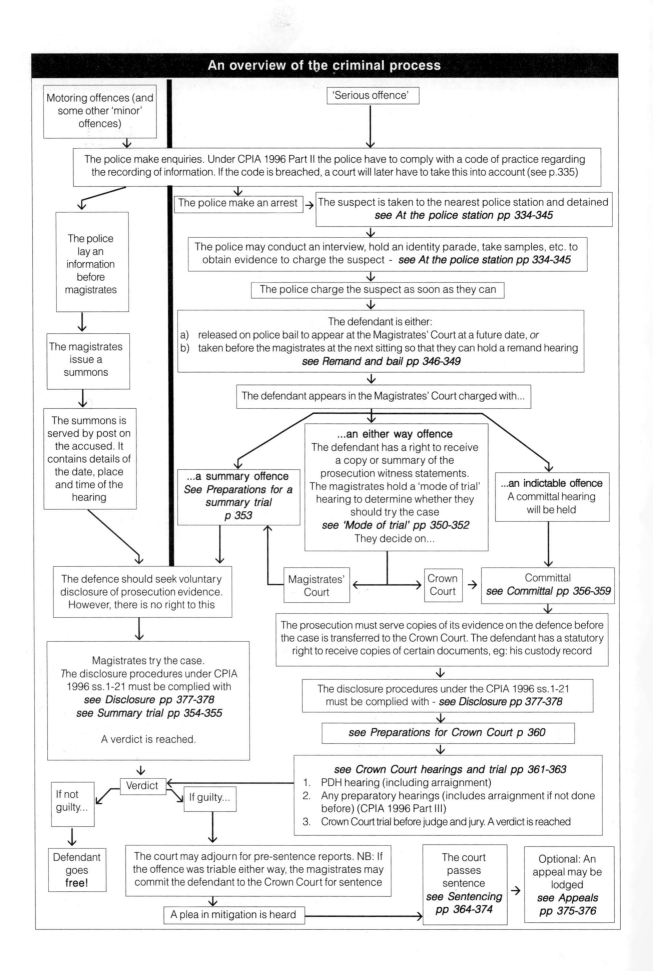

An overview of the criminal process

Motoring offences (and some other 'minor' offences)

'Serious offence'

The police make enquiries. Under CPIA 1996 Part II the police have to comply with a code of practice regarding the recording of information. If the code is breached, a court will later have to take this into account (see p.335)

The police make an arrest → The suspect is taken to the nearest police station and detained *see At the police station pp 334-345*

The police may conduct an interview, hold an identity parade, take samples, etc. to obtain evidence to charge the suspect - *see At the police station pp 334-345*

The police charge the suspect as soon as they can

The defendant is either:
a) released on police bail to appear at the Magistrates' Court at a future date, *or*
b) taken before the magistrates at the next sitting so that they can hold a remand hearing *see Remand and bail pp 346-349*

The defendant appears in the Magistrates' Court charged with...

The police lay an information before magistrates

The magistrates issue a summons

The summons is served by post on the accused. It contains details of the date, place and time of the hearing

...an either way offence
The defendant has a right to receive a copy or summary of the prosecution witness statements. The magistrates hold a 'mode of trial' hearing to determine whether they should try the case
see 'Mode of trial' pp 350-352
They decide on...

...a summary offence
See Preparations for a summary trial p 353

...an indictable offence
A committal hearing will be held

The defence should seek voluntary disclosure of prosecution evidence. However, there is no right to this

Magistrates' Court ← Crown Court → Committal *see Committal pp 356-359*

The prosecution must serve copies of its evidence on the defence before the case is transferred to the Crown Court. The defendant has a statutory right to receive copies of certain documents, eg: his custody record

Magistrates try the case.
The disclosure procedures under CPIA 1996 ss.1-21 must be complied with
see Disclosure pp 377-378
see Summary trial pp 354-355

A verdict is reached.

The disclosure procedures under the CPIA 1996 ss.1-21 must be complied with - *see Disclosure pp 377-378*

see Preparations for Crown Court p 360

see Crown Court hearings and trial pp 361-363
1. PDH hearing (including arraignment)
2. Any preparatory hearings (includes arraignment if not done before) (CPIA 1996 Part III)
3. Crown Court trial before judge and jury. A verdict is reached

Verdict

If not guilty...

If guilty...

Defendant goes **free!**

The court may adjourn for pre-sentence reports. NB: If the offence was triable either way, the magistrates may commit the defendant to the Crown Court for sentence

The court passes sentence
see Sentencing pp 364-374

Optional: An appeal may be lodged
see Appeals pp 375-376

A plea in mitigation is heard

Table of various offences

Offence	Power to arrest without warrant? (PACE s.24)		Type	Magistrates' maximum penalty	Crown court maximum penalty cf: Mandatory sentences p.360
Theft (TA 1968 s.1)	✓		Either way	6 months (TA 1968 s.1(7); s.9(4))	7 years (TA 1968 s.7) Unlimited fine (PCCA 1973 s.10)
Burglary (TA 1968 s.9)	✓		Either way / Indictment*	£5,000 fine (MCA 1980 s.32)	10 (14 years) (TA 1968 s.9(4)) Unlimited fine (PCCA 1973 s.10)
Robbery (TA 1968 s.8)	✓		Indictment	Not applicable	Life (TA 1968 s.8(2)) Unlimited fine (PCCA 1973 s.10)
Harassment, alarm or distress (POA 1986 s.5)	✗ ✓ POA 1986 s.5(4)		Summary	£1,000 fine (POA 1986 s.5(6))	Not applicable
Fear or provocation of violence (POA 1986 s.4)	✗ ✓ POA 1986 s.4(3)		Summary	6 months (POA 1986 s.4(4)) £5,000 fine (POA 1986 s.4(4))	
Actual bodily harm (OAPA 1861 s.47)	✓		Either way	6 months £5,000 fine	5 years (OAPA 1861 s.47) Unlimited fine (PCCA 1973 s.10)
Collective trespass (CJPO 1994 s.61)	✗ ✓ CJPO s.61(5)		Summary	3 months £2,500 fine	Not applicable
Careless driving (RTA 1988 s.3)	✗		Summary	£2,500 fine Endorsement of licence is obligatory Disqualification is discretionary, otherwise endorse 3-9 points Disqualification until a re-test is discretionary	
Dangerous driving (RTA 1988 s.2)	✗		Either way	6 months, £5,000 fine	2 years, unlimited fine
				Disqualification is obligatory Endorsement of offence on licence is obligatory with 3-11 points A re-test before requalifying is obligatory Forfeiture of vehicle is discretionary (PCCA 1973 s.43)	
Taking a conveyance (TA 1968 s.12)	✓		Summary	6 months, £5,000 fine (TA 1968 s.12(2)) Disqualification is discretionary (RTA 1988 Schedule 2)	Not applicable
Aggravated vehicle taking (TA 1968 s.12A)	✓	Either way		6 months, £5,000 fine	2 years (5 years if death results) Unlimited fine
		Summary if aggravating feature is that damage is worth £5,000 or less		and Endorsement on licence is obligatory - endorse 3-11 points Disqualification is obligatory	

Serious arrestable offences (PACE s.116)

➤ Whether an offence is a serious arrestable offence can affect how long someone is detained (see p.336), and can give the police extra powers.

➤ An offence which is 'arrestable' (PACE s.24) is a 'serious arrestable offence' if:
- the offence is serious as defined in PACE Schedule 5 Part I, eg: treason, murder, manslaughter, rape, kidnapping, or

- it is on a list of certain statutory offences in PACE Schedule 5 Part II, eg: causing an explosion likely to endanger life or property, death by dangerous driving, possession of, or use of, or carrying of firearms with certain intents. CJPO s.85 has recently added to the Part II list certain offences to do with obscene material. This list is varied from time to time, or

- the offence led to, or was intended to lead to: a) death, or b) serious injury, or c) serious financial loss (subjectively from the victim's viewpoint), or d) substantial financial gain (from an objective viewpoint).

A At the police station

All references in this section are to PACE, unless otherwise stated. References to the Code are to the PACE Codes of Practice. The Codes do not have statutory force, but in some situations the police are under a duty to comply (eg: s.39(1)).

I	Criminal investigations - code of practice
II	Voluntary attendance
III	Arrest
IV	Detention before charge
V	Interviewing
VI	Inferences from silence
VII	Identification
VIII	Samples (brief overview)
IX	Detention after charge
X	Charges
XI	Other rights at a police station

Safeguards at the police station

➤ **Generally**

◆ Cautions

- Wording: 'You do not have to say anything. But it may harm your defence if you do not mention when questioned something which you later rely on in court. Anything you do say may be given in evidence.' (*C:10*, see pp.338-339)

- A caution *must* be given:

  a) on, or just before, arrest, *and*

  b) on a custody officer authorising detention, *and*

  c) before an interview, *and*

  d) following a break in questioning (*C:10*).

➤ **On interview at a police station**

◆ **Rest:**	for a continuous period of 8 hours in 24 hours, preferably at night (*C:12.2*).
◆ **Drink or drugs:**	no questioning if the suspect is unable to grasp the significance of the questions, *unless* the superintendent or an officer of higher rank authorises it for the protection of people or property (*C:12.3, Annex C*).
◆ **Interview room:**	heated, lighted, ventilated; chair for the defendant to sit on (*C:12.4, 12.5*).
◆ **Breaks:**	at recognised meal times, refreshments every 2 hours (*C:12.7*).
◆ **Identification:**	a policeman must identify himself by name and rank before interview (*C:12.6*).
◆ **Juveniles (under 17):**	accompanied by an 'appropriate' adult (a parent/guardian or social worker) for certain situations (*C:1.7*).
◆ **Mentally disordered:**	accompanied by an 'appropriate' adult (a relative/other responsible person or a special social worker) for certain situations (*C:1.7*).

I   Criminal investigations - code of practice

➤   A code of practice applies for criminal investigations conducted by police officers (*CPIA* ...).

➤   The code provides that there are different functions to be performed by (para 3.1):

◆   the investigator,

◆   the officer in charge of an investigation,

◆   the disclosure officer.

Duty to retain material

➤   The investigator has a duty to retain material obtained in a criminal investigation which may be relevant to the investigation (para 5.1).

Time to retain material

➤   All material which may be relevant to an investigation must be retained until a decision is taken whether to institute proceedings against a person for an offence (para 5.6).

➤   If a criminal investigation results in proceedings being instituted, all material which may be relevant must be retained at least until (para 5.7-5.9):

◆   the prosecutor decides not to proceed with the case, *or*

◆   the accused is acquitted, *or*

◆   the accused is convicted.

●   If the accused is convicted the material must be retained until the latter of:

■   the convicted person is released from custody, *or*

■   6 months from the date of conviction, *or*

■   if an appeal is in progress, the time that the appeal is determined, *or*

■   if the Criminal Cases Review Commission (see p.376) is considering an application:

-   the time it decides not to refer the case to the Court of Appeal,

-   the time that the appeal is determined.

Preparation of schedules (para 6.6 and 7.1)

➤   The following schedules must be prepared and given to the prosectuor if:

◆   the accused is charged, *and*

a)   the offence is triable only on indictment, *or*

b)   the offence is triable summarily *and* the accused is considered likely to plead not guilty, *or*

c)   the offence is triable either way *and*

i)   it is considered that the offence is likely to be tried on indictment, *or*

ii)   it is considered that the accused is likely to plead not guilty at a summary trial.

NB: If, in (b) or (c)(ii) above, it is considered that the accused will plead guilty, and contrary to this, he pleads not guilty, then a schedule must be prepared as soon as practicable.

➤   Material which may be relevant to an investigation, which the disclosure officer believes will *not* form part of the prosecution case must be listed on a schedule (para 6.2).

Non - sensitive material (para 6.3)	Sensitive material (para 6.4)
Material which the disclosure officer does not believe is sensitive must be listed on a schedule of non-sensitive material	Material which is believed to be sensitive must be: ◆ listed on a schedule of sensitive material, *or* ◆ (in exceptional circumstances) revealed to the prosecution.

II   Voluntary attendance

➤ The individual may leave at will (*s.29*).

➤ If the individual is prevented from leaving at will, he must be informed that he is under arrest (*s.29*).

III   Arrest

➤ A suspect should be taken to the police station as soon as possible (*s.30*).

➤ The custody officer (at least a sergeant) must decide to:

a) charge the suspect immediately (*s.37(7)*), *or*

◆ The test is whether:
- there is sufficient evidence for a successful prosecution, *and*
- the officer is satisfied that the suspect has said all he wishes about the possible offence (*C:16.1*).

b) release the suspect (whether on bail or not) without charge (*s.37(7)*), *or*

c) detain the suspect before charge (only if there are special reasons - see Section IV below).

➤ A suspect is treated as arrested if he has returned to a police station to answer to bail (*s.24(7)*).

IV   Detention before charge

➤ Following arrest

◆ Detention is permitted if the custody officer has reasonable grounds to believe *either* (*s.37(2)*):

a) that there is insufficient evidence to charge the suspect and detention is necessary to obtain that evidence by questioning, *or*

b) it is necessary to secure or preserve evidence, or to obtain it by questioning.

➤ The police should interview the suspect as soon as possible and decide immediately after an interview whether a charge will be brought - if no charge is brought, release should be immediate (*s.34(2), s.41(7)*).

Detention timetable (before charge)			Authority: c = custody officer, i = inspector, s = superintendent, m = magistrate	
Monday 1.00 pm	Arrival at the police station. Detention clock begins to run (*s.41(2)(a)(1)*)		Tuesday 1.00 pm cont.	b) it is a serious arrestable offence, *and* c) the investigation is being conducted diligently and expeditiously NB: This new authorisation is only possible if it is: i) before 24 hours from when the detention clock began to run (*s.42(4)*), *and* ii) after the second review	s
Monday 1.10 pm	Detention is 'authorised' by the custody officer under the grounds in *s.37(2)*	c		
Monday 7.10 pm	Latest time for first review of detention - by an inspector. Detention may continue if the original grounds are still valid (*s.40(3)*) NB: The suspect or his solicitor may make representations	i	Wednesday 1.00 am	The authority of the superintendent expires. Charge or release *unless* a magistrate grants warrant of further detention (*s.43*)	m
Tuesday 4.10 am	Latest time for second review; thereafter reviews at 9 hourly intervals (*s.40(3)*)	i	Thursday 1.00 pm	The magistrate's warrant expires. Charge or release *unless* a magistrate grants extension of warrant of further detention (*s.44*)	m
Tuesday 1.00 pm	Charge, or release (*s.41(1)*) *unless* a superintendent has reasonable grounds to believe: a) the grounds in *s.37(2)* still exist, *and*	s	Friday 1.00 pm	Charge or release (*s.44 (3)(b)*) MAXIMUM LIMIT	

V   Interviewing

➤   An interview is the questioning of a person regarding his involvement or suspected involvement in a criminal offence or offences (for which a caution would need to be given under *C:10.1*).

➤   An interview should not be held until the suspect reaches the police station *unless* delay would endanger persons or evidence, alert others, or hinder the recovery of property (*C:11.1*).

➤   For an interview at a police station, see **Safeguards at the police station**, p.334.

➤   The suspect must be reminded that he has a right to free legal advice and that the interview can be delayed for this (*C:11.2*), see p.343.

➤   At the beginning of an interview at a police station, the officer must put to the suspect any significant statement or silence made before the suspect's arrival at the police station, and ask if he would like to confirm, deny, or add anything (*C:11.2A*).

➤   No oppression may be used by police during questioning (*C:11.3*).

➤   When police believe that a prosecution should be brought against the suspect, they must ask the suspect if he wishes to say anything further. If he does not, further questioning is forbidden (*C:11.4*).

➤   A record must be made during an interview (or as soon as practicable after it) (*C:11.5-11.7*).

➤   Interviewing is forbidden after the suspect has been charged, *unless* it is necessary to (*C:16.5*):
a) minimise harm to a person or the public, *or*
b) clarify ambiguity in an answer or statement, *or*
c) enable the defendant to comment on new information unearthed since he was charged.

➤   See interviews and other legal rights (p.345) and advice on the qualified right to silence (pp.338-339).

Recording an interview	
Taped interview (*Code E*)	Non-taped interview

➤ Compulsory *unless* the offence is a purely summary offence
◆ 2 tapes are recorded (*E:2*)
◆ The master tape is sealed, and signed by the suspect and the interviewing officer (*E:2*)
◆ A written summary is sent to the defence
◆ The defence has access to the working copy of the tape:
  • if the defence agrees, the summary is admissible as evidence
  • if the defence objects, a full transcript is made and the seal on the master tape is broken in court
	➤ Summary offences only
	◆ An accurate written record must be made (*C:11.5*)
	◆ The record must be made during the interview or as soon as possible after it (*C:11.5-11.7*)
	◆ An interviewee must read and sign the record (*C:11.10*). Refusals to do so must be recorded. Note: *C:11D* says that if the suspect agrees, the words to be used are 'I agree that this is a correct record of what was said' and he signs with his signature
	◆ The interview record will be served on the defence
	  • If the defence agrees, the record is admissible
	  • If the defence objects, oral evidence is admissible and the officer may refresh his memory from contemporaneous notes
	  • Any refusal to sign should be recorded

Outside the context of an interview
➤ Comments made by the suspect should be: ◆ recorded in writing and signed by the officer concerned, *and* ◆ shown to the suspect, who should have an opportunity to read, time and sign them - any refusal to sign should be recorded (*C:11.13*)

Written statement under caution
This is a prepared statement by the suspect setting out his version of events. It may also be a confession. The rules and the form are set out in *Annex D to Code C*

VI   Inferences from silence

➤   The *CJPO 1994* cuts down on a suspect's/accused's right to remain silent.

➤   The rules are now as follows:

	s.34		s.36	s.37
Situation	a) Before being charged, *and* b) while being questioned under caution by a constable, *and* c) the constable is trying to discover whether, or by whom, an offence has been committed	On a suspect being charged or officially informed he may be prosecuted for an offence	a) On being arrested, *and* b) with an object, substance or mark: i) on his person, *or* ii) in or on his clothing or footwear, *or* iii) in his possession, *or* iv) in any place in which he is, at the time of his arrest, *and* c) the constable reasonably believes that the object, substance or mark has something to do with the suspect participating in a specified offence, *and* d) the constable informs the suspect of his suspicions and asks for an explanation	a) On being arrested, *and* b) the suspect is at a place where a constable reasonably believes that the person's presence may be to do with participation in an offence, *and* c) the constable reasonably believes that the object, substance or mark has something to do with the suspect participating in a specified offence, *and* d) the constable informs the suspect of his suspicions and asks for an explanation
	ss. 34, 36 and 37 will most often apply only to interviews in police stations (because of the general rule prohibiting interviews outside police stations). The usual interview safeguards for police station interviews will, of course, still apply - see pp.334, 336, 343.			
Necessary factors for consequences to apply	a) Suspect fails to mention a fact he might reasonably be expected to mention, *and* b) he later relies on that fact in his defence	Suspect fails to mention a fact he might reasonably be expected to mention	Suspect fails or refuses to provide an explanation	Suspect fails or refuses to provide an explanation
Consequences	The court or magistrates can 'draw such inferences as appear proper' from the silence as applied to: 1 a submission of 'no case to answer' in a trial (see p.354 and p.361) 2 determining the guilt or innocence of a defendant at trial NB: Such inferences must *not* decide the matter alone - there must be other factors too (*CJPO 1994 s.38*)			

➤   If a solicitor does advise the suspect to remain silent for a particular reason, it is advisable to have this reason recorded to avoid 'adverse inferences' at trial - see p.389.

➤   It is wrong to advise clients to answer only some questions but not others, as the *whole* interview will be admissible and the silences will be hard to explain.

Principles from *R v Cowan* [1995] 4 All ER 939

➤ In normal circumstances, the burden of proof of proving the silence and inferences from it, is on the prosecution.

➤ The defendant's entitlement to remain silent is his right and choice.

➤ An inference from a failure to answer questions cannot on its own prove guilt (*CJPO 1994 s.38(3)*)

➤ A tribunal of fact (eg: the trial court) must first have established a case to answer before drawing a s.34 inference.

➤ A tribunal of fact (eg: the trial court) might draw an adverse inference, if despite:

◆ any evidence relied on to explain the silence, *or*

◆ the absence of any evidence to explain the silence,

the tribunal concluded that silence could only sensibly be attributed to:

◆ the defendant having no answer, *or*

◆ the defendant has no answer that would stand up to interrogation.

Advising on silence at police stations

Effect of keeping silent	Risk of damage to client's case (see factors below)	Best advice to a client
Adverse inferences will be drawn	**Low risk** There is no risk or a minimal risk in terms of possible damage to the client from the interview	Advise the client to answer the questions
Adverse inferences may or may not be drawn	**Medium risk** The risk from the interview is that the client might not perform well ormight come across badly	Advise the client to give a written statement
No adverse inferences will be drawn	**High risk** The risk from the interview is that the client will say something damning, possibly because he is frightened, confused or does not understand what is happening	Advise the client not to answer any questions but to remain totally silent or respond 'no comment' to everything that is asked

Factors to consider in evaluating risk

◆ whether an early explanation will avoid the suspect being charged at all
◆ the evidence the police already have - if this is overwhelming, a confession may be advisable to help later in mitigation
◆ the capacity of a suspect to handle the stresses of an interview (eg: maturity, age and psychological ability to handle the interview)
◆ the gravity of the offence
◆ whether the suspect has any prior experience of either questioning or custody

VII Identification

➤ There are identification issues if there is disputed identification evidence (see Disputed identification (Turnbull guidelines) and the warning at trial, p.382).

1 Suspect is not known

➤ Evidence of identity is admissible if the witness is taken to the neighbourhood to identify the suspect (*D:2.17*).

➤ Evidence is *in*admissible if the witness is shown a police photograph (because this reveals to the witness that the suspect has a criminal record).

2 Suspect is known

➤ There are five methods of identification (the first four are listed in *D:2.1*):

1 Identification parade.

2 Group identification.

3 Video identification.

4 Confrontation.

5 Court identification.

➤ The suspect is initially offered a parade. If he refuses (*D:2.3*):

♦ the police may use any of the other methods (*D:2.6*).

♦ the suspect's refusal is noted **and this may be used in evidence against him at trial.**

1 Identification parade

➤ This is held if *either* (*D:2.3*):

♦ the suspect disputes an identification, *or*

♦ the investigating officer considers it would be useful *and* the suspect agrees.

➤ The procedure is set out in *Code D:Annex A* - a summary follows.

➤ It is conducted by a uniformed officer who is an inspector (or higher), and who is unconnected with the investigation (*D:2.2*).

➤ The suspect is told that (*D:2.15*):

a) he has a right to free legal advice, *and*

b) he may have a solicitor or friend present, *and*

c) he or his solicitor may see the first description of the suspect by the witnesses who will attend the parade, *and*

d) he is entitled to refuse, *and* the consequences of refusal (ie: confrontation at trial), *and*

e) he is entitled to know whether the witness has seen any photographs of himself.

➤ 8 persons *in addition* to the suspect take part (*D:8 Annex A*).

➤ Participants must resemble the suspect in height, age, general appearance, position in life (*D:9 Annex A*).

➤ The witness is segregated before and after the parade (*D:12 Annex A*).

➤ The witness must *not* be told if another witness has made an identification (*D:13 Annex A*).

➤ A video recording or colour photograph must be taken of the parade (*D:2.5*).

2 Group identification

➤ The witness is asked whether he recognises the suspect in an informal group of people (usually a public place) (*D:2.7*).

➤ The procedure is set out in *Code D Annex E* - a summary follows.

➤ The suspect must consent, but the police can proceed if necessary without it (*D:2.8*).

➤ It is conducted in a public place (*D:3 Annex E*).

➤ It is conducted by a uniformed officer who is an inspector (or higher), and who is unconnected with the investigation (*D:2.2*).

➤ The suspect is told that:

    a) he or his solicitor may see the first description of the suspect by witnesses who will attend the identification (*D:11 Annex E*), *and*

    b) he may have a solicitor or friend present (but only if he consents to the group identification - there is no such right if he does not consent.) (*D:34*), *and*

    c) he is entitled to refuse, *and* the consequences of refusal (ie: confrontation at trial),

    d) he is entitled to know whether the witness has seen any photographs of himself (*D:Annex A*).

➤ The witness must be able to see others whose appearance is broadly similar to that of the suspect (*D:5 Annex E*).

➤ The witness is segregated before and after the group identification (*D:17 Annex E*).

➤ The witness must *not* be told if another witness has made an identification (*D:15 Annex E*).

➤ A video or colour photograph should be taken of the general scene (*D:7 Annex E*).

3 Video identification

➤ The witness is shown a video tape with several people doing similar things, and asked whether he recognises the suspect.

➤ The suspect's consent is required, but the police can proceed if necessary without it (*D:2.11*).

➤ The procedure is set out in *Code D Annex B* - a summary follows.

➤ It is conducted by a uniformed officer who is an inspector (or higher), and who is unconnected with the investigation (*D:2.2*).

➤ The suspect is told that (*D:2.15*):

    a) he has a right to free legal advice, *and*

    b) he or his solicitor may see the first description of the suspect by the witnesses who will attend the parade, *and*

    c) he is entitled to refuse, *and* the consequences of refusal (ie: confrontation at trial), *and*

    d) he is entitled to know whether the witness has seen any photographs of himself.

➤ At least 8 others *in addition* to the suspect are shown on the film (*D:3 Annex B*).

➤ All the subjects are filmed in the same position, in similar conditions, doing similar things (*D:4 Annex B*).

➤ Only 1 witness views the film at any one time (*D:10 Annex B*).

➤ The witness may freeze the film, and there is no limit on the number of times he may rerun it (*D:11 Annex B*).

➤ The witness must *not* be told if another witness has made an identification.

4   Confrontation

➤ A witness is confronted with the suspect and asked whether this is the correct person (*Code D: Annex C*).

➤ This is conducted by a uniformed officer who is an inspector (or higher), and who is unconnected with the investigation (*D:2.2*).

➤ Consent is *not* required.

➤ This is used if the alternative methods (above) are impracticable.

5   Court identification

➤ The witness is asked whether he recognises the prisoner in the dock.

➤ Consent is *not* required.

➤ Used as a last resort (its evidential value is limited as the witness is 'identifying' a man in the dock).

VIII   Samples (brief overview)

1   Non-intimate samples in police detention (*s.63*)

➤ Nails, non-pubic hair, a swab from the mouth (*s.58*) and saliva.

➤ **When in police detention:** the suspect's consent is *not* needed if one of the following situations apply:

   a)   A superintendent (or higher officer) authorises the taking of the sample which he can only do if:

   i)   he has reasonable grounds for believing that the suspect has committed a 'recordable offence', *and*

   ii)   the search will tend to confirm or disprove a suspect's involvement.

or **b)**   i)   the suspect has been charged with a recordable offence (or informed that he will be reported for such), *and*

   ii)   - the suspect must not have had an intimate sample taken in relation to the offence being investigated, *or*

   - the suspect must not have had a non-intimate sample taken which has proved unsuitable or insufficient for analysis.

or **c)**   the suspect has been convicted of a recordable offence.

   NB: this does not apply to anyone convicted before 10th April 1995 unless the conviction was for certain sexual offences.

   ◆   b and c above also apply if the suspect is not in police detention.

   ◆   If any of a or b or c are not true then the suspect's consent is needed and must be given in writing (*s.63(2)*).

2   Intimate samples in police detention (*s.62*)

➤ Blood, semen, urine, pubic hair, a swab taken from anywhere but the mouth (*s.58*).

➤ Consent is needed unless the suspect has been convicted of a recordable offence.

➤ Refusal means that the jury may draw such inference as they like. (It also currently amounts to corroboration, although this will change when *s.168(3)* and *Schedule 11* of the *CJPO 1994* come into force.)

IX   Detention after charge

➤   One of the three following alternatives applies:

1   The custody officer *must* release the accused (*s.38(1)*):

a) unconditionally (this is an unusual occurrence), *or*

b) on police bail. This might be conditional upon the accused attending court on a particular date, etc. **(This is the most usual and likely occurence.)** Conditions that the police may impose are listed in *BA 1976 s.3A*; these may be set to ensure the accused:

    i)   surrenders to custody, *and*

    ii)   does not commit an offence while on bail, *and*

    iii)   does not interfere with a witness, or obstruct the course of justice in rela⟨...⟩ ⟨him⟩self or another.

    NB: The police have a power of arrest if a suspect fails to answer to police bail (*s.46A*).

2   The custody officer *must* keep the accused in police detention if (*CJPO 1994 s.25*):

➤   ... the suspect is charged with, and has previously been convicted of, one of the following: murder, attempted murder, manslaughter (and has been given a custodial sentence), rape or attempted rape.

➤   He must then be brought before a magistrate as soon as possible (*s.46(1)*).

3   The custody officer *may* keep the accused in police detention if (*s.38(1)*):

a) his name or address is unascertainable or doubtful, *or*

b) detention is necessary because he has reasonable grounds to believe the suspect will fail to appear at court to answer to bail, *or*

c) (if the suspect is arrested for an imprisonable offence), detention is necessary to prevent the suspect committing an offence, *or*

d) (if the suspect is arrested for a non-imprisonable offence), detention is necessary to protect anyone else from physical injury or damage to property, *or*

e) detention is necessary to prevent interference with the administration of justice or the investigation of offences, *or*

f) detention is necessary for the suspect's own protection.

➤   He must then be brought before a magistrate as soon as possible (*s.46(1)*).

➤   Note: 'imprisonable offence' is defined in the *Schedule* to the *BA 1976*.

X   Charges

1   **Summary offences**

➤ The police must 'lay an information' at a Magistrates' Court within 6 months of the commission of the offence (*MCA 1980 ss.18,127*).

➤ An 'information' may only concern one offence, otherwise it is void for duplicity (*Magistrates' Courts Rules 1981 rule 12(1)*).

➤ When an 'information' is laid, the court issues a summons directing the defendant when to appear at court.

2   **Indictable offences (including 'either way' offences)**

➤ An indictment must be drawn up.

➤ It should be drawn up within 28 days of committal, but this time can be extended (*I(P)R 1971 r.5*).

3   **Dangerous or careless driving (*RTOA 1988 s.1*)**

➤ If there is no accident as a result of these offences, there can be no conviction for these offences, unless as a preliminary:

a)   the defendant is warned at the time of the offence that a prosecution is possible, *or*

b)   a summons is served on the defendant within 14 days, *or*

c)   within 14 days, a notice of intended prosecution is served on the registered keeper (at the time of the offence) of the vehicle.

4   **Summary offence linked with indictable or 'either way' offence: see 'Mode of trial', p.350.**

A solicitor's role at the police station
A solicitor should...

➤ ... go prepared. Take:

◆ *PACE, Codes of Practice*, the Law Society's *Guide to the Conduct of a Solicitor at a Police Station*, copies of a *Green Form* and a legal aid application form.

◆ a letter to be handed to the suspect explaining the solicitor's offer to advise the suspect if he requests it.

◆ a standard proforma for taking instructions.

◆ a pen and paper.

◆ cigarettes (tobacco!), as many people request these.

➤ ... keep account of passing time with reference to the time limits for detention.

➤ ... attend any interview at which the client is questioned.

➤ ... listen to his client, and offer advice calmly; his role is to advise.

➤ ... ask for the investigating officer; seek details of why a client is detained and evidence against him.

➤ ... ask, as soon as he arrives at the police station, to see the custody record - the police must agree under *C:2.4*.

➤ ... keep a contemporaneous note of all that occurs. The solicitor may later be a witness!

➤ If a relative or friend has requested the solicitor's presence, it is up to the suspect whether or not to see the solicitor.

XI   Other rights at a police station

Right to legal advice

Attending the police station voluntarily

➤ There is an unconditional right to legal representation (*C: Note 1A*).

➤ There is a right to legal advice in person, in writing, or by telephone, from the suspect's own solicitor (or from a duty solicitor, which is free of charge) (*C: 6.1*).

On arrest (*PACE s.58*)

➤ This is a right which a suspect has on arrival at the police station, and subsequently whenever he requests it.

➤ Legal advice from a *particular* solicitor can be delayed for up to 36 hours from the time detention was originally authorised if:

   a)   a superintendent, or a higher officer, authorises the delay, *and*

   b)   the investigation concerns a serious arrestable offence, and

   c)   there are reasonable grounds for believing that this will prevent interference with evidence or people, alert others still at large, or hinder the recovery of property.

➤ If legal advice is delayed because of a concern that a particular solicitor will pass a message on to someone inappropriate, access to another solicitor on the duty solicitor scheme must be offered (*Code C, Annex B, Paragraph B4*).

➤ The defendant must be told of an attempt by a solicitor (on the solicitor's arrival) to contact him (*Code C:6.15*).

At interview

➤ A person who has requested legal advice may not be interviewed (or continue to be interviewed) unless he has received that legal advice, unless *either* (*C:6.6*):

   a)   legal advice is barred under *PACE s.58* (see above) *or:*

   b)   a superintendent, or a higher officer has reasonable grounds for believing that
     i)   delay will harm persons or property, *or*
     ii)   waiting for a solicitor's arrival will unduly delay the investigation (*C:6.6*), or

   c)   an inspector authorises an interview and *either:*
     i)   the nominated solicitor cannot be contacted or will not attend, *and* the defendant refuses the duty solicitor, *or*
     ii)   the defendant changes his mind and agrees in writing or on tape (*C:6.6*).

➤ The solicitor may intervene during the interview (*C:6D*):
   ◆ to clarify or challenge improper questions.
   ◆ to advise the client not to reply.
   ◆ to give further legal advice.

➤ The interviewer may not exclude a solicitor from the interview unless a superintendent is first consulted and he first speaks to the solicitor.

Reminders of the right to legal advice (*C: 6.5*)

➤ There is a right to be reminded of the right to legal advice:

   ◆ before the start or recommencement of an interview at a police station.
   ◆ before a review of detention.
   ◆ after a charge if:
     ● a police officer wants to draw a suspect's attention to the written or oral statement of another person, *or*
     ● if further questions are to be put to a suspect about the offence (see p.336).
   ◆ before an identification parade or a request for an intimate body sample.

Right to have someone informed of arrival at the police station (*s.56*)

➤ The right can be delayed for up to 36 hours if:

   a)   a superintendent, or higher officer, authorises the delay, *and*
   b)   the investigation concerns a serious arrestable offence, *and*
   c)   there are reasonable grounds for believing that this will prevent interference with evidence or people, alert others still at large, or hinder the recovery of property.

B Remand and bail

I	Remand generally - in custody or on bail ?
II	Bail

I Remand generally - in custody or on bail ?

➤ Remand is considered at every adjournment. It is to ensure the defendant will appear at the next hearing.

➤ The defendant has a right to bail - it is for the prosecution to show why this should not be granted.

1 Remand before conviction or committal for trial (*MCA 1980 s.128*)

a) In custody

  ➤ For a maximum of 8 days at a time.

  ➤ This can be extended for another 8 days at a time if another hearing approves it.

  ➤ However, custody can be extended for 8 days at a time *without the defendant being present* at the hearing if:
  - the defendant consents, *and*
  - a solicitor is acting, *and*
  - there have not been more than 3 consecutive remand hearings in the defendant's absence.

  ➤ A court can remand a defendant in custody for up to 28 days (*MCA 1980 s.128A*) if:
  - it has previously remanded him in custody for the same offence, *and*
  - he is in court, *and*
  - it is able to set a date for when the next stage of the proceedings will occur, so he can be remanded until then.

  ➤ The maximum time limits for the cumulative detention for an either way or indictable offence are (*PO(CTL)R 1987 (as amended)*):
  - for up to 56 days in a Magistrates' Court before a summary trial.
  - for up to 70 days before committal proceedings.
  - for up to 112 days in the Crown Court between committal for trial and the start of the trial.
    - Solicitors should mark the Crown Court file with the 112 day period so as to make an application for bail when this period has expired.

  NB: The defence owes a duty to its client not to warn the prosecution when the time limits are about to run out.

  NB: Thereafter bail must be granted, unless an extension is 'reasonable' in the circumstances.

b) On bail

  ➤ The maximum time limit is unlimited (!) with the defendant's consent.

2 Remand after committal (*MCA 1980 s.6(3)*)

a) In custody: until the case is heard (this can take months).

b) On bail: on conditions set by the court until the case is heard.

3 Remand after conviction, until the next hearing (most probably sentencing) (*MCA 1980 s.10(3)*)

a) In custody: The Magistrates' Court may remand in custody for up to 3 weeks.
   The Crown Court may remand until the next hearing, whenever that is.

b) On bail: The Magistrates' Court can remand on bail for up to 4 weeks.
   The Crown Court may remand until the next hearing, whenever that is.

II   Bail

A. Right to bail *(BA 1976 s.4)*

➤   The following have the right to bail:

a) defendants before conviction, *and*

b) defendants after conviction during an adjournment for reports, *and*

c) offenders before magistrates for breaching a probation or community service order.

➤   BUT there is *no* right to bail for a defendant before the Crown Court awaiting:

a) sentence, *or*

b) appeal against conviction or sentence.

➤   There is *no* right to bail for someone with a previous conviction for murder, attempted murder, manslaughter, rape or attempted rape and who is now charged with any one of these (*BA 1976 4(8), CJPO 1994 s.25*).

B. Procedure for bail hearings

Steps	
1	The prosecution objects to bail (see box overleaf).
2	The defence applies for bail.
3	Evidence is called (rules of evidence do not apply - *Re Moles* [1981] Crim.L.R. 170).
4	The court decides on remand in custody or on bail.
5	The court must give the defendant a note stating whether or not bail will be granted, together with reasons why and a list of any conditions it imposes.

Duty to hear further applications (*MCA 1980 ss.5,10,18* and *SCA 1981 s.81*)	
Magistrates' Court	Crown Court

◆ There is a duty on the court to hear further applications for bail if a defendant is still in custody and the right to bail still applies
  • On a first re-hearing the court hears any argument of fact or law
  • On subsequent hearings, the court can only hear new arguments
	◆ There is a duty on the court to hear further applications for bail if a defendant is still in custody and the right to bail still applies
	  • On a first re-hearing the court hears any argument of fact or law
	  • On subsequent hearings, the court can only hear new arguments
	◆ There is a duty to hear further applications from those in custody:
	  • prior to trial, sentence and appeals *and*
	  • when a Magistrates' Court has refused bail after an adjournment *and* a certificate of full argument is presented to the court
	    ▪ Whenever the case has *not* been sent to the Crown Court for trial, sentence or appeal, a certificate of full argument is required from the Magistrates' Court before a bail hearing is possible

Hearing before a High Court judge in chambers (a last resort if neither of the above courts grant bail) (*CJA 1967 s.22*)	
✘ No criminal legal aid is available - this is a civil matter	✘ As a matter of practice, no court will grant bail later if the judge in the High Court refuses it

C. Refusing bail

➤ The court considers various grounds in relation to the following 5 factors:

a) the nature and seriousness of the offence, and the method of dealing with the defendant for it.

b) character, antecedents (criminal records are admissible on bail applications), associations and community ties.

c) record for previous grants of bail (criminal records are admissible on bail applications).

d) the strength of evidence against the defendant (except for considering ground **1f** below).

e) any other relevant factors.

➤ Strictly speaking, these factors only apply to **1a** and **1b** below, but in practice, they apply to all the grounds.

➤ The set of grounds that applies depends upon on whether an offence is imprisonable *or* not imprisonable.

1 Imprisonable offences

➤ Grounds for refusing bail (*BA 1976 Schedule I Part I*)

a) ◆ Failure to surrender to custody, *and/or*

◆ probability of committing another offence, *and/or*

◆ likelihood of interfering with witnesses or obstructing the course of justice in relation to the defendant himself *or* to others.

b) The offence is an indictable offence or an either way offence *and* the defendant was on bail at the time of the offence.

c) The defendant's own protection, or if he is young, his welfare.

d) The defendant is in custody pursuant to a court sentence.

e) Not enough information has been obtained about the defendant.

f) The defendant was arrested for absconding or breaking the bail conditions set for *this* offence.

g) Adjournment for enquiries or a report for which the defendant needs to be kept in custody.

2 Non-imprisonable offences

➤ Grounds for refusing bail (*BA 1976 Schedule I Part II*)

a) The defendant's previous conduct on bail suggests he would not surrender.

b) The defendant's own protection, or if he is young, his welfare.

c) The defendant is in custody pursuant to a court sentence.

d) Adjournment for enquiries or a report for which the defendant needs to be kept in custody.

Prosecution objections to bail (*B(A)A 1993 s.1(1)*)
If new evidence comes to light after bail has been granted by a Magistrates' Court for an either way or indictable offence, the prosecution can ask the court to reconsider the decision to grant bail (*BA 1976 s.5B*).
If a Magistrates' Court does grant bail against prosecution objections to a defendant charged with, or convicted of: ◆ an offence punishable by 5 years' or more imprisonment, *or* ◆ taking a conveyance, *or* ◆ aggravated vehicle taking ... ... the prosecution can appeal to a Crown Court judge.

D. Bail conditions (*BA 1976 s.3*)

➤ The court may impose conditions to ensure that the defendant:

 ◆ surrenders to custody, *and*

 ◆ does not commit an offence while on bail, *and*

 ◆ does not interfere with a witness, or obstruct the course of justice in relation to himself *or* another, *and*

 ◆ makes himself available for enquiries to be made to assist the court in dealing with him for the offence.

➤ Conditions which the court *may* set include:

 ◆ **surety:** the sum depends on a surety's wealth, character, previous convictions, or his proximity to the defendant. The surety pays the money to the court if the defendant defaults on his bail conditions - no money is paid to the court on bail being granted.

 ◆ **security:** the defendant surrenders his money, chattels, passport, etc.

 ◆ **reporting:** to the police station at specified intervals.

 ◆ **curfew:** compulsory attendance between certain times at a certain place.

 ◆ **residence:** this may be, for example, in a bail hostel. (If so, the defendant may also be required to comply with bail hostel rules (*BA 1976 s.3(6ZA)*.)

 ◆ **non-communication with a prosecution witness:**

   this may involve alternative accommodation for the defendant (possibly in a bail hostel) if a prosecution witness is a relative living in the same house.

➤ Conditions which the court *must* set are:

 ◆ if the defendant is accused of murder, a requirement that he be medically examined (unless previous reports of his medical condition are satisfactory) (*BA 1976 s.6A*).

E. Surrender and absconding

Refusing Bail
Bail conditions
surrender
absconding

1 Surrender

➤ A defendant granted bail must surrender at the time and place appointed (*BA 1976 s.6*).

➤ Failure to surrender is an offence unless there is a 'reasonable' cause - the defendant has the burden of proof (*BA 1976 ss.6(2)*, *6(3)*). The court may issue a warrant for the defendant's arrest (*BA 1976 s.7(1)-(2)*).

➤ Breach of a bail condition entitles the police to arrest the defendant - the breach is not an offence, but it may provide a ground on which bail can be withdrawn (*BA 1976 s.7*).

2 Absconding

➤ Magistrates may impose a fine of up to £5,000 and a sentence of up to 3 months (*BA 1976 s.6(7)*).

➤ The Crown Court may impose an unlimited fine and a sentence of up to 1 year (*BA 1976 s.6(7)*).

C Mode of trial on an 'either way' offence

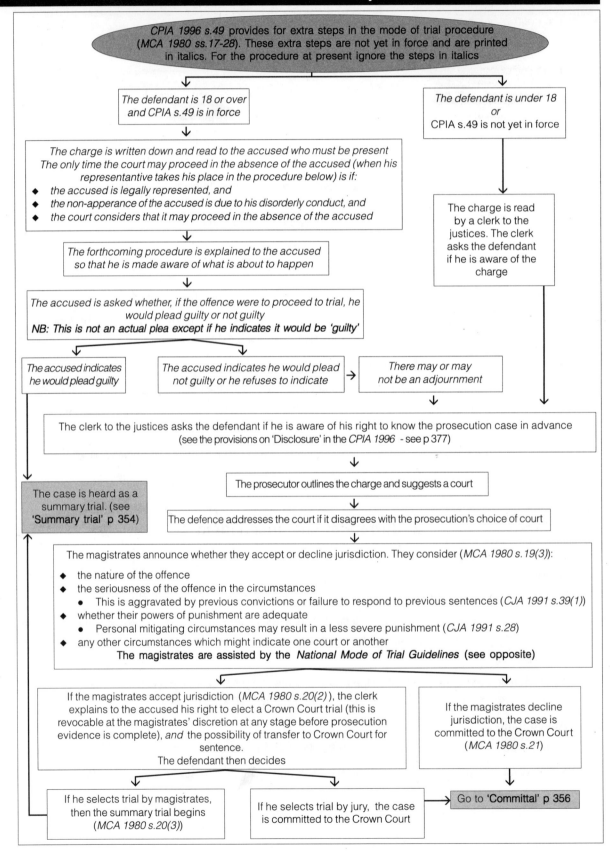

CPIA 1996 s.49 provides for extra steps in the mode of trial procedure (*MCA 1980 ss.17-28*). These extra steps are not yet in force and are printed in italics. For the procedure at present ignore the steps in italics

---

The defendant is 18 or over and CPIA s.49 is in force

The charge is written down and read to the accused who must be present The only time the court may proceed in the absence of the accused (when his representantive takes his place in the procedure below) is if:
- *the accused is legally represented, and*
- *the non-apperance of the accused is due to his disorderly conduct, and*
- *the court considers that it may proceed in the absence of the accused*

The forthcoming procedure is explained to the accused so that he is made aware of what is about to happen

The accused is asked whether, if the offence were to proceed to trial, he would plead guilty or not guilty
NB: This is not an actual plea except if he indicates it would be 'guilty'

The accused indicates he would plead guilty

The accused indicates he would plead not guilty or he refuses to indicate → *There may or may not be an adjournment*

The defendant is under 18 or CPIA s.49 is not yet in force

The charge is read by a clerk to the justices. The clerk asks the defendant if he is aware of the charge

---

The clerk to the justices asks the defendant if he is aware of his right to know the prosecution case in advance (see the provisions on 'Disclosure' in the *CPIA 1996* - see p 377)

The prosecutor outlines the charge and suggests a court

The case is heard as a summary trial. (see **'Summary trial' p 354**)

The defence addresses the court if it disagrees with the prosecution's choice of court

The magistrates announce whether they accept or decline jurisdiction. They consider (*MCA 1980 s.19(3)*):
- the nature of the offence
- the seriousness of the offence in the circumstances
  - This is aggravated by previous convictions or failure to respond to previous sentences (*CJA 1991 s.39(1)*)
- whether their powers of punishment are adequate
  - Personal mitigating circumstances may result in a less severe punishment (*CJA 1991 s.28*)
- any other circumstances which might indicate one court or another
  The magistrates are assisted by the *National Mode of Trial Guidelines* **(see opposite)**

If the magistrates accept jurisdiction (*MCA 1980 s.20(2)*), the clerk explains to the accused his right to elect a Crown Court trial (this is revocable at the magistrates' discretion at any stage before prosecution evidence is complete), *and* the possibility of transfer to Crown Court for sentence.
The defendant then decides

If the magistrates decline jurisdiction, the case is committed to the Crown Court (*MCA 1980 s.21*)

If he selects trial by magistrates, then the summary trial begins (*MCA 1980 s.20(3)*)

If he selects trial by jury, the case is committed to the Crown Court

Go to **'Committal' p 356**

Defendant elects summary trial and subsequently changes his mind before all the prosecution evidence has been heard

The magistrates have discretion to refer the case to the Crown Court (*MCA 1980 s.25*).

National Mode of Trial Guidelines

a) Magistrates should assume that the prosecution version of the facts is correct.
b) If there is a complex question of law or fact, then magistrates should consider transferring the matter to the Crown Court.
c) If more than one defendant is charged, each may select a different court regardless of the choice of the other(s). Advance indication for preference for a particular court by one defendant in such a case is irrelevant at the mode of trial hearing stage - *R. v. Ipswich Justices ex parte Callaghan* 159 J.P. 748.
d) The magistrates must assume there will be a summary trial unless:
   ◆ magistrates' sentencing powers will be insufficient (although they may later change their minds about whatever decision they reach (*R. v. Flax Bourton Magistrates' Court, ex parte Commissioners of Customs & Excise* (1996) The Times, 6th February)), *or*
   ◆ one of the aggravating factors below exists.

List of aggravating factors, per offence, that suggest a summary trial is *not* suitable

1 **Burglary**
   ◆ Dwelling: daytime - house occupied, night-time - house usually occupied, series of offences, soiling, damage, vandalism, professional hallmarks, high value of unrecovered property (greater than £10,000). NB: Violence or the threat of violence means it *must* be sent to the Crown Court (*MCA 1980 Schedule I para 28(c)*).
   ◆ Non-dwelling: fear or violence caused to anyone lawfully on the premises, professional hallmarks, substantial vandalism, high value of unrecovered property (greater than £10,000).
2 **Theft**
   ◆ Breach of trust by one in authority, committed or disguised in a sophisticated manner, organised gang, vulnerable victim, high value of unrecovered property (greater than £10,000).
3 **Assault** (*OAPA 1861 ss.20, 47*)
   ◆ Weapon likely to cause serious injury, more than minor injury by kicking or head-butting, serious violence to a victim whose work brings him in contact with the public.
4 **Dangerous driving**
   ◆ Defendant on alcohol or drugs, grossly excessive speed, racing, prolonged course of such driving, related offences.

Summary offences linked to indictable offences which may be tried in the Crown Court

CJA 1988 s.40(1): Defendant accused of...	CJA 1988 s.41(1): Defendant accused of an offence which is...
common assault, taking a conveyance, driving whilst disqualified, certain types of criminal damage, assaulting a prison custody officer or a secure training centre custody officer *and* a) i) the summary offence is based on the same facts or evidence as the indictable offence, *or* ii) the summary offence is of a similar character to the indictable offence with which the defendant is also charged, *and* b) facts/evidence relating to the offence were disclosed in an examination taken before a justice in the presence of the person charged	a) punishable with imprisonment or involves obligatory or discretionary disqualification from driving, *and* b) it appears to the court that the summary offence arises out of circumstances which are the same as, or connected with, those giving rise to the offence that is triable 'either way'

Subsequent procedure for trial

The Crown Court must treat the summary offence as an indictable offence, but must deal with the offender as a Magistrates' Court would have done	Evidence for the summary offence is not heard at committal. In the Crown Court the procedure depends on the plea: a) guilty plea: the court sentences for the summary offence with the same powers as a Magistrates' Court b) not-guilty plea: the summary offence is sent to the magistrates for trial

Advice to a client about selecting a court for trial

➤ There are 3 main factors to consider, together with their pros and cons:

1 Conviction

✗ Magistrates may be seen as case-hardened, and may already be familiar with a police officer or with the defendant.

✓ Conviction is thought by some to be less likely in a Crown Court where juries can be seen as sympathetic.

Note: There is no objective proof to support either of these contentions.

2 Evidence

✗ Magistrates decide matters of fact and law (ie: when giving a verdict, magistrates must attempt to 'forget' evidence which they have heard before holding it to be inadmissible).

✓ A Crown Court judge rules on the law, the jury decides matters of fact (ie: the jury is sent out while the judge decides evidential matters, so the jurors never hear evidence unless it is admissible).

3 Costs, stress, speed, sentence

✓ In the Magistrates' Court these will be lower, eg: less publicity means less stress.

✗ In the Crown Court these will be higher.

✗ If the defendant is remanded in custody, then he is likely to be detained for much longer before a Crown Court trial.

D   Preparations for a summary trial

➤   The solicitor should:

- ensure that he has a copy of the custody record (see *Code C:2.4,* p.344).

- ensure, where identification is disputed, that he has a copy of the original description from which the identification was made - see p.340 and note points on p.382.

- obtain a copy of the charge sheet.

- interview the client and take a detailed statement and full instructions as soon as possible.

- interview witnesses: take a proof of evidence signed and dated by the witness.
  - When interviewing a prosecution witness, it is good practice to have an independent party present, and to write to the prosecution to let them know the interview has taken place; this avoids any suspicion of putting pressure on a witness.
  - During an interview, challenge the witness's version of events. (**Note:** 'preparing a witness' for cross-examination is forbidden.)

- visit the area of the alleged offence, and prepare plans if appropriate.

- seek expert evidence: if the client is legally aided, obtain the Legal Aid Board's authorisation for the expenditure (cf: p.387 for disclosure of expert evidence).

- write to the prosecution asking for:
  - disclosure of the prosecution case. In either way cases, the prosecution provides this before a mode of trial hearing (*Magistrates' Court (Advance Information) Rules 1985 r.4*).   The prosecution does not *have* to disclose in purely summary trials, but a solicitor should request it.
    - *CPIA 1996 ss.1-21* contain the new disclosure rules (see p.377). It is likely that the *Magistrates' Court (Advance Information) Rules 1985* may be amended to lessen disclosure at this stage. However, this does not stop a solicitor asking the prosecution for voluntary disclosure at this point as the main statutory disclosure will be after plea.
  - details of any evidence the prosecution possesses which is favourable to the defence.
  - a record of any prosecution interviews with the defendant.
  - the names and addresses of witnesses the prosecution will not call.
  - a list of the witnesses interviewed by the police who the prosecution do *not* intend to call.
  - a statement of the defendant's criminal record. (This should be checked for inaccuracies.)
  - details of the criminal records of prosecution witnesses and co-defendants.

- put the prosecution case to the defendant, and note any comments he makes on it.

- decide whether witnesses should attend. (**Note:** where a witness will not need to be cross-examined, a statement submitted under *CJA 1967 s.9* will be sufficient - see pp.386-387.)

- if a witness's presence is desirable, write to him asking for written confirmation that he will turn up at a specified time.
  - If this confirmation is not forthcoming, the solicitor should write to the clerk using the unanswered letter as proof that the witness is unlikely to attend of his own accord. The clerk issues a summons which is served personally on each witness (*MCA 1980 s.97*) or he can summons the releuctant witness to give a deposition (*MCA 1980 s.97A*).
    - The summons should be issued as soon as reasonably practicable, else delay could amount to a refusal to grant the process.

E Summary trial

1 Joinder

➤ Co-defendants tried on one 'information' for the same offence are tried together, unless there is a conflict of interest. The conviction of one does not prevent the acquittal of the other (eg: *Barsted v. Jones* (1964) 124 JP 400).

➤ Defendants tried on separate 'informations' can be tried together if the defence agrees. But the court always has discretion to consider that as the facts are the same, or that as the offences are similar and related, a joint trial is 'in the interests of justice' (*Chief Constable of Norfolk v. Clayton* [1983] 2 AC 473).

2 Defect in process

➤ If the defence is misled by an error in the 'information', summons or warrant, then it may seek an adjournment to rethink its case. It has no other remedy in these circumstances (*MCA 1980 s.123*).

3 Procedure

Steps	
1	The charge is read to the defendant *(unless summary trial has started straight from a mode of trial hearing where the charge has already been read to the defendant - CPIA 1996 [not yet in force])*.
2	The defendant pleads 'guilty' *(except if he has already indicated this on a mode of trial hearing (MCA 1980 s.17(6) [not yet in force]))* or 'not guilty'. He can alter this at any time before sentence.
	◆ If the plea is 'guilty', the court proceeds to sentence (perhaps holding a Newton hearing beforehand, see p.374).
3	The statutory disclosure procedure applies from this point (see p.377) and the disclosure of expert evidence procedure applies too (see p.387).
4	The prosecution makes an opening speech outlining the facts and issues (*MCR 1981 r.13(1)*).
5	The prosecution calls evidence.
6	The legal representative of the defence must tell the court at this point that the defendant will give evidence, else the magistrate will give a 'silence warning' (see p.389) (*CJPO 1994 s.35*).
7	The defence may submit 'no case to answer' (*Practice Direction (Submission of No Case)* [1962] 1 WLR 227) (see p.357 for a discussion of this) if *either:*
	• there is no evidence to prove an essential element of the offence, *or*
	• the prosecution evidence is so discredited under cross-examination *or* so manifestly unreliable that no reasonable tribunal could convict on it.
	◆ For the effect of 'adverse inferences' on a defendant's decision not to testify, see p.389.
	◆ The prosecution may reply to this submission.
	◆ If the submission is accepted, the case is dismissed, otherwise step 8 applies.
8	The defence may make an opening speech, or may immediately move to calling evidence (*MCR 1981 r.13(2)-13(6)*).
9	If the defence evidence throws up unforeseeable surprises, the prosecution can seek leave to call more evidence.
10	If the defence did *not* make an opening speech, it has the right to address the court last.
11	The magistrates reach a majority verdict and then consider an appropriate sentence and costs.

Points of law at the trial

➤ A magistrate's clerk can advise the bench on matters of law, but not of fact.

➤ If a point of law is raised at any stage, the other party always has a right to reply.

---

4   Costs

a) **The defendant is acquitted (not legally aided)** *(POA 1985 s.16(1))*.

➤   Costs are met from central funds, *unless* the defendant brought suspicion on himself by his own conduct *(POA 1985 s.16(7))*.

b) **The defendant is acquitted (legally aided).**

➤   Costs are not met by central funds, but by the Legal Aid Board. Any contribution the defendant has made may be refunded *(POA 1985 s.21(4A))*.

c) **The defendant is convicted.**

➤   Costs must be met by the defendant where the court is satisfied that he has the means and ability to pay *(POA 1985 s.18(1))*. (Costs must be met by the Legal Aid Board if the offender is an assisted person.) The court makes an order for a specified sum *(POA 1985 s.18(3))*.

F   Committal

➤ Committal proceedings are the means by which a Magistrates' Court decides if there is sufficient evidence to send a defendant to the Crown Court, after:

   ◆ he comes before a Magistrates' Court charged with an offence triable on indictment, *or*

   ◆ he comes before a Magistrates' Court charged with an offence triable either way.

➤ There are 2 types of committal hearing, both in *MCA 1980 s.6 - s.6(1) committal and s.6(2) committal.*

Why choose a *s.6(2)* committal?

➤ A *s.6(2)* committal is quicker and will usually be preferable.

➤ A *s.6(2)* committal can only take place if:

a) all the evidence tendered by the prosecution at this stage is in the form of the following (see p.358 for in-depth definitions):

   ◆ written statements, *or*

   ◆ documents or exhibits referred to in the written statements, *or*

   ◆ depositions, *or*

   ◆ documents or exhibits referred to in depositions, *or*

   ◆ any particular document allowed by statute, *and*

b) the defendant has a solicitor acting for him, *and*

c) the defence do not claim that the prosecution has insufficient evidence.

Why choose a *s.6(1)* committal?

Prosecution reasons:	Defence reasons:
◆ identification is at issue - the Attorney General has advised that a *s.6(2)* committal is only suitable if the prosecution, defence and court are satisfied as to the reliability of the identification evidence	◆ to submit no case to answer, *or* ◆ to obtain publicity. This may help to trace witnesses.

Committal procedure

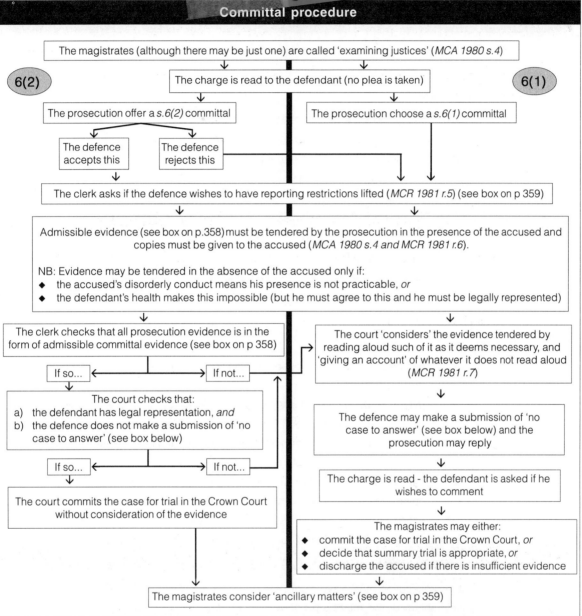

The magistrates (although there may be just one) are called 'examining justices' (*MCA 1980 s.4*)

6(2)   The charge is read to the defendant (no plea is taken)   6(1)

The prosecution offer a *s.6(2)* committal   The prosecution choose a *s.6(1)* committal

The defence accepts this   The defence rejects this

The clerk asks if the defence wishes to have reporting restrictions lifted (*MCR 1981 r.5*) (see box on p 359)

Admissible evidence (see box on p.358) must be tendered by the prosecution in the presence of the accused and copies must be given to the accused (*MCA 1980 s.4 and MCR 1981 r.6*).

NB: Evidence may be tendered in the absence of the accused only if:
- the accused's disorderly conduct means his presence is not practicable, *or*
- the defendant's health makes this impossible (but he must agree to this and he must be legally represented)

The clerk checks that all prosecution evidence is in the form of admissible committal evidence (see box on p 358)

The court 'considers' the evidence tendered by reading aloud such of it as it deems necessary, and 'giving an account' of whatever it does not read aloud (*MCR 1981 r.7*)

If so...   If not...

The court checks that:
a) the defendant has legal representation, *and*
b) the defence does not make a submission of 'no case to answer' (see box below)

The defence may make a submission of 'no case to answer' (see box below) and the prosecution may reply

If so...   If not...

The charge is read - the defendant is asked if he wishes to comment

The court commits the case for trial in the Crown Court without consideration of the evidence

The magistrates may either:
- commit the case for trial in the Crown Court, *or*
- decide that summary trial is appropriate, *or*
- discharge the accused if there is insufficient evidence

The magistrates consider 'ancillary matters' (see box on p 359)

Test for a submission of 'no case to answer'

➤ *R. v. Galbraith* [1981] 1 WLR 1039 - taken at its highest, could a jury convict on the evidence?
- This 'depends on the view to be taken of a witness's reliability, or other matters which are generally speaking within the jury's province, and where *one possible view* of the facts is that there is evidence on which the jury could properly convict [and if all these apply, then a submission will fail]'.

➤ *Practice Direction (Submission of No Case)* [1962] 1 WLR 227 (there is some doubt if this applies to committal as well as to a summary trial) - says that to succeed in a submission of 'no case to answer', one must show *either* that:
- evidence in support of an essential element of the offence is absent, *or*
- the case is so unreliable that a jury could not possibly convict.

Admissible committal evidence

➤ Admissible committal evidence is evidence that is tendered **by, or on behalf of, the prosecutor,** *and is*:

- ◆ **a written statement**, *or*
  - this is a statement that:
    - purports to be signed by the person making it, *and*
    - contains a declaration by that person that:
      - it is true to his best knowledge and belief *and*
      - if tendered in evidence the person would be liable to prosecution if it contained anything he knew to be false or untrue, *and*
    - has been given together with any documents or exhibits it refers to (or copies have been given) (these must be inspectable if copies are not available) to each of the other parties before being tendered by the prosecutor, *and*
    - contains the defendant's age (but only if he is under 18).

- ◆ **a deposition**, *or*
  - this is a document that:
    - has been sent to the prosecutor after the new *MCA 1980 s.97A(9)* procedure, *and*
      - (**NB:** the new *MCA 1980 s.97A* procedure is when a statement of evidence has been taken from someone who will not voluntarily give evidence at committal and is made to do so pursuant to a witness summons, or is arrested to do so - see p.353.)
    - has been given together with any documents or exhibits it refers to (or copies have been given) (these must be inspectable if copies are not available) to each of the other parties before the inquiry as 'examining justices' begins.

- ◆ **documents or other exhibits referred to in written statements or depositions**, *or*

- ◆ **a documentary hearsay statement** (*CJA 1988 ss.23-24* - see p.386), *or*
  - the prosecution must have signed a certificate that there is reasonable cause to believe the evidence may be properly used at trial.

- ◆ **any other document allowed by statute.**

A document is anything in which any
information of any description
is recorded
(*MCA 1980 s.5A(6)*)

Test for committal to the Crown Court

➤ The test is whether, having heard the case, there is sufficient evidence to put the accused on trial for indictment (ie: if a reasonably minded jury, properly directed, would convict on the evidence provided). If so, then the magistrates will commit the case to the Crown Court for trial.

Ancillary matters

1   Witness summons to ensure witnesses attend the Crown Court trial

> ➤ If the defendant is committed for trial in the Crown Court, the Magistrates' Court must remind the defendant of his right to object (within 14 days) to any statement or deposition being read at trial instead of the witness giving oral evidence (which of course allows cross-examination *(MCR 1981 r.8, CCR r.22)*).

> ◆ The general rule, if the defendant does not object, is that all statements of a particular wintess forming part of the committal bundle will be read at trial instead of the witness being called to give oral evidence.

> ➤ *Criminal Procedure (Attendance of Witnesses) Act 1965 s.2 contains the rules for issue of a witness summons. This ensures that any witness with material evidence will attend trial.*

> ◆ *CPIA 1996 ss.66-67 is not yet in force, but when it is, the present CP(AW)A 1965 s.2 procedure will be replaced by the following procedure:*

> • *parties must make an application for a witness summons as soon as reasonably practicable after committal, and they may need a detailed affidavit for this.*

> • *the court may also make a witness summons of its own motion.*

> • *Crown Court rules (yet to be made) will govern the procedure.*

> • *a Crown Court judge will punish contempt.*

2   Legal aid *(LAA 1988 s.20)*

> ➤ The defence applies for an extension of legal aid to cover a Crown Court trial. It also confirms whether or not the defendant's financial circumstances are altered. The grant of legal aid by the court is discretionary (see p.12).

3   Bail *(MCA 1980 s.6(3))*

> ➤ Bail is usually extended until trial. If the defendant is in custody, a bail application can be made.

4   Fix a date for a PDH

> ➤ The magistrates fix a date for a plea and directions hearing (see pp.361-362).

Reporting restrictions (*MCA 1980 s.8*)

> ➤ The press may report the names of defendants/witnesses, the charge and result of the proceedings.

> ➤ The press may not report evidence (to prevent a jury being prejudiced).

> ➤ A single defendant may ask that restrictions be lifted (eg: to obtain publicity to help trace witnesses).

> ◆ If a co-defendant requests, restrictions are lifted if it is 'in the interests of justice' (*MCA 1980 s.8(2A)*).

G Preparations for Crown Court hearings and trial

Between committal and trial

1 Make all relevant preparations as for summary trial (see p.353) *and get the committal bundle.*

2 Apply to the Crown Court or a High Court judge in chambers for bail, if necessary.

3 Brief counsel (see box below for '*Format of a brief to counsel*').

4 Ensure that the prosecution has turned over all relevant material (following the disclosure procedure - see p.377).

5 Ensure that witnesses can attend as planned.

➤ This is achieved by applying for any necessary witness summons (see p.xxx).

6 Exchange any expert witness statements with the prosecution as soon as practicable after committal (*The Crown Court (Advance Notice of Expert Evidence) (Amendment) Rules 1997*) (see p.387)

6 Take instructions on mitigation.

7 Obtain disclosure of materials unused by the prosecution (a common law right and cf: *R. v. Ward* (1993) 96 Cr.App.Rep. 1).

Format of a brief to counsel

1 **Heading:** case, title, court, legal aid certificate or fee, case number.

2 List of enclosures

➤ Eg: legal aid order, list of previous convictions, bundle of witness statements, comments on witness statements, bail notice, indictment, custody record.

3 Prosecution allegations

➤ Direct counsel to specific allegations in the witness statements.

➤ Define facts which are not in dispute.

4 Defence allegations

➤ Give a brief statement of the relevant law.

➤ Apply the law to the circumstances of the case.

5 Note any evidential problems

➤ Character: *CEA 1898 s.1(f)(ii)-(iii)* (Note the effect that any 'unspent' convictions may have on the defendant's character (see p.381). Rules for when convictions are spent are in *ROA 1974*).

➤ Evidence: admissible as an exception to the rule against hearsay (ie: opinion, *res gestae*, etc).

➤ Confessions: point out any grounds for exclusion.

➤ Corroboration: note where this is needed, and highlight any suitable evidence, see p.382.

➤ Discuss briefly the reasons for and against the defendant testifying, see p.381. State:

a) why the difficulty is likely to arise, *and*

b) any consequences which follow.

6 **Mitigation:** give any relevant information.

7 **Request:** 'Would counsel please advise ... and attend court on ... at ...'.

H Crown Court hearings and trial

1 The indictment

➤ The prosecution is responsible for seeing that an indictment is drafted.

➤ An indictment is a statement of offences (called 'counts') with which an accused is charged.

➤ A 'count' is an individual charge.

➤ Each count in an indictment must allege only one offence (*Indictment Rules 1971 r.4(2)*).

2 Joinder (*Indictment Rules 1971 r.9*)

➤ Charges for any offences may be joined in the same indictment if the charges are founded on the same facts, or a part of a series of offences of the same, or a similar character.

➤ 2 or more accused may be joined in one indictment.

3 Procedure

A Plea and Directions Hearing ('PDH') is held (see flowchart on p.362) - this includes arraignment. This also falls into the definition of a pre-trial hearing (see box left below)

Any pre-trial hearings are held to rule on:
♦ questions of admissibility of evidence, *and/or*
♦ questions of law
((*CPIA 1996 ss.39-43*)
NB: Stringent reporting restrictions apply to such hearings similar to those for preparatory hearings

Any preparatory hearings may be held (*CPIA 1996 ss.28-38*) (see box on p.363)

Steps	The trial
1	The prosecution makes an opening speech outlining the facts and the issues of the case.
2	The prosecution calls evidence.
3	The legal representative of the defence must tell the court at this point that the defendant will give evidence, else the judge will give a 'silence warning' (see p.389) (*CJPO 1994 s.35*).
4	The defence may submit that there is no case to answer. ♦ The prosecution may reply to this submission. ♦ If the submission is accepted the case is dismissed, otherwise proceed to the next step.
5	If the defence will be producing evidence other than just from the accused, they have a right to an opening speech, otherwise they do not.
6	The defence calls evidence.
7	If defence evidence throws up unforeseeable surprises, the prosecution can seek leave to call more evidence.
8	The prosecution delivers its closing speech to the jury.
9	The defence delivers its closing speech to the jury.
10	The judge sums up and directs the jury as necessary.
11	The jury must deliver a unanimous verdict. ♦ A majority verdict (11:1, 10:2) is acceptable if unanimity is impossible after a reasonable time (minimum of 2 hours) (*Juries Act 1974 s.17(1)*).
12	If the jurors cannot agree on a unanimous or a majority verdict, a retrial may be held. The prosecution have discretion to ask for a retrial.

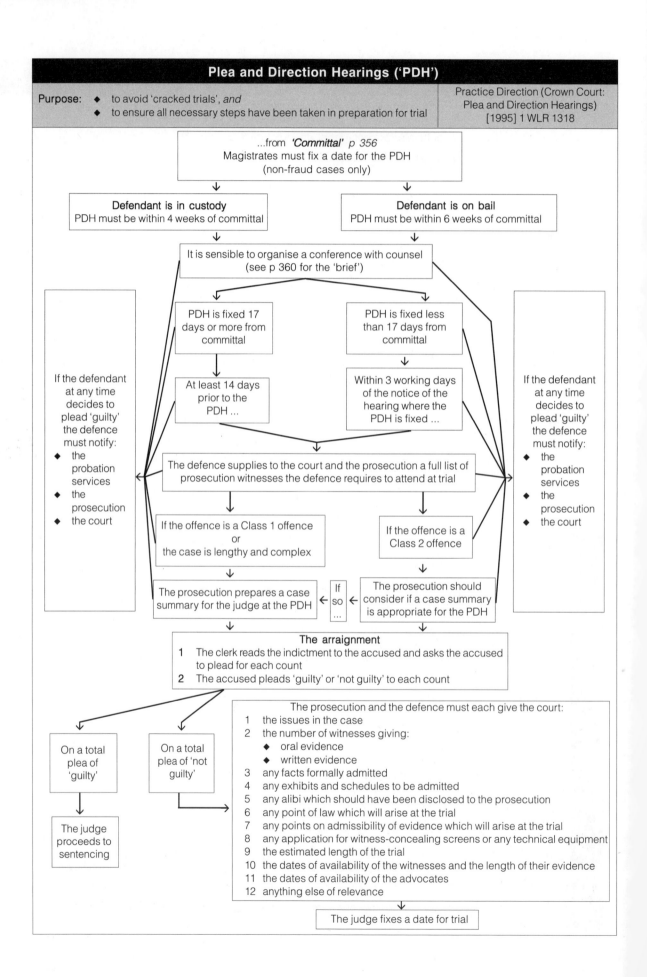

Plea and Direction Hearings ('PDH')

Purpose:
- to avoid 'cracked trials', *and*
- to ensure all necessary steps have been taken in preparation for trial

Practice Direction (Crown Court: Plea and Direction Hearings) [1995] 1 WLR 1318

...from *'Committal' p 356*
Magistrates must fix a date for the PDH
(non-fraud cases only)

Defendant is in custody
PDH must be within 4 weeks of committal

Defendant is on bail
PDH must be within 6 weeks of committal

It is sensible to organise a conference with counsel
(see p 360 for the 'brief')

PDH is fixed 17 days or more from committal

PDH is fixed less than 17 days from committal

At least 14 days prior to the PDH ...

Within 3 working days of the notice of the hearing where the PDH is fixed ...

If the defendant at any time decides to plead 'guilty' the defence must notify:
- the probation services
- the prosecution
- the court

The defence supplies to the court and the prosecution a full list of prosecution witnesses the defence requires to attend at trial

If the defendant at any time decides to plead 'guilty' the defence must notify:
- the probation services
- the prosecution
- the court

If the offence is a Class 1 offence
or
the case is lengthy and complex

If the offence is a Class 2 offence

The prosecution prepares a case summary for the judge at the PDH

If so ...

The prosecution should consider if a case summary is appropriate for the PDH

The arraignment
1. The clerk reads the indictment to the accused and asks the accused to plead for each count
2. The accused pleads 'guilty' or 'not guilty' to each count

On a total plea of 'guilty'

On a total plea of 'not guilty'

The judge proceeds to sentencing

The prosecution and the defence must each give the court:
1. the issues in the case
2. the number of witnesses giving:
   - oral evidence
   - written evidence
3. any facts formally admitted
4. any exhibits and schedules to be admitted
5. any alibi which should have been disclosed to the prosecution
6. any point of law which will arise at the trial
7. any points on admissibility of evidence which will arise at the trial
8. any application for witness-concealing screens or any technical equipment
9. the estimated length of the trial
10. the dates of availability of the witnesses and the length of their evidence
11. the dates of availability of the advocates
12. anything else of relevance

The judge fixes a date for trial

Preparatory hearings (*CPIA 1996 ss.28-38*)

➤ Any time after committal but before a jury has been sworn, a Crown Court judge may hold a preparatory hearing (in a non-fraud case only), if he decides that a trial will be so complex or so long that there will be a substantial benefit for one of the following purposes:
- ◆ to identify the issues likely to be material to the verdict of the jury.
- ◆ to assist the jury's comprehension of such issues.
- ◆ to expedite proceedings before the jury.
- ◆ to assist the judge in the management of the trial.

➤ The hearing starts with arraignment (see p.362) (unless it has been done before, eg: at the PDH).

➤ The powers of the judge at a preparatory hearing are (*s.31*):
- ◆ to rule on the admissibility of evidence.
  - • There may be an appeal to the Court of Appeal (only with leave of the judge or the Court of Appeal) (*s.35*). No jury may be sworn until after the appeal is heard.
- ◆ to rule on a question of law.
  - • There may be an appeal to the Court of Appeal (only with leave of the judge or the Court of Appeal) (*s.35*). No jury may be sworn until after the appeal is heard.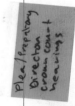
- ◆ to order the prosecutor to give a written statement of:
  - a) the principal facts of the prosecution case, *and/or*
  - b) witnesses, *and/or*
  - c) exhibits, *and/or*
  - d) a proposition of law on which the prosecutor will rely, *and/or*
  - e) the consequences of the above.
- ◆ to order, *but only following any order to the prosecution to give a statement*, the defence to give the prosecution and the court a statement of:
  - • its defence in general terms and the principal matters in dispute with the prosecution, *and/or*
  - • written notice of objections to the prosecution case statement, *and/or*
  - • written notice of points of law it might raise, *and/or*
  - • written notice of points of admissibility of evidence.
- ◆ to order the prosecution to prepare the case in a form that the jury will understand.
- ◆ to order the prosecution to give a list of documents or matters with which it agrees.
- ◆ to order the prosecution to change its case if there are valid objections raised after the written statement ordered above.

➤ The judge must warn the accused of the consequences of later departing from the case outlined in the defence statement above (*s.31(8)*).
- ◆ The consequences are that at trial a jury may draw 'adverse inferences' following:
  - • the judge's comment on this, *and/or*
  - • other parties' comments on this (with leave).
  - NB: The judge must point out that the jury must have regard to the extent of departure from the case and any justifications for such departure (*s.34*).

Reporting restrictions (*CPIA 1996 ss.37-38*)

➤ There is no reporting allowed of the preparatory hearing (or an appeal from it) until after trial unless a judge authorises it. The following details are allowed to be reported however:
- ◆ the identity of the court and the name of the judge.
- ◆ the details of the accused and witnesses.
- ◆ the details of the offence(s).
- ◆ the name of counsel and solicitors.
- ◆ the details of any adjournment.
- ◆ the details of any bail arrangements.
- ◆ the details of whether legal aid was granted or not.

I   Sentencing powers

NB: *All sentences are subject to the statutory limits laid down for particular offences.*

NB: *The rules in this chapter apply to adults only unless youth are mentioned specifically.*

> I   Custodial sentences
> II   Suspended sentences
> III   Fines
> IV   Community sentences
> V   Discharges
> VI   Motoring penalties
> VII   Ancillary orders
> VIII   Custodial sentences for youth

I   Custodial sentences

A. Main principles

1   First custodial sentence

> ➤ The offender cannot be given a custodial sentence for the first time if he is not legally represented during the sentencing process *unless* (*PCCA 1973 s.21(1)*):
>   ◆ a legal aid application has been refused under the means test, *or*
>   ◆ the offender has not applied for legal aid despite previous opportunity to do so.

2   Imposition

> ➤ A custodial sentence can be imposed if ...
>   a) ... the 'seriousness test' is satisfied (*CJA 1991 s.1(2)(a)*), *or* ...
>   ◆ The seriousness test is satisfied if: a 'combination of the offence and one or more offences associated with it was so serious that only a...[custodial] sentence can be justified for [it]' (*CJA 1991 s.1(2)(a)*).
>   ◆ Factors that can affect seriousness are:
>   • information about the circumstances of the offence (*CJA 1991 s.3(3)*).
>   • previous convictions: 'take into account any previous convictions of the offender or any failure of his to respond to previous sentences' (*CJA 1991 s.29(1)*).
>   • if the offence was committed on bail, the 'court shall treat the fact that it was committed in those circumstances as an aggravating factor' (*CJA 1991 s.29(2)*).
>   b) ... the offence was a 'violent' or 'sexual' offence (defined in *CJA 1991 s.31(1)*) and the public needs protection from serious harm (*CJA 1991 s.1(2)(b)*), *or* ...
>   ◆ The factors relevant for this are:
>   • information about the circumstances of the offence or the offender (*CJA 1991 s.3(3)*).

364

- imprisonment is necessary to protect the public from physical or psychological injury.
- previous convictions.
- likelihood of long-term danger.

c) ... the offender refuses a community sentence which requires his consent (*CJA 1991 s.1(3)*).

- ◆ A community sentence is: probation, community service, combination order, curfew order, attendance centre order.

3 Length (*CJA 1991 s.2*)

➤ This term should:

a) be 'such term as the court considers is commensurate with the seriousness of the offence or the combination of the offence and one or more offences associated with it', *and*

b) be, for violent or sexual offences, for 'such longer term as the ... court [considers] necessary to protect the public from the offender' (but not more than the statutory maximum for the offence), *and*

c) have regard to mitigating circumstances (*CJA 1991 s.28(1)*).

4 Limits on length

➤ **Magistrates' Court:** maximum 6 months unless an offence presents a lower maximum penalty (*MCA 1980 s.31*). The minimum is 5 days (*MCA 1980 s.132*).

- ◆ There is a maximum of 12 months for 2 offences triable either way (*MCA 1980 s.32*).

➤ **Crown Court:** up to the maximum set by statute for the offence.

NB: *C(S)A 1997 s.9(3) [not yet in force] says that time served on remand in custody, is counted as time served as part of sentence **unless** remand was concurrent with an existing term of imprisonment (under a set of rules that are yet to be made) or it is unjust not to give effect to this.*

5 *Early release under C(S)A 1997 [not yet in force]*

➤ *A prisoner may be released early on compassionate grounds if the Home Secretary considers there are exceptional circumstances.*

➤ *If a prisoner is sentenced for a term of greater than 2 months and less than 3 years, he may qualify for early release days for good behaviour.*

➤ *If a prisoner is sentenced to a term of 3 years or more and the prisoner has served 5/6 of his sentence, the Parole Board may recommend the prisoner for release.*

NB: *In certain circumstances, early release may be subject to a release supervision order which is a type of probation order subject to certain conditions.*

Custodial Sentences

B. Mandatory sentences under C(S)A 1997 [not yet in force]

1   Life (s.2)

> If:

  a) a person is 18 or over at the time of the offence, and

  b) a person has previously been convicted of:

   ♦ attempt to, conspiracy to, incitement or solicitation of murder, or

   ♦ manslaughter, or

   ♦ wounding or grievous bodily harm, or

   ♦ certain firearms offences, or

   ♦ robbery with a real or imitation firearm, and

  c) a person is convicted a second time of any one of the above list (although it does not have to be the same offence second time round),

  then a court must impose a life sentence unless there are exceptional circumstances.

2   Minimum 3 years (s.4)

> A court must sentence a convicted burglar to a minimum of 3 years for a third domestic burglary.

II   Suspended sentences (PCCA 1973 s.22)

---

1   Imposition

> Under certain circumstances a court may suspend a custodial sentence.

> The court must decide to immediately imprison, but due to certain *exceptional* circumstances does not do so (ie: it is not to be used to frighten a small-time offender into behaving himself).

> A suspended sentence may be combined with a fine, compensation order, or community sentence.

2   Activation (PCCA 1973 s.23)

> The sentence becomes activated on a subsequent conviction for an imprisonable offence within the suspended sentence's 'operational period'.

> A court has discretion not to activate a suspended sentence in full (or at all) if in the circumstances this would be unjust (ie: the new offence is trivial and unconnected with the original offence, *or* the new offence was committed towards the end of the operational period).

> An activated sentence runs consecutively with any new term which the court imposes.

Suspended sentencing powers	
Magistrates' Court	Crown Court
➤ Imprisonment term limits are: up to 6 months (unless a particular offence presents a lower maximum penalty) ➤ Imprisonment term limits are: consecutive sentences of up to 1 year in aggregate for 2 or more either way offences *(MCA 1980 s.32)* ➤ The court may suspend the sentence of imprisonment over the same 'operational period' as the Crown Court *(PCCA 1977 s.23)* **Note:** If a Crown Court has imposed a suspended sentence and an offender is subsequently convicted of an offence in the Magistrates' Court, he should normally be sent to the Crown Court for the activation of the original sentence and the new sentence *(PCCA 1973 s.24(2), CJA 1967 s.56)*.	➤ Imprisonment term limits are: up to the maximum term set by statute for the offence ➤ The court may suspend, for between 1 and 2 years (called the 'operational period'), a sentence of imprisonment not exceeding 2 years *(PCCA 1973 s.22)*

III Fines (CJA 1991 s.18)

➤ Before fixing a sum the court must:

a) inquire into the offender's financial circumstances. (The court is empowered to order the defendant to provide a statement of means (*CJA 1991 s.18(1)*) called 'a financial circumstances order' (*CJA 1991 s.20(1)*)), *and*

b) ensure that the penalty reflects the seriousness of the offence (*CJA 1991 s.18(2)*), *and*

c) consider the case circumstances, including the state of an offender's finances insofar as they are known, or appear to the court (*CJA 1991 s.18(3)*).

◆ The offender's finances can lead to a reduction or increase in the amount of the fine.

➤ If the offender is under 18, the parents are liable to pay the fine (*CYPA 1933 s.55*).

➤ The court has the power to make an attachment of earnings order to ensure that the fine is paid (*CPIA 1996 s.53*).

◆ Consent of the offender is required.

IV Community sentences (CJA 1991 s.6)

1 Imposition

➤ The court considers:

a) whether an offence (or combination of one or more associated offences) is serious enough to warrant a community sentence, *and*

b) whether particular order(s) are most suitable for a particular defendant, *and*

c) whether the restrictions on liberty are commensurate with the seriousness of the offence (and any associated offences).

◆ Seriousness is ascertained with reference to the same criteria as those used for imprisonment (see above p.364).

➤ For certain orders a pre-sentence report is needed (*CJA 1991 s.7*).

➤ For crimes against property and minor violence, the court must be satisfied that the offence is too serious for a financial penalty.

2 Breach of a community sentence

➤ Magistrates can revoke an order which they imposed.

➤ The Crown Court alone may revoke the order if it imposed the original sentence.

➤ Penalties for non-compliance: a) a fine, *or* b) if non-compliance is wilful and persistent, then custody (see *CJA 1991 Schedule 2*).

➤ If the defendant re-offends, re-sentencing is possible.

Types of community sentence					
Order	Probation	Community service	Combination	Curfew	Attendance centre
Statutory authority	*PCCA 1973 s.2*	*PCCA 1973 s.14*	*CJA 1991 s.11*	*CJA 1991 s.12*	*CJA 1982 ss.17-19*
Age	16 or over	16 or over	16 or over	16 or over	Under 21
Consent of offender needed?	✓	✓	✓	✓	✗
Combine with suspended sentence?	✓ By means of a suspended sentence supervision order	✓	✓	✓	✓
Combine with fine?	✓	✓	✓	✓	✓
Description	The offender must be under the supervision of a probation officer and must comply with probation requirements	The offender must perform unpaid work	This is a combination of a probation order and a community service order	This specifes a time and place for a curfew. The court appoints someone to monitor the offender	The order specifies a time and place for the offender to partake in a specified activity
Period	6 months to 3 years	40 - 240 hours	1 - 3 years' probation 40 - 100 hours unpaid work	Up to 6 months for a period between 2 and 12 hours per day	Maximum 3 hours a day up to a different aggregate maximum depending on age
Grounds for, and aims of, the order and restrictions that the order imposes	For any offence where there is no fixed sentence, *and* the court feels that it is desirable *either* to: a) secure the defendant's rehabilitation, *or* b) protect the public from harm, *or* c) prevent the offender committing further offences 'Probation requirements' can include: ◆ treatment for drug dependency or psychiatric illness, *and* ◆ residence requirements, *and* ◆ supervision, *and* ◆ attendance at a probation centre	The offender is convicted of an imprisonable offence, *and* the offender must be a suitable person to do work, *and* there must be work available The aim is to restrict leisure time, and make reparation to the community for the offence	The offender is convicted of an imprisonable offence, *and* the court believes that the order will: a) help rehabilitate the offender, *and* b) protect the public from harm, *and* c) prevent further offences being committed	For any offence where there is no fixed sentence. Electronic monitoring may be used (*CJA 1991 s.13(1)*). The aim is to prevent the offender reoffending *The C(S)A 1997 s.43 [not yet in force] allows a curfew order to be made for a person of any age. However, if the person is less than 16 the order can only be made for up to 3 months*	The offender is convicted of an imprisonable offence The aim is to deprive the offender of leisure This was introduced with 'football hooligans' in mind

➤ Generally the courts decide on the appropriate community sentence using the following 'rules':
   ◆ the offence warrants the punishment
   ◆ the order is suitable for the offender
   ◆ restrictions on liberty are commensurate with the seriousness of the offence(s)

V   Discharges *(PCCA 1973 s.1A)*

➤ A court can issue a discharge if in the circumstances (the nature of the offence, the defendant's character), punishment is inexpedient.

   ◆ **An absolute discharge:** if the offender is morally blameless, but technically guilty.

   ◆ **A conditional discharge:** if the offender has a previously clean record, the offence is trivial, and the publicity and court appearance are sufficient ordeal.

      • A conditional discharge is for up to 3 years only.

      • If the offender commits any offence during this time, he may be re-sentenced for the original offence.

A summary of non-community sentence sentencing provisions		
Penalty	Imposition	Effect
Custody	➤ Seriousness test ➤ Protect the public from violent/sexual offences ➤ Community sentence refused	➤ Prison if aged over 21 ➤ If aged under 21, sent to a young offender's institution (see p.372)
Suspended sentence	➤ *Not* for those aged under 21 ➤ When the court has decided to imprison but there are 'exceptional' circumstances	➤ Court has discretion whether to activate the sentence
Fine	➤ Seriousness of the offence ➤ Circumstances of the case	➤ Consider the offender's financial circumstances when deciding to increase or decrease the fine

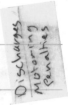

VI   Motoring penalties

1   Endorsement

➤ This is mandatory for i) dangerous driving, ii) aggravated vehicle taking, iii) careless driving.

➤ Conviction for 2 (or more) offences on the same occasion leads to an endorsement for the offence with the 'higher' number of points allowed.   However, the court may wish to exercise its discretion and award more than just the points for the 'higher' offence *(RTOA 1988 ss.28(4)-28(6))*.

2   Disqualification

   a) **Obligatory** (for at least 1 year): for i) dangerous driving, ii) aggravated vehicle taking.

   b) **Discretionary** (for a period): i) careless driving, ii) taking a conveyance, iii) theft of a motor vehicle.

c) Under the penalty points system (*RTOA 1988 s.35*)

➤ If the offender has no previous disqualification of at least 56 days (imposed within 3 years of the commission of the offence now being sentenced), the minimum period of disqualification is 6 months.

♦ If there is one previous disqualification, disqualification is for 1 year.

♦ If there are 2 or more previous disqualifications, disqualification is for a minimum of 2 years.

➤ Penalty points are dealt with first.

♦ If there are 12 or more penalty points from:

• the current conviction (disregarding any order for disqualification for committing the offence) *plus*

• points previously endorsed for offences within 3 years immediately before the commission of the present offence,

THEN disqualification is obligatory.

➤ Points prior to a previous disqualification are ignored.

➤ The court will go on to consider discretionary disqualification if the driver is not automatically disqualified by having 12 points or more.

d) *C(S)A 1997 [not yet in force]: if convicted of an offence where the sentence is fixed by law or a mandatory sentence is imposed (see p.366) the court may disqualify a driver for as long as it thinks fit.*

3   Avoiding disqualification

a) Avoiding obligatory disqualification or obligatory endorsement

➤ A 'special reason' is present.

➤ This is a mitigating circumstance (eg: a boomerang thrown across the windscreen).

➤ 'Special reasons' are connected with the commission of the offence, but are *not* personal to the offender (*Whittal v. Kirby* [1947] KB 194).

➤ A 'special reason' is not anything which could constitute a defence to the charge in law.

b) Avoiding discretionary disqualification

➤ *Any* mitigating factor relevant to the offence should be used to avoid discretionary disqualification.

➤ The factor may be *either* connected with the circumstances *or* personal to the offender. (For example, an obligatory situation or loss of job is relevant here.)

c) Avoiding disqualification under the points system

➤ Disqualification is mandatory unless there are mitigating circumstances.

➤ All circumstances are relevant except (*(RTOA 1988 s.35(4))*:

i) the triviality of the offence.

ii) hardship (unless exceptional).

iii) circumstances taken into account to avoid or reduce disqualification under the points system during the last 3 years.

Note: i) a driver can have 7-12 points and escape disqualification.

ii) disqualification wipes a licence clean of all the old points.

iii) if 2 offences are committed simultaneously, both of which carry a point penalty, the court only adds the 'higher' of the penalties to the licence, unless it sees fit to order otherwise.

VII Ancillary orders

1 **Compensation order** *(PCCA 1973 ss.35-38)*

➤ The order is for the offender to pay compensation to a victim.

➤ This order is *not* available for motoring offences (the victim can seek redress from the offender's insurers).

➤ Magistrates' limit: £5,000 *(MCA 1980 s.40(1))*; Crown Court: unlimited.

➤ The court has the power to make an attachment of earnings order to ensure that the compensation is paid *(CPIA 1996 s.53)*.

♦ Consent of the offender is required.

2 **Forfeiture order** *(PCCA 1973 s.43)*

➤ Property in the offender's possession, or control, is forfeit by this order if the property is:

a) used for committing or facilitating the offence, *or*

b) intended for use in connection with the offence, *or*

c) held unlawfully.

3 **Confiscation order** *(CJA 1988 & PCA 1995)*

➤ An order confiscates the proceeds of crime.

➤ The prosecution have a right to insist on this order.

➤ Interest is payable on unpaid orders, with custody in default.

➤ The prosecution can apply for a revaluation of the offender's proceeds of crime for up to 6 years after conviction.

➤ The court may assume that any of the offender's goods that were obtained or held up to 6 years previously are the proceeds of crime in cases where:

♦ the offender has been convicted of 2 or more acquiring offences at one time, *or*

♦ the offender has been convicted of 1 acquiring offence on one occasion and another such offence within the previous 6 years.

➤ NB: The *Drug Trafficking Act 1994 s.2* deals with confiscation of profits from lucrative drug crimes.

4 **Restitution order** *(TA 1968 s.28)*

➤ The order is to compensate, or restore to a victim, goods stolen from him.

5 **Costs order** *(POA 1985 s.18)*

➤ On conviction, such costs as are 'just and reasonable' may be awarded to the prosecution and are payable by the offender.

➤ On acquittal where the defendant is not legally aided, the court can order his costs to be paid from central funds. This will usually be done unless, for example, the acquittal was on a technicality *or* the defendant brought suspicion on himself by his conduct *(POA 1985 s.16, Practice Direction (Crime Costs)* [1991] 1 WLR 498).

➤ On acquittal, contributions paid by a legally aided defendant may be repaid (subject to the above).

6   **Deferment of sentence** *(PCCA 1973 s.1)*

➤ Passing a sentence may be deferred for up to 6 months.

➤ The offender must consent.

➤ If the offender is convicted during the interval of another offence, he can be sentenced for both offences. The court will have the same powers as on conviction for the original offence.

➤ The power to defer a sentence is used to assess:

◆ the offender's conduct after conviction, *or*

◆ any change in the offender's circumstances (marriage, etc).

➤ The court specifies the conduct it expects, and the sentence it intends to impose if this standard of behaviour is not reached.

7   **Committal to the Crown Court for sentence** *(MCA 1980 s.38)*

➤ The offender must be aged over 18.

➤ The conviction must be for an either way offence *and* when:

a) the offence (or a combination of associated offences) is so serious that a punishment greater than that which a Magistrates' Court is authorised to impose, is warranted, *or*

b) the offence is a violent or sexual offence, and a custodial sentence is necessary to protect the public from serious harm, *or*

c) the offender unexpectedly asks for previous offences to be taken into consideration. This is rare and is usually the result of evidence (unknown at the mode of trial hearing) coming to light during the trial.

VIII   Custodial sentences for youth

Custodial sentences for youths under 21			
Age	Detention in Young Offender's Institution *CJA 1982 ss.1-3*	Secure Training Order *CJPO 1994 ss.1-15* *(not yet in force)*	Detention under *CYPA 1933 s.53*
18 to 20	Minimum term: 21 days Maximum term: the maximum term for the offence	Not applicable	Not applicable
15 to 17	Minimum term: 2 months Maximum term: 2 years		a) If the offence is punishable with 14 years imprisonment *or* b) indecent assault on a woman *or* c) death by dangerous/careless driving while affected by alcohol
14 and below	Not applicable	Available from aged 12 (Gradual availability over lower age ranges down to 12)	a) If the offence is punishable with 14 years imprisonment *or* b) indecent assault on a woman

J   Sentencing procedure and mitigation

I   Preparing a plea in mitigation
II   Newton hearing
III   Pre-sentence report
IV   Court proceedings

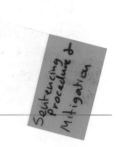

I   Preparing a plea in mitigation

Preparing a plea in mitigation

➤ The defence must present a plea in mitigation for the accused in order to:

◆ reduce the severity of sentence, *and/or*

◆ persuade the court that a particular punishment is not suitable, and that another sentence would help the offender.

➤ Preparation:

1 Make a realistic assessment of the likely penalties. (Consult the Magistrates' Association Guidelines.)

2 Consider any relevant factors such as:

◆ the offender's age and history: youth or old-age may induce sympathy.

◆ the circumstances of the offence: provocation, stress, drug dependency.

    ● **Note**: voluntary ingestion is *not* good mitigation.

◆ the likely effect on the offender of sentence and conviction;

    ● **Note:** failure to respond to previous sentences is relevant (*CJA 1991*).

◆ subsequent behaviour:

    ● **remorse.**

    ● **guilty plea and the time and circumstances of this plea** (*CJPO 1994 s.48*).

      ■ There is usually a discount on custodial sentences of up to a third, but probably not on a non-custodial sentence.

      ■ If the evidence is so overwhelming that the defendant has no choice but to plead guilty, there is no discount under *CJPO 1994 s.48* - *R. v. Hastings* 1 Cr.App.Rep.(S) 167.

    ● **assisting police.**

      ■ Naming others, revealing the whereabouts of stolen property, confessing to save police time.

    ● **reparation.**

      ■ Voluntary rectification of damage and motive are important.

➤ Character witnesses and letters of reference are admissible in a plea for mitigation.

II Newton hearing

➤ A Newton hearing comes from *R. v. Newton* (1982) 77 Cr.App.R.13.

➤ This is held after a guilty plea. Evidence is heard to ascertain the facts relevant to sentencing, *either*:

  ◆ because the prosecution and defence accounts of the facts differ greatly, *or*

  ◆ to resolve the respective liability of 2 or more defendants.

III Pre-sentence report

➤ This is compiled by a probation officer or social worker.

➤ It *must* be ordered (if the offender is aged over 18) before:

  ◆ imposing a custodial sentence *unless* the court feels it is unnecessary (*CJA 1991 s.3*), *or*

  ◆ making a probation order with 'requirements' (*CJA 1991 s.7(3)*) *unless* the court considers it unnecessary (*CJA 1991 s.7(3A)*), *or*

  ◆ making a community service order (*CJA 1991 s.7(3)*) *unless* the court considers it unnecessary (*CJA 1991 s.7(3A)*), *or*

  ◆ making a combination order (*CJA 1991 s.7(3)*) *unless* the court considers it unnecessary (*CJA 1991 s.7(3A)*).

  NB: There are slightly altered rules for offenders aged under 18 (*CJA 1991 s.3(2A)* and *s.7(3B) and also C(S)A 1997 s.50 [which is not yet in force]*).

➤ It *may* be ordered before imposing any other sentence, usually when it is anticipated that the accused will plead guilty and he is aged 30 or less.

IV Court proceedings

1 **The prosecution summarises:**

  ◆ the nature of the offence.

  ◆ the offender's background and previous convictions.

  ◆ any other offences of similar or less serious nature to be taken into consideration (admitted by the offender). The offender may not be subsequently charged with these. A compensation order can be made in respect of these offences.

    • The offender signs a 'taking into consideration' form, provided by the police.

2 **The pre-sentence report is presented to the court.**

3 **The defence gives a plea in mitigation.**

  ➤ On a driving offence for which disqualification is an issue, 'special reasons' for avoiding disqualification are given by the defendant on oath.

4 **The judge passes sentence.**

K Appeals

➤ Some main details of 3 different appellate courts are outlined below.

1 **From Magistrates' Court to Crown Court** (*MCA 1980 ss.108-110* and the *Crown Court Rules 1982*)

➤ Against either conviction or sentence.

➤ Conviction:

♦ if the offender pleaded guilty, there is only a right to appeal against a conviction if the plea was equivocal (ie: a non-genuine plea of guilty) (*MCA 1980 s.108*).

♦ the Crown Court can remit an equivocal plea to the Magistrates' Court with a direction to enter a plea of 'not guilty'.

➤ **Sentence:** may be heavier or lighter, provided the magistrates would be empowered to impose it.

➤ Procedure:

Steps	
1	Send a notice of appeal to the magistrates' clerk and the prosecution within 21 days of sentence or conviction.
	♦ The Crown Court can grant leave to appeal after this (*Crown Court Rules 1982 r.7(5)*).
2	The appeal is heard by a Crown Court judge *or* a recorder sitting with 2 to 4 magistrates.
	♦ If the appeal is against conviction, there is a rehearing following exactly the same process as for a summary trial (*SCA 1981 s.79(3)*).
	♦ If the appeal is against sentencing, the prosecution merely outlines the case facts, and the defence makes a plea in mitigation.
3	The court can confirm, reverse or vary the magistrates' decision. It can also remit the matter (with its opinion) to the Magistrates' Court, *or* it may make any order it thinks just, exercising any powers the magistrates might have used (eg: concerning costs and compensation) (*SCA 1981 s.48*).

2 **From Magistrates' Court to Divisional Court** (the QBD of the High Court) **by way of case stated:**

➤ Grounds: the magistrates' decision is wrong in law, or exceeds their authority (*MCA 1980 s.111*).

➤ There is a hearing of legal argument (no evidence is called).

➤ The Divisional Court may reverse, affirm, or vary the decision. It can also remit the matter (with its opinion) to the Magistrates' Court, *or* it may make any order it thinks fit, exercising any powers the magistrates might have used (eg: concerning costs and compensation) (*SCA 1981 s.28A*).

3 **From Crown Court to the Court of Appeal**

➤ Against conviction or sentence (*CAA 1968 ss.1,2,9,11 and CAA 1995*).

➤ On a question of law or fact, leave is required.

➤ The prosecution cannot appeal against acquittal or sentence.

➤ The Attorney General may, with leave of the Court of Appeal, refer lenient Crown Court sentences to the Court of Appeal for review. The Court of Appeal passes the appropriate sentence in accordance with the Crown Court's powers (*CJA 1988 ss.33-36*).

➤ If the defendant is acquitted in the Crown Court, the prosecution can appeal on a point of law. The defendant stays acquitted, but the Court of Appeal will nonetheless rule on the point of law.

A summary table of appeals to higher courts		
Who appeals	Reason for appeal	Court where the appeal is heard
Appeal from the Magistrates' Court (*MCA 1980 s.108*)		
Defence only	Perverse conviction against the evidence	Crown Court appeal hearing
	Excessive sentence	
Defence *or* Prosecution	*Ultra vires*	Queen's Bench Division of the High Court (Divisional Court) for judicial review cf: *R v Hereford Magistrates' Court ex parte Rowlands* [1997] The Times 17 Feb
Prosecution only	Lenient sentence	No right of appeal
	Perverse acquittal against the evidence	
Appeal from the Crown Court (*CAA 1968, CAA 1995*)		
Defence only	Excessive sentence	Court of Appeal
	Conviction unsafe (ie: law or fact)	Court of Appeal, with leave
Defence *or* Prosecution	*Ultra vires*	No provision for judicial review in the High Court
Prosecution only	Lenient sentence	Attorney General can refer the case to the Court of Appeal (Note: in the Magistrates' Court there is no such right)
	Perverse acquittal against the evidence	No right of appeal
	Question of law following acquittal	Court of Appeal The defendant *stays* acquitted, but the court can rule on the point of law anyway

➤ It should also be noted that the Magistrates' Court has power to hear 'appeals' from itself under certain circumstances (*MCA 1980 s.142 (as amended by ss.26-28 CAA 1995)*). However, this topic is not dealt with in this chapter.

➤ The *CAA 1995* provides for the Criminal Cases Review Commission which was set up on 31st March 1997 with powers to refer certain types of cases to appeal.

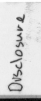

Disclosure

L Disclosure

All references in this section are to the CPIA 1996.

➤ *CPIA 1996 ss.1-21* introduces a new procedure for advance disclosure of evidence by both sides.

  ◆ Common law rules applying to the prosecution are disapplied (see box below).

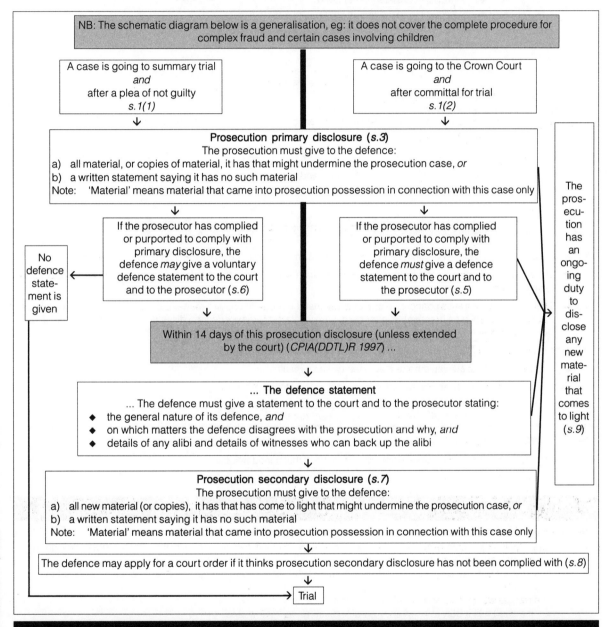

NB: The schematic diagram below is a generalisation, eg: it does not cover the complete procedure for complex fraud and certain cases involving children

| A case is going to summary trial *and* after a plea of not guilty *s.1(1)* | A case is going to the Crown Court *and* after committal for trial *s.1(2)* |

Prosecution primary disclosure (*s.3*)
The prosecution must give to the defence:
a)   all material, or copies of material, it has that might undermine the prosecution case, *or*
b)   a written statement saying it has no such material
Note: 'Material' means material that came into prosecution possession in connection with this case only

If the prosecutor has complied or purported to comply with primary disclosure, the defence *may* give a voluntary defence statement to the court and to the prosecutor (*s.6*)

If the prosecutor has complied or purported to comply with primary disclosure, the defence *must* give a defence statement to the court and to the prosecutor (*s.5*)

No defence statement is given

Within 14 days of this prosecution disclosure (unless extended by the court) (*CPIA(DDTL)R 1997*) ...

... The defence statement
... The defence must give a statement to the court and to the prosecutor stating:
  ◆ the general nature of its defence, *and*
  ◆ on which matters the defence disagrees with the prosecution and why, *and*
  ◆ details of any alibi and details of witnesses who can back up the alibi

The prosecution has an ongoing duty to disclose any new material that comes to light (*s.9*)

Prosecution secondary disclosure (*s.7*)
The prosecution must give to the defence:
a)   all new material (or copies), it has that has come to light that might undermine the prosecution case, *or*
b)   a written statement saying it has no such material
Note: 'Material' means material that came into prosecution possession in connection with this case only

The defence may apply for a court order if it thinks prosecution secondary disclosure has not been complied with (*s.8*)

Trial

Changes to common law rules (*s.21*)

➤ For *s.1(1)* disclosure, all common law rules relating to disclosure after the accused has pleaded 'not guilty' are abolished.

➤ For *s.1(2)* disclosure, all common law rules relating to disclosure after the accused has been committed for trial are abolished.

➤ It is arguable that common law rules continue to apply in the period between accusation (charge or summons) and a plea of not guilty/committal (see also p.353).

Problems with ...

... the defence statement and the final defence

If the defence statement (*s.11*):
- is not given (under *s.5* disclosure), *or*
- is out of time (according to the periods laid down by rules made under *s.12*, *or*
- contains inconsistent defences, *or*
- is different from a defence later put forward at trial, *or*
- does not contain details of an alibi and details of those who will support that alibi, but such evidence is later introduced at trial

At trial (*s.11*):
- the court can comment on this
- any other party can comment on this (with leave)

Note: it must have regard to the degree of any difference between the defence and the defence statement and the justification for any difference

The jury and the court:
may draw adverse inferences as to guilt (but cannot convict solely on this)

... time limits for disclosure

➤ All prosecution and defence disclosure must occur within time limits set down by the Secretary of State (under *s.12*).

- These time limits may be set as the Secretary of State sees fit (eg: the 14 day rule for defence disclosure - see previous page).

- There are various transitional provisions that say that if no regulations are made, the various stages of disclosure must occur 'as soon as practicable' after certain events listed (eg: prosecution disclosure is as soon as reasonably practicable after certain events such as a plea of 'not guilty' or committal for trial) (*s.13*).

➤ If the prosecutor does not comply with his time limits (*s.10*), then ...

- ... unless the accused would be denied a fair trial as a result ...

- ... this is not on its own an abuse of process leading to a stay of proceedings.

... confidentiality

➤ *ss.17-18* provide that any material disclosed by the prosecutor is confidential.

- Various new criminal offences are set out for breach of that confidentiality.

Prosecutor will not disclose material 'in the public interest' (*ss.14-16*)

➤ The prosecutor as a general rule must disclose all material.

➤ However, the prosecutor may apply to the court for non-disclosure if it would not be 'in the public interest'. The court may grant such an application.

- **In summary trial**, as long as it is before the verdict, the accused can apply at any time for a review of non-disclosure.

- **In other cases**, as long as it is before the verdict:
  - the court has a duty to keep any non-disclosure under review, *and*
  - notwithstanding the court's duty, the accused can apply at any time for a court review.

➤ If:
- a person claiming to have an interest in the material applies for a review of the non-disclosure, *and*
- he shows that he was involved in bringing the material to the attention of the prosecutor,

then he must be heard before any order for non-disclosure is made.

➤ A third party who has material which has previously been inspected by the prosecution or which is in the possession of the prosecution, may be required to disclose this to the defence.

- This will be subject to a hearing if necessary on:
  - public interest, *or*
  - confidentiality.

M Evidence at trial

I   Evidential proof

A. Burden of proof

➤ **The prosecution** must prove guilt 'beyond reasonable doubt'.

➤ **The defence** has an 'evidential burden' (ie: it must introduce necessary evidence before the court).

  ◆ Occasionally, a defence may need to satisfy the court on the balance of probabilities:

     a) insane automatism (*Bratty v. AG for Northern Ireland* [1963] AC 386).

     b) insanity *(Sodeman v. The King* [1936] 2 All ER 1138).

     c) diminished responsibility (*Homicide Act 1957 s.2(2)*).

B. Proof by evidence

➤ Everything must be proved *except*:

  ◆ facts which are formally admitted by the defence and the prosecution (*CJA 1967 s.10*).

  ◆ where judicial notice is taken of a point of fact (eg: dogs bark, they do not quack).

  ◆ where judicial notice is taken of a point of law (eg: traffic must stop at a red light).

  ◆ circumstantial evidence (rebuttable): where there is an *inference* of fact drawn from *proven* facts.

    • Examples include:

       i) doctrine of recent possession - someone possessing goods illegally came by them illicitly.

       ii) doctrine of continuance - a given state of affairs continues (*R. v. Balloz* (1908) 1 Cr.App.R. 258).

C. Types of evidence

➤ **Oral evidence:** this carries most weight.

➤ **Real evidence:** this consists of objects (eg: weapons).

➤ **Documentary evidence:** this includes recordings and photographs.

  ◆ A document must be authenticated by demonstrating in what circumstances it was created.

  ◆ A copy is admissible (*CJA 1988 s.27*).

➤ **Written statements and depositions (see p.358):** any that were used at committal may be used at trial, as long as they have been signed by a magistrate.

D. Finding the facts

Sequence for examination of witnesses

Steps	
1	Examination-in-chief
2	Cross-examination
3	Re-examination

1   Examination-in-chief

➤ This is where a side calls its own witness and asks questions of that witness.

➤ A witness may refresh his memory from a contemporaneous document.

➤ No leading questions are permitted, except to obtain a rebuttal or denial of the opponent's case.

➤ Even if a witness gives unfavourable answers, the side which called the witness cannot contradict or discredit the witness *unless*:

♦ the witness is declared hostile. To achieve this, an application must be made to the judge (*CPA 1865 s.3*)). If this is done:

• the party calling a witness may cross-examine him and ask leading questions, *and*

• the witness can be confronted with statements made previously by him which are inconsistent with his testimony. **Note:** These previous inconsistent statements are not admissible as evidence, but they go to the credibility of the witness.

2   Cross-examination

➤ After a side has called its witness for examination-in-chief, the other side may cross-examine the witness.

➤ The cross-examiner will seek to:

a) put his view of the case to a witness, *and*

b) extract useful information from the witness, *and*

c) challenge a witness's credibility.

♦ The questions must be relevant to the evidence about the offence before the court.

♦ A witness's answer is *final* unless the witness:

i) is biased (*R. v. Shaw* (1888) 16 Cox 503), *or*

ii) has given evidence which is inconsistent with a previous statement (*CPA 1865 ss.4, 5*), *or*

• These previous inconsistent statements are not admissible as evidence, but they go to the credibility of the witness.

iii) has a relevant conviction (*CPA 1865 s.6*), *or*

iv) has a reputation for untruthfulness (*Toohey v. Metropolitan Police Comm.* [1965] AC 595).

3   Re-examination

➤ There may now be a re-examination by the other side after the cross-examination on matters brought up during the cross-examination.

➤ This may be done in an attempt to undo any damage from the cross-examination.

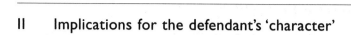

II   Implications for the defendant's 'character'

➤   The general rule is that the prosecution may not call evidence about the defendant's character or previous convictions.

♦   This is a kind of 'shield' that the defendant has *(CEA 1898 s.1(1))*.

➤   There are 3 exceptions to the general rule:

1   To rebut an assertion of a defendant's good character.

♦   If a defendant testifies and asserts his good character, then the prosecution may call evidence to rebut this.

♦   If a defendant does not testify, and the defence makes character an issue, the prosecution can apply for leave to bring evidence of the defendant's bad character.

♦   The weight this evidence carries depends on the aspect of character (eg: violence need not imply dishonesty, so evidence of violence might not suggest that a defendant has stolen).

2   Similar fact evidence *(CEA 1898 s.1(f)(i))*.   See p.385.

3   If the defendant testifies *and* the defence's conduct at the trial leads to the defendant 'losing his shield'.

♦   If a defendant chooses to give oral evidence, then special rules apply governing what sorts of questions the prosecution can put to him.

♦   **The general rule is that the prosecution may not cross-examine the defendant on his character (encompassing both reputation and disposition of the defendant) or previous convictions.**

♦   *CEA 1898 s.1(f)* provides the defendant with a 'shield' against cross-examination in relation to bad character and past misconduct. However, the 'shield' can be lost under a) or b) below:

a)   *CEA 1898 s.1(f)(ii)*

•   **Limb 1:**   a defendant has established (or tried to establish) his own good character.

•   **Limb 2:**   the defence has 'cast imputations' on the character of the prosecution, or a prosecution witness.

b)   *CEA 1898 s.1(f)(iii)*

•   A defendant has given evidence against a co-defendant (ie: a 'cut-throat defence').

♦   The court has discretion to prevent *s.1(f)* cross-examination if it would prejudice the defence *(Selvey v. DPP* [1970] AC 304).

♦   This discretion does not extend to cross-examination by a co-defendant under *s.1(f)(iii)* *(Murdoch v. Taylor* [1965] AC 547).

➤   Notes:

♦   **'cast imputations':** this bears its ordinary meaning, but does not include an assertion of innocence.

♦   **previous convictions:** only go to character. This merits a judicial warning that previous convictions merely show that the defendant's allegations against the prosecution are less likely to be true. The fact of a conviction can be raised, not the evidence for it.

♦   **'cut-throat' defence:** this occurs when a co-defendant can only rebut an implication of his guilt by imputing bad character to the other defendant. Both defendants lose their 'shields'. The defence can seek to avoid this by adopting an alternative argument (eg: the victim suffered harm another way).

♦   **character is indivisible:** ie: once some aspects of character emerge (good or bad), they all can be brought up (including previous convictions).

III   Evidential safeguards

1   Corroboration

➤ At common law, one witness is sufficient in all cases.

➤ By statute, corroboration (ie: independent supporting evidence) is required to convict a defendant of treason (*Treason Act 1795 s.1*), perjury (*Perjury Act 1911 s.13*) and speeding (except if the evidence is from a speed camera). The judge must tell the jury this.

➤ In other cases, where it is felt that further proof might be needed to support certain evidence, it is within the discretion of the judge to give the jury a corroboration warning - ie: the jury should be warned that further proof is desirable.

➤ Contents of a corroboration warning:

   ◆ A judge should point out to the jury why evidence is suspect, or identify corroborative evidence and non-corroborative evidence, as a warning that there is a danger in relying on the evidence.

   ◆ Magistrates warn themselves (!) - the defence can remind them in its closing speech.

When is a warning necessary?		
When corroboration itself is essential	When a corroboration warning is mandatory	When a corroboration warning is desirable

For charges of:
◆ treason
◆ perjury
◆ speeding
	There *used to be* a mandatory warning for the following 2 instances, but this has now been abolished by *CJPO 1994 ss.32-33*. However, a court may still give such a warning even though this is undesirable as it is contrary to the intention of the *CJPO 1994* (*R. v. Makanjuola; R. v. Easton*, [1995] 2 Cr. App. R. 469)
	   ◆ An accomplice gives evidence
	   ◆ A victim of an alleged sexual offence gives evidence
		◆ A prosecution witness has an interest in giving false evidence (eg: to preserve his own reputation or he bears a grudge) (*R. v. Cheema* [1994] 1 WLR 147)
		◆ A defendant tries to incriminate a co-defendant
		◆ A witness is shown to be unreliable (eg: a mental patient)

2   Disputed identification (Turnbull guidelines) (*R. v. Turnbull* [1977] QB 224)

➤ In a case where disputed identification of the defendant is the sole or a substantial issue, there is a danger of wrongful conviction unless the following procedure is complied with:

Steps

1   Evidence of identification is admissible if:

   ◆ the evidence is visual *and*

   ◆ on at least 2 occasions, the defendant was purported to be seen (eg: at the crime and at an identification parade).

2   The judge or magistrates must consider the soundness of the evidence by contemplating the following 6 factors:

1 the length of observation.	4	conditions.
2 whether the defendant was already known to the witness.	5	distance.
3 how close the witness's description is to the police description.	6	lighting.

3   If the identifying evidence is poor, then the judge or magistrates must order an acquittal.

4   If the evidence is sound, the judge gives the jury a **Turnbull warning.** He must warn the jury (or magistrates must warn themselves!):

   ◆ of the dangers of relying on identification evidence, *and*

   ◆ to consider factors 1 - 6 above in evaluating the evidence.

IV   Witness's competence and compellability

➤   **Competent:**   a witness is competent if he can lawfully give evidence.

➤   **Compellable:**   a witness is 'compellable' if he can be required to testify.

1   Defendant as a prosecution witness

➤   *Not* compellable.

➤   A co-defendant can only be called if he ceases to be a co-defendant either because he:

♦   pleads guilty, *or*

♦   is tried separately, *or*

♦   is acquitted, *or*

♦   the Attorney General ends proceedings against him.

2   Defendant as a defence witness

➤   Competent, but *not* compellable (*CEA 1898 s.1*).

➤   His evidence is admissible against a co-defendant that he implicates.

➤   If the defendant testifies, he must be called before any other witnesses for the defence (*PACE s.79*).

➤   If the defendant decides not to testify, this can have adverse consequences, see p.389.

➤   The judge will comment adversely if the defence has raised an issue, but not given evidence in support of it.

➤   The prosecution may comment on a defendant's refusal to testify (*CJPO 1994 Schedule 10 para 2*).

➤   A co-accused may comment freely on a defendant's refusal to give evidence.

3   Present spouse as a prosecution witness (*PACE s.80*)

➤   Competent.

➤   Compellable only if the defendant is charged with:

♦   an assault on the spouse.

♦   an assault or sexual offence on a victim aged under 16.

4   Former spouse as a prosecution witness (*PACE s.80(5)*)

➤   Competent and compellable.

5   Present spouse as a defence witness (*PACE s.80(2), s.80(4)*)

➤   Competent and compellable (unless the accused and the spouse are jointly charged).

6   Child aged under 14 (*CJA 1988 s.33A, CJA 1991 s.52*)

➤   The child must give unsworn evidence.

➤   Competent (unless the court thinks the child is incapable of giving intelligent testimony), and compellable.

7   Co-defendant

➤   Whether a co-defendant is competent or compellable to testify against a fellow defendant, and the admissibility of his evidence depends on the co-defendant's plea (see box overleaf).

The co-defendant on a plea of...	
'guilty' (and therefore no longer on trial)	'not guilty'
Competent and compellable	Competent, but *not* compellable
He is like any other witness, so any statements made to the police, or a confession, will be inadmissible against the defendant as they will be hearsay	His confession, or statements made to the police, are only admissible against himself. (Evidence not made on oath by the co-defendant is not evidence against the defendant - it is inadmissible and must be disregarded)
A corroboration warning is no longer necessary (*CJPO 1994 s.32,* see p.382)	Some corroboration warning is desirable, see p.382
Cross-examinable on his record	Cross-examination *per s.1(f)(iii),* see p.381
Note: A defendant is innocent until he *pleads* guilty	**Note:** A defendant is competent as witness to his own alibi, or to authenticate a document

V   Admissibility of evidence

➤   There are 8 primary types of *in*admissible evidence:

1   At common law

➤   The common law discretion of a judge to prevent an unfair trial is preserved by *PACE s.82(3).*

➤   There is discretion to exclude evidence improperly obtained by the prosecution (*R. v. Sang* [1980] AC 402).

➤   Usually the discretion might be applied if the prejudicial effect on the jury of the evidence outweighs its true probitive value.

➤   However, the discretion is very rarely exercised because as a *matter of law* much improperly obtained evidence is admissible.   The following examples are admissible:

◆   evidence from the illegal search of a person (*Kuruma, Son of Kariu v. The Queen* [1955] AC 197).

◆   evidence obtained by an agent provocateur (*R. v. Sang* [1980] AC 402).

2   *PACE s.78*

➤   The court has a general discretion:

a)   to exclude evidence, if an admission of the evidence 'would have such an adverse effect on the fairness of the proceedings that the court ought not to admit it' given all the circumstances, including how the evidence was obtained, *and*

b)   to prevent cross-examination of a defendant as to his character even if the prosecution are permitted to do this under *CEA 1898 s.1(f)(i)-(ii).* Prejudice must be overwhelming to qualify for exclusion on this ground. This caveat does not apply to *s.1(f)(iii)* (*Selvey v. DPP* [1970] AC 304).

3   Irrelevant evidence

4 Self-made evidence

➤ A witness may not support his evidence at trial by introducing a statement he made on a previous occasion.

➤ This is inadmissible unless it involves:

   a) previous exculpatory statements to the police, *or*

   b) statements that come under *res gestae* - 'circumstances of spontaneity or involvement in the event', so there is no possibility of concoction or distortion (see '*res gestae*' on p.387), *or*

   c) evidence that rebuts the suggestion that the witness has recently fabricated his testimony.

5 Privileged evidence

➤ Privileged material is inadmissible and falls within these categories:

   a) legal professional privilege: (eg: client-solicitor communications, or those with third parties, in contemplation of proceedings (*Parkins v. Hawkshaw* (1817) 2 Stark N.P. 239).

   b) against self-incrimination: an answer which may lead to a criminal charge for a witness (*R. v. Garbett* (1847) 2 C&K 474, and *Evidence Act 1851 s.3*). However, this does not apply if a defendant elects to testify (*CEA 1898 s.1(e)*).

6 Public interest immunity

➤ Evidence that for reasons of public interest is inadmissible (cf: the *Matrix Churchill* case).

➤ Such reasons include:

   ◆ state interests (*D v. NSPCC* [1978] AC 171).

   ◆ details of the prevention, detection and investigation of crime, eg: identity of a police informant, unless this is necessary to prove a defendant's innocence (*R. v. Turner* [1995] 1 WLR 264).

7 Similar fact evidence

➤ This is evidence that the defendant has committed offences before, similar to the ones now before the court.

➤ This is inadmissible because:

   a) the prejudice created by such evidence outweighs any probative value it may have (*DPP v. Kilbourne* [1973] AC 729), *and*

   b) it is irrelevant, since irrespective of the number of similar crimes which have been committed, these crimes cannot connect a person with the crime in front of the court (*R. v. Miller* [1952] 2 All ER 667).

➤ However, if the prosecution can convince the judge/magistrates that in a particular case a) and b) are untrue *and* that the evidence is relevant, the judge/magistrates may rule that the similar fact evidence is admissible.

➤ An accused can *always* introduce similar evidence against a co-accused because the judge has no discretion to exclude it (*R. v. Miller* [1952] 2 All ER 667).

8   Hearsay evidence

➤ Hearsay is a statement made out of court, now being repeated in court, intended to prove the truth of the matter stated out of court.

➤ Hearsay evidence is inadmissible.

➤ The following are *prima facie* hearsay, but admissible anyway as exceptions to the rules of hearsay:

A. Documentary hearsay (*CJA 1988 ss.23-24*).

B. Written statements (usually a statement not in dispute) (*CJA 1967 s.9*).

C. *Res gestae.*

D. Opinion.

E. Confessions (*PACE s.76*).

A. Documentary hearsay - admissible

Witness statements	Business documents
First hand hearsay only (*CJA 1988 s.23*)	First hand and multiple hearsay (*CJA 1988 s.24*)
A statement in a DOCUMENT...	
...and the witness is unable to attend due to...	...and the document was...
a) death, bodily or mental condition, *or* b) not being present in the UK and his attendance is not reasonably practical, *or* c) he is untraceable despite reasonable efforts to find him, *or* d) i) the statement was made to: ◆ a police officer, *or* ◆ another under a duty to investigate offences or charge offenders, *and* ii) the witness is unavailable as he is fearful, *or* because he is being kept out of the way	a) created *or* received by a person in the course of a trade, business, profession, occupation, or office, *and* b) the information was supplied by a person having, or reasonably supposed to have had, personal knowledge of the matter (and each member of the chain between the original witness and the compiler of the document must be under a duty in a) above) NB: A document prepared for criminal proceedings or a criminal investigation is only admissible if either: a) the witness is not present due to: i) death, his bodily or mental condition, *or* ii) not being present in the UK and his attendance is not reasonably practical, *or* iii) he is untraceable despite reasonable efforts to find him *OR* b) i) the statement was made to: ◆ a police officer, *or* ◆ another under a duty to investigate offences or charge offenders, *and* ii) the witness is unavailable as he is fearful, *or* because he is being kept out of the way *OR* c) the maker of the statement cannot be expected to recall the information after such a lapse of time
Excluding hearsay 'in the interests of justice' (*CJA 1988 s.25*)	

➤ The court has discretion to exclude hearsay which would otherwise be admissible under *s.23 or s.24* if its probative force is outweighed by the prejudice it might cause to a fair trial

➤ Prejudice might be caused because:

◆ a witness may not be cross-examined, *or*

◆ a witness is not liable for perjury if the evidence is fabricated

When leave of the court is required (*CJA 1988 s.26*)
If a statement under *s.23 or s.24* has been made for the purpose of criminal proceedings or a criminal investigation, leave of the court is needed to introduce it. Leave will be given if it is 'in the interests of justice'

B. Written statements - admissible

➤ If:

a) the statement purports to be made by the signatory, *and*

b) there is a declaration that it is true to the best of the witness's knowledge and belief, and it was made in full knowledge of the danger of a prosecution for falsehood, *and*

c) a copy is served before any hearing on all parties *and* none object within 7 days of service,

... **then** these statements are admissible in trials (*CJA 1967 s.9(1)*).

C. *Res gestae* (*Ratten v. R.* [1972] AC 378) - admissible

➤ *Res gestae* is:

◆ a statement by the doer of an act, which is related to the act and is contemporaneous with it.

◆ a spontaneous statement at the time of an event.

◆ a statement which was made at the time of an event, and which shows a state of mind, emotion or intention.

◆ an expression of physical sensation felt at the time.

➤ *Res gestae* is admissible if a judge can disregard the possibility that the statement was concocted or distorted (*R. v. Andrews (Donald)* [1987] AC 281).

➤ A classic example of *res gestae* is a dying declaration (*R. v. Mills* [1995] 3 All ER 865).

D. Opinion - admissible

➤ Opinion is admissible if *either*:

a) a witness recalls his personal perception at the time, *or*

b) the evidence is from an expert witness. The opinion must be pertinent to the expert's expertise.

◆ If an expert is present, all can see copies of his report.

◆ If an expert is absent, leave of court is required to admit an expert's report (*CJA 1988 s.30(2)*).

➤ **Magistrates' Court:** advance disclosure of an expert witness's evidence is compulsory (*MC(ANEE) R 1997*).

➤ **Crown Court:** advance disclosure of an expert witness's evidence is compulsory (*PACE s.81* and *Crown Court (Advance Notice of Expert Evidence) Rules 1987*). Leave of the court is needed if the evidence is not disclosed as soon as possible after committal according to *rule 5* of the *Crown Court (Advance Notice of Expert Evidence) Rules 1987*.

E. Confessions - admissible

i) Confessions generally

➤ A confession is:

'any statement wholly or partly adverse to the person who made it, whether made to a person in authority or not and whether made in words or otherwise' (*PACE s.82(1)*).

➤ A part-confession is admissible in total. If there are periods of silence followed by periods of speaking, the whole is admissible.

➤ A confession implicating a co-defendant is:

◆ admissible purely against the confessor.

◆ hearsay against a co-defendant (*R. v. Rudd 32 Cr. App.R. 138*).

ii) Excluding confessions

➤ The following 3 points show ways to attempt to exclude a confession:

❶ *PACE s.76(2)*

◆ A confession is inadmissible *unless* the prosecution show 'beyond reasonable doubt' that the confession was not obtained in one of the following two ways:

• by **oppression** of the person who made it, *or*

• in consequence of anything said or done which was likely, in the circumstances existing at the time, to render **unreliable** any confession which might be made by him in consequence thereof'.

◆ **Oppression:** the Court of Appeal has defined this as the 'exercise of authority or power in a burdensome, harsh or wrongful manner; unjust or cruel treatment of subjects ... the imposition of unjust or unreasonable burdens' (*R. v. Fulling* [1987] QB 426). ('Oppression' includes 'torture, inhuman and degrading treatment and the use or threat of violence' (*PACE s.76(8)*).)

◆ **Unreliability:** a breach of a *PACE* Code is, in itself, not sufficient. There must be a causal link between the breach and the unreliability. There is no need for any police misconduct to be shown.

❷ *PACE s.78* - see p.384

❸ **At common law** - see p.384

iii) The admission of evidence from an excluded confession

➤ Factual evidence gained from an excluded confession.

◆ Facts are admissible (*PACE s.76(4)(a)*).

➤ Expression

◆ A confession is admissible as evidence that the defendant writes, speaks or expresses himself in a certain way, irrespective of whether the confession itself is excluded (*PACE s.76(4)(b)*).

VI   Inferences from silence at trial

➤ The following sections of the *CJPO 1994* can each adversly affect the defendant at trial.

s.35 CJPO 1994

The defendant is 14 years old or above, and fails to give evidence at trial

↓

Sub-procedure for *s.35*

➤ At the end of the prosecution case, *unless the legal representative of the defendant informs the court that the defendant will give evidence,* the judge will ensure that the defendant knows that inferences may be drawn from his refusal to testify

➤ In the Crown Court this procedure is covered by *Practice Direction (Crown Court: Defendant's Evidence)* [1995] 1 WLR 657.

s.34 CJPO 1994
Situation 1

a) The defendant had not yet been charged, *and*
b) was being questioned under caution by a constable, *and*
c) the constable was trying to discover whether, or by whom, an offence had been committed, *and*
d) the defendant failed to mention a fact he might reasonably be expected to mention at the time, *and*
e) **the defendant later (at trial) relies on that fact in his defence**

Situation 2

a) At the time that the defendant was charged or officially informed he might be prosecuted for an offence, *and*
b) the defendant failed to mention a fact he might reasonably be expected to mention at the time

s.37 CJPO 1994

a) At the time that the defendant was arrested, *and*
b) the defendant was at a place where a constable reasonably believed that the person's presence might be to do with participation in an offence, *and*
c) the constable reasonably believed that the object, substance or mark had something to do with the defendant participating in a specified offence, *and*
d) the constable informed the defendant of his suspicions and asked for an explanation, *and*
e) the defendant failed or refused to provide an explanation

s.36 CJPO 1994

a) The defendant was arrested, *and*
b) with an object, substance or mark:
   i) on his person, *or*
   ii) in or on his clothing or footwear, *or*
   iii) in his possession, *or*
   iv) in any place in which he was at the time of his arrest, *and*
c) the constable reasonably believed that the object, substance or mark had something to do with the defendant participating in a specified offence, *and*
d) the constable informed the defendant of his suspicions and asked for an explanation, *and*
e) the defendant failed or refused to provide an explanation

Consequences of an adverse inference of silence

➤ In the Crown Court, arguments about the admissibility of the defendant's silence when previously being interviewed (ie: any case above apart from *s.35*) take place in the absence of the jury.
  ◆ The judge decides on admissibility and the jury decides whether inferences may be drawn.

➤ In the Magistrates' Court, the magistrates decide everything.

➤ The magistrates or jury can 'draw such inferences as appear proper' from the silence as applied to:
1 a submission of 'no case to answer' in a trial (see p.354 and p.361).
2 determining the guilt or innocence of a defendant at trial.

Note: such inferences must *not* decide the matter alone - there must be other factors too (*CJPO 1994 s.38*).
➤ The defence needs to introduce evidence in order to put forward a 'good reason' for the defendant's silence, so as to avoid the 'adverse inferences' from the silence (*R. v. Cowan; Gayle; Ricciardi* [1995] 3 WLR 818 CA).
  ◆ This case also shows that *s.35* is not only meant to be invoked in exceptional cases.

Appendices and Index

Telephone numbers

Organisation	Telephone	Organisation	Telephone
A		**D**	
Attorney General	0171 828 7155	DHL (Couriers)	0345 100 300
B		**E**	
Bar Council	0171 242 0082	Employment Appeals Tribunal	0171 273 1041
Baker & MacKenzie	0171 919 1000	Enquiry Agents, Process Servers	
Benefits Agency	0800 666 555	Thames Law	01474 702 006
British Standards Institution	0181 996 9000	Equal Opportunities Commission	0161 833 9244
C		European Commission	0171 973 1992
Central Law Training Limited	0121 355 0900	Eurostar	01233 617 575
Certificated Bailiffs		**F**	
Jefferies & Pennicott	0181 877 1945	**G**	
Chambers (London sets of high repute)		Government Departments of State	
(Crime), 3 Raymond Buidlings	0171 831 3833	Defence	0171 218 9000
(Company), Erskine Chambers	0171 242 5532	Education and Employment	0171 273 3000
(Chancery, Commercial),		Environment	0171 276 0900
13 Old Square	0171 242 6105	Health	0171 210 4850
(Commercial, Employment),		Home Office	0171 273 3000
11 King's Bench Walk	0171 583 0610	Lord Chancellor	0171 210 8500
(Property), Falcon Chambers	0171 353 2484	Social Security	0171 210 5983
(Taxation), Gray's Inn Chambers	0171 242 2642	Trade and Industry (DTI)	0171 215 5000
Charity Commission	0171 210 4477	Treasury	0171 270 5000
Clifford Chance	0171 600 1000	**H**	
Companies House		High Court (London)	
Birmingham	0121 233 9047	General	0171 936 6000
Cardiff	01222 388 588	Clerk of the Lists	0171 936 6021
Edinburgh	0131 535 5800	Family Division, Probate Registry	0171 936 6569
London	0171 253 9393	Funds Office	0171 936 6016
Leeds	0113 233 8338	Crown Office (for Judicial Review)	0171 936 6653
Manchester	0161 236 7500	Masters' Secretaries, Ch. Division	0171 936 6095
County Courts		Masters' Secretaries, QB Division	0171 936 6474
Central London	0171 917 5000	Winding up petitions	0171 936 7328
Ipswich	01473 214 256	Health and Safety Executive	0171 717 6000
Leeds	0113 283 0040	HM Customs & Excise	
Plymouth	01752 674 808	General	0171 202 4227
West London	0171 602 8444	VAT Registration	0345 112 114
York	01904 629935		
.... otherwise see the list in the back of the Green Book			
Court of Protection	0171 269 7000		
Crown Prosecution Service	0171 273 8000		

Organisation	Telephone	Organisation	Telephone
HMSO		Official Receiver	0171 637 1110
Books	0171 873 0011	Official Solicitor	0171 911 7127
British Standards Hotline	0171 404 1213	OYEZ Stationery Group	01908 371 111
House of Commons	0171 219 4272	**P**	
House of Lords	0171 219 3000	Parcelforce	0800 224 446
I		Personal Investment Authority (PIA)	0171 379 0444
Inland Revenue		Prison Department	0181 317 2436
Capital Taxes Office	0115 974 2400	Probation Service (Head Office, SE London)	0181 464 3430
Financial Intermediaries and Claims Office	0151 472 6000	Public Prosecutions, Director of (DPP)	0171 273 3000
Technical Division	0171 438 6622	Public Record Office	0181 876 3444
J		**Q**	
K		**R**	
L		Royal Mail	0345 950 950
Land Charges Department	01752 635 635	**S**	
Land Registry, Central London	0171-917 8888	Samaritans	0345 909090
Law Society	0171 242 1222	Securities and Investment Board (SIB)	0171 638 1240
Legal Aid Board	0171 813 1000	Stamp Office (Worthing)	01903 700 222
London Gazette	0171 873 8300	Stock Exchange	0171 588 2358
M		**T**	
N		Trains	0345 48 49 50
O			
Office of Fair Trading	0171 242 2858	**U- Z**	

Key Number (for telephoning HM Land Registry/Land Charges Department) . . . .

Account Number (for telephoning Companies House) . . . .

Account Number (for telephoning the Law Society Library) . . . .

The organisations selected for inclusion in this directory have been chosen in the belief that readers may find them useful. Neither the authors, nor the publishers have received payment for inclusion. No warranty, representation or assurance is given in relation to any of the organisations listed.

Notes

Fees, costs and penalties

All tables of fees, costs and penalties are in outline only, in some circumstances different figures may apply.

Although these tables are believed to be accurate at the time of going to press, they may change - if in doubt telephone the relevant organisation to check.

I   Companies House fees and penalties for late filing

II   HM Land Registry fees

III   Court fees

I   Companies House fees and penalties for late filing

A. Fees

1   Registration services

➤ Same day incorporation, change of name or re-registration - £100.

➤ Incorporation - £20.

➤ Re-registration (usually about 7days) - £20.

➤ Change of name (usually about 7days) - £10.

➤ Filing an annual return - £15.

2   Searches

➤ Microfiche ordered by telephone or post - £5, same day service - £20.

➤ Microfiche if collected personally - £3.50.

3   Copy documents

Certified photocopy - £15, same day service - £30.

Additional certificate for a company - £10.

B. Penalties

1   Late filing of accounts

	Plc (£)	Ltd (£)
Not more than 3 months	500	100
Over 3 months but not more than 6 months	1,000	250
Over 6 months but not more than 1 year	2,000	500
More than 1 year	5,000	1,000

For a private company, the time for filing is 10 months from the end of the accounting period
For a public company, the time for filing is 7 months from the end of the accounting period

2   Late filing of other documents

➤ Up to £5,000

II   HM Land Registry fees

➤   From 1 April 1997, fees for services are as follows (*HMLRFO 1997*):

- ◆ Office copies and inspection of the Register

    - A copy of an OCE or an index map plan - £4.

    - Making an inspection by direct access - £2.

- ◆ Searches: conducting an official search, or an index map search - £4.

- ◆ Cautions, notices and inhibitions

    - In each case, for the first title affected £40, then £20 for subsequent titles.

- ◆ Lost or destroyed documents

    - Replacing a land or charge certificate - £40 (£20 if no certificate is issued).

Consideration (Scale 1)			No consideration (Scale 2)	
Value (£) (incl. VAT if charged)	Fee for transfer of registered land (£)	Fee for registering a new lease (£)	Value (£)	Fee for transfer of land (£)
Up to 30,000	40	According to the formula: A = P+ (R x 10) 'A' is the amount (in the extreme left hand column of this table) on which the fee is to be paid 'P' is the premium paid 'R' is the greatest ascertainable annual rent. If: • R is 0, *or* • R is unascertainable, and • P is 0, the Registrar certifies the value of the lease (minimum fee is £40)	To 100,000	40
30,001 to 40,000	50		100,001 to 200,000	50
40,001 to 50,000	70		200,001 to 500,000	70
50,001 to 60,000	90		500,001 to 1,000,000	100
60,001 to 70,000	110		From 1,000,001	200
70,001 to 80,000	130			
80,001 to 90,000	160			
90,001 to 100,000	190			
100,001 to 150,000	220			
150,001 to 200,000	260			
200,001 to 300,000	300			
300,001 to 500,000	400			
500,001 to 700,000	500			
700,001 to 1,000,000	600			
1,000,001 to 2,000,000	900			
2,000,001 to 5,000,000	1200			
From 5,000,000	1800			

Formula in the "Fee for registering a new lease" column:

$$A = P + (R \times 10)$$

➤ Deduct anything outstanding on a registered charge, but pay a fee for each charge, and any advances

➤ If the borrower is also submitting an application to register a freehold or leasehold interest, there is no charge under this scale

➤ If a charge is transferred for no value, calculate the fee using the amount outstanding under the loan

This scale also applies to:
- surrenders in consideration of the grant of a registerable lease to the existing registered proprietor
- surrenders for no value
- assents and transmissions on death or bankruptcy
- transfers under court orders - *MHA 1983 / FLA 1996*

This scale also applies to:
- first registrations
- exchanges
- surrenders for value of registered leases
- cancellations of unregistered leases which are noted on the Register

If an application for first registration is over a year after a sale, or it follows a gift or a part disposal, the Registrar certifies the market value of the property at the time of registration

The following are free:
- discharging a registered charge
- registering an *MHA 1983 / FLA 1996* notice, caution or renewal or their renewal
- cancelling a notice, caution or inhibition
- changing description of proprietor (eg: on marriage)
- PRs of a deceased proprietor registering a disposition not for value
- registering a joint proprietorship restriction or a joint proprietor's death

A. Originating documents

➤ From 15 January 1997, the court principle fees are as set out on these pages (*SCF(A)O 1996, CCF(A)O 1996*). Note that these fees and costs may be altered from time to time by statutory instrument - if in any doubt (**or if it is feared that a limitation period has, or may be about to, expire**) always telephone the court to cheque that the correct figures are used in respect of fees and costs.

High Court			
Fee	(£)	Fixed costs (£)	
Relief:		Service by post in jurisdiction for liquidated claims	
recovery of possession of property or does not include the payment of money -		Claim 600 but under 1,000	126.25
or	120	Claim 1,000 but under 2,000	131.25
is or includes the payment of money (other than money charged on property possession of which is also claimed) and is limited to -		Claim 2,000 but under 3,000	139.00
		Claim 3,000 but under 5,000	159.25
not exceeding 10,000	120	Claim 5,000 or over	209.25
exceeds 10,000 but not exceeding 50,000	150		
exceeds 50,000 but not exceeding 100,000	300	**Personal service**	
exceeding 100,000	500	Claim 600 but under 2,000	7.75
		Claim 2,000 but under 3,000	6.65
		Extra defendants	
		Claim 600 but under 3,000	9.50
		Claim 3,000 or more	12.25
		Substituted service	
		Claim 600 but under 3,000	22.25
		Claim over 3,000	47.75

Court fees to issue bankruptcy proceedings

➤ Debtor's petition - £50, creditor's petition - £80.

➤ Application before a Registrar (Chancery Division), or a District Judge - £50.

   ◆ These fees apply in the High Court and the County Court, irrespective of whether the petition is in relation to an individual or a company.

County Court				
Fee (£)		**Fixed costs (£)**		
		Service by	.... the court	.... by a solicitor
Claim for money alone:				
Claim not more than 100	10	Claim over 25 up to 250	27.50	31.25
Claim not more than 200	20			
Claim not more than 300	30	Claim over 250 up to 600	36.75	43.50
Claim not more than 400	40			
Claim not more than 500	50	Claim over 600 up to 2,000	62.25	69.00
Claim not more than 600	60			
Claim not more than 1,000	60	Claim over 2,000	67.75	73.50
Claim not more than 5,000	80			
Claim not more than 10,000	100			
Claim not more than 50,000	150			
Claim not more than 100,000	300			
Claim exceeding 100,000	500			
Claim not just for money	65			
Service by bailiff (per person) 10				
If making a counterclaim for more than the original claim, the fee is the difference between the two figures				

B. Interlocutory judgments, trial and appeal

High Court

Fee (in both cases) (£)	Fixed costs (£)	Judgment in default of notice to defend (£)	Summary judgment
30.00	**Service by post in jurisdiction when writ is served by post**		
	Recover under 600	Discretionary	Discretionary
	Recover 600 but under 1,000	145.75	227.00
	Recover 1,000 but under 2,000	150.75	232.00
	Recover 2,000 but under 3,000	159.25	239.00
	Recover 3,000 but under 5,000	199.00	274.00
	Recover 5,000 or over	249.00	324.00
	Personal service		
	Recover 600 but under 2,000	6.25	7.00
	Recover 2,000 but under 3,000	5.25	7.00
	Extra defendants		
	Recover 600 but under 3,000	9.50	9.50
	Recover 3,000 or more	12.25	12.25

County Court

Fee (all judgment summons) (£)	Fixed costs (£)	In default of defence (£)	Acceptance of admission and offer (£)	Decisions by court on payment rate (£)
£50	over 25 to 600	9.75	17.25	23.25
	over 600 to 3,000	18.25	36.25	46.25
	over 3,000	20.25	42.25	54.50
	Summary judgment			
	over 500 to 3,000	79.50		
	over 3,000	91.25		

Trial and appeal (below the Court of Appeal)

▲ Ex parte application and consent applicatons (not requiring attendance) before a Master or Registrar, High Court - £20, County Court - £10.

▲ Setting down in the County Court - £100, Queens Bench Division or Chancery Division - £150, or a commercial or admiralty matter - £500.

▲ Notice of appeal in the County Court, or to set aside arbitrators' award (small claims procedure), or in the High Court from a Master to Judge in Chambers - £50

C. Enforcement of judgments

1   Application for an oral examination

➤ Issue fee in the County Court - £30.

➤ Issue fee in the High Court - £35.

2   Application for a garnishee order

➤ Issue fee in the County Court - £50.

➤ Fixed costs in the County Court - as for originating documents.

➤ Issue fee in the High Court - £60.

➤ Fixed costs in the High Court.

◆ A sum deducted from the garnishee's debt before any payment is made to the creditor - £20.75.

◆ If under £150 is recovered, the creditor's fixed costs are half the amount recovered plus the £30 fee, otherwise £118.50 is allowed, with an extra £16.25 for an affidavit of service if the garnishee does not attend the hearing.

3   Application for a charging order

➤ Issue fee in the County Court - £50.

➤ Fixed costs in the County Court - as for originating documents.

➤ Issue fee in the High Court - £60.

➤ Fixed costs in the High Court where the order is granted and made absolute - £129 plus £16.25 if an affidavit of service is needed and reasonable costs for search fees and registering the order.

4   Application for an attachment of earnings order

➤ Issue fee (in the County Court only) - £50.

5   Application to issue a warrant of execution

➤ Issue fee in the County Court - if the sum to be recovered is under £125 - £20, otherwise £40.

➤ Fixed costs in the County Court - if the sum to be recovered exceeds £25 - £2.

➤ Issue fee in the High Court for a writ of Fi Fa - £20.

➤ Fixed costs in the High Court for a writ of Fi Fa, provided the judgment *either* includes costs *or* is for £600 or more - £66.50 (otherwise no costs are allowed).

D. Probate Registry fees

Value assessed for IHT ...	Fee
... not exceeding £10,000	No fee (free!)
... exceeds £10,000 but not £25,000	£40
... exceeds £25,000 but not £40,000	£80
... exceeds £40,000 but not £70,000	£150
... exceeds £70,000 but not £100,000	£215
... exceeds £100,000 but not £200,000	£300
... exceeds £200,000, then an additional fee for every extra £100,000 or part thereof	£50

Index

405